MADE
NOT BORN

To Marilyn,
 Thank you for being interested in any/our
stories. In explaining the title of this book, I
used the phrase, "We are nothing more than
the product of our experiences." Our experience
with you in these later years of our lives,
here at Beverwyck add some nice finishing
touches.
 I enjoyed reading your stories and as a
one-time writer, I can appreciate the shared
experience. Thank you for your comments,
coaching, and guidance in "Letting My
Inner Book Out," to paraphrase Troy
Book Makers slogan.

                    Sincerely,
                    Jack

Book design by The Troy Book Makers
Printed in the United States of America
The Troy Book Makers • Schodack Landing, New York • thetroybookmakers.com

To order additional copies of this title,
contact your favorite local bookstore
or visit www.shoptbmbooks.com

ISBN: 978-1-61468-972-0

MADE NOT BORN

John "Jack" Kolman

Dedicated to my wife Verna
who helped make me

ON THE COVER

The picture of me on the tricycle represents the Beginning/Before/Then. The other picture portrays the Ending/After/Now. I was five and a half years old when my picture was taken. I have no idea who took it. My parents did not own a camera. I only have one other snapshot of me, First Communion, and a picture of my eighth-grade graduating class until I was in high school. It was summer. We were living at my grandmother's house. Something in the recesses of my memory tells me that it was a Sunday afternoon. I rode my trike up and down the sidewalk in my grandmother's yard. It was long (about two hundred feet). To the right of where I was sitting on my trike, there was a rose trellis. I would back my trike into it and pretend it was my garage. I do not look happy in the picture. I guess it captures my disposition during those early years. I look far too serious for my age, which also says a lot about me during that time of my life.

Fast forward twenty-four years, from 1943 to 1967, and the photo of Verna and me. I am twenty-nine years old and have come a long way, represented by several things. I am not alone anymore, and standing alongside me is the most important person in my life, my wife Verna. In addition, there are three "firsts" in the photo. The mobile home is our first home (future story). Second, you can barely see it, but in the lower right-hand corner, you can see the right front corner of our first new car. It was a red and white 1966 Ambassador. Coincidentally, our mobile home was also an Ambassador. Verna and I represent the third first. We are formally dressed to attend the first formal event of our new lives as an officer and officer's wife at the Officers' Club. I am smiling, and Verna is too. She looks so beautiful. And we both look very happy.

There are not enough words to describe what these pictures mean and the contrast they represent. I tried to do so in the stories of this book, but as I stare at the pictures, I am dumbstruck. I have no more words to offer; these pictures say it all.

ABOUT THE TITLE

About three years ago, while writing these memoirs, I ran across a statement by a Renaissance philosopher, Erasmus, that caught my attention. "Men are not born but made." By coincidence, a similar phrase caught my attention a short time later as Verna and I were watching a movie on TV. "We are nothing more than the product of our experiences." Now, that's a quantum leap of five hundred years from a sixteenth-century philosopher to a casual remark in a twenty-first-century movie. Yet the two phrases pretty much say the same thing.

When I was born, did I start as an empty shell, blank canvas, and skeletal framework that had to be filled, painted upon, and fleshed out, respectively? Of course, there is the nature/nurture phenomenon. But what made me who I am today? How did I become the person I am? I can't help but conclude that I started to be "made right after I was born." Each decision I made and every experience I encountered from the moment I was born up until this very moment had not only a specific effect on me but also a cumulative effect. That process is still going on. I am not done being "made." I am not yet finished! Is it possible to scientifically analyze each work, deed, and experience I encountered to show how all of the pieces came together to create a unique individual? I'll leave all that to the professionals who delve into such matters. That is enough psychology and philosophy to digest. What is important is that we all have our memoirs (decisions and experiences) that made us. Therefore, "Made Not Born" is a fitting title for everyone's memoirs.

As I further contemplated this title to be sure it would suffice, the word "made" caught my attention. Who did the making? Since the "born" applies to me, one would naturally assume that I did the making all by myself. Not really; despite what that Dutch humanist Erasmus said, I owe very much to my wife, Verna. We have been together since I was seventeen years old. She played a significant role in making me. Our children, David and Kevin, have also contributed to my making in various and subtle ways that they are probably unaware of. Yes, children can learn from their parents. To take it to a higher level, I think a more powerful and Divine intervention took place in my life. These stories include numerous circumstances, decisions, good news/bad news happenings, and four life-changing events that have to have been part of something that I am unworthy to take credit for. As you read the episodes, I hope you will agree with me when, in summary, I say that there has to have been Divine Intervention at work making me after I was born, and I am still a work in process. Thank you, God!

PREFACE

Over the years and more recently, I found myself telling family members and friends various stories about things I had experienced during my life. Invariably, there were comments such as, "You have to write these stories down." More specifically, our nephew Michael made that exact comment at a family gathering in April 2019. Shortly after Verna and I returned home, I joined a Memoir Writing Club in The Villages, Florida. The club met weekly to share common interests and provide helpful hints, encouragement, and constructive criticisms. I liked the members, the format of the meetings, and the fact that everyone was encouraged to share a written story every week. I am a very organized and methodical person, so the weekly assignments fit my self-disciplined mindset.

At the first Memoirs Writing Club meeting I attended, the leaders asked for whom am I writing my memoirs. My response was my children, naturally. At that same time, I had envisioned writing the stories, doing the editing, having them printed in some fashion, and then giving each of our sons a copy of the book. Those two ideas quickly changed. As I completed each story, I got into the routine of sending it to our sons via MESSENGER on our computer. That mailing list expanded to their children, Verna's brother Raymond and his wife, Carol, our nephew Michael, and our niece Andrea. That turned out to be a good move. It generated interest, comments, and feedback. As I completed each story, I felt relieved that I no longer had the burden of carrying all the information in my head, which could vanish at any moment. It is now on paper and in the computer, on a backup hard drive, and on a couple of flash drives. Whew!

I planned to write my stories chronologically, starting with my earliest memories and continuing until I reached the present. That pattern held up reasonably well except for a few stories that spanned a period of time. Once I chronologically reached my high school years, I began writing stories that were no longer only about me but also included Verna. The first one is "Life-Changing Event Number One," about how we started going together in high school. Including Verna in this collection added a nice dimension to them.

I was cranking out the stories at a pretty good pace and was up to date by the middle of 2022. The next phase in the process was to edit and publish my collection of seventy-five stories. However, about that time, a series of additional life-changing events took place in our lives that caused me to put this project on the back burner. It took another twelve stories to explain what happened and bring this epic up to date.

That two-year gap presented some problems regarding handling some stories that were written too many years ago, needed to be updated, and changed the tense from the present to the past. For example, I had to update this preface to set the stage and give the reader a correct and current explanation of how our life story played out. I did not have to rewrite any story completely.

I enjoyed writing each story. They came easily to me. The content was in my head. All I had to do was pick up a pen and paper and write. I never struggled to get the words down. The words flowed as soon as I started writing, and I had to write quickly to keep up with the pace.

Finally, I would like to thank a few people who have been instrumental in this accomplishment; first of all, our nephew, Michael, for getting me started. If Michael pushed the starter button, my wife, Verna, represented the horsepower that made the engine run so well. The first years of my life, flying solo constituted only twenty-five percent of my living years. Once we joined Hearts at age seventeen, she became a guiding spirit, mentor, and someone to share problems, challenges, and achievements with. We make a good team, and as they say, "There is no 'I' in team." So, these memoirs are more of a "We" story than an "I" story. I may have used the word I more often than we, but she was the unsung heroine behind me all the time. I can't imagine how my story would have turned out without Verna, and I don't even like to think about it. It would probably not even be worth writing.

On a more practical note, I thank Verna for her editorial corrections and other suggestions. She was the first person to read each story when it came out of the printer, and I also had to rely on her computer skills on numerous occasions.

I would also like to thank the members of our family whom I identified earlier and my fellow memoir writers for their comments, suggestions, and feedback. Finally, I would like to thank our dear friend Esther Brown, who we met in our new Lifestyle arrangement, for doing an excellent job of final editing and proofreading my manuscript. I hope this little preface gives you an idea about the "story behind the story."

CONTENTS

I. EIGHTY-SIX YEARS IN A FLASH!

"It was on a cold and windy day" in November 1938 (just kidding, how would I know, but isn't that how great stories usually begin?) that I was born and grew up in a small coal-mining area in northeast Pennsylvania. I came from a family that I would classify as lower-middle class and had a Slavic ethnic background.

I attended a parochial school for eight years and then a public high school. Upon graduating in 1956, I joined the Air Force. It was a popular thing to do because the word "college" was not part of my vocabulary, and the local employment opportunities were scarce. The coal mines had peaked in the forties.

I met my wife Verna Klapal in high school, and we have been together ever since. I made two significant decisions in my life: joining the Air Force and marrying Verna.

We married in 1958, and two years later, we decided to make the Air Force my career. My first job was as a radar operator, and I subsequently became a Procurement/Contracting Officer. I took advantage of the education opportunities provided by the military, and by the time my Air Force career was over, I had a BS degree in Business Administration and an MBA degree.

My military assignments ranged from lonely radar sites to large bases and a final assignment in a civilian environment monitoring Department of Defense contractors. Geographically, we found ourselves in Texas, Tennessee, Kentucky, Pennsylvania, Iceland, California twice, Wisconsin, New York, Germany, and finally, New Jersey. While still in the Air Force, I became an adjunct university professor. My military career was over in 1977, and after being "retired" for the weekend, I went to work for the Lockheed Corporation as a Contract Administrator and then Manager of Subcontracts.

My last Air Force assignment was in New Jersey, where our children David and Kevin spent most of their childhood and remaining school years. They were excellent students and became top-notch engineers for General Electric. They have always been and still are our pride and joy.

We lived in a small iron-mining town called Ironia in New Jersey. After we sent our boys off to college, we became empty nesters. Verna became a medical secretary and administrative assistant working for the county government.

We took our first cruise for our twenty-fifth wedding anniversary and got hooked on them.

In 2004, we moved to The Villages, Florida. Because of health concerns and a desire to be closer to family, we moved from The Villages to an independent living facility in upstate New York in 2023, where we currently reside.

2. NOVEMBER 13, 1938 - MY BIRTHDAY

What was going on in the world in 1938?

- Franklin D. Roosevelt was president.
- The Great Depression had passed in the United States and Europe, but World War II had not yet begun.
- German troops occupied Austria, and Hitler announced the *Anschluss* (union) of Germany and Austria.
- British Prime Minister Neville Chamberlain met with Hitler to discuss German demands on Czechoslovakia. That's ironic because both Verna and I have roots in that country.
- A conference of European leaders met at Munich and decided to permit the annexation of the Sudetenland region of Czechoslovakia; Poland and Hungary also gained areas of Czech territory.
- Jewish shops and businesses were smashed in Germany in what came to be called Kristallnacht, the Night of Broken Glass.
- Nylon was invented.
- A Hungarian engineer invented the ballpoint pen based on ball bearings.
- A process of photocopying documents was invented.
- Orson Wells panicked radio audiences with the performance of "*War of the Worlds.*"

My birthday, November 13, 1938, was never recognized or celebrated by anyone (family or friends) until November 13, 1955. But that is another story.

3. EARLIEST MEMORIES

FEBRUARY 1942 - SEPTEMBER 1943 AGES 4 to 5

Shortly after I joined the Air Force, I was told I needed a security clearance because I would become a radar operator. I was given a form entitled "Statement of Personal History," which asked for information regarding my parents and if I had any relatives living in a foreign country. I had to contact my parents about it. To my surprise, I learned that my father's father died in 1917, but his mother, an uncle, and two aunts were living in Czechoslovakia. I also discovered that for the first four years of my life, I lived in Duryea, Pennsylvania, a small town close to Exeter, Pennsylvania, where I lived the remaining years of my childhood. My father must have had relatives in Duryea because I remember them visiting us while I was growing up. I further learned that my parents must have moved to live with my maternal grandmother at 1279 Pershing Street, Exeter, Pennsylvania, from February 1942 until September 1943. My parents then purchased a home at 242 Harland Street, close to my grandmother's house.

My grandmother was the only grandparent I ever knew. She and her husband were Slovak, and her husband died before I was born. We called my grandmother "Bobbie," the Slavic name for grandma.

Whenever I ask our children if they remember certain things from their early years, they say, "I don't know if I remember that or if I remember it from a home movie or video you took of me." In my first memory years (early 1940s), there were no home movies or videos of me. So, my early memories are indeed memories.

These first memories are not associated with any stories. They are more or less flashes in a pan. I have to get them down on paper before I forget them.

- My first memory is one I have been lugging around for over 80 years and has no meaning. I am sitting on the kitchen floor eating a box of pretzel sticks(something tells me it was the Duryea house) with other people at the table. There, it is now on paper, and it's okay if I forget it. Phew!

- Playing with three metal soldiers (World War II in progress): one carrying an American flag, a machine gunner, and one standing and shooting a rifle. They would be worth a lot of money today!

- Drinking a cup of coffee with pieces of bread broken up in it.

- Riding my trike up and down a long sidewalk, underneath a huge grapevine, and parking it under a rose trellis (photo on the cover of this book).

- Sitting on the front porch looking across the Susquehanna River at a gigantic coal breaker, which is a tall building where huge chunks of coal are dumped into a gravity-fed large chute that has a mechanism to break the coal into smaller sizes depending on the type of furnace in which it will be used. The breaker had four large windows at the top. I don't know why, but I used to tell myself that those four windows were where the four seasons of the year came from. That was a stupid thought, yet I knew enough to identify the four seasons. I have never figured out how I came up with that theory.

- Waking up from a nightmare more than once, and Bobbie lighting matches, then putting them out in a glass of water and rubbing the water on my forehead. I recently checked that out but found no explanation for the old Slavic wife's tale.

- Sitting on the front porch on a Fourth of July morning, waiting to go to the Slovak Day celebration at Sans Souci amusement park. Bobbie had given me a handkerchief tied in the corner with a few coins, and she warned me not to lose it.

- Bobbie had a large yard with huge fruit trees, a vegetable garden, a grapevine, flower beds, hedges, and rose bushes. It was always neat and well-manicured. And that is very likely why, to this day, I love to do yard work.

- The day we moved to our own house, a couple of miles away, my father borrowed a truck from a local farmer. It was drizzling. I was helping by carrying some small boxes up the stairs. That was the first of numerous chores and home improvements to that house that I helped my father with for the remainder of my childhood years.

4. 242 HARLAND STREET AND ME

1943 - 1956 AGES 5 to 17

The above street address is the place where I grew up. We moved there when I was four, and I left at seventeen to join the Air Force. The house was built in the early nineteen twenties or late teens and was called a bungalow. It had three bedrooms, and I slept in all three over the years. So much of me became a part of that house.

A doctor had lived in the house before us. The first time I dug up an area in the backyard for a vegetable garden, I found a lot of glass medicine bottles. As you entered the front door, you saw a little room I imagined was the waiting room for the patients. We referred to it as the "Reception Room." There were glass French doors to what was probably the doctor's office, which later became our living room. There was another set of French doors to another room, which was our dining room. There was no direct entry to the kitchen, so one of the first projects was to make an entry from the reception room into the kitchen. The French doors to the doctor's office were removed, and an archway was built. My mother wanted two lights in the living room, one on each side of the arch. I remember the holes being there, but I don't recall if there was any wiring. For as long as I lived there, the lights were never installed.

Another priority project was to move a coal-burning stove from the kitchen to the cellar and remove the chimney that had been installed for it. My father built a new chimney outside the house. He later used the old chimney bricks to build a coal bin in the cellar. He gave me the job of removing the old mortar from the chimney bricks with a chisel and hammer.

Some other changes took place after I left the house. My father opened up the kitchen to the previous dining room. He also enclosed the addition to the back porch for a storage area. He also added a closet to the upstairs bedroom, which previously had none. There is now an addition to a single-car garage my father built after I left. He said he tore down the old garage except for the left and rear walls, then extended it to what it is today.

Whenever my father was doing something around the house, I found myself by his side watching and helping by handing him nails one at a time, holding a board while he cut it, mixing cement, lugging shingles on my shoulder up the ladder to the roof; cleaning up the wood shavings, sawdust, and other debris, and putting the tools away. By the time I got to high school, my father had started doing carpentry jobs for other people after he came home from working in the coal mines. I went with him whenever I could and helped him the same way.

One day, we were demolishing an old barn for use in a future project. The roof and upper section were already down; my father stood on the second floor. All of a sudden, the whole structure started to collapse. My father yelled my name. He was concerned that I was underneath, but I wasn't. That was the only time I ever saw my father get so emotional regarding me.

At the end of each job, he had me prepare the invoice by writing what he paid for the materials and how much he charged for his labor. My father never had an education. He could read printed material but could not write or read handwriting. I always wondered where and how he learned to figure out how to cut a board with double angles to put a roof on a garage that he built. Or how to apply the trigonometric Pythagorean principle of "*a squared plus b squared equals c squared*" to be sure that the corners of a wall are perfectly square. I wish I had asked him. He built a double-car garage on a piece of property on the town's main street where we lived (corner of Schooley Street and Wyoming Avenue). Of course, I was part of that. The garage is still standing; every time I passed it over the last sixty years, I had to glance at it. It became somewhat of a memorial of my father (and me).

When I was in the fourth grade, my father decided to expand our back porch. He had to build a foundation about three feet high to match the level of the existing porch. Then he had to fill it. He started to dig a hole in the backyard to use for fill. I don't remember how that hole ever got refilled. Nor do I remember him specifically telling me to continue with the digging, but I do remember digging it when I was in the fourth grade because the huge shovel I was using had the number "4" embossed on the metal part of the handle and every time I shoved it into the ground I saw the number. The other part of that project I spent a lot of time on was painting the lattice. There was a lot of it enclosing the porch surrounding the entire back of the house. To paint a lattice, you need two people, one on each side, painting simultaneously to catch the paint running down the lattice strips from the other side as each person painted. My mother was on one side, and I was on the other.

A few years later, he rebuilt the front porch. That project involved removing soil to expand the cellar under the porch. Why didn't he do the front porch first and use the soil to fill the back porch? I don't remember what we did with all the soil we dug out. I remember that we used some of it to make concrete for the foundation because the soil was a mixture of sand and gravel; all it needed was cement and water to make concrete.

When I was about ten years old, I undertook my first Mr. Fixit Project. I have been a Mr. Fixit ever since. I can't stand it when something needs to be repaired. I am not satisfied until it's done. I have a knack for fixing things, and in doing so, I tend to think outside the box when a "not-too-obvious" repair will not work. My first repair job was an electrical plug that was not working. I pulled it from the wall and reconnected the wires to the plug. However, I did not know enough to go into the cellar to remove that circuit's fuse. Those were the days before circuit breakers. After I repaired the plug, I put it back into the wall, and there was a flash of sparks. I didn't realize that two bare wires should never touch each other. I honestly don't remember what happened afterward.

Throughout those years, I was involved in painting the house. The clapboards were a deep yellow, and the trim was maroon (which turned out to be my high school colors). As part of that project, I was on the front porch roof painting the clapboards yellow. My father was still at work in the mines and would not be home for another few hours. While painting, I accidentally knocked over a gallon of that yellow paint which ran down the green roof. My father is going to kill me! When he got home, he said, "No problem, I was undecided whether to replace the roof; now I know what to do." Phew!

We had a small garden in the backyard, and my father made a simple fence around it out of old galvanized pipe. I didn't like the way it looked so drab. So I went to the Woolworth's Five and Dime store and, with my own money, bought a small can of white paint and another of green paint. I painted the lengths of the pipe white and the fittings connecting them green. It looked better (at least to me).

The woodwork inside our house was hardwood with handsome grain that had been painted ivory by the previous owner. My parents thought it would look better if the woodgrain were shown. We removed the paint with paint remover, and my job was to sand the wood. That job went on for over a year.

One day, I saved our house from being burnt down. My parents were in the house, and I was burning papers in the backyard. I casually looked back toward the house and saw the kitchen through the glass in the kitchen door. I saw in the glass what I thought was a reflection of the fire I was using. But I then realized it was a fire in the kitchen. I ran inside the house. My mother had put an empty can that had contained shortening on the stove to melt the remains in it. It was an electric stove. The burner was shut off but still warm enough to cause the heated oil to flame up. My mother was in the living room, and I yelled for her. She came, grabbed the burning can with a towel, and threw it outside.

On a more routine basis, I cut the grass, shoveled the snow, swept the cellar, took the ashes from the coal furnace, and put the metal tubs on the street for the trash man to pick up. They were heavy.

I don't remember ever being told to do all of those things. I just did them because they needed to be done. Of course, I never got an allowance. Our generation didn't know that word. I had a brother, six years older than me. I don't remember him ever doing any of the above with me. I also had two younger brothers, nine and twelve years younger. Of course, they were much too young to be involved. I have a lot of memories of 242 Harland Street. The house still stands, and little do the people there know how much of me is embedded in its walls.

5. FUN AND GAMES

What did I do for fun? Looking back over my early years, I see that they seemed filled with all work and no play. I had my first job at about age ten, which will be a later story. There were about five years between the ages of five and ten that I vividly remember having fun.

Significant gaps existed between my older and younger brothers, so I was somewhat of an only child and had no siblings to play with.

Let me begin by listing my toys and games. It is not a long list. Our two sons' lists would be very difficult, if not impossible, for them to reconstruct. As parents, we tend to provide our children with what we did not have. On the other hand, a current child's list of toys and games would be straightforward to complete: one iPhone!

Here is my list:

- metal soldiers
- marbles
- tinker toys
- pump ping-pong ball gun
- Lincoln logs
- the Parcheesi game
- set of bricks (like Legos)
- Erector set (my favorite)
- American Flyer wagon
- sled
- five small construction vehicles
- checkers
- Roy Rogers gun & holster

- Buck Rogers space gun
- Chinese checkers
- Presidents game
- a small rifle that shot corks at crows sitting on a fence
- home-made slingshot from a tree branch that formed a "Y" with strips of rubber from an old inner tube
- pea shooter made from a piece of wood from a sumac tree with a soft core that was easy to gouge. We picked green berries from a tree for ammo.

When I was seven, my father built a garage in the backyard. One day, I picked up a scrap piece of lumber about a foot long and six inches wide. I cut the front with a saw to make a point, nailed a couple of small blocks of wood in the center, pounded nails around the edges, and finally wrapped string around the nails. What did I make? A ship, the first of many woodworking projects I completed over the future years. When my father came home from work, I showed it to him, and he smiled.

To amuse myself, I had three hobbies: stamp collecting, jigsaw puzzles, and building model airplanes with balsa wood sticks for the frame and tissue paper to cover them. The trick for making the paper nice and tight was to spray it with water. One time, I sliced my finger with a razor blade I was using to cut the balsa wood.

On the street I grew up on, there were eight other boys. We were all within three years of age. These were my playmates. There were also three girls, but we did not play with them. Those were the days before "equal rights."

If we wanted to play with someone, we walked up to their back porch and yelled, "Hello, Eddie, Stevie, Alex, Billy, Paul, or Bobby" (three of them had the same name). That makes eight. I wonder what became of all of them?

The games we played and the things we did together need explanation. A list does not capture the fun.

BASEBALL—It was softball because nobody could afford a glove. Between us, we had only one ball and one bat. We played in an empty lot. Half of the lots on the street had no houses; some were open, and some had trees and shrubbery. There are none vacant today. Those were the days before Little League and other organized sports for kids.

BASKETBALL—We nailed a backboard to a utility pole and used a barrel ring (a small ring, of course) for a hoop. The pole had a light on it so we could play at night.

FOOTBALL—We had never heard of flag football. We played touch football on the road and tackled on the fields. We also created a game called Kicking Glories. One guy kicked the ball as far as he could. The other guy had to kick it back from wherever he stopped it. Behind each guy was a goal marker. You got one point once you made the other guy go over that line to stop the ball.

ICE HOCKEY—We played on a frozen "swamp" now called a "wetland." For a hockey stick, we used a tree branch with a good curve at the bottom. For a puck, we used a small tin can. After a few smacks, it became crushed and had plenty of sharp edges. How stupid! I remember only one guy getting a gash on his forehead. To stay warm, we built a fire from old tires (the swamp was being used as a landfill). We smelled awful when we got home.

FISHING—We used a long tree branch, string, a cork from a bottle, and worms. We only had to buy hooks—shades of Huckleberry Finn. We caught small bluegills we called "sunnies" and catfish—nothing edible, too small, and from the landfill swamp.

WAR—One side hid in an empty wooded lot, and the other tried to find them. When we saw the enemy, we would shout, "Bang." I don't know how we ever knew who won. Eventually, we all had ping-pong ball pump guns, so it was easier to tell who got hit.

COWBOYS & INDIANS—We usually played this on Saturday afternoons coming home from the movie matinee. For seven cents, you saw one of the following: *Roy Rogers, Gene Autry, Hopalong Cassidy, Red Ryder and Little Beaver,* etc., plus a cartoon and a short movie called a "Chapter" that always had a cliffhanger ending that brought you back next week. Just like war, there was a lot of shouting between the cowboys and Indians. You couldn't tell who won, but supposedly, the Indians lost, just like in the movie—a lot of yelling but simple fun.

TRADING FUNNY BOOKS—That's what we call comics. We all had a stack of about twenty. I don't remember where the stack started, but each cost about five cents. *Donald Duck, Mickey Mouse, Goofy, Superman, Batman, Archie, Tom and Jerry, and Mutt and Jeff,* to name a few. I used to laugh at the "funny" things Mutt and Jeff would say or do. Every so often, you got together with another kid and traded one for one. That was the extent of my literary enrichment. I've come a long way since then, as you will learn in future stories!

HOPSCOTCH—Two versions of this. On the road, with a piece of chalk, you draw a rectangle and divide it into ten small rectangles. We printed categories such as boys' names, girls' names, games, colors, animals, and countries in each one. I don't remember the details, but you had to bounce a ball through the rectangle and rattle off ten names for the category you were up to. I don't remember how you won. Oh well, it didn't matter. We were just having fun. The second version was a diagram of squares numbered one through ten. You threw a stone to land on the numbers sequentially. The stone had to stay within the line of the number you were up to. The flatter the stone, the better the chance of not jumping out. We spit on both sides to help it stick. If your stone stayed in your number, you jumped into the other squares, skipping the number you were up to and back to the beginning. The first one to go through all ten numbers won. These sound like girls' games. Oh well, what did we care?

MARBLES—Two versions again. We all had a "steely," a sold iron ball about the size of a golf ball. One kid rolled his on the ground. After it stops, the other kid rolls his and tries to hit yours. If he did, you gave him two marbles. You would give him one marble if he came close enough to "span it"(touch both steelies with his outstretched palm). In another game, we made a circle in the dirt about six feet across. Everybody placed five marbles inside of it. Then we took turns trying to knock the marbles out with our steely. If you got at least one, you got another turn. If you didn't, it was the next kid's turn.

CARDS—Not your usual Old Maids. We collected World War II and Korean War cards. Like baseball cards, they came wrapped with bubble gum inside. Again, we had two versions of this. One kid flipped a card onto the ground. It ended up with the picture side up or the writing side up. Then the other kid flipped his. If it matched the card on the ground, he would win both cards. If it did not, the first kid won both cards. The other thing we did with the cards was toss one of them against a wall. The other kid then threw one of his. Whoever came closest to the wall wins both cards.

JACKKNIFE—We used a Camp King knife with four blades and used the one that looked like an awl. You flipped the open knife from your hand, arms, elbows, face parts, and knees through all parts of your body, plus some other gyrations. The knife had to stick in the ground so you could get two fingers under the handle. Whoever made it through all the gyrations first won.

COPS & ROBBERS—-Not really a game. During the summer, we hung around under the street light and played hide and seek (there were plenty of good hiding places in the empty wooded lots). Our little town had only one policeman on duty, who patrolled the streets at night. We would all run and hide if we saw his car coming down the street. I don't know why; maybe we feared him, unlike the kids today.

SLEIGH-RIDING—(A near-death experience). We didn't call it sledding. There are two forms of it again. In one, you held your sled in front of you while running down the street that was nice and icy from compacted snow (before the days of salt, although the town would eventually get around to spreading coal ashes on the road using two guys with shovels off the back of a dump truck). After you built up some running speed, you dropped the sled to the ground, then jumped on it (belly-flopped) and lay on it until it stopped. The other thrill was going down hills. The hills went down into the frozen swamp. Beyond the swamp was the Susquehanna River. One sunny, cold winter day, it was a Sunday; I remember it well: I went sleigh-riding down one of those hills alone. I passed the frozen swamp and still had some momentum and hill left, so I continued toward the river, which appeared to be frozen thick. As I approached the river's edge, my guardian angel made me make a hard right turn with my sled. I lay on the sled for a few seconds, then poked my finger through the river ice; it was only about one-quarter inch thick. I shudder every time I think of that scene. Thank you, God!

We got a lot of fun out of a few simple and inexpensive things and some imagination. There will never be another era like that. Ah! The good old days.

6. SCHOOL DAYS - GRADES ONE THROUGH EIGHT

1944 - 1952

I started school in 1944 at age five and would be six in November. Parochial school did not have kindergarten. For some reason, for first grade, my parents sent me to a parochial school, St. Cecilia's, within walking distance of home and not the parochial school my older brother Leonard was going to.

FIRST GRADE—I remember only two things from the first grade. One is walking/marching to the music of John Philip Sousa through the hallways, going to lunch, and leaving class at the end of the day. The other is a bit more of a story. I had spent the night at my grandmother's house. It was a tradition in Catholic schools during May to have a little altar set up in each classroom dedicated to Mary, Jesus' mother. There always was a small vase of flowers at that little altar. The evening before, my grandmother told me to go into her yard and pick a bunch of lilies of the valley to take to school the following day for the altar. On the way to school that morning, I had to go past a florist shop. As I walked by it, the owner came out and said, "Hey kid, I'll give you five cents for that bunch of flowers." I said okay and went to school with a nickel in my pocket. I don't remember anything more than that. That florist shop is still there, and I feel guilty whenever I pass it. Am I going to go to hell?

I started attending St. John the Baptist School in the second grade, and where Leonard was in the eighth. We had to take the city bus. It was a Slovak parish school, and the nuns were from the Order of Saints Cyril and Methodius. First and second grades were in the same room. I still have my report cards for grades two through seven. I can't imagine why I don't have the one from the eighth grade.

The report cards have some interesting features. For the first three years, there is a numerical grade for each subject for each month, plus a mid-year grade and final grade for each subject, and then an overall numerical grade for all subjects for the entire year. The only subject that was letter-graded was the Slovak language. After having these report cards for all these years, I am analyzing them for the first time.

SECOND GRADE (SISTER JUDITH)—My average grade for the year was 81. My two best subjects were Religion and Spelling. Three subjects tied for my poorest: English, Penmanship, and Art. There were numerical grades for Penmanship and Deportment (Conduct). I averaged 75 in Penmanship and 92 in Deportment. Now I ask you, why did I not get a 76 in Penmanship and 93 in Deportment? What would I have to have done to be one digit better? The nuns were ahead of their time with the "digital age." Another interesting thing about the second grade is that I was absent for fourteen days in May. I had measles and missed the Sunday that I would have received First Holy Communion, but I remember receiving it on the same day as my brother's eighth-grade graduation Mass. I have a picture of me taken that day, one of only three I have of me until high school. I have a lasting image of that classroom. In the back of the classroom was a sandbox about four feet square on legs about table height. A replica of the Garden of Eden was created in the white sand.

THIRD GRADE (SISTER REGINA)—My average grade for the year was 88, up from 81 in the second grade. I remember struggling in the second grade, but it all began to click in the third. I got three gold stars on my report card for April, May, and Final Tests. My best subject was Spelling, and my worst was English. I got the same grade in Behavior as in the second grade. What did I have to do to get a 93?

FOURTH GRADE (DON'T RECALL SISTER'S NAME)—I increased my average grade for the year by one point to 89. My best subject was spelling again. I improved my English from 77 to 88. The poorest subject was Slovak. I finally improved my Deportment from 92 to 94. Wow! I did not receive any grades for March. I had scarlet fever. I remember staying home for a long time and a "Quarantine" sign on the front of the house. I don't remember being sick or in any pain.

FIFTH GRADE (SISTER THERESA)—New report card format. There are no numbers except for mid-year and final letter grades for three grading periods in the year's first half and three for the second half. I guess the world was not yet ready to go digital! My average grade for the year was 89.4, up four-tenths of a point; the trend continues. The best subject was Religion, with a 94; I'm going to heaven. Poorest was Handwriting. No more numerical grades for Deportment. There were twelve character traits in a section called "Progress in Growth of Personality," a letter grade was given for each. I started with A's, B's, and C's in the first half of the year and ended up with all A's for the entire second half. Wow!

SIXTH GRADE (SISTER VENERANDA)—Back to numbers, not letters, for academic subjects. There is hope for the digital world. My average grade was 92, up three points from the fifth grade. The best subject was Religion again. My poorest was Art. I received straight A's for all twelve traits in all grading periods. Sixth grade is one of my most memorable for a few reasons. First of all, on the very first day, Sister Veneranda told us that we would be studying Ancient History and that it was more interesting than other history. Secondly, throughout the year, she placed arithmetic flashcards on the chalk tray beneath the blackboard and quickly walked by them, pointing at each one with a pointing stick. When called on, we had to rattle the answers as fast as she walked. Thirdly, one day, a man came into the classroom to demonstrate the "Palmer" method of penmanship and sell Palmer fountain pens. I couldn't afford one. Fourthly, I had perfect attendance that year, which was the only time that would happen. Finally, Sister Veneranda was the tallest and meanest of all the nuns. She was also in charge of the altar boys, and I was one. That will be a future story.

SEVENTH GRADE (SISTER ULPHIA)—My average for the year was 91, down one point from last year. For my character traits, I received all B's for the year for the Works to Ability trait. The previous year, I received all A's. Sister Ulphia knew that I could do better. The best subject was Spelling, with a 97, but Religion was second, with a 95. The poorest was Handwriting. I should have bought the Palmer pen.

EIGHTH GRADE (SISTER ANGELINA)—I do not have my report card for that year. I remember that another boy and I were tied for the highest average for the year. One last thing about my grades that I noticed is that the core subjects, such as Arithmetic, History, Reading, and Geography, were never my best but never my poorest. We never had Science or pre-algebra courses.

That is enough with the numbers. Here are a few snippets from those eight years.

- I liked school, the routine, regimentation, scheduling, discipline, structure, being in the same classroom with the same kids every year, and having my own desk for the whole year. We could leave any books in them that we did not have to take home for homework.
- Small cardboard pencil boxes with a lid and pull-out drawer holding two or three pencils, an eraser, a couple of crayons, a pencil sharpener, a protractor, a six-inch ruler, and other similar school supplies.
- Book bags were made from plastic and cardboard and looked like toy briefcases.
- After I'd been taking the city bus for a couple of years, the school purchased a school bus. We were not allowed to talk on the bus.
- The school had somewhat of a kangaroo court. I got arrested one day for leaving the playground during recess to get a ball that went astray. I had to go to court, which

the eighth graders conducted. I remember being found guilty, but I don't recall my sentence.

- I was a patrol boy with a badge and white shoulder strap. Duties included keeping the kids in a straight line as they went from one place to another, enforcing "No Talking" rules, and just standing around looking important and fearsome.

- Hot lunch in the cafeteria in the church basement. Warm milk. The only meal I hated was the one with sauerkraut, but I like it today. Not allowed to talk during lunch.

- Going to Mass every morning before school.

- The first class was always religion.

- The first question in the Baltimore Catechism: Who made you? Answer: God made me. Second question: Why did God make you? Answer: God made me to love Him, honor Him, and be happy with Him in Heaven.

- A thicker Catechism book every year.

- I have never seen a Bible.

- I bought a World War II knapsack from the Army Surplus store to use as a backpack. We were ahead of our time.

- Going to an amusement park called Rocky Glenn at the end of each school year. Food and rides were free. The seventh-grade boys played the eighth-grade boys in softball first thing in the morning. The eighth graders usually won. They were bigger and heavier hitters. A new pair of jeans (called overalls then) and high-top sneakers for the event and the rest of the summer. The park is no longer there.

- Ballpoint pens replacing fountain pens. The first ones leaked a lot.

- About 20 kids in our class.

- Learning Latin music. Why? A Latin note is called a "punctum." That is all I remember.

- The principal has a cat-o-nine tail. I got it once when I was about ten years old for having too much body movement (fidgeting) while serving Mass as an altar boy.

- Having to bring in a Sunday collection envelope every Monday morning. I put five cents in it.

- I got a bill for lunch, bus, book rental, etc., and paid it out of my own money starting in about the fifth grade when I started working on the farm.

- Sister Veneranda selling candy during recess. I never bought any.

- An inkwell is a small glass jar with a plastic top and a hole for the pen to dip into. It is set in the upper right-hand corner of the desk.

- Going to our state capital in Harrisburg and the sisters' summer home in Danville, Pennsylvania, for our eighth-grade class outing.

- Having a fiftieth reunion in 2002. About one-half of the class attended.

St. John the Baptist School and the church are no longer there. They were demolished ten years ago and three years ago because of declining attendance. Those days were a pleasant part of my life, and I don't remember ever being bitter or remorseful about that school experience, even though there were some rough spots. My high school years took on a poorer flavor academically and in other ways, except for one life-changing event.

JACK'S FIRST COMMUNION

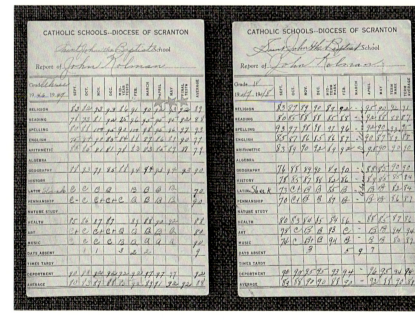

2ND GRADE REPORT CARD

3RD GRADE REPORT CARD

4TH GRADE REPORT CARD

5TH GRADE REPORT CARD

PROGRESS IN GROWTH OF PERSONALITY

Parents should acknowledge not only the weak traits in their children but also their good traits and strive to co-operate honestly with the teacher in the elimination of the former by assisting in the positive development of the latter.

The attitudes and habits listed below are desirable traits for Christian living.

A — Always   B — Usually   C — Sometimes   D — Never

1st	2nd	Mid-Year		1st	2nd	Final
A	A	A	Shows Religious Spirit	A	A	A
A	A	A	Is Courteous	A	A	A
A	A	A	Attends to Personal Appearance	A	A	A
A	A	A	Is Attentive	A	A	A
A	A	A	Co-operates with Others	A	A	A
A	A	A	Comes Well Prepared	A	A	A
A	A	A	Begins Work Promptly	A	A	A
A	A	A	Works to Ability	A	A	A
A	A	A	Works Carefully	A	A	A
A	A	A	Completes Tasks	A	A	A
A	A	A	Respects Rights of Others	A	A	A
A	A	A	Respects Property of Others	A	A	A

The following attitudes and habits seriously interfere with the proper development of your child's personality. A check mark signifies the necessity of investigation.

1st	2nd	Mid-Year		1st	2nd	Final
			Lacking in Self-Control			
			Not Attentive			
			Disrespectful			
			Annoys Others			
			Finds Work too Difficult			
			Seems Unwell			

SCHOOL SUBJECTS

Since abilities differ among pupils, the school attempts to estimate the accomplishments of the children in accordance with their respective abilities. A child who is doing all that may be expected and is clearly profiting by experience in the assigned grade is given a satisfactory rating. Unsatisfactory means that a child has ability but is not using it.

EXPLANATION OF MARKS

100—95 — Excellent   84—75 — Fair
94—90 — Very Good   74—70 — Passing
89—85 — Good   S — Satisfactory
U — Unsatisfactory

SUBJECT		1st	2nd	Mid-Year	1st	2nd	Final	Gen. Ave.
Religion		95	96	96	95	95	94	95
English	Oral	90	90		90	90		
	Written	90	90		95	86		
	Grammar	92	94	89	88	90	94	91
	Reading	95	96	94	92	90	80	89
	Spelling	98	94	88	90	94	90	90
History		90	92	86	87	90	94	90
Civics								
Geography		90	94	88	89	91	92	90
Arithmetic		90	96	89	92	95	94	90
Handwriting		90	90	89	86	88	88	88
Music		85	89	86	88	95	88	89
Art		85	88	89	88	85	82	84
Health Education		88	89	89	90	90	92	91
Slovak		B	B	B	B	B		B
Homework		✓	✓		✓	✓		
Period Average		94	95.2	91.4	90.3	92.1	91.1	89.4

(No child should be permitted to spend more than one hour on homework. The homework assigned by the teacher will be in keeping with the ability of the child so that he will require no help from those at home.)

6TH GRADE REPORT CARD

PROGRESS IN GROWTH OF PERSONALITY

Parents should acknowledge not only the weak traits in their children but also their good traits and strive to co-operate honestly with the teacher in the elimination of the former by assisting in the positive development of the latter.

The attitudes and habits listed below are desirable traits for Christian living.

A — Always   B — Usually   C — Sometimes   D — Never

1st	2nd	Mid-Year		1st	2nd	Final
B	A	A	Shows Religious Spirit	A	A	A
B	B	B	Is Courteous	A	A	A
A	B	B	Attends to Personal Appearance	A	A	A
B	B	B	Is Attentive	A	A	A
A	A	A	Co-operates with Others	A	A	A
A	A	A	Comes Well Prepared	A	A	A
B	B	B	Begins Work Promptly	B	B	B
B	B	B	Works to Ability	A	A	A
A	A	A	Works Carefully	A	A	A
A	A	A	Completes Tasks	A	A	A
B	B	B	Respects Rights of Others	A	A	A
B	B	B	Respects Property of Others	A	A	A

The following attitudes and habits seriously interfere with the proper development of your child's personality. A check mark signifies the necessity of investigation.

1st	2nd	Mid-Year		1st	2nd	Final
			Lacking in Self-Control			
			Not Attentive			
			Disrespectful			
			Annoys Others			
			Finds Work too Difficult			
			Seems Unwell			

SCHOOL SUBJECTS

Since abilities differ among pupils, the school attempts to estimate the accomplishments of the children in accordance with their respective abilities. A child who is doing all that may be expected and is clearly profiting by experience in the assigned grade is given a satisfactory rating. Unsatisfactory means that a child has ability but is not using it.

EXPLANATION OF MARKS

100—95 — Excellent   84—75 — Fair
94—90 — Very Good   74—70 — Passing
89—85 — Good   S — Satisfactory
U — Unsatisfactory

SUBJECT		1st	2nd	Mid-Year	1st	2nd	Final	Gen. Ave.
Religion		90	93	94	96	98	95	95
English	Oral	80	84		86	88		
	Written	82	84		88	89		
	Grammar	85	88	90	89	92	91	91
	Reading	88	92	88	92	94	93	91
	Spelling	95	96	96	97	98	98	97
History		85	88	89	92	95	90	90
Civics		80	85		88	90		
Geography		88	89	90	92	95	95	93
Arithmetic		85	90	90	95	96	92	91
Handwriting		80	82	80	83	84	84	82
Music		75	76	82	78	82	84	83
Art		76	78	81	80	85	85	83
Health Education		80	83	88	89	90	82	85
Slovak		80	82	82	83	84	85	84
Homework		✓	✓		✓	✓		
Period Average		86	88	90	93	94	91	91

(No child should be permitted to spend more than one hour on homework. The homework assigned by the teacher will be in keeping with the ability of the child so that he will require no help from those at home.)

PROGRESS IN GROWTH OF PERSONALITY

Parents should acknowledge not only the weak traits in their children but also their good traits and strive to co-operate honestly with the teacher in the elimination of the former by assisting in the positive development of the latter.

The attitudes and habits listed below are desirable traits for Christian living.

A — Always   B — Usually   C — Sometimes   D — Never

1st	2nd	3rd	Mid-Year		1st	2nd	3rd	Final
C	B	A	A	Shows Religious Spirit	A	A	A	A
B	A	A	A	Is Courteous	A	A	A	A
B	A	A	A	Attends to Personal Appearance	A	A	A	A
C	B	A	A	Is Attentive	A	A	A	A
B	B	A	A	Co-operates with Others	A	A	A	A
B	B	A	A	Comes Well Prepared	A	A	A	A
C	B	B	B	Begins Work Promptly	A	A	A	A
C	B	A	A	Works to Ability	A	A	A	A
B	B	A	A	Works Carefully	A	A	A	A
B	B	B	A	Completes Tasks	A	A	A	A
B	B	A	A	Respects Rights of Others	A	A	A	A
B	B	A	A	Respects Property of Others	A	A	A	A

The following attitudes and habits seriously interfere with the proper development of your child's personality. A check mark signifies the necessity of investigation.

1st	2nd	3rd	Mid-Year		1st	2nd	3rd	Final
·				Lacking in Self-Control				
				Not Attentive				
				Disrespectful				
				Annoys Others				
				Finds Work too Difficult				
				Seems Unwell				

SCHOOL SUBJECTS

Since abilities differ among pupils, the school attempts to estimate the accomplishments of the children in accordance with their respective abilities. A child who is doing all that may be expected and is clearly profiting by experience in the assigned grade is given a satisfactory rating.

EXPLANATIONS OF MARKS

A or 100 — 95	D or 84 — 75
B or 94 — 90	E or 74 — 70
C or 89 — 85	F — Failure

S — Satisfactory

SUBJECT		1st	2nd	3rd	Mid-Year	1st	2nd	3rd	Final
Religion		B	A	A	93	A	B	B	94
English	Oral	C	C	C		C	C	C	
	Writing	C	C	C	88	C	C	C	84
	Reading	C	B	B		C	B	B	89
	Spelling	B	A	A	93	A	A	A	94
History		C	B	B	86	B	B	B	89
Civics						C	C	C	
Geography		C	B	B	88	B	B	B	91
Arithmetic		C	B	B	83	C	C	B	88
Handwriting		D	C	C	77	C	C	C	79
Music		C	C	C	94	C	C	C	89
Art		C	C	C	88	C	C	C	80
Health Education		C	C	C	83	C	C	C	84
Slovak		C	C	C		C	C	C	87
Average					88.3				89.4
Homework		C	B	A	A	A	A	A	

(No child should be permitted to spend more than one hour on homework. The homework assigned by the teacher will be in keeping with the ability of the child so that he will require no help from those at home.)

7TH GRADE REPORT CARD

7. ALTAR BOY

1946 - 1952 AGES 8 to 14

When I was in the third grade at St. John the Baptist School, my mother told me to become an altar boy in the church associated with that school. There were eight boys in my class. Three of us were altar boys.

My first memory of being an altar boy was memorizing the Latin responses to the priest's prayers. Those were the days before the Mass started to be said in the vernacular rather than Latin. The first prayer uttered by the priest was, "In the name of the Father, the Son, and the Holy Ghost. I will go unto the altar of God." Of course, it was in Latin. The altar boy responded, "To God Who gives joy to my youth," and in Latin, " Ad *Deum qi laetificat iuventutem meam.*" I've remembered those words all of these years. I guess I can forget them now since they are down on paper.

EVERYDAY MASS—There were usually four boys serving a Mass. Two were more experienced than the others, and that is how the younger ones learned the movements and other ritualistic maneuvers at the altar. Also, sometimes, there were training sessions that we had to go to during recess and lunch. One of the tasks we performed was ringing bells when the priest made certain gestures during the Mass. The bells were an arrangement of four bells of different sizes attached to a metal framework with a handle. Another ritual was pouring water over the priest's fingers into a dish. This signified him purifying his hands before he touched the Host. One altar boy pours the water and holds the dish underneath to catch the runoff—the other hands the priest a small cloth to dry his fingers.

The next event was presenting cruets (small glass containers with a narrow top) to the priest. One cruet contained water and the other wine. We had to kiss the cruets before handing them to him. The priest poured the wine into a chalice and added very little water, which he later drank during the service.

Sometime during the 1960s, the Catholic Church made some changes to the Mass service in addition to the use of the vernacular language. One change was the removal of the Communion rail (this was to make the people feel more a part of the service). Before this, the people knelt at the rail, and the priest placed a Host on their tongue. The altar boy followed him and held a "paten" (round tray about eight inches in diameter with a handle) under the person's chin so that any fragments of the Host fell on it and not on the floor.

In addition to the four altar boys, there was one in the sacristy, a little room off the altar. His job was to light the candles before Mass and put them out when it was over. There was an exact sequence in which the candles had to be lit and which ones to extinguish first. Sometimes, after a Mass, there was an added ritual called Benediction. The boy in the sacristy had to light a small piece of charcoal by holding it with tongs over a burning candle until it was red hot. He then places it in a brass container on a chain. One of the serving altar boys comes to get it from him and takes it to the priest, who then puts some incense over the hot charcoal with a small spoon. The priest then waves the brass container on the chain with the smoking incense toward a huge device called a Monstrance. The Monstrance looked like a brass sunburst about a foot in diameter with a two-foot handle and transparent receptacle in the middle that contained a concentrated Host. After that, he raises the Monstrance toward the people, and the altar boy rings the bells three times. During all these activities at the altar, we had to stand and kneel rigidly and move about the altar with very sharp and snappy turns with our hands held in a praying position. For Masses during the week, we wore black cassocks and white linen pleated surplices like oversized short-sleeved shirts. On Sundays, the cassock was red, and the surplice was white lace.

CHRISTMAS AND EASTER MASSES—There are three types of Masses. One is called a Low Mass and is pretty much the everyday Mass. The second type is a High Mass usually performed on Sundays. It included more prayers and always a Benediction. The ultimate Mass is a Solemn High Mass, which is reserved for Christmas, Easter, or other special occasions such as the ordination of a priest. There are four regular altar boys and another twelve in such a Mass. During the ceremony, the additional twelve stood there holding brass lanterns lit with candles in a red glass container, all placed on top of a wooden pole like a broomstick. All the altar boys wore silk cream-colored cassocks with a bright red sash tied around the waist and a small red cape. The sash and capes had gold fringes. We were the cat's meow!

DUTY SCHEDULE—Throughout the school year, we were scheduled to serve Mass for an entire week. On weekdays, there were three Masses before school started: 7:00, 7:30, and 8:00. To be there for the 7:00 Mass, I had to get up at 6:00 and take the city bus to school. There was only an 8:00 Mass on Saturday. On Sunday, there were two Masses. The boys starting their week had the 9:00 Mass, and those ending their week had the 11:00 High Mass. For the summer, we were also on a weekly schedule.

FUNERALS—Funeral Masses were later in the morning, meaning we were out of school for about two to three hours. Two altar boys served the Mass. The first task was to get in the back of the priest's car and go to either the funeral home or a private residence where the deceased was still in an open casket. Our role was to respond to a few prayers and prepare the charcoal for incense. Then we went to the church for the Mass and after that to the cemetery and more prayers and incense. Sometimes, it was raining, cold, snowing, or all three. It was always sad to see the casket lowered into the ground and everyone grieving. Then, I went back to school in time for lunch.

WEDDINGS—Every so often, we were scheduled to serve a wedding on a Saturday morning. It was a regular Mass, but a bonus for us. The groom, best man, or usher, and sometimes all of them, gave each of us some cash. This never amounted to more than a couple of dollars.

BLESSING HOUSES—Our church had a tradition of the priest visiting each parish household at the beginning of each year to bless it. Two altar boys accompanied him. It took about ten minutes to do a house. The parishioners knew the day that the priest was coming. Those were the days when women stayed home. Upon entering the house, we responded to some prayers from the priest. Then, one boy entered the kitchen and sprinkled incense over a hot coal stove. The other boy went to the front door and, with a piece of white chalk, wrote the year and the initials " M, C, B" on the top of the door frame after wiping it clean from the previous year's marking. What did those initials stand for? The names of the Three Wise Men are Melchior, Caspar, and Balthazar. Back then, house woodwork was stained dark, not painted white. Then, on to the next house. Somewhere along the way, we had lunch at one of the houses. The table was always nicely set as the woman of the house had to impress the priest. We got back to school in time for the bus home. No money earned!

CHRISTMAS CAROLING—Before we left school for Christmas break, three or four altar boys from the same neighborhood were given a list of names and addresses of parishioners in their area. One boy was given a small bank about the size of a cup with a handle on top and a slot for the money. The bank had to be taken to an actual bank to be opened by them. On Christmas Eve after dinner, we had to go to the addresses on the list, ring the doorbell, and when someone answered, sing a carol and hold out the bank for the occupant to put something in it. Then, on to the next house. We did that until 9:00. After that, there was Midnight Mass to serve, and we went back home sometime after 1:00 a.m. Then up in the morning to serve the Solemn High Mass. More caroling for a couple of hours in the afternoon and after dinner to finish up. When we returned to school after the first of the year, we gave the bank to Sister Veneranda, the nun in charge of the altar boys. At recess, the other kids would ask, "Did you have a nice Christmas?" What could I say?

OUR REWARD— At the end of each school year, the altar boys and choir girls went to Father's Farm in the mountains of Pennsylvania. There was a house, a barn, a vast field, and a large cold creek too cold for swimming. It most likely was a vacation home for our priests. There were treats available, and we played games. It wasn't much fun.

One last comment: when my grandmother died in 1956 when I was a senior in high school, my older brother, who had also been an altar boy, and I served at her funeral Mass. After not using them for four years, I remembered all the Latin responses since the eighth grade. "*Ad Deum qui laetificat iuventutem meam*" lives on.

8. FARM BOY

1948 - 1954 AGES 10 to 16

When I was about ten, my mother told me to go to a nearby farm and ask for a job. I did. It was a weekday spring morning, and there was no school, probably during the Easter break. I walked there. It was about twenty minutes away. The farm had been in the Lukash family for generations and was operated by two brothers. One of the brothers had the nickname "Yazzie," the Slavic version of Joseph. The farm was located in my hometown of Exeter in the "flats," which ran along the Susquehanna River. At some point, while working on that farm, I learned how to swim in that river, which is a scary thought. As I mentioned in a previous story, I almost drowned in the Susquehanna a few years earlier had it not been for my guardian angel. Another strange thing about that river and me is that when I was in the third grade, a girl who was a classmate of mine and was born on the same day as me drowned in the river. At one point in my life, I intended to have my ashes poured into it. I had this weird feeling that the river was my destiny, but I have since changed my mind.

About ten guys, ranging from my age of ten to sixteen, were working on the farm. Since it was spring, the crew was planting lettuce that had been started from seed in a hothouse earlier in the year. I don't remember asking or being told how much I would be paid. I do remember Yazzie telling me to grab a trowel and start planting.

This was my first job in many future and varied ways of making money. It paid fifteen cents an hour. Wow! Every year, we automatically got a five-cent raise. We did not get our first pay (always cash in an envelope) until the first load of produce went to the market, usually in early May. We had probably already worked about two months before that. After that, we got paid every two weeks. During my first year, after working ten hours a day for two weeks, or one hundred hours, I had a total of $15. One payday, I remember a co-worker getting paid, taking part of his pay, and giving it back to Yazzie. I asked him why he did that, and he said he usually ran out of money before payday, so he borrowed money against his pay. Even at ten years old, that did not make sense to me.

I'd get home from school at about 3:30, quickly change clothes, jump on my bike, rush to the farm, and work until it got dark. Incidentally, I did not have a bike when I first got the job, so I had to walk to the farm. An older boy who lived next to me had a bike he no longer used. His mother said she would sell it to me for $15. I told her I did not have the money then but would when I got my first pay. She let me have the bike, and I paid her later. So, after one hundred hours of work, I bought a used bicycle. I wonder how that equates today regarding work hours for a comparable item.

During the summer, the work hours were seven a.m. to noon, one hour for lunch, and then one o'clock until six. A nearby church had a routine of ringing the bells at six in the morning, noon, and six in the evening for something called "*The Angelus*" (*Calling the Angels*, I think). So precisely at noon and six in the evening, at the first sound of the bell, it was common practice to immediately stop working, get onto the truck, and head back up the hill.

In addition to the regular ten-hour days, other work was usually done on Saturdays, but they only needed part of the crew. I always volunteered for the extra hours. Some Saturdays, I was the only one working with Yazzie. One particular job was carrying a machine in front of me and spraying cabbage plants with DDT to kill insects. DDT is no longer used because of its toxicity. Nobody told me to wear a mask. Cough! Cough!

Once the planting was done and the crops started to produce, there was a daily routine throughout the summer months. The first task in the morning was to pick tomatoes. We grabbed a bunch of empty baskets and filled them up as we went down the long rows. As the baskets got filled, they were left in the row. When the end of the row was reached, we carried the filled baskets to the truck.

The tomatoes were picked first because it took a couple of guys all afternoon to sort them out and prepare them for the market. Sorting entailed dividing the tomatoes into three categories. One was "toppers," which were the nicest looking and well-shaped and were placed on the top of the baskets to make them appealing. The next was "seconds." They were good but did not look as appealing as the toppers, so they went under them. The last group was the "others," which were not very appealing. They were edible and sold at the farmer's stand at reduced prices. I never became a sorter.

After picking tomatoes, the next most time-consuming job in the summer was picking beans. There were two ways to pick beans: kneel between the rows and pick or stand up, bend over the bush, and pick. We usually switched from one position to the other. Some guys were faster pickers than others.

A couple of guys spent the last couple of hours in the afternoon washing the vegetables, putting them in crates or baskets, and then loading them on the truck for the three a.m. trip the following day to market. I never got into that part of the job.

Other crops being picked were cabbage, lettuce, and beets. We cut the cabbage and threw the heads into a bushel. A bushel of cabbage is a lot heavier than a bushel of lettuce. A bushel of red beets with the greens cut off is almost as heavy as a bushel of stones.

Of course, there was work every day, regardless of the weather. There were some cold spring days. I remember my knees getting numb from kneeling on the cold, wet ground. Summer days could be scorching, wet, or both. Many days, I took my shirt off. You could always tell the farm boys at the beach. We were brown above the waist and white below. One day, I came home with severe sunburn, plus I happened to be allergic to something that made it difficult for me to breathe. My mother put a mustard plaster on my chest, which burned; between that and my sunburn, I tossed and turned all night.

When we went to work after lunch, we filled glass gallon jugs with water and kept them in the truck's shade. Then, as we went to empty our basket of beans, we grabbed a sip of warm water. Ice water would have been much more refreshing. Once in a while, Yazzie's brother, who happened to be up by the barns, would stop an ice cream truck selling ice cream throughout the neighborhood and send down an ice cream bar for each of us. It hit the spot.

With summer over, it was back to school, but there was still farming to be done through October, harvesting fall crops plus the last of the summer crops. One major fall job was to cut the strings used to tie tomatoes to the sticks, pull the sticks out, lug them to the truck, take the truck up the hill, and stack the sticks for next year.

The farm is no longer in operation, but I have passed it by numerous times and can still see that little boy bent over a row of beans. I sometimes have dreams about those days. I remember the last day I worked there, and Yazzie told me that I was a good worker and that he would always have a job for me if I ever needed it. I never did, but he made me feel good, and I still am proud of myself for that life experience.

JACK - TOP ROW MIDDLE

9. BOY SCOUTS

1950 - 1953 AGES 12 to 15

Of the eight boys on our street that I grew up with, there was one I respected more than any others. His name was Bobby Mayovich, and he became the Best Man at our wedding. He was the only one of us that went to college right after high school. Bobby was one year older than me. We had a few things in common. He got me a job on a soda delivery truck; he had an afternoon paper route in our town, and I had the morning route. When I was twelve, he asked me to join the Boy Scouts; he was already a member. He took me to the first meeting to see if I was interested, and I was. I liked the idea of hiking, camping, and the outdoor life, but I outgrew all that once I entered high school. I also liked the structure and challenge of advancing through the ranks of Tenderfoot, Second Class Scout, First Class Scout, Star Scout, Life Scout, and ultimately, Eagle Scout. There were particular requirements for the first three ranks. To advance through the last three, you accumulated merit badges, which covered a variety of subjects with specific requirements regarding knowledge and activities. In addition, to become an Eagle Scout, you had to select, design, and complete a community project. I was working on my First Class badge when I left the Scouts.

I have one classic outdoor "survival" story that sticks with me. It was a sunny but cool spring day. Four of us hiked up a mountain to spend the day. We brought a light lunch and a mix to make hot chocolate. We were messing around in a small creek and got wet and chilled. We decided it would be a good time to get a fire going and make our hot chocolate using water from the creek. (I would not do that today). We gathered tinder and small sticks to get a fire going but had some trouble and were down to our last two matches. A significant violation of the Scout motto, "Be Prepared." We started to panic. Then we settled down and took our time and extra care in placing the tinder and small sticks in the most optimal arrangement. We struck the next to our last match, and a little flame started. We patiently nursed the fire along, then heated the water in a small pot by hanging it from a stick placed across two other sticks with "Y"-shaped notches. We were very careful not to allow the water to dump on the fire. Success, boy, did that hot chocolate hit the spot!

Every three years, there was a Scout Rally, where troops from neighboring towns gathered in the winter in one of the school's gyms to compete in scouting activities. Some were knot tying (speed and accuracy), first aid (neat bandages and correct answers to first aid questions), human pyramid building (speed and strength), signaling (speed and accuracy), and starting a fire by rubbing two pieces of wood together (speed).

One of the activities I participated in was signaling using Morse Code and flags. I was the sender waving the flag left for dot and right for dash. Another boy stood behind me and was given a message involving a couple of sentences. He told me one letter at a time, and I had to wave the flag for that letter. At the end of that letter, you dip the flag to the ground then send the following letter. Across from us, on the other side of the gym floor, there were two other guys. One watched my flag and told the letter to a boy behind him who wrote it down. We were graded on speed and accuracy. Our team won first place in that event.

Our troop had one Eagle Scout who was about eighteen years old. He always competed in fire-starting. You could purchase a fire-starting kit with a bow, spindle, flat board, and tinder. However, he made his own kit, which included the same pieces; it was legal to do that. He could have a flame going in seven seconds and won every year.

One of our sons was in the Cub Scouts, and the other was in Webelos, for the age group between Cub Scouts and Boy Scouts. My wife, Verna, became a Den Mother in the Cub Scouts, and I became a Den Father in the Webelos. Our older son, David, briefly belonged to the Boy Scouts, and I became an Assistant Scout Master. He didn't care for the other boys in the troop, and the scouting experience was not as enjoyable as I had remembered it, so we quit.

Scouting has changed over the years, and like so many other things, it has lost its charm. Every so often, I repeat the Boy Scout motto, slogan, oath, and laws. You had to memorize them to become a Tenderfoot. Over the years, they have provided me with good guideposts as I stumble along life's journey.

- Boy Scout Motto - Be Prepared
- Boy Scout Slogan - Do a Good Turn Daily
- Boy Scout Oath - On my honor, I will do my best to do my duty to God and my Country. To obey the Scout Laws, to help other people at all times, and to keep myself physically strong, mentally awake, and morally straight.
- Boy Scout Laws - A Scout is Trustworthy, Loyal, Helpful, Friendly, Courteous, Kind, Obedient, Cheerful, Thrifty, Brave, Clean, and Reverent.

10. EXTRA, EXTRA, READ ALL ABOUT IT!

1952 - 1956 AGES 13 to 17

When I was in the eighth grade, an office for the area's newspaper was around the corner from the school I was attending. One day, I took it upon myself to go there and put in an application to deliver papers for them. Two newspapers were serving the city of Wilkes-Barre, Pennsylvania, and the surrounding communities. There was a morning edition called *The Wilkes-Barre Record* and an evening edition named *The Times-Leader* that hit the streets in the afternoon; that was the more popular one. I wanted a morning route because it would not interrupt my days.

In late August 1952, just before my high school days began, I came home from working on the farm, and my mother told me that I had received a phone call from the newspaper office. The message was that if I wanted the job, I should be at the Exeter (my home town) Town Hall at 5:15 the next morning with my bike.

I told my mother to wake me up the next morning at five; she did that every day after that for four years except on Sundays when no paper was published. The town hall was about a ten-minute bike ride. It was still dark. I got there and met the guy I was going to replace. His name was Norm Salus, and he was one year ahead of me in high school. There was another guy there. Our town was divided into two routes. We both started at the Town Hall, going in opposite directions.

I had five days to learn the route and other bits of information. Norm gave me a green book with all of the customers' names and addresses in the order of the route, with spaces between each one to add new names. There were seventy-some names. Over the four years I had the route, I never had fewer nor more than seventy-some customers.

The first thing I had to do was count the newspapers to be sure I had the exact number. If a new customer was added or deleted, an envelope with the name and address was in the bundle. It was no problem if there were some extra copies. But if I was short, I had to call the newspaper office, and they got me the copies I needed by sending them on the next bus leaving the city with instructions on what stop to drop them off. It happened sometimes.

After counting, I folded the papers. I got faster at that as time went on. Our town was small, with only one cop on duty all night in the Town Hall. Sometimes, he folded the papers for me, saving about five minutes. Once in a while, he took one of my papers to a local all-night diner, which was one of my customers. If he did, he left me a note. At one point during my four-year tour, I got into the habit of stopping at that diner for a cup of tea and toast for ten cents on my way to the Town Hall. That didn't last long.

I had to revise the route, so it ended up at my house instead of Norm's. After following Norm for three days, he gave me the bag to put on my bike and followed me. I had my first problem. When I bought my bike a few years earlier, I did not like the shape of the handlebars, so I bought new ones that were extra wide. When I went to put the bag of papers on them, it did not fit. When I got home that morning, I had to attach some brackets further down the bars; after a few modifications, the problem was solved.

In those days, we had to be sure that the paper was on a porch, not the lawn. In most cases, I hit the porch by riding down the sidewalk and throwing the paper. For some houses, I had to stop and walk a little. Sometimes, there was a house with a corpse in it. Back in the fifties, it was common to have a recently deceased person laid out in their home for a few nights rather than in a funeral home. You could tell from the wreath on the door and a light in the front window. It was always weird when I came to a house like that.

I was back home at about 6:30. During school days, I went back to sleep for an hour and then got up for school. When working on the farm in the summer, I made myself a hearty breakfast of bacon, eggs, toast, and coffee. Whenever I finished my route and ended up with an extra paper, it meant I missed someone. Not good! Over the four years, I know it happened a couple of times. Of course, I had no idea who I missed unless I got a phone call. Then I had to take the paper there.

Our house was one of my customers. The price of the paper was $1.04 per month, which stayed at that price for the entire four years. My parents never paid me for their copy. They assumed it was free, and I never asked them for the $1.04. So, $1.04 a month times forty-eight months equals $49.92 they owe me.

Three things can make a bicycle immediately useless: a flat tire, a broken chain, and a broken pedal. All three happened to me more than once. When it did, I had to push the bike for the remainder of the route, and then sometime before the next morning (unless it was a Saturday), I had to repair it. Years after I was through my paper boy career, it occurred to me that I could have carried a spare inner tube, chain, pedal, and some tools in a small pouch that would fit under the seat. Then, I could make the repair on my route. Speaking of bikes, I always had a headlight and tail light operated by batteries. I always thought the headlight was for me to see where I was going, but when I started driving an automobile later in life, I realized it was more for on-coming cars to see me. Thank God I never got hit by a car.

I was always worried about going into our garage in the morning to get my bike and finding out it had a flat tire. I mentioned this to a friend on our street. He said not to worry; if it ever happened, just take his bike off his porch and use it. I never had to do that.

Now for the weather. In northeast Pennsylvania, you get all kinds. The only type of weather I never experienced was hot. I never sweated to peddle my bike in the early morning hours. I got drenched many times because of rain. The worst was deep snow. Anything over about four inches, and I had to walk. Instead of being back home at 6:30, it would be about 8:30. I was late for school unless there was a late opening or closing.

I was not healthy during those years, and I do remember being sick at times but still getting out of bed and doing my job. Having a brother to take over whenever that happened would have been nice.

Sometimes, when I woke up to go to school, I wondered if I had gotten up at five and delivered the papers. I was scared until I went downstairs and saw our copy of the paper on the kitchen table. Whew!

Once a month, I got a bill from the newspaper company for fifty-some dollars, payable in a couple of days. So after school, after work on the farm, or on Saturdays, I had to go to all the houses and start collecting money to be sure I had enough money to pay the bill on time. I eventually knew which customers I could count on to pay me the first time. There were always some who said, "Come back tomorrow." But it's only $1.04! About half of the people paid to the penny. The others gave a small tip, but nobody ever gave me more than a quarter, not even at Christmas. The customers had a card that hung on a nail on their door frame. As they paid me, I marked the card "paid," annotated my book likewise, and then put the money in a little canvas bag with a drawstring that I got from the local bank. Then, on to the next house. I cleared about $30 a month or $1.00 a day. Wow! All that for only one dollar.

I grew to like Saturday nights since there was no paper to deliver on Sunday morning. However, my Saturday nights were spoiled by my father. He worked hard in the mines all week and usually did extra carpentry work on Saturday, and I give him credit for that. But every Saturday night, he got dressed up in a suit and tie, went to his favorite "Beer Garden," and got drunk. I remember being woken up in the early morning hours by my mother calling the beer garden for him to come home. The phone number was "9015." I cannot get it out of my head. Eventually, he came home, and there was a heated argument. But we all went to church Sunday morning. I never developed a taste for beer. I tried a sip on two occasions, but I didn't even like the smell of it. Then guess what? I ended up marrying a girl who lived and grew up in a family-owned tavern. I lived there with her for two years (future stories).

In May 1956, my paper boy career is coming to an end. I got a phone call from the office that my replacement will be at the Town Hall the next morning. My last day will be May 31. I remember walking to school on the morning of June 1. I started to cry because I felt so normal. Every year, the newspaper company puts a picture of all the graduating paper boys in the paper. They have a large banquet and give you a certificate. My mother was going to go with me. The night of the banquet, June 19, I was in the hospital with rheumatic fever. After all those mornings in rain, snow, sleet, and sometimes sick, I missed the grand finale. They mailed me the certificate. It reads, "John Kolman has faithfully fulfilled his contract as a *Wilkes-Barre Record* Newspaper Carrier Boy."

I have been back to that town and through those streets many times. I see myself on my bike throwing a paper on a porch. For the longest time, I've had this recurring dream. It's approaching June 1, 1956. I'm supposed to call the newspaper office to let them know I'm graduating soon. But the only time I remember to call is during the night when the office is closed. I tell myself I better remember to call the next day, but I never do—end of dream. I haven't had that dream for several years now. When I recall those four years, I honestly can't believe I did what I did.

II. HIGH SCHOOL PART I - GOT NOTHING OUT OF IT

1952 - 1956

After attending a parochial school for eight years that had no high school, I attended a public high school in my hometown. If the parochial school had a high school, I would most likely have gone to it, and my life would have been so much different than it turned out. You'll see why I'm saying this in my next story.

When I think back on my high school experience, so many thoughts and words go through my mind. Such as different, freedom, wasted time, pathetic, work and jobs, no fun, sick, did not do well, did not contribute or participate, got nothing out of it, **GOT EVERYTHING OUT OF IT.** (NEXT STORY)

What makes me say these things? Well, for one thing, I have a general feeling about those years. But let me be more specific and start with grades. I still have my ninth, tenth, and eleventh grade report cards. I don't know what became of grade twelve. But it was just as bad, if not worse, than the other three. I never really looked at them until now. They are not good! I counted all the letters and numerical grades on them, totaling 215. Of that many, only 13 were A's or, in the nineties, only about 6%. When I compared my average for actual academics, I scored ten points lower than I had for my previous eight years. Letter grades for Conduct were B, C, C, D, and F. I am ashamed of myself when I look at my record.

The obvious questions are: Why? What happened? What went wrong? Who is to blame? Of course, my parents never asked, and our school had no counselors. Plus, I was new to all of my teachers, so they did not know that I should have been doing better. These questions got me thinking, so I started to do some soul-searching and came up with the following observations:

- The whole academic environment was different.

- Different teachers for every subject.

- I was no longer an altar boy.

- I did not start every school day by attending Mass and one hour of catechism.

- Did I no longer feel "Holy" because of the above?

- A sense of freedom without the previous eight years' nuns, discipline, and structure.

- I did not feel studious.

- I was inattentive in classes.

- I did not take my homework seriously.

- I was not involved. There were no clubs. One teacher who was a relative of my mother suggested that I join the band. I went to see the music director, and he looked at my fingers and lips and said, "Saxophone." I never went back, and I don't know why. I guess I was just not interested.

- I played football in my junior year. I was not good and too small, only weighing 135 pounds. I went out for the team in my senior year but did not pass the physical; the doctor said I had high blood pressure. My parents should have been notified, but there was never any follow-up, so I guess they were not.

- I bounced between jobs the entire four years: farm work, paper route, caddying, soda delivery truck, and helping my father.

- I did not have a happy home and family life.

Do the above thirteen points provide any answers, or are they just excuses? Well, it's all history now, and there is no need to dwell on it. But they do help describe my high school experience.

Here are a few words about the academic structure at Exeter High School. All students took the same courses in the ninth grade. At the end of that year, you had to decide between the Academic Program or the Commercial Program. Nobody pointed me in any direction, so I chose the commercial because no higher education was planned for my future, and I wanted an easier path. Both groups took the same state-required courses. But instead of Chemistry, Physics, Algebra II, Geometry, and Trigonometry, I had Bookkeeping, Typing, Shorthand, Business Math, and no Languages.

My best subject was Bookkeeping. Typing was useful throughout my entire life. I have never once used Shorthand, but I still remember the first two sentences I learned to write in Shorthand: "Mary ate a meal late in the day." "Will Mary eat a meal on the train?"

Forty-eight students were in our class, just about equally divided between the Academic and Commercial groups. None of us in the Commercial class went to college right after high school, but a few Academics did.

In addition to not having any counselors, we had no yearbook. There were only three sports, football, basketball, and baseball, and all had more losing than winning seasons. I don't want to criticize the teachers because, in all fairness, I did not do my part. Our town was the only one in the area that did not have a library and still does not have one. I have more to say about my high school years in my next story, "High School-Got Everything Out of It."

12. LIFE-CHANGING EVENT NUMBER ONE - HIGH SCHOOL PART 2 - GOT EVERYTHING OUT OF IT

1952 - 1956

As I said in Part 1, everyone took the same courses in the ninth grade. The only difference was that we were in two separate home rooms next to each other. In the room next to mine was a girl named Veronica Klapal. I don't remember recognizing her, knowing her name, or being aware of her through our first year of high school.

Like me, she chose the Commercial curriculum after the ninth grade, so in the tenth grade, we were in the same room and had all of our classes together. I don't remember ever talking to her during that year. We must have sat next to each other because she told this story about a biology test that we were taking. She saw that I was not doing well and gave me some answers. She told me about this in our later years, but I did not remember her doing it. That began her lifelong calling of looking out after me!

Saint John the Baptist parish did not have a high school. It was a given that I attended Exeter High School. The second step in that life-determining event occurred as I entered the eleventh grade. After the tenth grade, I changed my mind and decided I wanted to transfer to the "smart" people classes in the Academic curriculum. So, I just took it upon myself to follow their class schedule. I was in a chemistry class around the second or third day of the new school year. Suddenly, the principal walked in, approached me, and asked what I was doing there. I told him I changed my mind about my choice, and he said, "No, no, Mr. Kolman, you missed Algebra II and Latin II and have to go back to the Commercial group." He marched me out of the classroom and back to Verna's room.

In the eleventh grade, I sat in the rear of the room, and Verna was in front and to the right. Sometime during that year, I became aware of where she lived. It was in a house/tavern combination on a road I went by as I went to caddy. A large sign in the front of the building read "Veronica

Shonk's Cafe." Veronica Shonk was Verna's grandmother. She established the business in 1933 when prohibition ended. Toward the end of high school, Verna wanted her classmates and teachers to call her Verna instead of Veronica.

No relationship developed between us in the eleventh grade until the spring. The prom was coming up in about a month. I said to myself, " I think I'll go to the prom, but who with?". It was a sunny spring morning with the sun filling the classroom. I started looking up and down the rows, evaluating all the girls as possible dates. There were sixteen of them. After considering about half of them, I still had not made a selection. Then I glanced towards the windows and saw Verna going up to the pencil sharpener with the sun shining gloriously on her. I think I even saw a halo at the top of her head! Just kidding about the halo! I can still see the dress she had on. It had broad rose-and-white horizontal stripes. I instantly said to myself. "Why not her?" She returned to her seat, and my eyes followed her the whole time. I did not look at any other girls after that.

When the bell rang for lunch, I asked her if she wanted to go to the prom with me. She said she would have to ask her mother when she went home for lunch. She came back from lunch and said, "Yes." In later years, she told me that when she went home for lunch, she "told" her mother she was going to the prom; that's not asking.

Our prom was low-budget, so different from our children's and grandchildren's years later. Verna wore a shrimp-colored, very full gown with a lot of netting material. She was then and still is very beautiful at age eighty-six. She was always neatly dressed and matched her shoes with her outfits. She was very meticulous about her hair and still is. I bought her a corsage to match her gown. She had a formal picture taken and looked like a movie star.

My father let me use his 1950 Chrysler Imperial, which was like a limo. Another couple went with us. The prom was held in the school gym. There was no fancy dinner afterward. After the prom, we went to the big city of Scranton, about ten miles away, to a very popular hamburger place.

After the prom, we started to develop a relationship. But it fizzled out when we got out of school for the summer. I made numerous phone calls to her during the summer with no success; either the line was busy, she was not home, or she was home but did not want to talk to me. I found out later in the summer that Verna had started dating a star football player, Timmy, in our class. By the time we returned to school, they had broken up. In later years, Verna told me that her parents and grandmother did not like Timmy because he had no respect for her. He blew the horn when he came in his car to pick her up instead of walking up and ringing the doorbell like me. They also said he always wore blue jeans, "Not gabardines like Jackie Kolman." I was called Jackie until we got married, and then Verna said to change it to Jack because it sounded more mature. Verna also told me that Timmy used to pinch her for no apparent reason.

The first couple of months of our senior year were insignificant regarding our relationship. Around mid-November, on a Friday, I built up enough courage to ask Verna if she would like to go to a drive-in movie with me on Sunday. She said okay. I remember that Sunday well. My father, uncle, and a hunting club they formed were in the process of building a cabin for deer hunting in the mountains of Northeast Pennsylvania. I went along to help as usual. It was a wet, dreary November day. When we got home, I ate, cleaned up, and picked Verna up in the '50 Chrysler. The movie we saw was *Strategic Air Command* with James Steward and June Allyson. Quite a coincidence because the Air Force was not yet in my plans, but within seven months of that day, I joined the Air Force. That Sunday was my seventeenth birthday (1955), and I always refer to that as our official get-together date. So, life-changing event number one is complete. Verna wore a red gown for the senior prom. I bought her a gardenia corsage. Our class trip was a one-day affair to a resort in the Pocono Mountains. In the evening, there was a ceremony where everyone received a token gift having something to do with their school days. I received a token "diamond" ring attached to a 3x5 card, which read, "To Jackie, who is going steady, we give this diamond ring to help you get ready!" To Verna, they gave a little toy airplane, the card reading, "To the wild blue yonder your sweetheart is bound, we give you this airplane to follow him around." We still have both items and cards.

And so ends the first seventeen years of my life, many memories, some good, some bad. I'm on my way to the next sixty-nine years of my life with **EVERYTHING I GOT FROM HIGH SCHOOL** (Verna) that I will need to make them happy, prosperous, fulfilling, and blessed!

PROM NIGHT

VERNA HIGH SCHOOL GRADUATION

JACK - HIGH SCHOOL SENIOR YEAR

GIVEN AT HIGH SCHOOL GRADUATION OUTING

Verna Klapal "To the wild blue yonder your sweetheart is bound. We give you this airplane to follow him around."

John Kolman "To Jackie who is going steady. We give you this diamond ring to help you get ready."

13. GRADUATION NIGHTMARE

1956 - AGE 17

After taking two stories to describe my high school years, a few details did not fit the themes of either one. However, they need to be documented because of their emotional content and include an incident that will be referred to in a future story when I was in Air Force basic training.

Verna and my last days of school and graduation were a nightmare for both of us. In March, my grandmother died. She had been very sick, but before that, she told me she wanted to buy me my high-school class ring, which was about $50. She gave me the money earlier. The day it came in, I picked the ring up and went to show it to her. She kissed it on my finger. She died one week later. I still have the ring and wear it around the anniversary date of her death.

There is an interesting little matter regarding my grandmother and Verna's grandmother. At some point, while we were going together in our senior year, they were both in a hospital in beds right next to each other, but neither knew of each other and, of course, that their respective grandchildren were going steady. Verna and I were not aware of this until months later after my grandmother died.

During our final year's examinations, I was very sick. I remember having a severe sore throat, which later developed into strep, which caused rheumatic fever and put me in the hospital after graduation. I was selected to carry the American flag with our high school marching band in the town's Memorial Day parade, but I could not because I was sick. Also, because I was ill, I recall missing some final tests and having to make them up, but being in somewhat of a delirious state of mind, I don't know how I passed.

Then, I discovered that someone had stolen my bookkeeping workbook, and I was told I would only graduate if it were returned. I don't remember what happened in that incident, except that I graduated.

On the day before our graduation ceremony, Verna's mother fell off a ladder while she was washing windows in preparation for Verna's graduation party. She was holding a glass Windex bottle that broke when she fell and cut her hand. She had to be rushed to the hospital. Verna is crying in all of her graduation pictures. What should have been an enjoyable milestone in our lives was a nightmare. However, it sets the stage for us and prepares us to face future mishaps.

14. LIFE-CHANGING EVENT NUMBER TWO

1956 - AGE 17

I don't recall exactly when I decided to join the Air Force after high school. I guess "why" rather than "when" is a more important question. It's not like I had a lot of choices. After all, you have to do something after high school, don't you? College was never a possibility. My older brother joined the Navy immediately after high school. Neither of my two younger brothers went to college after high school. One went into the army, and the other just sort of hung around. So you see, "college" was not in our family's vocabulary. I don't even remember my parents asking me what my plans were.

Many youngsters in our area went to work in factories after graduation. But I never seriously considered that because, when I looked at myself ten years down the road, I saw no future in it. The primary job market in the area had been coal mining, but our generation had seen the end of that.

Joining the military was a common and popular thing to do in our town in the mid-50s. Six guys in my age group signed up on the same day, so that was it. The decision was a given rather than something to work on.

But why the Air Force and not the Army, Navy, Marines, or Coast Guard? Although I liked to play "war" as a kid, sleeping in a tent or foxhole did not appeal to me. Eliminate the Navy and Coast Guard because who wants to always be on the water? The Marines are a breed of their own and the "first to hit the beach." That left the Air Force, which provided the opportunity for the most normal lifestyle. From watching many war movies and learning more about the military branches, I've greatly respected the Army ground soldiers and the Marines. They are facing the enemy, and my hat is off to them.

As a requirement to graduate from high school, we had to write a research paper on a topic of our choice, subject to approval by the principal. I chose "The Air Force as a Career." I submitted it as my choice but was told to expand it to "The Air Force Versus the Navy as a Career." This occurred about two months before we graduated, so at that point, I had already made up my mind. The paper was not very scholarly because I was not studious. I did not do any research. I paraphrased the Air Force recruiting brochure and used my imagination to put down the Navy. Not very fair!

During the last months of our senior year, recruiters from all military branches visited the school to do their thing. It must have been then that I decided, and the recruitment process started. One day, the recruiter came to the school and said we had to be at the recruiting office the following day for our physical examinations. I suddenly started to worry about passing the physical because I remembered the doctor telling me I could not play football six months earlier because I had high blood pressure. How was I going to pass the Air Force physical? I just had to. The Air Force was my ticket out of an environment that included an unhappy home life, poor economic conditions, and a general feeling of "no future here." We were all in line at the doctor's office (you get the picture), and I got called in next. I told myself, "Settle down," my whole future depends on the next few minutes. I passed! Thank God!

Our paperwork was done, our physicals completed, and we were told that the only thing left was to take the swearing-in oath and depart for basic training on July 16, 1956 (Verna's birthday was July 15).

Sometime during the end of the school year, I was out collecting money as part of my paperboy job. I remember the day well. It was a Saturday, and I had a severe sore throat that hurt awfully when I swallowed. I stopped in the local ice cream parlor to get a cold orange soda to soothe it. A month or so later, after graduation, I suddenly developed severe pains in my knees and ended up in the hospital for one week. I had rheumatic fever, which comes from strep throat that's not treated with an antibiotic.

15. INTO THE WILD BLUE YONDER

1956 - AGE 17

On the morning of July 16, 1956, five of my classmates and I had to go to the Air Force recruiting station in Wilkes-Barre, Pennsylvania, to take the final steps in joining the Air Force. One of the guy's father picked me up at my house. We had completed all of the preliminary paperwork and physical examinations. All we had to do was get sworn into the Air Force and be on our way to basic training. We were given vouchers for lunch, dinner, and a movie theatre. We were scheduled to board a train at midnight that took us to Lackland Air Force Base in San Antonio, Texas. As soon as we got on the train, we were assigned a sleeper, and I was off into the Wild Blue Yonder in the darkness of night!

The only two events I remember on the train ride were waking up the first morning, looking out the window from my sleeper, and seeing a massive statue of a buffalo staring at me. We were stopped in Buffalo, New York. The second memory is stopping in St. Louis, Missouri, around midnight and having about a half hour before the train departed. We stepped outside for a little walk, and it felt like somebody turned off our air supply. It was so hot and humid.

We arrived in San Antonio at sunrise on Thursday morning. We were taken to the base by bus, and the first stop was the mess hall for breakfast. You are familiar with the classic scene where the drill sergeant addresses the recruits for the first time and fills them with the fear of God. Well, there he was, and there I was.

Basic training was a six-week program. An additional six weeks took place while we were going to a technical school for the career for which we were selected. All of the recruits are broken up into flights of sixty airmen. One of the first things we did as a flight was to get in a formation of four rows with fifteen guys in a row. The drill sergeant shouted, "If you are shorter than the person in front of you, tap him on the shoulder and change places with him." After that, he commanded us to turn left and repeat the same thing. Then, a command to turn right and so on until the formation made a smooth plane across the top of everyone's head, angled diagonally from one corner to the other. You had to remember your position by knowing whom you stood next to so that every time you were given the command "Fall In," the formation looked the same.

We wore our civilian clothes for the first few days of training until we were given uniforms. Flights still dressed up in civilian clothes were called "Rainbows." And as harassment, when a flight of uniformed recruits marched past a flight of Rainbows, they chanted the cadence, "Rainbow, Rainbow, don't be blue, I was once a Rainbow too. Sound-off, one two. Sound-off 3 4. Sound-off, 1,2,3,4, 3,4." Do you feel the beat?

When we marched, we had to dig our heels into the pavement so that a loud thump could be heard. If it weren't loud enough, the drill sergeant would shout "Heels, Heels, Heels, Heels . . ." to get us all in step.

The days were filled with revelry at 5 a.m., rise and shine, make your bed, clean the barracks, and then march to breakfast. I loved the food. I had never had so much to eat in all my life. Various activities during the day included classrooms, marching, and policing the area (picking up the tinniest items not part of the natural ground). Sometimes, the entire day was spent on KP (Kitchen Police washing dishes, pots and pans, etc.). We had that once, and it was a twelve-hour day. One other day, we went to the motor pool and had to wash every vehicle there. There must have been a hundred. We were often awakened (harassed) during the middle of the night and commanded to fall in on the road for no apparent reason, then back to sleep. Part of basic training was going on a bivouac, where we marched to the desert and spent a few nights there sleeping in two-man tents. While there, we learned how to fire a rifle and had to achieve a specific score in hitting a target. One night, we went on an all-night march that included running through a burning building, then putting on gas masks and going into a gas-filled building for an extended time. The ultimate challenge was the obstacle course.

Within a few weeks of basic training, I started to have severe pains in my ankles, very similar to the ones I had in my knees when I had rheumatic fever a couple of months earlier. I could not bring myself to seek medical aid because I was afraid that I would not be able to stay in the Air Force. So I endured the extricating pain. Somehow, miraculously, the pains went away. I don't recall the exact number of days that I had them. Very likely, it was about two weeks. I seemed to be okay for the first two weeks, and I know I was well toward the end of the six-week training period. That whole episode was a positive turning point in my general health condition. I never again had similar pains, and over a twenty-plus-year career in the Air Force, I never missed more than a couple of days of work for health reasons. This is another one of my stories that, when I think about it, makes it hard to believe that it happened to me!

FIRST AIR FORCE PHOTO

Air Force assault, or run, basic, run ...

Swinging across the water obstacle ...   ... then footing across requires balance ...

Assault ramp slows up at the barrel barricade ...

Whereas low-down tactics are necessary for the "mine field" crossing ...

BASIC TRAINING OBSTACLE COURSE

16. SCOPE DOPE SCHOOL

AUGUST - NOVEMBER 1956 AGE 17

The term "Scope Dope" was a nickname given to radar operators during the 1950s. It comes from the mesmerizing effect of sitting in a dark room, looking at a radar scope for an hour, and watching a straight green illuminated strobe of light trace itself 360 degrees around a 15-inch cathode ray tube (similar to a TV screen). The strobe of light is a beam of radio signals transmitted through a rotating antenna, hitting an object and returning it to the scope. The object the signal hits produces a half-inch bright green light called a "blip" on the radar screen. Its intensity begins to fade slowly but becomes brighter once the antenna hits it again in a few seconds. The circular radar screen is divided into 360 degrees, which gives direction to the radar antenna. The screen is also calibrated with concentric circles that provide the distance from the location of the antenna. This information enables the viewer to track the object across the sky. RADAR is an acronym for Radio Detection and Ranging. Radar was developed in the 1930s. It was available in World War II and spotted Japanese planes as they headed for Pearl Harbor, but no one took any action against them because, by the time it was realized what was happening, it was too late. Radar became significant in the Battle of Britain and was a turning point in saving that country from German bombers.

I arrived at Keesler Air Force Base in August 1956 after basic training at Lackland Air Force Base in San Antonio, Texas. The pipeline for the radar operator school was backed up for about six weeks, so they had to find something for us to do. Some guys were assigned to permanent KP duty. I got assigned to assist the Air Police. I would have preferred KP. I have a lot of respect for law enforcement people, but you could not pay me enough to be one.

I was assigned the "swing" shift (4 p.m. to midnight). Every day, I worked with a different Air Policeman or was assigned to guard something independently. One stupid example was being given a rifle but no bullets and told to walk around a finance building for eight hours.

After a few weeks of that routine, I got assigned to a stockade, where I again got an empty rifle and walked around the stockade fence for eight hours. A week later, I became a prisoner chaser. We hung around the stockade, and if one of the prisoners had a medical or dental appointment, it would be our job to escort him there and back. I was not given any weapon. There was a rumor going around, handed down from the more veteran prisoner chasers, that if your prisoner escaped from you, you had to serve whatever his remaining time in prison was. So, the first thing we asked the prisoner when we got an assignment was how much time he had left to serve. One day, I got an assignment to take this prisoner to the dentist. He had eighteen more months to serve. On the walk to the dentist, we started chatting. On the way back, he asked me if it would be okay if we stopped at his old barracks so he could say hello to his buddy. I stupidly said okay. When we got there, he told me to wait outside while he went upstairs to see him. After a few minutes, he was not coming down. I panicked. Oh my God, eighteen months in the stockade for me! I had no idea what to do. Then he showed up and had a good laugh. " Gotcha," he chuckled. We both laughed on the way back, he more than me.

Finally, school started. Basic training is in the morning, with a little free time after lunch, and then class from four until ten for six weeks. Towards the end of the six weeks, we all got anxious about where we would be assigned for our first radar operator duty. The whole class before us got sent to Saudi Arabia. There are no good radar operator assignments. They are all in remote areas on the top of mountains to increase radar coverage. The school had a policy of granting the honor student from each class their choice of the available assignments. I was the honor student in our class but was unaware of it until later. I vaguely remember that before we all left Keesler, there were rumors about someone cheating on the final examination. Then, a few months later, while reviewing my records with someone from personnel, I found a certificate for being the honor student; oh well! As it turned out, I ended up in the same place. Of all available assignments, I would have chosen Wright-Patterson Air Force Base in Ohio, the closest one to Pennsylvania, where it was convenient to see Verna regularly.

I left Keesler on a train to Pennsylvania in the middle of the night. When Verna saw me for the first time, she was shocked and said, "Oh my God, how fat you got!" I had gained forty pounds in four months. I was 135 when I left and was now 175. I loved the food. I still remember walking out of the dining hall and having to adjust my belt after every meal. I was unaware that if you gained or lost significant weight within the first six months of your enlistment, you could have exchanged your uniforms for a more correct size. When I went in, I had a 28-inch waist; four months later, it was 34. After a week home, I was on a Greyhound bus to my first permanent assignment as a radar operator to fight the Cold War.

17. FALSE START

NOVEMBER 1956 - JULY 1957

When I arrived at Wright-Patterson Air Force Base in Dayton, Ohio, in November 1956 for my first assignment as a radar operator, they told me I was at the wrong place. I panicked and thought I made a mistake! I checked my orders, and they said, "799th AC&W (Aircraft Control and Warning) Squadron, Wright-Patterson Air Force Base, Dayton, Ohio. I showed them to the person I reported to, and to my relief, he told me that it was not my mistake, but the personnel's at the radar operator's school. I should have been sent to a radar site outside of Nashville, Tennessee, one of the others in that part of the country that reported to their headquarters in Dayton. A few of us in Dayton were in the same predicament. It was the day before Thanksgiving. We got on a Greyhound bus to our correct destination, Joelton, near Nashville. We arrived in Nashville about 3 a.m. on Thanksgiving, but nobody at the bus station had ever heard of Joelton. Another mistake? Finally, a cab driver knew that it was about twenty-five miles outside of Nashville in the hills of Tennessee and took us there. We arrived at the radar site at about 7 a.m. It was a bright, sunny, cold November morning. We went straight to the dining hall, which was open, and we were just there in time for breakfast.

The site was still under construction, almost completed, but not fully operational as a radar site. We were assigned to our barracks, slept all day, and had Thanksgiving dinner. The next morning, we discovered that since we had no jobs to do as radar operators, we would be doing odd jobs and attending training sessions regarding the specifics of our duties as radar operators until all of the radar equipment was up and running. I was disappointed because I was anxious to apply my newly acquired knowledge and skills as a radar operator.

During this waiting period, I was introduced to the workday ritual of a coffee break. The first day we were cleaning construction debris, the sergeant in charge blew his whistle at 9:30 a.m. and shouted, "Okay, you guys, coffee break, everybody to the dining hall." When we arrived, there was freshly made coffee cake to go with the coffee. I asked the sergeant in charge of us how long a coffee break is, and he said it is as long as it takes everyone to drink his coffee. To this day, I can get half an hour out of a cup of coffee! My wife Verna says I take too long to drink my coffee. I tell her that I developed that habit a long time ago.

After a few months of hanging around and waiting for the site to become operational, they sent all radar operators to other radar sites within the Southeast. In January, three of us went to a small radar site in Owingsville, Kentucky. A regular radar site has about 200 troops and 40 radar operators, with ten on each crew. At this smaller radar site called an "Early Warning" site, there were only 50 guys and 12 radar operators, with three on a crew. These sites were gap fillers located at various spots to provide 100% radar air space coverage. After six months, I was sent back to Joelton, the site became operational, and I was finally applying my skills and knowledge to fight the Cold War.

18. KIDNAPPED

1957 - AGE 19

Within three months after arriving at Joelton Air Force Base in Tennessee for the second time, I was called into the First Sergeant's Office. The First Sergeant is in charge of all of the enlisted airmen on the radar site. He is not your immediate supervisor in terms of your job specialty but is somewhat of an overseer. In a sense, within the military, anyone with a higher rank than you has a degree of control over you. Getting called into the First Sergeant's office usually means you are in trouble. So, on my way to his office, I racked my brains out, trying to figure out what I did wrong.

When I got there, he said, "Airman Kolman, you are going to be the Fire Marshal for the radar site." I responded appropriately, "Yes, sir," while thinking, "Why me? I'm one of the youngest guys there and have only one stripe." He told me that my responsibility was to perform a monthly inspection of all the buildings on the site using a checklist of potential fire hazards and submit a report of my findings.

A few months later, I received another call from the First Sergeant. What now? Since we were a small facility, we needed the support of a nearby larger Air Force Base. The Fire Chief from that base had shown up at our radar site and told the First Sergeant that he was there to perform a mandatory annual fire inspection. The First Sergeant said to take him wherever he wanted to go. So we both grabbed our clipboards and went through all the buildings; he was taking notes and chatting with me but not indicating whether we were passing the inspection. On the site, the radar operations building has restricted access and is guarded by one of the radar operators as part of their hourly rotation schedule. We approached the guard, told him who we were, and he said, "Go ahead in" (Ah, the power of a clipboard). After we inspected the buildings, the Fire Chief told me to get into his car. I did, and he zoomed toward the main gate, speeding right through it without stopping. He then drove down the country road for about a mile, turned around, and returned to the radar site. It all happened so quickly that I did not have time to digest it. When we arrived at the First Sergeant's office, I was dismissed. It was all a test of the security of the site. I don't know who was at fault. I was not at fault and did not lose my extra-duty job. Too bad!

19. DETECT IDENTIFY DESTROY

1956 - 1964 AGES 18 to 26

"DETECT, IDENTIFY, AND DESTROY" captures the air defense mission. They appear in Latin on a patch (photo attached) created for the 799th AC&W (AIRCRAFT CONTROL AND WARNING) Squadron, my first assignment as a radar operator. The black and yellow background depicts the 24/7 (day and night) vigil associated with air defense. You can also notice the radar beams going out to the aircraft and returning to the radar scope.

Let me explain the AC&W or RADAR DEFENSE system as it existed in the United States in the late 1950s. Radar sites were placed around the perimeter of the United States. Since the country's northern boundary was most susceptible to attack from the Soviet Union, two lines of radar coverage were expanded to the North. One was the DEW (Distant Early Warning) Line that stretched from Alaska to Iceland. The second was a line of radar sites across mid-Canada called the Pine-Tree Line. On the eastern and western coasts, radar coverage was expanded by Texas Towers and Picket ships. Texas Towers were so named because they resembled oil drilling rigs in the Gulf of Mexico off of Texas. They were radar sites with the same equipment and capabilities as land-based ones. If assigned to one, the tour of duty was two months on the tower and then one month on shore. It was the most dreaded assignment. The standard joke about such an assignment was that when you got one, you also got sixty feet of fishing line because they were fifty feet above the water. You worked twelve-hour shifts every day. Pickett ships were floating radar sites operated by the Navy and patrolled beyond the Texas Towers.

The radar operators at a site were divided into crews of about twelve guys. We changed shifts every three days and then had three days off. The radar operations room was very dark, like a movie theatre. This was necessary for reading the radar scopes, plexiglass plotting board, and similar information boards. One officer was called a director, and a non-commissioned officer was named the crew chief on each crew. The lower-ranked airmen rotated every hour through the following positions.

RADAR SCOPE—Watch the radar screen wearing a headset (earphones and microphone). When a blip appears, call it into a plotter, giving the azimuth in degrees and the range in miles.

PLOTTER—The plotter stood behind a large plexiglass board with a map outline of the area under radar coverage. As the radar operator gave the position of the blip to the plotter, the plotter put a dot on the board and connected the dots as the plane traveled across the sky. Each flight path was given a unique alphanumeric number. Since he was standing behind the board, he had to print the alphanumeric number of the plane backward and from right to left. It's a simple skill once you get the hang of it. However, as I learned later in life, it was a skill that had no value in the civilian job market. Three colors were used: white for a friendly aircraft, yellow for an unidentified one, and red for a hostile. We called the markers "grease pencils." The plotter stood behind the board rather than in front of it so that other crew members could always follow the traffic, which would have been blocked had the plotter stood in front of it.

RECORDER—The recorder sat facing the plotting board and recorded each plot of the planes on a form. Pencil and paper record keeping was the state of the art. I wonder what ever became of all of the forms?

TELLER—The teller wore a headset and communicated the planes' movements to a central control center for monitoring at a higher command level.

The more senior airmen performed the following tasks on upper levels above the main floor to provide visibility of the plotting and other information boards.

AIR SURVEILLANCE TECHNICIAN—Prepared the lower-ranked airmen's rotation and lunch schedules. It was similar to being a first-level supervisor. This was my first promotion. Out of all the lower airmen, I was selected for this position within six months. On my first day with this new responsibility, I made my first mistake by sending too many guys to lunch at the same time and had to run to the mess hall to get some of them back. I never made that mistake again.

IDENTIFICATION TECHNICIAN—There was no concern regarding air traffic originating within the US. While I was stationed in Tennessee, an Air Defense Identification Zone (ADIZ) stretched between the southeast states and Cuba, which was a potential threat to us at the time. Only planes approaching the country from that direction were of concern. Such planes were required to file a flight plan with the FAA before departure, giving the place and time of departure, their destination, and arrival time. The FAA transmitted that information to us. The Identification Technician had a plotting board table and pre-plotted the flight plans. Then, when a plane appeared approaching the ADIZ, he correlated it with a pre-plot to confirm that it was a known friendly aircraft. The criteria for determining it friendly was plus or minus five miles or five minutes from where it should be. We contacted the pilot by radio if it was not within those parameters. If there was no response, we scrambled two armed interceptor jets to check him out. It always turned out friendly when I was stationed in the US, not so when I was in Iceland a few years later (later story).

INTERCEPT TECHNICIAN—The Officer Director controlled the interceptor aircraft. One of the more senior airmen was his assistant during an intercept. That eventually became my specialty. At some time during an eight-hour shift, there were practice intercepts. Arrangements were made to use planes as targets to train pilots on how to fly. After they took off and when we identified them on the radar, the officer called the Interceptor Squadron to scramble the interceptors. When the interceptors were airborne and identified, we contacted them and directed them to find the target. In the late 1950s, the interceptors were F-86 jets left over from the Korean War. More sophisticated planes and control techniques were developed in subsequent years, incorporating computers. As the Intercept Technician, I had eight tasks while sitting beside the officer.

1. Listen in on his conversations with the pilot wearing a headset.

2. Receive the call from the base from which the targets took off and coordinate the handoff of those planes from the control tower.

3. Know the type of armament the interceptor had on board. This was necessary so that we used the proper angle of attack. There were two major types of armaments. One was heat-seeking that homed in on the target's exhaust, and the other was radar-controlled. For the heat-seeking missile, you had to attack from the rear. With a radar-guided missile, a broadside attack was optimum.

4. Know the cruise range of the interceptor based on fuel capacity.

5. Next to the plotting board was a "Winds Aloft" board, which gave the wind direction at every 5,000 feet of altitude up to 30,000 feet. The purpose of this was to determine the effect that the wind had on the angle of attack. In addition to the Winds Aloft information, there was a Weather Status Board. This information was obtained from the local US Weather Service via teletype and was plotted on the board.

6. Use a circular slide-rule-type device called an "Abalon Computer" to determine the effect of the wind on the actual speed of the aircraft.

7. Draw two lines with a black marking pencil on a 3x5 clear plastic card called a "Handy Dandy"- I know, not a very technical term. One line represents the track of the target,

and the other is the line that the interceptor pilot has to stay on to get close enough to the target. After drawing the lines, I gave the Handy Dandy to the officer. He placed it on the radar scope and transmitted information to the pilot to keep him on track toward the target.

8. Keep a hand-written record of what transpired during the mission, which generally lasted one to two hours.

At the end of the mission, I was mentally exhausted because of all the multitasking, even though that word was not as common as it is today. There were three skill levels for the officer/technician team. The minimum skill level was to handle three interceptors at a time and receive a score of 85% on a written test. The next level was four interceptors and a score of 90%. The ultimate level was five interceptors and 95%. I was at the middle level when I left the AC&W career.

CONTROL TECHNICIAN—Overall monitoring and recording of significant activities during the shift.

Every so often, there was a significant performance evaluation of the entire operation. These were scheduled and prepared for and lasted about three hours. Whenever we had one, they assembled a "Tiger Team" of the best radar operators. I am proud to say that I was a part of that team. One fallacy of those exercises was that there would not always be the luxury of a warning or a Tiger Team on duty in the real world.

DETECT - IDENTIFY - DESTROY

ABALON COMPUTER

INSIDE RADAR OPERATIONS ROOM

20. GOONEY BIRD

JUNE 1958 AGE 19

When I left Joelton Air Force Station in Tennessee to go home to Exeter, Pennsylvania, to get married, I got a hop (free ride) on an Air Force cargo plane going to Olmsted Air Force Base near Harrisburg, Pennsylvania. This was a common practice if there was space available on the aircraft. This would be the first time in my life on an airplane. The plane was a C-47, a converted DC-3 built by Douglas Aircraft. It had the nickname "Gooney Bird." One source of that name is that it was the first aircraft to land on Midway Island, home to the albatross. A more common source of the nickname is the word "gooney" itself. I ran across the following synonyms: clumsy, foolish, silly, and awkward. And the word "goon" is used to describe a simpleton or stupid person which came into use in the 1920s. Was that some negative omen regarding my first time in an airplane?

I had to take a bus to get to Seward Air Force Base, a larger base about twenty-five miles south of Joelton, to get on the plane. Fort Campbell, Kentucky, is an Army training base for paratroopers just a little north of Joelton. When I arrived at Seward, eight paratroopers from Fort Campbell were waiting to get on the same plane as me. Before we got on the plane, this Air Force sergeant approached us and told us we had to wear parachutes during the flight. The paratroopers jokingly complained that they were on leave and the last thing they expected was to have to wear a parachute on leave. Here they were, having a grand old time, making light of the ordeal as I began shaking in my boots, and they weren't even paratrooper boots! (We had to wear our uniforms). The sergeant instructed us on what to do if we had to jump. It was a one-on-one presentation to me. The army paratroopers were having a good laugh at me. Anyway, the sergeant strapped the parachute on me and said, "If you have to jump, pull this metal handle attached to the parachute, but by all means, don't pull it until you clear the rudder of the plane. Otherwise, your chute will get hung up in the plane's rudder, and you'll end up going down with the plane. Got it?" I said, "Yes, Sir."

So we got on the plane, metal bucket seats down the length of the plane, parachute on my back, and hot inside as we rumbled down the runway. Finally, we are airborne, and the plane is vibrating, noisy, and bouncing. I broke out in a cold sweat but did not lose my breakfast. My fingers are tight on the metal ring, and I keep repeating, "Don't pull the ring until I clear the rudder. Don't pull the ring until I clear the rudder." The veteran paratroopers are all sleeping. No flight attendant came down the aisle serving coffee or peanuts. A truly "no-frills" flight. How long will the flight be? I had no idea.

About two hours later, we landed, bouncing down the runway and coming to a stop. My hand was cramped onto the metal ring. I pry it loose. The troopers woke up disappointed that we didn't have to jump. I jokingly said, "Me too!" They laughed. Thank you, Gooney Bird, for not living up to your reputation.

21. PRE-WEDDING DAYS

JUNE 1958 AGE 19

On June 10, 1958, I left Joelton Air Force Station in Tennessee to go home to Exeter, Pennsylvania, to marry my high school sweetheart, Verna, on June 21 (the longest day of the year)! To comply with the Catholic Church's restrictions on birth control, the only one authorized by them being the rhythm method, Verna selected that date. We've come a long way since then. Before I left Joelton, I purchased two pieces of blue Samsonite luggage, one large and one small. Talk about a good omen: at Verna's wedding shower, she received two pieces of Samsonite luggage, the same color but a medium one, and a train case. So, we were a complete and complementary set from the very beginning, just like our marriage turned out to be.

We started making wedding plans via letters immediately after my nontraditional botched proposal, as I will explain in a future story. I recall coming home about ten days before the wedding date. We were both nineteen; Verna would be twenty in one month, and I would be twenty in four months. We were young kids, and the consensus among the naysayers was, "It won't last." Well, it has been 66 years, and there's a good chance it will!

Right off the bat, we ran into a lot of roadblocks. For some unknown reason, my mother tried to prevent the marriage from taking place. She claimed that I was not a Roman Catholic, and since Verna was, I could not marry her. Her basis for that ridiculous idea was that my father was an Orthodox Catholic, which he probably was because of his Slavic heritage. Still, he went to a Roman Catholic church and received Holy Communion. And since I was his son, I was automatically an Orthodox Catholic. That made no sense because I had a Baptism Certificate from a Roman Catholic Church. All we had to do was show that to the priest who would perform the marriage ceremony, and that roadblock was knocked down.

The next hurdle was the fact that since I was under twenty-one years of age, I needed my parents' written consent to get married. Shortly after I first arrived home, my mother put herself in the hospital for no apparent reason. I had to take the approval form to her to sign while she was in the hospital. Verna's mother told us that if she did not sign it, she would drive Verna and me to Maryland, where we would not have to get parental approval to get married. My mother signed it.

A third hurdle we had to deal with involved Verna's choice of a Maid of Honor. She wanted her favorite Aunt Bertha to have that honor. But Aunt Bertha was not a Catholic in good standing with the Catholic Church because she was divorced, and my mother made a big stink about it. Rather than create a possible scene at the church service, Verna reluctantly agreed to select another Maid of Honor. That's enough for the hurdles; there were no others, but the damper was already placed on the whole affair.

There was a little complication regarding my choice of Best Man. I wanted to keep the wedding party in the family, so I selected my favorite cousin, Jerry Kolman, my father's nephew, as Best Man. He could not accept because of a conflict with the date, and he joined the Navy around the same time. So, I asked a neighbor friend, Bobby Mayovich, who was somewhat of my role model. It turned out that Jerry did become available, but it was too late, so he became an usher.

Ours was a low-budget, do-it-yourself wedding. First, instead of purchasing a costly wedding gown, Verna took a white gown she wore for high school graduation Class Night and had it enhanced to make it a more modest, beautiful wedding gown (money saved). Years later, she used it to decorate our first son's (David's) bassinet. When she did, her grandmother, on her deathbed, commented that the bassinet was fit for a king. That's where David got this name. Forty-two years later, we sold that wedding gown on eBay. I need to take that off the cost of the wedding. Ha Ha! Secondly, there was no fancy, high-priced facility for the reception. We rented the local VFW Hall. Plus, Verna, her mother, grandmother, and Aunt Bertha prepared all of the food, not only for dinner but also for breakfast for those who attended the wedding Mass.

Thirdly, the limo and driver were donated by a friend of Verna's family, a funeral director. The driver, Tucker Nardone, was a regular customer at Verna's grandmother's neighborhood tavern. He interceded on our behalf and had the funeral director let him use a 1958 Cadillac with him as the chauffeur. Fourthly, music was provided by an accordion player and two other elderly musicians who were friends of Verna's family. I don't remember if we paid them or not.

Of course, there was no rehearsal dinner or bachelor party—something I had not heard of then. Other details that didn't generate any complications or hurdles were the marriage license, blood test, church arrangements, and photographer. So, we are ready for the Big Day. I hope my mother doesn't drop any bombs!

22. WEDDING DAY

JUNE 21, 1958 AGE 19

Verna and I had been going steady since we were seniors at Exeter High School. June is one of the nicest months in northeast Pennsylvania. But it was drizzling when I woke up that Saturday morning and the whole day remained cloudy and dreary.

We were married in St. Casimir's Lithuanian Church in Pittston, Pennsylvania. Because most attendees were immigrants or descendants of immigrants from European countries, all churches in that area were referred to by an ethnic name. The more popular ones were the Irish Church, the Polish Church, and the Italian Church. The Mass was at 9 a.m.

I did not have a car and don't remember how I got to the church. I don't remember any of the details of the Mass nor the actual marriage proceedings except for one moment. That was when, after Verna's father walked her down the aisle, we shook hands. Then, he lifted her veil and said, "God bless you," to Verna, kissing her. Of course, Verna also remembers that touching gesture. We each did not have our own prepared vows but followed the canned script interwoven within the Mass. In a picture taken at the altar, Verna and I look like two scared rabbits. Some good captions would be: What are we doing? What are they doing to us? What happens next? How did we get into this situation?

We made it through the Mass with no incidents. Then, off to the VFW Hall for breakfast. The reception at the same place was scheduled for later in the day. As good as I am about remembering details from my early years, I honestly don't recall how I spent the time between breakfast and the reception. Verna reminisces with her Maid of Honor, Anna, about how they plopped down on Verna's bed during the afternoon to catch their breath, as suggested by her grandmother. Verna and Anna relate that to a scene from the movie *Little Women*. But I don't recall what I did, where I went, or who I was with.

The first thing I remember about the reception was Verna and me standing in the receiving line and receiving congratulations and best wishes from everyone. Occasionally, someone wished us well, and then Verna and I asked each other who they were. I know I had relatives there from my father's side who lived in New Jersey, but I had never met them. Verna also had relatives from her father's side with whom she was unfamiliar.

There was no DJ or master of ceremonies, so I don't know who directed the evening's events. There was a head table for the wedding party and our immediate families. The hall was set up with long tables and open seating. We have a picture of it with beer and liquor bottles on the table. As I mentioned in the previous story, the food was prepared by Verna's grandmother, mother, and Aunt Bertha. We don't remember who served it.

My mother went into the kitchen during dinner to complain that the food was cold. Verna's grandmother responded with an appropriate comment unsuitable for printing here. One of my uncles on my mother's side was a heavy cigar smoker. I remember going up to him and giving him a handful of cigars. Music for dancing was provided by an accordion player and two other musicians. Toward the end of the evening, there was this Slavic tradition called the "Bridal Dance." The bride puts on a "Babushka," which is a Slavic name for a head scarf. This symbolizes that she is now an old married lady. Her Maid of Honor sits on a chair, using the bride's folded veil to collect money on her lap. People then line up to dance a polka with the bride for a few seconds, but before they do, they must place money into the apron. After everyone has danced with the bride, all of the men join hands and form a circle around her. The purpose is to make it difficult for the groom to get to his bride. When the groom finally breaks through the circle (I did not have to put any money in the veil, but I will shell out much in the future. HA HA!). The groom dances for a few seconds, picks his bride up in his arms, carries her off the floor out of the hall and into the future, and the wedding ceremony ends. One more dark spot. During the Bridal Dance, Verna's Aunt Bertha told my mother she should dance with her daughter-in-law. She did and purposely tried to trip her. Tears started rolling down Verna's eyes.

Someone must have driven us to Verna's house because I only remember going back to my house to get my suitcase to take to Verna's. I don't remember if someone drove me or if I used someone's car. I only recall going into the dark, empty house (242 Harland Street) and feeling very emotional leaving it for the last time. It was a feeling of escape.

Back at Verna's house, we proceeded to the bedroom. We both vividly remember sitting in our wedding attire on the edge of the bed, opening the wedding cards we received, noting the cards with the amount given, and totaling the money. We remember that some families came to the breakfast and dinner with all of their children and gave $3.50 or $5.00. We called it a night before we went through all of the envelopes. It felt strange lying next to Verna in the bed. We had never been in that position next to each other. It felt "RIGHT." We both immediately fell asleep. I've relived that day so many times. There was no happy moment on that day, but the last sixty-six years of "Happy Days" since then far outweighed that one day. I feel deeply sorry for Verna. A wedding day should be one of the happiest and most enjoyable in a girl's life, but it was not for her. I try to make it up to her, but I know that is impossible.

WE LOOK LIKE TWO SCARED RABBITS

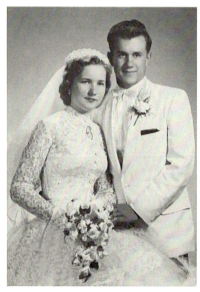

19-YEAR-OLD NEWLYWEDS

VERNA'S AND JACK'S FAMILIES

Left to right: Verna's father - Verna's mother - Verna's grandmother (Baba) - Verna - Jack - Jack's mother - Jack's father

LOW-BUDGET WEDDING RECEPTION

SLAVIC CUSTOMARY BRIDAL DANCE

23. POST-WEDDING DAYS

JUNE 1958 AGE 19

After spending our first night together in bed, Verna and I woke up Sunday morning and went to Mass as Mr. & Mrs. John J. Kolman. After church, another Slavic tradition was underway at Verna's house as we prepared to leave on our honeymoon. This was called a mock wedding. The best man dresses as the bride, and the maid of honor as the groom. Since we did not have my mother to contend with, Verna gave the groom's honor to her favorite Aunt Bertha, who played the role well. Also, in a variation on the theme, my father's brother and my favorite uncle played the role of the bride. The couple was older and more Slavic than their counterparts, and they had more appreciation for the tradition. We were involved in getting ready to leave, so neither Verna nor I witnessed the whole affair. One scene we did catch was the appearance of a Slavic neighbor arriving at the marriage ceremony with a shotgun, playing the role of the bride's father. Do you get the picture? Of course, it turned out to be a day of eating, drinking, and plain old fun with a lot of laughs. We heard all about it when we returned from our honeymoon. The tradition originated in the "Old Country" (as our parents referred to their heritage), where funerals, weddings, and christenings presented the few opportunities for families and friends to gather socially, so they had to maximize the gathering of the clan.

Off to our honeymoon after lunch. Just like our wedding, our honeymoon was low-budget and do-it-yourself. Verna had an uncle who lived in Connecticut near the beach. He and his family were visiting family in Pennsylvania for our wedding. Their daughters were bridesmaids. Since their house was empty for the week, they offered it to us for our "romantic" getaway. Verna and I still did not own a car, but my father came to the rescue and offered us the use of his 1955 cream and green Chrysler Imperial hardtop. Verna and I still don't understand where that kind gesture came from. The drive to Connecticut was about four hours on a perfectly lovely June day, such a contrast to the previous cloudy and bittersweet day. Things are looking up.

Verna's Aunt Mary had stocked the refrigerator with food for our first breakfast on Monday morning. As we gathered in the kitchen, Verna put the frying pan on the stove and then placed butter in it to fry the bacon. I stopped her and told her you did not need the butter. I knew that from cooking my breakfast before I went to work on the farm during my earlier years. Let me tell you, after that first minor mistake, Verna turned out to be the best cook a husband could have. In sixty-six years of marriage, I think there were only three meals that were not satisfying. We still laugh when we reminisce about her first cooking attempt. Verna has a story about her grandmother (Baba) telling her to watch her cook when she was growing up. Verna responded, "Baba, when I get married, I'll learn then; I don't have to learn now." Well, she did learn and is self-taught. She is very creative in the kitchen. She will start with a recipe, close the book, and improvise and taste as she goes along. She is very efficient and thrifty in the kitchen. Her favorite routine is, "While the oven is hot, I think I'll make some cookies in addition to the lasagna." I have no kitchen skills. I make the salad, and yes, I can make bacon and eggs; that's about it. My specialty and contribution is cleaning up. You don't need two cooks, but you do need someone to clean up the mess. You've read how much I loved the food in the Air Force. The emphasis was more on quantity, not quality. Verna has taught me to appreciate quality, not quantity. And I always know that when I sit down to eat, it will be great before I even taste it.

We returned home on Friday and had about ten days to take care of some post-wedding matters, buy a car, pack up, and head for Tennessee, where I was stationed. We received about $400 in wedding gifts and other household presents, so we just about broke even on the cost of the wedding.

Once we started making plans to go to Tennessee, Verna's family became disappointed. They were under the impression that after we got married, Verna would stay home, and I would return to Tennessee or wherever the Air Force sent me. I still had two years to serve. Verna's Aunt

Bertha stepped in and convinced her parents that Verna's place was with her husband. But I'm sure they were still disappointed.

We purchased our first car, a used 1955 Chevrolet Belair, a turquoise and white four-door sedan. It cost about $1,200, and our monthly payments were $50 for two years. About thirty years later, I purchased a '55 Chevy for $250 and restored it (future story). Imagine taking everything you needed to set up housekeeping and fitting it into a four-door car.

So here we go, two newly married nineteen-year-old kids with all of their worldly possessions packed into a '55 Chevy heading south on US Route 11 (now Interstate 81) to the hills of Tennessee to begin a new life adventure loaded with many unknowns. What does the future hold for us?

SLAVIC CUSTOMARY MOCK WEDDING

Left to right: Jack's Uncle George (honorary best man, now maid of honor) - Verna's Aunt Bertha (honorary maid of honor, now best man) - Ann (Verna's best friend and maid of honor, now groom) - Bob (Jack's best man, now bride) - friend of Verna's family (now father of the bride, with a shotgun!).

24. ROUGH START

JUNE - DECEMBER 1958 AGES 19 to 20

The drive from Exeter, Pennsylvania, to Joelton, Tennessee, was about 19 hours in 1958. Verna and I tried to do it nonstop, but we had to stop at a motel in the wee hours of the morning. Verna was a basket case. She felt very close to her family and did not like the idea of being so far away from them for an extended period. I still had two years to serve in the Air Force. At one point, I tried to distract and amuse her by telling her to look at the hills of Tennessee, and she may see a wisp of smoke rising into the sky that would be a telltale sign of someone making moonshine. It did not work.

Before I left Joelton, I had arranged to have a fellow radar operator find an apartment for us and mail us the address. That was a mistake on my part. I don't know why I did not do it myself. So, upon arriving in Joelton, we went to that address and were immediately disappointed. It was not pleasant; it was far from work and in an area where no other Air Force people lived. The couple who owned it and lived in the same duplex were lovely, but we did not want to stay there. Within one month, we found a newly refurbished apartment that the owner had added to a garage in a trailer park that he owned. Air Force people were there, and it was close to the base.

Our next problem became financial. In the 1950s, the military had a system of increasing your pay when you got married. It was called an allotment. You had to provide the finance personnel with proof of marriage. The military then took a certain amount of money from your paycheck, added some, and sent a check to your house. Well, they immediately took the money out of my check, but there was about a two-month delay before the first allotment check arrived, which meant there was instantly less money for us to live on for a while. Our monthly income at the time was about $200 (my pay, the allotment, and the extra $50 I was getting for cleaning the NCO Club). Our rent was $55, and our car payment was $50. That was over one-half of our money. We still had an electric bill, food, gas, insurance, etc., to cover. We had pennies left at the end of the month. Things got so bad that one night, I had to siphon gas out of one of the owner's lawnmowers in the attached garage to get to work. On another occasion, there was an inspection the next day at the base, and I needed a haircut. We did not have enough money to go to the barber, so Verna cut my hair with her electric razor. When I came home the next day after the inspection, I told her the sergeant chewed me out for such a botched-up haircut. She cried. I was only kidding. We still retell that story. A few weeks later, before I needed another haircut, we went to a pawn shop in Nashville and bought a used hair clipper for $15. From that time on, Verna cut my hair. Assuming an average price of $12 a haircut over those years, twelve haircuts a year times sixty-six years equals $9,504 saved. Wow! In addition to that, she cut our two sons' hair until they went to college. Plus, while we were in the Air Force for eighteen years of our marriage, she cut her father's hair whenever we went to her parent's house. On top of that, she had a few regular paying customers who frequented her family's tavern and had their hair cut in the basement of their house. That totaled up to a good dollar return on a $15 original investment. During this period, our social life was minimal. I was working shift work. Three swing shifts, twenty four hours off, three midnight shifts, twenty four hours off, three day shifts, seventy two hours off. So, our acquaintances were limited to the married guys on my crew. There are only two couples that we developed a relationship with. We are still in touch with one of them. We never went out for a meal during our one year in Joelton.

On July 24, 1958, less than one month after we left Exeter, Verna's brother, Sonny (Andy), was in a tragic car accident. He was sixteen years old and driving his first car that he had just purchased. The car hit a pothole and rolled over. There were five boys in the car. Her brother was thrown from the vehicle and ended up with severe head injuries and in a coma for nineteen days. One boy was killed instantly. The ordeal affected my brother-in-law physically and mentally for the rest of his life. He never went back to school. He would have had a promising football career because he illegally started on the high school team in the eighth grade. He was big, 350 pounds, and over six feet tall. The whole town held him responsible for the death of that boy. Finally, a good friend of

Verna's family wrote a letter to the local newspaper to give Sonny peace of mind. Every year after that, until he died in 2019, he remembered July 24. We learned about this accident in a letter from Verna's mother once Sonny came out of the coma. Verna was devastated and felt that something terrible had happened at home. Coincidentally, she received the letter bearing the bad news on the day our first allotment check arrived. That's life, a mixed bag of good news and bad.

Given all of the above going on during the first months of our marriage, Verna just had to get back to Pennsylvania and see her family. Christmas is an exceptional family time for her; this would be the first one she would not spend with them. So, I put in for leave but had to return before New Year's Day. We found a couple of other airmen who wanted to go north for the holidays, so we arranged to have them chip in for gas. They only gave a couple of bucks. We dropped them off and picked them up on the way back. Cheap door-to-door service, but it helped financially.

When we got home, Sonny was a different person. He had always been outgoing and fun-loving. Now, he never left the house since the accident and was very distraught. We finally got him and his brother Raymond to go bowling one day. It did him good, and Verna felt a little better. It was agony all over again when we had to return to Tennessee. There was more bad news during the next six months that required drastic action on our part to alleviate.

FIRST CAR - 1955 CHEVY

25. POLITICAL INFLUENCE

JANUARY - JULY 1959

Shortly after returning to Tennessee after visiting Verna's family for Christmas in 1958, another problem arose for her family. In the 1950s, a law in Pennsylvania prohibited taverns from being open and selling alcohol on Sundays. However, Verna's family never opened their tavern on Sundays, but they occasionally sold a six-pack of beer to someone if they came to a private door other than the door to the tavern. Was this a violation of the law? Of course. My father was habitually going to his favorite tavern every Sunday afternoon. And seeing numerous cars parked near taverns in the local town on Sundays was very common. As I mentioned in a previous story, there were grounds for my mother resenting that practice because of my father's drinking habits and wanting to do something to prevent it, such as reporting the owner of that tavern to the proper state authorities. We later learned that she notified the Pennsylvania Liquor Control Board that they should investigate Verna's parents for possible violation of the law. Verna's mother found out it was my mother when she attended the court hearing regarding the incident. Why would she do that, who knows? Possible resentment over my marrying Verna? The authorities did catch my in-laws for selling alcohol on a Sunday, and their tavern was closed for ninety days. This eliminated their primary source of income for that period.

Verna was devastated, and I shared her concern when we learned about this in a letter from her mother. This was on top of her brother's situation regarding his accident, as I mentioned in the previous story. Verna felt she could help them emotionally during that difficult time if she were there. We obviously could not help them financially.

I still had a year and a half to serve in the Air Force, but that was far too long for us to wait until we could live closer to her family. I knew there was a radar site about an hour from her parents' home. The Air Force had a Compassionate transfer policy, but I don't recall how I became aware of it. I requested a transfer to that site, but it was denied because the facts did not justify it. Rather than accept that, somebody in Pennsylvania (probably a tavern customer) suggested that we bring the matter to the attention of our Congressman, who was very popular in the community. I remember sending him a handwritten letter on a sheet from a legal pad. And I know I did not even use the proper address form in the salutation or the envelope address. It was a "Hail Mary" letter. Within a relatively short period, the owner of our apartment knocked on our door one evening and said we had an important call in his office (we could not afford a phone). It was the Congressman's secretary informing us that our transfer was approved. We were elated. When I went to work the following day, I had a call directing me to report to the officer who had denied my request. I knew what it was about. I entered his office, saluted, and reported in proper military fashion. The first words out of his mouth were, "Airman Kolman, did you write your Congressman?" I responded, "Yes, sir." He then told me what I already knew and probably was worried at the same time that his career was in jeopardy for having an adverse action on his part come to the attention of a member of Congress. I felt that he would have liked to chew me out, but he knew better not to. The paperwork for the transfer began right then and there. So sometime in July 1959, one month after our first wedding anniversary, we repacked our worldly possessions into the 1955 Chevy and headed north on US Route 11.

Once word got around about my transfer, we started to hear rumors from guys I knew that my military record folder would now have the large letters "PI" stamped on the outer cover. What did this indicate? Simply, **POLITICAL INFLUENCE.**

26. 724 TUNKHANNOCK AVENUE

1959 - 2019

Verna and I arrived at Verna's parent's house at 724 Tunkhannock (Indian name), Exeter, Pennsylvania, in July 1959 due to my Compassionate transfer while in the Air Force. I had a ten-day leave before I had to report to my new assignment. This was the beginning of a new experience for me. Verna's parent's house was a newly constructed dwelling with part typical living quarters and part neighborhood tavern, which were common in the local neighborhoods then. At the time, Verna's parents, grandmother, and two brothers lived in the house.

Verna's parents owned a much older dual-purpose structure next door, which they moved from and converted into a double-block rental. Two roofs in the kitchens there needed to be replaced. I don't recall how it came about, but I must have volunteered my services to impress Verna's family, and within a day or two after arriving, I was in charge of replacing the roofs. I learned the procedure from watching and helping my father replace roofs in my childhood years. Verna and her father helped me. Her older brother, Andy, was 17 years old at the time. I don't know why he wasn't part of the crew. Her younger brother, Raymond, was 13. I would not have expected much from him. But when I was 13, I lugged shingles up a ladder of two-story houses and did other chores, helping my father replace roofs. Remember, I had just married Verna one year earlier and was still somewhat of a stranger to her family. Suddenly, I am living with them and getting to know them daily. The project took four days to complete. We removed the old shingles and installed the new ones on one-half of each roof daily.

That roofing job became the first of numerous projects I did on both houses for the two years we lived there and for the next fifty-nine years whenever Verna and I visited her family. There was always something that needed to be taken care of, and I was the go-to guy as soon as I walked through the doorway. The reason it came to an end in 2019 is that Andy died that year, and Raymond moved out some time before. Andy's wife, Georgia, still lives there, and her nephew lives upstairs in an apartment created when the tavern area was converted into a living space. He is very handy and takes care of the household. It wasn't only me spending all of our visits doing things around the house. Verna was just as busy cleaning and doing other domestic tasks. That career is also over for her. We never had a chance to visit other friends we knew from school or relax and enjoy the visit. However, the best quality time was sitting around the kitchen table for meals for the longest time, hearing stories, and enjoying each other's company. I had never experienced something like that in my childhood years. And despite always being involved in one task or another, those were good memories. Ironically, I lived under the same roof, covering a barroom, and experienced wholesome family living. But in my childhood years, a barroom somewhere near the house I lived in was one of the root causes of an unhappy childhood. On top of that, I didn't even like beer, and here it was in the next room, free, well, not really! I never developed a taste for beer. There was quite a difference between the two dwellings, 242 Harland Street, my childhood dwelling, and 724 Tunkhannock Avenue, both in the same town, about three miles apart. I have many memories from both places, bad from one but good from the other. Seventeen years in one and 59 years associated with the other. Not only does 724 top 242 in terms of the number of years, but more importantly it is when it comes to the quality of lifetime experiences and memories.

VERNA AND JACK REPLACING ROOF
My first week living at 724 Tunk Ave.

JACK WORKING OFF THE RENT

27. WHERE'S THE PLOTTING BOARD?

1959 - 1960

My Compassionate transfer took me to Benton Air Force Station, a radar site about thirty miles from 724 Tunkhannock Avenue. It was located on one of the highest mountain tops in that vicinity. At times in the winter, driving became treacherous. When I arrived there, I was on a crew that included some guys I could carpool with. As I entered the radar operations room for the first time, I was shocked that it was so small, about eight by sixteen feet, and had no dais. My first question was, "Where's the plotting board?" The crew chief answered, "Welcome to the high-tech age of air defense." There was only one radar scope operating, but nobody was sitting in front of it, and there were two height-finder radar scopes. There were only four guys on a crew where I came from in Tennessee.

The air defense system in the U.S. at that time was computer-based and called SAGE (Semi-Automatic Ground Environment). The radar site at Benton, plus other sites in the northeast part of the country, picked up air traffic and automatically transmitted it to a control center in Syracuse, New York. That facility used massive computers built by Sperry Rand to perform all the essential functions of identifying the traffic and controlling intercepts if needed. We did not have to sit in front of a radar scope, nor do all of the functions I outlined in a previous story. However, there was one task we had to perform. We would get a signal from Syracuse on one of the height-finder radar sets for the altitude of a particular aircraft. We then rotated a dial on the set to the direction indicated. When we spotted the blip, we ran a cursor beam dissecting the target and pushed a button, sending the information to Syracuse. Burroughs built the computer that ran the system at Benton. It consisted of four rows of computer hardware. Each row was about sixty feet long, and four rows of large cabinets about the size of an upright freezer. The four rows included two identical systems so that if there was a problem with one, the other took over. Every so often, the system had to be checked for calibration using the sun when it rose or set. One radar operator sat in front of the surveillance radar set, and another was in front of the height finder scope, with the antenna picking up the signal of the setting or rising sun. Another radar operator was in the room where all the computer hardware was and had to read off the numbers of little lights as they became lit when the operators in front of the scopes told him to. Once a crew started a test, we could not change shifts until the test was completed. I would be late getting home after a long midnight shift on more than one occasion.

Once, during my tour at Benton, our crew went on a field trip to the Control Center in Syracuse. It was interesting and impressive to see what became of our radar inputs once they got into their system. A few years later, I had an assignment at a Control Center in California.

After one year at Benton, my Air Force enlistment, which had lasted four years, was ending in July 1960. It was time to start looking for a job in the Exeter, Pennsylvania, area. Is anyone looking for a scope dope who can print backward?

RADAR SITE - PENNSYLVANIA

28. LIFE-CHANGING EVENT NUMBER THREE

JULY 1960 AGE 22

After four years of receiving a paycheck every two weeks, there was a date on the calendar when that would end: July 15, 1960. I started looking for a job about three months before that date. What did I have to offer? Nothing. A high school diploma at best and no trade skills. I remember going to a lumber yard and applying for a job. I may have inherited some woodworking skills from my father that would emerge, plus I always and still do like to work with wood. There is a lot of satisfaction from constructing something. But, I struck out at the lumber yard. I saw an ad in a magazine for a heavy equipment operator school in New Jersey. Driving a bulldozer had a certain appeal to me at the time. It's a real man's job, and in control of all of that horsepower. It was a two-week course and cost about $500, which we did not have.

I don't know why I did not go to more places seeking a job. There were factories, stores, and offices around. College was still not a part of my vocabulary. I don't know the precise moment it happened or what inspired it, but Verna and I started to consider reenlisting in the Air Force for another four years. I think there was a voice telling me there was no future for me in the Exeter area. Your best choice is somewhere out there in a larger world where there are more opportunities.

Having made this big decision presented two problem situations. Sometime during the late 1950s, the Air Force instituted a "fat boy" program based on a Canadian physical fitness plan. As you recall, four years earlier, when I joined the Air Force, I weighed 135 pounds; four months later, I was up to 175. I was now 192 pounds. Verna's mother and grandmother were good cooks, and her mother made delicious apple pies. I need to note here that as soon as we arrived in Exeter, Verna went to work full-time sewing in a pants factory. Verna helped with many chores around the house. Back to the problem, if

I weighed more than 190, I could not reenlist. I cut back and tipped the scale at 188.

The second concern was Verna being away from her family for another extended period. As soon as I reenlisted, there was a high probability of being transferred to another location. Well, we had made the decision and were aware of this possibility. Verna's parents did not try to talk us out of it. One day before we married, Verna's grandmother looked out the kitchen window and saw Verna and me walking into the house holding hands. As we entered the house, Verna recalls her grandmother telling her, "Verna, marry a veteran." Her husband was a veteran. Although Verna's parents were content with us living there, they realized we had to leave someday and accepted the fact.

By the way, I did receive a bonus of about $500 for signing up for four more years. This was quite a windfall for us in those years. So, I had secured a steady income for the next four years. But what will my status be at the end of that period?

One final comment. Although I called the previous story about joining the Air Force a life-changing event, I also called this decision to join the Air Force **AGAIN** a life-changing event because it created a significant fourth life-changing event that I did not expect 481481in July 1960.

29. BACK TO SCHOOL

JULY 1960 - JULY 1961

Now that I committed to four more years in the Air Force, for lack of any other viable options, I took stock of myself and my future. In four years, I would see the last of a regular paycheck again, and the pathetic scenario I just went through would repeat itself unless something changed.

It must have been within months after I reenlisted in July 1960 that something told me I had to do something about my lack of education. I had no specific plans or goals. I did not feel ready for a college classroom even though I could have started taking courses in a local community college. One day, on my shift, I went to the Education office at Benton Air Force Station and asked for suggestions. The Education Officer looked at my high school record. The first thing he noticed was that I was lacking a solid base in math and science. He went to a bookshelf, pulled down a book, handed it to me, and said, "I'm putting you in eighth-grade Pre-Algebra. After that, you will move on to high school Algebra I, II, Geometry, Chemistry, and Physics."

The military had an organization called "USAFI" (United States Armed Forces Institute) in Madison, Wisconsin. They had a catalog of vocational and academic courses. It was free. You get a textbook and a workbook. After going through a chapter, practice problems were sent to USAFI and graded. You had to achieve a specific score on those practice problems. After completing the book, you took a controlled test sent to USAFI that you had to pass.

So I hit the books. You can take two courses at a time once you complete one course successfully. We were still living at Verna's parents' house. I don't recall studying in that house. We arranged to live there at no expense, but I would maintain both of their homes, including the business portion inside and out. I did my "homework" at work during my lunchtime and breaks. The nature of my radar operator duties at the time was such that there was downtime when nothing had to be done, but you did have to be there. During this downtime, some guys just sat around and "Batted the Breeze." Others slept or played cards. I was learning the fundamentals of Algebra and solving equations. I completed Pre-Algebra and then enrolled In Algebra I and a college-level American History course from USAFI.

In December 1960, I was nominated for Airman of the Month at Benton. I still have the letters regarding my nomination. A recommendation by my crew chief reads:

"During the past year, it has been my good fortune to have A/1C Kolman on my crew. Working very closely with Airman Kolman, I have observed that he conducts himself in an orderly fashion on and off duty. Airman Kolman is neat and courteous, and it is a pleasure and satisfaction to know that any job assigned to him is in capable hands. He is very loyal to his supervisor as well as to his crew members. Airman Kolman did not limit his time and talents to the operations section alone. He has taken USAFI courses in his spare time and is presently engaged in an Officer Correspondence Course and the Air Defense Command Management course. Because I believe in him, it is with great satisfaction that I submit Airman Kolman for Airman of the Month. Since he has recently re-enlisted and is a confirmed career airman, I feel he will remain a great asset to his unit and the Air Force."

Additional comments from the Non-Commissioned Officer in charge of Radar Operations reads:

"Without a doubt, Airman Kolman must be given prime consideration for this award. No matter what may be asked of this airman, excellent results can be expected. His military appearance is always neat, and he is always polite when dealing with his seniors. This airman is a great asset to his section, squadron, and the Air Force."

And finally, approval by the radar site commanding officer: "You have been selected as Airman of the Month. You are to be complimented on your outstanding achievements while a member of this organization and the United States Air Force. With great pleasure, I commend you for your efforts and express my appreciation for the exemplary manner in which you have performed your duties. I congratulate you on a job well done."

So, the second leg of my Air Force career is off to a good start. I am building a good record and have taken steps for future improvement. Who knows how it will all play out over the next four years?

30. LAND OF FIRE AND ICE

AUGUST 1961 - JULY 1962

About six months after I had reenlisted in the Air Force for another four years, Verna and I decided it would be a good time to start a family. I was guaranteed an income for the next four years, and since we were living in her parent's house, her mother was there to help with the baby. Verna got pregnant, and the baby was due in November 1961.

Sometime in July of that year, I went to work and had a message waiting for me stating that I had received orders to be transferred to a radar site in Iceland. We were not surprised. I had been at Benton for two years, and after being a radar operator for four and a half years, I knew I was due for an overseas assignment. It was a twelve-month assignment. Enlisted airmen could not bring their wives, but officers could. I could have gotten out of the assignment since Verna was pregnant, but as soon as the baby was born, I would be on the top of the list for an overseas assignment. We decided to take the assignment, and I left on August 10, 1961.

Iceland is a unique country. It is called the "Land of Fire and Ice" because of the glaciers and volcanoes. The topography is sparse, with no trees but plenty of volcanic rocks. There are no railroads. Thermal springs are used to heat homes and grow tropical crops. Although it touches the Arctic Circle, the climate is relatively mild because it lies in the Gulf Stream, which brings in warm air in the winter, reverses its path, and brings in cool air in the summer. There are much more severe winters in the States. The temperature never got over sixty degrees the whole time I was there. There are extremes of daylight hours. There was an annual traditional softball game between the officers and enlisted airmen at midnight on June 21 (the longest day of the year). I don't remember who won.

When I was there, there were four radar sites in Iceland—one in each corner of the country and on the highest peak of land. I was assigned to Rockville Air Force Station in the southwest corner of the country near the fishing village of Keflavik, about an hour out of Reykjavik. It was the best assignment of the four sites. The other three were much more remote and had more extreme weather and exceptionally high wind. Shortly after I left, two of them had to be abandoned. The wind was so strong that it blew down the radome bubbles covering the radar antenna. Forty years after I left Iceland, Verna and I visited Rockville on a cruise. Then, a couple of years ago, we were on another cruise that stopped at a site in the country's northwest corner—stories to follow.

As we did earlier during our courtship, Verna and I wrote each other letters daily. But we did not save them this time. The romance was over, and we were now an old married couple. HAHA!

When I walked into the radar operations room for the first time, I said, "Aha, there's the plotting board." No computer-driven Air Defense system here. I picked up where I left off two years ago when I left Joelton as an Intercept Control Technician. However, this time, I was in a much more sensitive and critical situation regarding the Soviet Union and the Cold War. There is a lot of open free-air space in that part of the world. It was very common to pick up Soviet Union strategic bombers on our radar. Just like the U.S., then and still does today, both countries have strategic long-range bombers in the skies at all times. They are of no concern as long as we know where they are and where they are heading. Radar sites were located in Iceland because they extended radar coverage 2,000 miles closer to our potential enemy. More intercepts of Soviet bombers were made in Iceland (over 3,000) than all other US radar sites combined. We were the Paul Revere's of the 20th Century!

The air traffic over the polar cap was minimal but regular. Most commercial flights out of Europe originated in the Scandinavian countries and Moscow. For example, if a blip appeared at a specific place at three a.m., we automatically knew it was a Scandinavian Air Systems (SAS) Flight from Stockholm to Idlewild (now JFK) airport. Another regular was the Russian airline Aeroflot, which flew from Moscow to Idlewild. Over my entire twenty-year Air Force career, I have only one good war story. It was a midnight shift, about 2 a.m. We picked up this blip that should have been the Aeroflot from Moscow, but he was not quite where he should have been. We made radio contact and asked him to confirm his position—the prime meridian (zero degrees longitude passes through Greenwich, England). Longitudes to the East are designated as so many degrees east and those to the West as so many degrees west. This aircraft had just crossed the prime meridian. The aircraft navigator kept reporting his position as so many degrees West, but his blip was at the same number of degrees but East. We could not help thinking he was testing us and playing a cat-and-mouse game. It was our Lieutenant Crew Director's decision as to whether to scramble some interceptors and check him out. Our whole crew shouted, "Sir, check him out, go get him, shoot him down!" The last part was in jest only. The Lieutenant pondered the situation and finally said, "We know who he is. Let him go." It took our crew some time to settle down. Nothing became of the situation. We could have started World War III or prevented it. What would you have done?

As the due date for our first child started to get closer, Verna's grandmother, Baba (Slavic for grandmother), was on her deathbed. The guys on my crew knew that we were expecting a baby soon. On the night Baba died, Verna sent a telegram to my radar site that read, "Baba died." When the teletype operator got the message, he thought "Baba" was a typo for Baby, and everyone started offering me condolences on the loss of our baby. Fortunately, I knew the circumstances involved, and everyone was relieved. Our first son, David, was born on November 26. That night, I wrote Verna a twelve-page letter expressing that joyous occasion. We did save that letter, but it burned in a fire a few years later. I took a leave to be home for the Christening, Christmas, and New Year.

While in Iceland, I continued with my USAFI correspondence courses. The University of Maryland had an extension division on the main base in Keflavik. I built up enough courage to enroll in English Composition and American Literature I. The classes were held in the evening. When I arrived for the first class, the instructor said, "Everyone take a sheet of paper and write an essay about a book you read." I panicked. I had never read any books that would be appropriate to write about. Then I settled down. There was one I read a couple of years earlier. Jack London's *The Call of the Wild*. Fortunately, it was a simple story, and

I remembered enough to fill the page. I entitled it "Local Dog Makes Good." I got an *A* on it. Phew! I kept that paper for the longest time but don't have it now—my confidence has increased. I went on to take English Composition II and Western Civilization I. Those courses, plus the American History USAFI course, gave me twelve college credits. In addition, I was pulling KP and working in the library for the rest of my spare time for extra money.

As an enlisted airman, once in a while, we got an extra duty called CQ (Charge of Quarters). It was a 24-hour shift. The main purpose was that you were the point of contact if something occurred that needed attention. As part of the duty, you had to go through all of the barracks and other buildings on the site in the morning's wee hours to ensure no fires were smoldering. The first night I had that duty, I went through the officer's barracks and club. I was impressed. Theirs was much more plush and comfortable than mine. I asked myself, "Wouldn't it be great to live like they do?"

As my tour in Iceland was coming to an end in June 1962, I put in for the East Coast for my next assignment. I got the West Coast, Beale Air Force Base, near Sacramento, California.

This would be Verna's and my second place to live on our own. The idea of paying rent did not appeal to us because, at the end of the year, all you had was a bunch of rent receipts with no equity. Since there would be future assignments, we did not want to get involved in buying a house and then have to sell it in a year or two. So we did the next best thing. We purchased a house with wheels (a mobile home). There was a manufacturer of top-line motor homes two blocks from Verna's parents' house. Verna sent me pictures, floor plans, and prices. We selected a 55'x10' three-bedroom Ambassador mobile home. They would have it ready to hit the road when I returned to the States in August. The price was $6,000. I don't recall the details of the financing. We could not have paid cash for it, so there had to be monthly payments.

On July 10, 1962, at about three in the afternoon, someone came through our barracks and announced that if there was anyone who was due to return to the States within thirty days and could be ready to get on an airplane to leave at 10 a.m. the following day, there were seats available. My tour was up on August 10. I jumped up and said. "I'll take it." I had to scramble, take care of the paperwork, pack, and say so long to everybody. It was an all-nighter, but I was on that plane. When it landed at Idlewild, I arranged to get to Port Authority, New York, to get a Greyhound bus to Exeter. When I got to Exeter that afternoon, I called Verna's Aunt Bertha to come and get me so I could surprise Verna. I pulled it off. So what could have been a twelve-month tour with no break turned out to be a ten-month deal with a month break in between. I was lucky. And so ends my Iceland adventure. A lot happened in that relatively short period. Now Westward Ho to California.

AT RIGHT: GOING TO 1ST
COLLEGE COURSE - ICELAND

BELOW: ICELAND - JACK
NOTIFIED OF DAVID'S BIRTH

31. WESTWARD HO!

AUGUST 1962

When I arrived home from a year-long Air Force assignment in Iceland, Verna and I had to start packing for our next assignment in California. On our journey to our first home a few years earlier, we had to load all our belongings into a 1955 Chevy. On this trip to California, we packed everything up the street from Verna's parent's house, where she had been living while I was in Iceland, into our brand new 55'x10' mobile home. The Air Force allowed us so much per mile for travel expenses and so much a mile to have our mobile home commercially towed to California. The rate for having it moved was much higher than we would be reimbursed for, so we had out-of-pocket expenses. Had I known we would get an assignment to California, we would not have purchased the mobile home when we did. We should have waited and bought one when we arrived at our new destination. We made a huge mistake, which was paid for again on three future reassignments.

The day to depart finally arrived. Our first son, David, was nine months old. The evening before we left Verna's family, he took his first steps. It was a bitter-sweet moment. They had grown very attached to David as their first grandchild. I'm sure they were heartbroken to see him leave, not knowing when they would see us again.

We had traded our 1955 Chevy for a used 1959 Chevy a few years earlier. That was the car with the flat fins on the back deck, which, many said, caused the vehicle to lift off the road at high speeds because of the aerodynamic design. I always wondered about that. So, while it was still under warranty, I decided to see for myself. On an open highway, while driving home from work with a couple of the guys in our carpool, I got it up to 90 miles an hour, and sure enough, I felt the sensation of losing control. It was a once-in-a-lifetime experience of going that fast and the first time in my life that I felt very stupid.

Now imagine this today. Jump into your car in Pennsylvania and head for California. No credit card, cell phone, or GPS, in a car with no air conditioning, and a nine-month-old teething baby. The Interstate Highway system was not yet fully completed. Here we go. The first couple of days were uneventful. To save money, we brought an electric frying pan with Verna's reputation as a *Heloise;* she put water in it to heat the TV dinners we purchased when we stopped for the night at motels. Long-distance phone calls were about $5 for three minutes, so every night, when we stopped, Verna called her parents, let the phone ring three times, and then hung up as we arranged with them so they knew we were okay.

Driving across the Great Plains states, the car's engine started to miss a few times. I'm a little concerned, but it keeps on running. We arrived in Denver that evening to spend the night. I looked up at the snow-capped Rocky Mountains and began to worry that the Chevy would not make it over them. We pulled into a gas station and told the mechanic about our concern. He says, "Don't worry about it; the high altitude with less oxygen affects the car's performance. You'll be okay."

The following day, we started climbing the Rockies. The car is huffing and puffing and gasping for breath. We roll backward off the two-lane hill. When we stopped, the sign read, "Elevation 12,000 feet." There are no guard rails, and as we look down, we see that the cars below appear to be the size of Matchbox toys. After a few minutes, the Chevy catches its breath, and we inch up the mountain. After a few more similar terrifying episodes, we reach the summit. Downhill for a few hours and then across the Utah and Nevada deserts. The signs read, "Fill up now, next gas station 200 miles away." Other cars on the road have canvas bags with water on their front ends. It is flat land, but the car is not running smoothly, and the engine is struggling, causing it to overheat. We turn on the heater (midsummer and in the middle of a desert) to dissipate some of the heat from the engine. David is crying. The radiator boils over. We pulled over, but no house or other cars on the road were in sight. Being from the Northeast, we have never seen such a sight. Watch out for rattlesnakes and Indians!

This nightmare repeats itself a few times for the remainder of the day. At about 6 p.m., we limp into Ely, Nevada. We fill up with gas. Since we are across the hot desert and David has settled down, we drive a little further while the day's heat is behind us. We pulled out of the gas station, and there was a slight hill. The Chevy dies, we roll back into the service station and have the mechanic look at it. After a few minutes, he says we need a fuel pump. He checks to see if he has one in stock. He does not. We ask him what can he do. He says maybe he could add a few connections to the fuel line to adapt the one he had to fit our car. We say thank you, please try. What is this going to cost us? How much cash do we have left in our pockets? It's Saturday, and we have been on the road all week. Within twenty minutes, he returns and says, "That will be $15." Phew! We thanked him profusely and resumed our journey. We will drive for an hour or so to check out the repair. It's cool; David is sleeping, and the Chevy is purring along. We start to climb the Sierra Nevada Mountains and go through Donner Pass. Do you remember where pioneers got stranded in a blizzard and reverted to cannibalism to survive? Thank God it is not winter. I told Verna to get out of the map and see the elevation of the upcoming peak. She reports about 8,000 feet. We go for it and reach the peak without a hiccup. Let's try the next one. We're on a roll, higher and higher. There is no stopping us now. Finally, at about 2 a.m., we're over the summit and going downhill. We deserve a break. I pull off the road and catch a couple of winks. Verna can't sleep. I wake up, drive a few hours, and arrive at our destination, Beale Air Force Base, at sunrise on Sunday morning. Alleluia! Thank God we made it! Our hats are off to the pioneers and Forty-niners who preceded us. Westward HO!

32. QUICK TURNAROUND

AUGUST 1962 - JULY 1963

We arrived at Beale Air Force Base, Marysville, California, in August 1962. After signing it at the base, we checked into a motel where we had to stay until our motor home arrived. This turned out to be a nightmare. We had no idea where our motor home was. We eventually got information from Morgan Drive-Away, the hauler towing it. Soon after the driver left the factory with it, he had to turn around and take it back because part of the undercarriage broke. It took a couple of days for the manufacturer to repair it. Then, someplace in the middle of the country, his rig blew an engine, and he had to replace it. Worst of all, tires kept blowing on our motor home along the way, and by the time it arrived in California, eight tires had blown. We would be responsible for the cost of replacing them. When the driver told me what had happened, I crawled under the motor home and saw where the wheels were rubbing against the undercarriage. I would think that the driver should have looked for the cause of the problem. The motor home was supposed to be high quality. I had a case against the manufacturer but didn't even consider it at the time, my fault. I also had a case against the negligence of the driver. We were just glad and relieved to have it arrive after waiting about ten days. More out-of-pocket expenses for us were the motel plus the difference in actual cost-per-mile and the amount we would be reimbursed. On top of that, the driver used one of the beds in the motor home to sleep in. Verna had put brand new linen on it, and here it was, filthy from his greasy hair. We reported the incident to the transportation inspector at the base, which was the end of the matter.

We had the motor home delivered to a motor home park on the base. The monthly rental was $15, electricity and water included. When we get the bill, cheap living will help pay for the recent damages and expenses.

One of the first things we purchased in California was a mechanical Brownie movie camera. I say mechanical because you had to crank it up to take a movie without batteries. We bought it to capture David's growing-up years to show Verna's grandparents. One of the first rolls of film we took was at a rodeo in Marysville (local culture). I remember the cost of a five-minute movie was about eight dollars (film plus developing of the film). Compare that with what it costs today to take a video (with sound on your cell phone or iPad). Over the years, we upgraded to battery-operated cameras, but still no sound. I spliced them onto 400-foot, half-hour reels as we accumulated five-minute reels. More than once, the splice jammed the movie projector. I had to shut it off quickly as the film melted, then splice it. Try explaining that to a millennial! We still have all of the original film in six-inch diameter metal cans. Finally, camcorders came out; now we have audio to accompany the video. Sometime in the 1970s, I transferred the reels of movie film to VCR tapes. The process consisted of a movie projector running the film pointed at a box containing angled mirrors at which a camcorder was aimed and recorded the movie film onto the camcorder. No more need for a movie projector and splicing. No sound except the click, click, click of the movie projector. You have to turn down the volume on the TV as you view the VCR tape. A few years ago, our son David obtained an app to transfer the VCR tapes to DVDs. I purposely saved one VCR to view the tapes until he completes the project. Who will be viewing our treasured memories, and with what medium will future generations use?

Time to get to work on my new assignment. Beale is a Strategic Air Command base for B-52 Bombers. On it, there was a gigantic concrete building that housed the control center for the San Francisco Air Defense Sector. It was identical to the one in Syracuse, where radar data was input from the radar site I was stationed at in Pennsylvania in 1959. All of the United States was divided into such Air Defense Sectors. Now, I was on the receiving end of that radar data. This was a new world to me. Shades of *Star Wars*. There was one large blue-lit room with numerous computer monitors. It gives you an eerie feeling when you enter it. As I stated in an earlier story, the Air Defense SAGE (SEMI-AUTOMATIC GROUND ENVIRONMENT) system was now computer-driven and quite sophisticated. I was still on shift work and continued with my specialty as an Intercept Control Technician. I had to learn how to operate the computer monitors, the language, and something called *Symbology*, which was how various symbols, letters, and numbers were presented on the monitors. The technology of the interceptor aircraft also increased significantly from the 1950s. Back then, the trigonometry of the intercept problem was solved manually and verbally transmitted to the pilot. In the next aircraft generation, a land-based computer calculated the intercept problem, and it was transmitted via data link to the aircraft. The pilot read the information off a screen in the cockpit and maneuvered the plane. By the time I left my duties as a radar operator, the state-of-the-art interceptor was the F-106. It had a computer on board, which turned the aircraft to complete the intercept when it received the solution to the intercept problem from the SAGE system. We used to razz the pilot by reminding him that he had nothing to do and was just along for the ride.

After about nine months as an Interceptor Control Technician, I wrangled myself into a position in the SAGE Training Office, straight day shift 8 to 5, five days a week. So this is how normal people live. While in that job, I got nominated for Airman of the Month. I still have the letter nominating me, it reads:

"Airman Kolman is responsible to the Intercept Director (IND) for the performance of switch actions in support of the Intercept Director's position. As an Intercept Technician, this airman also maintains forms and reports, monitors air-to-ground radio communications, logs appropriate items, and coordinates between appropriate control agencies in the performance of the Sector's assigned mission. In addition to his duties as an Intercept Technician, Airman Kolman is directly responsible to the Direction Center Training Officer for the control and maintenance of operational proficiency training records. For the past three (3) months, Airman Kolman had managed the entire Records Section for this Headquarters. His duties in this function encompass maintaining current records on every officer and enlisted man assigned to the Office of Combat Operations, currently 300 in number. Airman Kolman is also required to prepare and submit four complex reports every month to the Air Defense Command about proficiency training completed for this Sector during the reporting month.

Airman Kolman's performance of duty is outstanding in every respect. He has absorbed the duties which previously required several men to accomplish. Since his assignment to the Records Section, he has sought new and improved methods of performing his duties. These methods have proven practical and have been the direct result of tremendous savings in manpower and hours for the Air Force.

Airman Kolman displays a high degree of personal initiative and drive in accomplishing all duties assigned to him. Through his initiative, he developed a condensed training requirement guide, which saved personnel in the blue-light area many hours of research time. It keeps them informed of their training requirements for maintenance of Combat Ready Status. Airman Kolman has achieved many other refinements in the administration of his function, which are too numerous to mention in the space allotted in this correspondence. In addition, he maintains proficiency in his Combat Ready Status as an Intercept Technician. Combining a winning personality with a profound technical knowledge and a fiery determination to excel in the performance of his assigned tasks. This airman truly demonstrates all the standards desirable for airmen of the finest caliber.

Airman Kolman readily accepts responsibility and is never reluctant to assume positions outside his primary duty. His great desire to learn is reflected in the many self-improvement areas into which he has plunged in a determination to possess a greater mastery of Sector Operations.

Airman Kolman's loyalty to both superiors and subordinates is beyond question. He is an ideal of reliability and thoroughness in his positions and reacts promptly and willingly to every request from his supervisors.

Airman Kolman's strict adherence to Air Force Standards of conduct, customs, and courtesies is highly commendable. He is a possessor of outstanding abilities for self-expression, incorporating clarity, conciseness, and persuasion to a rare and unique degree.

Airman Kolman's appearance on and off duty reflects the high standards and ideals of the modern airman with conscientious regard for himself and the United States Air Force. He is always neat and well-groomed, presenting a fine soldierly appearance. His bearing is very well executed, and high military potential is evidenced. Due to the nature of his duties, he is often in direct contact with high-ranking officials within and without the Sector and has never failed to make a favorable impression for his exemplary courtesy and conduct.

Airman Kolman's conduct off duty includes a heavy educational program through night school at Yuba College, through which he hopes to acquire the necessary credits for qualification to enter the Airman Education and Commissioning Program as soon as possible. Besides the night course, he takes correspondence courses in various military subjects. A most complimentary record." Signed by Major James G. Barnett, Direction Center Training Officer.

The San Francisco Air Defense Sector was in the process of closing. There was some consolidation going on. Anyway, I would be the last Airman of the Month for that organization. As a reward, Verna, David, and I received a four-day trip to Santa Cruz, California. Motel and meals were paid for, plus the balance of cash they had in their fund for other expenses. It was about $50. It was a nice trip. Let's go to the video!

This would be Verna's first Christmas away from her family. We could not afford to fly home. As the next best thing, Verna's mother came out to see us right after Christmas. It eased the pain a little bit.

I continued with my USAFI high school correspondence courses and picked up nine more college credits at Yuba City Community College and Sacramento State College. I had previously completed a college-level Accounting I course from USAFI, so I now had 24 credits. On one of my visits to the base Education Office, I became aware of a program the Air Force recently created called AECP (Airman Education and Commissioning Program). If accepted, the Air Force sends you to college for two years to complete your degree. You are still on active duty receiving full pay and benefits. If you were not already a Staff Sergeant (4 stripes, I now had three stripes), they promoted you to that rank. However, you did not have to wear a uniform the whole time. After completing your degree, you go to Officer Training School for twelve weeks at Lackland Air Force Base and be commissioned a Second Lieutenant. The requirements for the program were: at least 30 college credits; pass a test similar to the SAT; meet a review board; be recommended by your Commanding

Officer. I did not have the thirty credits, so I could not apply, but the Education Officer advised me to take the test. I did, but barely passed.

Sometime in the early summer of 1963, I received orders reassigning me to the Chicago Air Defense Sector at Truax Field in Madison, Wisconsin. So now we had to have the motor home hauled back two-thirds of the way across the country. More expenses. We had not yet received the bill for the trip to California. Maybe it got lost and we're home free. I did not inquire. To get the motor home ready for the trip, I had to disconnect the water supply and sewage lines, fasten the appliances to the floor, and place the furniture in a position so the pieces don't slide around. Also, I had to take everything out of the kitchen cabinets and store them in boxes that would not move around during the trip. You just don't walk out the door and have the driver hook up the motor home and drive away.

We still had the '59 Chevy. But rather than risk the higher peaks of the Colorado Rockies, we planned on taking what was known as the northern route through Wyoming, where the peaks were not as high. So, after a short stay in California, we hit the road again. I hope this trip is not as exciting.

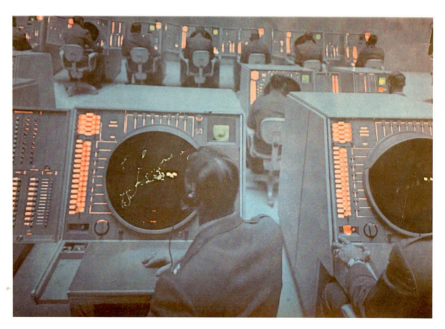

SAGE BLUE-LIGHT ROOM

33. LIFE-CHANGING EVENT NUMBER FOUR

JULY 1963 - DECEMBER 1964

Sometime in the summer of 1963, Verna, David (age one and a half), and I left Beale Air Force Base for our new assignment at Truax Field in Madison, Wisconsin. As I stated in the previous story, we took the northern route through Wyoming instead of the lower one through Colorado to avoid the highest peaks of the Rockies. The Interstate System was still incomplete, and we still did not have credit cards, cell phones, or GPS.

Verna made a batch of cookies for the road and put some in a brown paper bag for David to keep in the back seat for himself. There were no seat belts or car seats in the rear, but I had installed after-manufacture seat belts in the front of our '59 Chevy. David hung on to that paper bag the whole trip and twisted the top into a round stick. It was the cutest sight to see him treasure that bag.

We drove to Chicago without incident—such a pleasure compared to the nightmare of the trip one year earlier. Verna and David flew from Chicago to Verna's parents' home in Pennsylvania, and I headed north to Madison. Wisconsin is a beautiful state and reminded us of Pennsylvania, where we grew up. One significant difference, though, was the more severe cold in the winter.

My first priority in Madison was to find a park for our motor home. It arrived there without blowing any tires, which was not understandable since it had blown eight on the trip to California. There were no parks on the base, so our monthly rental fee will be more than the $15 it was at Beale.

My second priority was enrolling in an evening course at the University of Wisconsin in Madison. I still needed six credit hours to qualify for the Airman's Education and Commissioning Program. The selections were limited, so I had to enroll in a math course, which was not my best subject. It became one of my most challenging college experiences. On the first night of class, this Greek professor walks into the room, goes directly to the blackboard, and writes, " *a x 0 = 0, prove it.*" He has to be kidding. In his hard-to-understand broken English, he goes on with five subsequent equations and ends with the last one reading "*a x 0= 0.*" Was all of that necessary? I believed him in step one. I'm in trouble. What's the point?

There were about sixty students in the class on that first night. The following week, only twenty-five showed up. By the end of the semester, we were down to twelve, with me hanging on by the skin of my teeth. I could not drop out. I needed those three credits. It came time for the final exam, and I just knew one of the problems would be "*'a x 0 = 0, prove it'.*" I memorized the steps in the process but did not understand them. One of the professor's favorite sayings regarding mathematical concepts was that it was intuitive. Mathematical theories and concepts are not intuitive to me. I am currently working on a self-study program to teach myself trigonometry and calculus, which I have never had in school. Four books are involved, and I have just started the third one. Back to the final exam, I am better at setting up and solving equations than proving mathematical concepts. Sure enough, the first problem was *x times 0 = 0, prove it*. I panicked. I had *a x 0 = 0* down pat. I settled down and realized that all I had to do was change the *x* to an *a* in the process, and I had it. I got a C in that course, one of only three Cs I had earned in six years of college. I enrolled in American History II in the spring semester, which gave me the thirty credits I needed.

I resumed my position as an Intercept Control Technician in the SAGE system. One last bit of information on that Air Defense System before I leave it. The computer system was a dual system, so if there was a problem with one, the other could be used. Additionally, periodically, one of the systems was used for training. It was similar to a war game. A film was inserted into it, portraying a mock air attack on the US. It ran for about two hours, and the crew was evaluated on how many enemy planes had penetrated our radar and the extent of the damage, not unlike video games today. After two hours, you were mentally drained.

Shortly after arriving at Truax, I got promoted to Staff Sergeant (four stripes). That caused a lot of resentment from my peers because they felt they deserved the promotion before me since they were stationed there longer than me. They also said that I got promoted only because I was going to night school. I facetiously said to myself, "I'm sorry I stole your stripe." In the military, you get a formal performance review by your supervisor every year, which is the criteria for rank advancement.

We drove to Pennsylvania for the Christmas of 1963. We had to be back for New Year's. We drove straight through for nineteen hours. When we returned home on the evening that I was supposed to go to work at midnight, our furnace was not working and the water pipes were frozen. I called in to get the night off and found a plumber to come to repair the pipes. I don't recall having to call anyone to fix the furnace. I must have gotten it going on my own.

Remember the bill I was expecting in California for the blown tires and dollars per mile for having our motor home towed across the country? Well, it showed up in the mail, eight hundred and some dollars. It had taken over a year to catch up with me. We never forgot about it but I did think it had fallen through the crack. When I took it to the base finance office to settle it, the clerk told me it should have been sent directly to them, not to me. And if I had not brought it to their attention, I would never have had to pay it. I'm glad I took it in. I would not have liked to have wondered about it for the rest of my life.

When I finally had my thirty college credits, I submitted my formal application for the AECP, met the board, and got a letter of recommendation from my commanding officer. I gave my application a few weeks to run through the system. Then, one day, I called Wright-Patterson Air Force Base in Ohio, where it was being considered. The person on the phone said yes, they did receive it, but I was not yet selected because I had the bare minimum of thirty credits, and they had applications from airmen who had more credits than me and were getting chosen before me. I told him I was enrolled in a correspondence college course in Economics for three credits and would complete it shortly. He said to have the school send in a transcript as soon as it was finished. About a month later, I called the Ohio office to see if they had received the transcript, and they said yes, they did. There was a moment of silence on the phone, and then I heard him say, "By the way, you are in the program." I can still hear those words. I about fell over and knew something big had just happened to me.

I asked the guy on the phone what happens now. He said, "We're going to send you to college." I asked where. He said, "Where do you want to go?" I said, "Can I go to any college in the country?" He said, "No, wait a minute; it depends on your background and what you're suited for." He started rattling off universities. I recall Arizona State and Florida State, but I don't remember any others until he said, "Syracuse University." I said, "Ok, I'll take that." Then I asked, "What next?" He said, "You'll start in January 1965 for the spring semester and graduate in January 1967 with a BS in Business Administration and a major in Production Management. Then, I will go to Officer Training School at Lackland AFB in Texas for twelve weeks and on to school to become a Procurement/Contracting Officer." He told me I would receive information from Syracuse and that the personnel at Truax would arrange my transfer. I told him to thank the committee for selecting me. I then called Verna to give her the big news, and we started to digest it. Was it a dream? Did I hear the guy correctly? We couldn't believe it. Our lives will never be the same. I had just experienced my **FOURTH LIFE-CHANGING EVENT**.

BEFORE JACK BECAME AN OFFICER

34. SYRACUSE UNIVERSITY

DECEMBER 1964 - JANUARY 1967 AGES 27 to 29

We departed Truax Field in Madison, Wisconsin, just before Christmas 1964 so I could start classes at Syracuse University in January. So our motor home is on its way back to the womb (close enough, Syracuse being only a few hours from where it had been born two and a half years earlier). It did not blow any tires on this leg of its epic journey.

Verna, David, and I went in the '59 Chevy, once again, non-stop, with no incidents. We arrived in Pennsylvania a few days before Christmas. Our motor home was due to arrive in Syracuse about a day or two later. I left Verna and David at Verna's parents' house while her brother Raymond and I scooted up to Syracuse to find a place to set up our motor home. We selected a place called "Shady Lane Mobile Home Park," about half an hour from the University. After the driver backed our home into the lot, we wished him a Merry Christmas and returned to Pennsylvania the day before Christmas Eve.

Once I signed out at Truax Field, I was off duty. I was officially still in the Air Force but had no duties to perform or even on call. My responsibilities were registering for classes, attending them, and completing three years of college in the next two years. I don't remember any requirement to maintain a certain GPA, but I ended up with a 3.2. When the school was off, I was off. I did have to take courses during the two summers I was there. In the military, you get thirty days leave each year. So, for the two years I was at Syracuse, I did not have to take leave and accumulated sixty days of vacation time. What a deal!

Soon after the holidays, Verna, her father, and I went to Shady Lane to hook up our home. We had to insert the 220-volt plug into the outlet on a pole. We had an electric range and clothes dryer that needed 220 volts. Then, connect the sewer line to the lot and a copper water line to the water supply line. I had to wrap the pipe with a thermostatically controlled heating tape to keep it from freezing. Next, mount the six-foot TV antenna to the side of the motor home. The furnace ran on oil with a fifty-five-gallon metal drum resting on cinder blocks under the mobile home. I don't recall where I got the drum for each place we parked the home. Nor do I remember what I did with each one every time we moved. I know I didn't put it inside for the trip. So when we got to Shady Lane, I had to get a barrel, hook it up to the furnace, and have oil delivered. After getting the furnace going and heating the motor home, the pipes started to leak in numerous places, including some within the walls, which was a disaster. When we left Wisconsin, I knew enough to put anti-freeze in the toilet and all the drains. I left all the faucets and the main drain open, thinking that any water remaining in those lines would drain out as the driver pulled it away and went down the road. I really should have had the water line blown out with an air compressor. That was a huge mistake on my part. Verna's father and I eventually repaired all the leaks, turned the heat down, and returned to Pennsylvania. I had to be back later in January to register and start classes.

There were about twenty of us in the program. We were at various stages in pursuit of our degrees. We always had the same meeting table in the cafeteria to chat over coffee between classes. There was always at least a couple of us at the table. The professors loved us. We were good students; we had been out into the world and appreciated the opportunity. We attended class, did our homework, participated, and contributed in class. We knew what jobs we were going into right after graduation. We also had a good reputation with other students.

Three notables attending Syracuse University then were Larry Czonka and Floyd Little, who are of football fame, and Dave Bing in basketball.

Our tuition was paid in full. The Air Force gave us a bookstore credit card for books, but we could not use it for supplies. I tracked how much my first thirty college credits cost me before Syracuse. I had to pay a small percentage of each night class I took. The correspondence courses, including books, were free. The night classes plus books came to about $250. So that's what four years of college cost me.

Speaking of registration, all of us Air Force types were offered jobs as cashiers during registration. Of course, I took advantage of that opportunity to make a couple of extra bucks. I remember one incident while registering students. This girl approached my table and said, "Tuition, room, and board, how much?" I said $800. Then she said, "I'll take two, one for me and one for my sister behind me." The $800 was insignificant to me at the time because I had no idea what college cost. It became more meaningful to Verna and me when we had to shell out $30,000 for David's education at RPI and $50,000 for Kevin at Cornell. It gets magnified when David's children cost him about $50,000 per year. What struck me about the girl's remark was that she treated it so casually, as if she was ordering two burgers at McDonald's. I thought, kid, you take it so much for granted. It's a "when I was your age moment" as I thought of myself at her age, with college not being a part of my world nor anywhere on the horizon.

Since we would be at Syracuse for two years, Verna and I decided it would be a good time to add to our family. Plus, I was there for the event this time, unlike in Iceland, when David was born four years earlier. And once again, Verna's mother will be on hand to help. Kevin was born on September 9, 1965. We went to the hospital around eight a.m. Verna's mother stayed with David. I took my schoolwork to do and was ready for the long haul because Verna was in labor for nineteen hours with David. In 1965, fathers had a waiting room, unlike today. Within a couple of hours, Kevin had entered the world.

During the semester break in January 1966, we went down to Pennsylvania for the holidays. On the way back to Syracuse, we ran into the historical "Blizzard of '66." It had snowed in Pennsylvania but cleared up as we left. We listened to a Scranton radio station in our '59 Chevy and kept it on to see how far north the station would last. We should have changed the radio station to something more local. As we approached Binghamton, the storm was getting worse by the mile. As we entered Cortland, it got bad. I pulled to the side of the road and started to put chains on the rear wheels. I was lying underneath the car with my feet sticking out. Then, some guy in a hooded parka knocked on the window and asked Verna if I had been run over. Verna told him what I was doing, and he strongly advised us not to go another mile. He invited us to spend the night at his house. We were apprehensive but took him up on the offer. David was a little over four years old, and Kevin was four months old. When we went to his house, it was being remolded with gutted walls. It was an Italian family. They invited other family members over for a storm party and made us feel a part of them. When we woke up in the morning, the snow had stopped. I shoveled their sidewalk as a thank-you gesture, and we left a few dollars on the bedside table. After breakfast, we headed north again on Interstate 81. As we approached Syracuse, all traffic came to a halt. After a couple of hours, a side road that ran through an Indian reservation opened. We finally arrived home at about four p.m. to find our motor home covered by twelve-foot drifts and the electricity down. A neighbor invited us into their place, where they used their gas stove for heat. We were praying that our pipes did not freeze. After a couple of hours, the electricity came back on. I dug into our home, and all was well.

Sometime in 1966, we purchased our first brand-new car. We had the '59 Chevy for about six years. We bought an Ambassador built by the Nash people, famous at the time for their Rambler, one of the more economical cars on the road. But Nash wanted to upgrade their image and go after a higher-end market, so they made it a point not to put the word "Rambler" anywhere on the vehicle or in any advertisements for it. Compare the names "Rambler" versus "Ambassador," and you get the idea. Since Nash wanted to kick it up a notch, and I was on my way to getting a college degree, I was in a "kick-it-up-a-notch" attitude. Our new car was red with a white top and a red interior and had air conditioning. It just occurred to me that the name of our mobile home was also "Ambassador," which was quite a coincidence.

While we were at Syracuse, it occurred to Verna and me that since I would be entering the officer ranks shortly, we had better develop our drinking skills. Until then, we had never had any beer, wine, or liquor in our house. I did not like beer, so we decided to start with wine; what else but Mogen David Manischewitz Concord grape? After one bottle, we never went back to it again; it was too sweet. Still, on a tight budget, we tried jug wines such as Thunderbird at $3.99 a gallon. But today, our go-to drink is a glass or two of chardonnay or cabernet sauvignon. We never really got into the hard liquor drinks except for an occasional brandy with dark chocolate. But to check them out, we bought the *Old Mr. Boston Bartenders Guide* and started on page one. We got hooked on Grasshoppers, Pink Squirrels, and Brandy Alexanders. They are all made with equal parts of heavy cream, creme de cocoa, with creme de menthe for the grasshoppers, almond-flavored cherry liquor for the pink squirrels, and cognac for the brandy alexanders. They were good! But after a while, the heavy cream started reading "**HEAVY**" on the bathroom scale. There were about 300 calories in each drink, and we got about two drinks each from a blender. So we had to move on in *Mr. Boston's* bar guide, and after a while, we felt that we could hold our own at Happy Hour in the Officers' Club.

Since I completed my degree requirements in January, there was no graduation ceremony to attend. After taking final exams in December, we arranged to leave Shady Lane. I had orders to start Officer Training School in Texas in February. After twelve weeks, I had to report to my next assignment, Oxnard Air Force Base, one hour north of Los Angeles. Oh no! Here we go again across the country. We had our motor home moved off our lot, parked in another area to be picked up later, and moved to California. This time, I knew enough to have the water lines blown out. Verna and the boys stayed with her parents while I attended Officer Training School.

So, exactly five years after I took my first college course in Iceland, I now have a college degree. I had come a long way since I graduated high school ten and a half years earlier. Unlike some of my nightmarish experiences in earlier years, this was a dream beyond my wildest expectations that came true.

"KNOWLEDGE CROWNS THOSE WHO SEEK HER" is Syracuse University's motto. It is embossed on my class ring. It could be a subtitle to my memoirs. I feel good about myself overtime I repeat those words.

35. TRANSITION POINT

FEBRUARY - AUGUST 1967

I started Officer Training School (OTS) for twelve weeks at Lackland Air Force Base in San Antonio, Texas. Ironically, it was the same base where I went through Air Force basic training as an enlisted airman ten and a half years earlier. This was a completely different experience. My first impression is that we were treated in a much better manner. The living conditions were nicer, and there was no harassment. A small cadre of us had prior military service experience, so we quickly adapted to the routine. The instructors used us as role models. The entire twelve weeks were very varied, structured, and demanding. Every day (except Sundays) started at five a.m., with a public address announcement in the barracks that was both a wake-up call and informing us what the uniform of the day was. The days were filled with inspections, classroom instruction, physical training, and drilling with no break in between. We were free after dinner, but there was still plenty to do until lights out at ten p.m. I had never felt so physically, mentally disciplined, and emotionally complete in all of my life. The only thing missing was the rest of my family, who were staying with Verna's parents in Pennsylvania.

Even though I had been in the Air Force when I started OTS and already had uniforms, I was issued a new set. Officers' uniforms were a little bit more flashy, and of course, I no longer had the rank of Staff Sergeant with four stripes on my sleeves. Speaking of uniforms, there were no "Rainbows" harassments, as I described in a previous story. Also, the first thing we had to do with our uniforms was to go through every item and cut off all pieces of extra threads. Dangling pieces of string were called "cables." During inspections, if you had a cable hanging on you, the instructor cut it off, and you got one demerit (gig) for each one. On top of that, you got one gig for every knot that the instructor could tie with it.

I don't know what happens if you have too many gigs in one week because I have never had "too many."

Our books had to be arranged on shelves from the tallest to the shortest. Shoes under the bed had to be lined up in a straight line side-by-side with no gaps in between. Hangers for clothes had to be evenly spaced. The purpose of all of that was to pay attention to detail. If you somewhat had OCD, like me, you would have no problem.

We were given tests on classroom subjects that we had to pass. I failed one on communism and had to retake it, but I passed it the second time. We had to run a mile and a half in twelve minutes to graduate. I passed that, but invariably, on graduation day, there were a couple of lonely souls out on the track being timed so that they could meet the requirement and go to the graduation.

After six weeks of training and halfway through, you were considered upperclassmen, and some of us were given an Officer Training rank. I was made a captain, became a mentor, and was responsible for a group of underclassmen. Some received higher ranks, became responsible for larger groups, and created a chain of command up to a colonel. It was a good training experience.

Another requirement was to march a group of forty-eight troops around the parade ground, shouting various commands and maneuvers using a strong "Command Voice" and bringing them back to the starting point. One thing they emphasized about that exercise was that if you give a wrong command, don't fall apart and lose your composure. Shout the commands necessary to recover and move on. We were told to develop that habit whenever we made a mistake about anything else. When you make a mistake, don't panic and fall apart; regroup and do what it takes to correct the situation. I've applied that idea numerous times in my life.

Verna flew down for graduation and the "pinning of the bars" on my collar. Immediately after the ceremony, Verna developed a urinary tract infection, and we had to rush to the dispensary. She was taken care of but told she would need a procedure.

We stayed with friends from Syracuse for a few days. We visited the Alamo and had a once-in-a-lifetime horseback riding experience. All

Texans assume that everyone knows how to ride a horse. Big mistake! After helping Verna and I get on our horses and ten seconds of instruction, the person slaps the horses on their behinds, and we are off and running. The horses sensed that we had no idea what we were doing and were out of control. Verna's horse was trying to bite her. Mine got too close to a soft river bank and started to slide down the slope. I don't know how I did not end up in the river with the horse. Another river is trying to get me, as I told of two other river incidents in previous stories. Somehow, we made it back to the stables. Never again!

We flew back to Pennsylvania. I was scheduled to report to Oxnard Air Force Base in California. I went to Lowry Air Force Base in Denver, Colorado, a month later to attend Procurement/Contracting Officer school for six weeks. I drove by myself to California in our newly purchased 1966 Ambassador. My daily stops for the nights were Dayton, Oklahoma City, Albuquerque, and Los Angeles, arriving at Oxnard the following day. We arranged for Verna and the boys to join me in Denver after I drove there and found us a furnished apartment for six weeks. We also arranged to have Verna's medical procedure taken care of there. We had to put David and Kevin in daycare for one day.

After Procurement school, we all jumped in the car and headed to California. Westward Ho again! But much better circumstances. It's a newer car with air conditioning and no babies cutting teeth. David is almost six, and Kevin is just about two. We make it to Las Vegas on the first day and home on the next. Our motor home was already there, and I had found a park for it. It had now crossed the country three times and was five years old. I now had been in the Air Force for ten years. I had an obligation to stay in for four more years because they had sent me to college for two years. A lot has happened and changed in the last ten years. What will the next ten years bring? Stay tuned.

JACK BECOMING AN AIR FORCE OFFICER

36. FIRST DAY ON THE JOB

AUGUST 1967 - JULY 1969

My first **JOB** in my new **JOB** as a Procurement/Contracting Officer was to learn the **JOB.** I attended procurement school for six weeks, and the curriculum was based on Department of Defense regulations regarding procurement procedures and policies. At this point, they were just words written in legalese. Only after being a part of the purchasing process did I see the reality of the written rules and regulations come to life. I attended various purchasing, contracting, and negotiation principles and practices courses as my career progressed. I had gotten so much more out of these courses because I already had real-time experiences to relate to the course content.

My role at Oxnard was that of an intern. I cycled through the various divisions of the Base Procurement Office, as it was officially called. There were about sixteen people in the office. About half were military, and the other half were civilian employees. An Air Force major was in charge and was called the "Base Procurement Officer." He had a civilian assistant. The civilians contributed local knowledge and continuity to the organization. The military personnel provided a sense of mission. There was one other officer like me going through the same intern process.

The purpose of the Base Procurement function was to purchase items from the local economy that were unavailable through regular Department of Defense supply channels and services beyond the base's capabilities. The major functions included contracts for construction and various services such as refuse collection, janitorial services, and mortuary services; purchase orders for smaller routine items; a separate division for items needed to be sent out for repair; and a petty cash fund for small and quick buys.

A funny incident occurred on the Friday afternoon of my first week in the office. The senior Non-commissioned Officer (NCO), who had one more stripe than me before I became an officer, shouts down the hall,

"OK, you guys, time to clean up." I jumped off my chair, conditioned to respond to such an order, and the sergeant said to me, "Not you, Lieutenant, you don't do this anymore." He said it in a friendly and jesting manner. The other enlisted airmen in that office and those who worked for me in future assignments had a certain respect for me because I had been in their shoes at one time, and I had a mutual respect for them.

We were in California for two Christmases and flew to Verna's parents' home both times. We were financially better off than we had been, which made me feel good for Verna as I became a better provider.

There was no motor home park on base so we had our motor home parked off base. After being in California for one year, we decided we had outgrown our motor home and wanted to live in a house without wheels. Plus, Verna wanted a formal dining room. We sold our motor home to a single guy for $3,000. We paid $6,000 for it six years prior. We used the $3,000 to purchase furniture, and I started to build furniture for the boys' bedrooms. We moved into base housing. No household expenses such as rent, utilities, taxes, or insurance, but you don't get the monthly monetary allowance you would get if you lived off base. The size and type of house you get depends on your rank. This was the nicest house we lived in so far.

As my two-year internship was coming to an end, I received orders to be the Base Procurement Officer at Kadena Air Base in Okinawa. After researching, we quickly concluded that we were not thrilled about going there. I saw the Personnel Officer, and he said, "No problem. We'll send you somewhere else." A month or so later, he had orders for me to go to Sembach Air Base in Germany to become the Base Procurement Officer. I said, "We'll take it." Europe appealed more to us than the Far East. It was a three-year assignment.

It's time for major decisions. Take the car or not? It was three years old and had low mileage. We decided to sell it. We ordered a Volkswagen Fastback that would be waiting for us as soon as we arrived in Germany. The next decision was what to take. Now imagine this: take everything you own and divide it into four categories. Category One included all the furniture and anything you could do without for three years. There was a weight limit on the things you could take. The items in this category would be stored in an environmentally controlled warehouse, and you would not see them for three years. Category Two was small household goods that would be transported to Germany in a container onboard a ship. These items would not get there before you. Category Three items would go on a plane to Germany and arrive at about the same time as us. Once again, there was a weight limit. Category Four was what we would take in our suitcases as regular passengers.

I had thirteen years in the Air Force as we got on the plane for Germany. I was single for the first two years, and Verna and I lived on letters. Then, we married and lived in six different places over eleven years. It's time for things to settle down. Our family is complete, and our sons are in their early school years. I have been educated and trained to embark on a new career. Verna is anxious to resume her role as a great homemaker in a house without wheels with a dining room, seeing her hubby off to work on a regular daily schedule (not shift work) and the boys off to school every morning. We represent a typical family with a normal lifestyle—shades of a fifties TV sitcom, Ozzie and Harriet, but in a foreign country. Life certainly has been exciting so far. It is time for us to begin enjoying the fruits of our labor.

37. SEMBACH, GERMANY

JULY - OCTOBER 1969

After spending time with Verna's parents in Pennsylvania, we departed in July 1969 for a new adventure to Sembach, Germany, where I would have my first "Command" as the Base Procurement/Contracting Officer for a small Air Force Base. Sembach is a small village in the Southwest corner of Germany called the Saarland. For history buffs, the region once famous as Alsace-Lorraine was lost to the Prussians during a giant war in the late 1880s. Then, the French regained it from the Germans after World War I. Sembach is near the French border, and while we were there, we had access to a French military establishment where we enjoyed shopping for French wines and escarole. Throughout the countryside, you could still see German bunker remains from World War II. The rolling open countryside was well-suited for tank warfare. The closest city to Sembach is Kaiserslautern, nicknamed "K-Town" by the local US military. There was a larger airbase close to Sembach called Ramstein Air Base and a nearby US Army facility called Vogelweh.

Sembach was a small air base that ironically was home to a radar site very similar to the ones I was stationed at in Tennessee and Iceland in previous years. I could have been stationed there at some point as a radar operator had I not become an officer. But here I was under entirely different circumstances, an officer compared to an enlisted airman. I was in charge of fifteen people compared to being one of fifteen other guys on a crew. Working straight days, five days a week, as compared to shift work, changing shifts every three days. How did all of this happen?

When you are transferred to a base in a foreign country, the Air Force has a policy of assigning someone at that base to be your sponsor. Our sponsor met us at the airport and helped us get settled.

After reporting to my new boss, the Base Commander, and checking in at the Base Procurement Office, my priority was to find a permanent place for our family to live. We had ordered a 1969 dark green Volkswagen Fastback before leaving the States. One of the German civilians in the Procurement Office drove us to the dealer to pick it up. There was housing on base, but there was a waiting list, and it would be at least six months before one was available for us. We had to "live on the economy," as it was called, so we had to do some house-hunting with the help of our sponsor. But in the meantime, we had temporary living quarters in a motel one-bedroom facility on base.

We had a list of available places "on the economy" that our sponsor had obtained for us. I parked the car with Verna and the boys as we drove to one of the addresses. I then proceeded to walk to the residence. As I approached it, I heard this dog barking, and as I turned around the corner of the house, a fully grown German shepherd leaped at me. One of his paws ripped my jeans at the hip, and the other scratched my elbow as I raised my arm to protect my face. The owners of the house were sitting in the backyard. They called the brut off me and said, "*Mox nix, mox nix,*" which translates to "No problem, no problem." They then told me that he does that all the time, had just received a rabies shot, and was under quarantine. That did not make me feel any better. I turned around and went to the car, and we scratched that address off the list. We later reported the incident to the base housing office, which had the homeowner reimburse me for my jeans and remove their name from the available housing list. Before too long, we found a recently renovated apartment on the upper floor of a small house in the village of Sembach. It was owned by Herr and Frau Hipp, older than us, who lived on the house's ground floor. Their son had a room on the same upper floor of the dwelling. It was somewhat strange, but we knew it was temporary until we got into base housing. The Hipps were a pleasant couple and spoke enough English to meet our needs. Shortly after moving in, Frau Hipp got into the habit of baking German cakes called *kugen,* topping them with the fruits in season and growing in their garden. She brought one to our door every couple of days. They were delicious, but we could not keep up with her production. We had no freezer to store them and only a small refrigerator. We could not throw them in the garbage because the Hipps habitually went through our garbage and removed certain items because they paid by the pound to have it picked up. As a solution, we are sorry to say Verna flushed the older cakes down the toilet. It's not a proud memory.

Speaking of moving in, none of our stuff was showing up. The items that were coming on the cargo airplane eventually did arrive. They had been delayed, and some boxes had gotten wet. All of the clothing was damaged from mold and had to be discarded. Verna had a mink stole in one of the boxes and it had to be reconditioned. We were reimbursed for all of those losses. After some time, we received a message that all of our household goods that were coming on the ship had been damaged by a fire. That was the extent of the information. We had no idea what to expect. Then for the next three months, boxes arrived in dribs and drabs with our items in various conditions. Some plastic items were melted beyond use. Some items were water-damaged. Some clothes had been dried and cleaned but still reeked of smoke. One pot still had seawater in it. Worst of all, we had a baby book of David and some baby photos of David and Kevin that were damaged or did not arrive-an irreplaceable loss. We had to submit a claim, listing everything in the cargo container with the date of purchase and original price. The boys would start school soon, and their newly purchased school clothes were lost. We had to go shopping. The base exchange stores where the military did most of their shopping had already sold out their inventory of boys' clothes. We had to shop on the economy. We had trouble finding the correct size. David and Kevin were thin in stature compared to the German boys, who were more on the chunky side from all of those potatoes and *kugen*. Also, there was a peculiarity regarding German shopping. All department stores were closed on Saturdays and Sundays except for the first Saturday of each month when they were open until noon.

Another difference between American and German weekends is that the Germans took Sundays off. The housewives prepared Sunday meals on Saturday, so they did not have to do it on Sunday. Walk through an American neighborhood on a Sunday, and you will see all sorts of projects and chores, such as mowing the lawn, painting the house, building a deck, etc., not so in Germany. Sundays are a solemn day off. People go to church, come home, and do <u>not</u> change their clothes. In the afternoon, you'll find them, men in coats and ties and women in high heels, walking the paths through forests and parks. We could learn something from them.

Before we left Verna's parents' home to fly to Germany, her parents planned a trip to visit us. They had never been out of the country. Verna's father's parents were from Germany, and he recalled a place called "Seven Churches" in Germany. He wanted to connect with his German heritage and possibly stumble across "Seven Churches." A lady friend of Verna's parents was from Germany and was planning to visit there, so they made plans to go on the same flight. They showed up about a month after we arrived. We preferred a little more time to get settled ourselves, but their heart was set on it, and their lady friend had no flexibility. Plus, we were more comfortable with her accompanying them. They arrived at the Luxembourg airport, about an hour away from Sembach. Their friend went on her way. I don't know how, but we squeezed Verna's parents, their luggage, David, Kevin, Verna, and me in that little VW. We also had to squeeze them into our small living quarters for a couple of weeks. After they were there about a week, we all took a four-day bus trip over the Labor Day weekend to Paris to see all the highlights. Before they left Germany, we all took a one-day Rhine River cruise and a train trip to Heidelberg, where, from a boat on the river, we saw the Heidelberg Castle lit up with fireworks. Verna's father never located the Seven Churches, but he felt a certain reconnection with his roots and German cuisine.

Time to get to the office. As the Base Procurement Officer, I was in charge of about fifteen people, a mix of German civilians and enlisted airmen. The officer I was replacing had to leave before I arrived, so I was on my own to get familiar with what we would have discussed regarding the office's operation, people, and peculiarities. I had a quick introduction to the rules that applied to the civilians. These were spelled out in a contract between the respective governments of the US and Germany. There was quite a difference regarding working conditions and benefits. For example, a male buyer came into my office one day and told me he was going on "Cure Leave" for 30 days. I said, "What do you mean?" He said, "Because of my health condition, once a year, I am entitled to a paid vacation at a spa for thirty days, paid for by the government." I picked up the phone and called the civilian personnel office to confirm this, and they did.

Another more sticky situation presented itself as the American holiday of Labor Day approached. Since it was an American holiday, the military day workers were off. I somehow learned that the German civilians in my office would also be off. But I told them it was an American holiday, not a German one. They said, "Oh, we take off on your holidays, and you take off on ours." The senior NCO in the office confirmed the practice. I didn't know what to do. I did not call the civilian personnel office to confirm this one. I decided to stop the practice. If the Germans had a legal right to a day off on an American holiday, I figured that one of them would call the office and have me adequately informed. Nothing became of the matter. Since I was in Paris over the Labor Day weekend, I could not stop by the office to see who was there. Would I have done it?

Soon after we arrived in Sembach, I saw a flyer for an MBA program being held by an extension of the University of Utah. It was a two-year program, and I knew I would be there for three years, so it was a good opportunity to pick up an MBA. You never know when it might come in handy. The military paid for tuition; my only cost was books. Although the financial cost was nil, the non-financial cost was significant. Classes were at night, and on more than one occasion, our son David would sadly ask, "Daddy, do you have school tonight?" However, there were offsetting benefits while we were in Germany. Since we did not own a house, I had no demands on my spare time to keep it up, so I had time to take trips with our family and spend time with the boys.

A major disruption occurred in October regarding my assignment to Sembach and our status there. To be continued.

38. BASE PROCUREMENT OFFICER, ZWEIBRUCKEN AIR BASE, GERMANY

1969 - 1973

We had been at Sembach only three months when it was announced that Ramstein Air Base would take over the Base Procurement function I was in charge of. The Air Force didn't know what to do with me. I can't believe it was a spur-of-the-moment decision regarding consolidating the procurement offices. Decisions do not happen that quickly in the government. The Air Force had to have had some inkling of it before they sent me there three months earlier. As it turned out, in the same time frame, the Air Force decided to take over an airbase in Zweibrucken (about an hour closer to the French border) that the Canadian Air Force had abandoned. They decided to send me there as the Base Procurement Officer. Perhaps they were also thinking of having the Ramstein Air Base procurement office support Zweibrucken, but since I was available, why not send me there to create one? The base was operational with a Tactical Reconnaissance Squadron flying out of it with a mission to take aerial photographs of potential threats in East Europe and the Middle East. There was also a Tactical Fighter Squadron whose mission was to disable potential or actual threats.

As I said above, my mission was to create and manage a Base Procurement function. After reporting to my boss, the Base Commander, he pointed to an empty building, gave me the keys to it, and said, "Get going." It was cold about a month before Christmas, and I remember it snowing every day for the first few months.

While at Sembach, the civilian personnel office sent me people to interview as buyers, contract administrators, and office staff. None of the civilians at Sembach chose to go to Zweibrucken; some went to Ramstein.

One contract administrator I interviewed at Sembach impressed me. She was French and had married a veteran. Her name was Mrs. Curtis, and she spoke fluent German. Her dossier was loaded with numerous letters of recommendation and extensive experience. I hired her on the spot! When I got to Zweibrucken, the civilian personnel office sent a buyer to me for an interview. His name was Alfred Pfarr. He had been a buyer for the Canadians when they operated the base. What impressed me about him was that he pulled out about six little black books during the interview. In each book, he had items, descriptions, part numbers, prices, and sources for almost every item on the base we would ever have to purchase. He was a walking buyers' catalog, very pleasant and mild-mannered. I hired him on the spot!

I had more trouble filling a clerical position. The state-of-the-art in 1969 for reproducing "boilerplate" military contractual provisions was a "Flexowriter." Boilerplate provisions (generally called terms and conditions) are legalese statements from United States laws as supplemented by Armed Service Procurement Regulations. They are called "boilerplates" because some must be included in all contracts, and some go into different contracts. You cannot change the words. So instead of retyping the numerous pages each time or using paper copies, which are inappropriate when an original document is required, a Flexowriter was used. A Flexowriter is a combination typewriter/perforated-tape punching machine (before the days of word processors, Word, Pages, and Spellcheck). The operator types the clauses on the typewriter, and a perforated tape is simultaneously produced. The tape is yellow, about an inch wide, and has holes representing the characters on a keyboard. The length would be commensurate with the size of the particular contract clause. The completed tape is labeled and then hung on a board of nails labeled for each clause. When needed, the contract administrator indicates which clauses are required, and the clerk inserts the tape into the flexowriter, and an original copy is printed. The first few candidates I interviewed for the position were apprehensive about operating the Flexowriter and did not want to even sit in front of it as I explained it to them. Then, Frau Steiner was sent in for an interview. She was amazed at the machine, so she sat down and started operating it, following my directions. I hired her on the spot! As a bonus, she had been working in the Civilian Personnel office and was intimately familiar with the regulations applying to the German civilian workers. She became an added asset to me and her fellow civilian workers.

All three employees, Mrs. Curtis, Herr Pfarr, and Frau Steiner, proved their value the entire time I was there and became my shining stars. Before I left Zweibrucken, I called all three of them into my office at the same time and told them how pleased and grateful I was to them for their performance and for making my job easier. I also told them I was writing a "To whom it may concern" letter regarding their outstanding performance. Off the record, I said to them that if I had a choice, I would have let all of the other civilians and airmen go, taken all the salaries being paid to them, and divided it among those three star performers. I could have run the whole operation with just those three employees. That's how strongly I felt about them. They reciprocated by saying they had enjoyed working for me for the last three and a half years.

I had a few more civilians to hire, and enlisted procurement and clerical airmen started joining my staff. In addition to staffing the office, I had to oversee furnishing and organizing it to begin buying and contracting. Once I got it going, I had to ensure it didn't break down. The government and military tend to overemphasize procedures, and our operation was subject to reviews, inspections, and audits from various echelons in the system, including the government financial watchdog GAO (Government Accounting Office). To ensure that we did not jump off the track and violate any procurement regulations and to make the operation efficient, I wrote procedures to be followed by all activities. Then, I wrote a series of checklist items to ensure the procedures were followed. I divided all of the procurement functions in the office into four sections and personally inspected one every three months. I am pleased to say that we passed all upper-level inspections and audits by outside agencies under my watch.

Let me tell you about four of my more interesting and memorable procurement experiences at Zweibrucken.

- The Canadians who left Zweibrucken could have done a better job of maintaining it. As a consequence, there were a lot of major construction and repair projects that had to be contracted for. In the first months, about fifteen construction projects were underway, and the priority was a major renovation of the base heating system. I reported directly to the Base Commander and would have to keep him informed on the status of these programs. To put more pressure on me, the Base Commander's boss, the Wing Commander, a tiger and micro-manager, kept a chart in his office to track the status of all the construction projects. Once a week, he called me and directed me to come immediately to his office and review each project's status. I was a First Lieutenant, and he was a full colonel, four ranks above me. I used to hate that experience, but he always treated me professionally. When, for example, I told him we had to solicit competitive bids, which took time for contractors to respond to, he understood.

- One of our contracted services was removing the trash from the base. We had the same contractor for two years with no problems. When we received the bids for the next year, a new contractor was the low bidder. I was reluctant to give him the contract, but his price was considerably lower, and I had no reason not to give him the contract. However, there was one issue of concern when we opened the bids on June 15: he did not have a refuse collection truck. He did tell me that if he were awarded the contract, he would have the truck on July 1, the first day he was required to start picking up the trash. I signed the contract. The contractor who lost the contract called my boss and expressed his disappointment. My boss called me, and I explained the situation. He said, "Captain Kolman, if that new contractor does not pick up the trash on July 1, you and your entire office will do it!" I said, "Yes sir," hung up the phone and started to panic. On June 29, the new contractor pulled up in front of my office with his shiny new monster trash hauler and blasted the air horn. I ran out to the truck, thanked him profusely, and jumped into the truck with him. I told him to drive to the Base Commander's office, blast his air horn, and then drive off. Phew!

- One day, Herr Pfarr received a purchase request for fifteen tanks, twenty-five army trucks, twenty jeeps, and eighteen cannons. That's all the purchase request said. He did not understand it, nor did I. We were not an army base, and such large items like those are surely not purchased from the local economy. I picked up the phone, called the Base Supply Officer, and asked him if that was a joke. He said he would look into it and call me back. After a few minutes, he called back and said it was a legitimate purchase request. It came from a group of Army photo interpreters on base who reviewed and interpreted aerial photographs. The purchase request was for **TOY** tanks, trucks, jeeps, and cannons. They were going to use them as training aids in interpreting aerial photos. Mystery solved, and Herr Pfarr went toy shopping with the smile of a four-year-old on his face. I wonder if he ever added those items to his little black books?

- One of my procurement responsibilities was to support the elementary school on base in their need for local services. A major requirement they had was providing school bus services. That was an annual challenge for us, with all the different routes to be described and priced by the potential contractors. However, one day, we received a more mundane purchase request from the school to find someone to assemble 150 metal lockers for the students. One of the interested contractors asked to see the disassembled lockers and be allowed to put one together so he could see how long it took. It was a reasonable and logical request, so the buyer observed him doing it. When he completed the assembly and timed himself, he multiplied the time by 150 and said that was his bid. I told the buyer when the guy was done to let me know the result of his task. The buyer did and said it was an honest and reasonable price and we should give him the job. I told the buyer no. He said why not? I asked him if he considered the "learning curve." He asked what I meant. The learning curve is a technique derived from the airplane manufacturing industry that states that as you repeat a task, the time to perform it decreases by 50% every time you double the quantity. I explained it in everyday terms to the guy. I said the second one the contractor put together would take him less time than the first one. By the time he gets to the last one, he will have "learned" a lot about putting the lockers together, and the time for that one will be a fraction of the first. We all can relate to this principle whenever we purchase an item that requires assembly. It always takes us a long time to follow the instructions, but we seldom do more than one, so we never get a chance to "learn" how to do it more efficiently. The contractor finally agreed to adjust his original bid accordingly.

It was a warm, sunny spring day in 1973. I had been at Zweibrucken for over three and a half years. I was sitting in my office with the warm sun on my back in the middle of the afternoon. The entire building was quiet, and I had a flashback to December 1969, when it was bitterly cold in an empty building with no furniture or people. All of a sudden, I felt a strong sense of accomplishment. I had created a well-oiled running machine out of nothing. I would leave Zweibrucken before my replacement arrived. He will have no idea how much of me I left behind as he sits at my desk for the first time and reaps the fruits of my labor.

My experiences as the Base Procurement Officer at Zweibrucken represent the highest achievement in my working career and the one I am most proud of.

39. ZWEIBRUCKEN EXPERIENCES I

1969 - 1973

HOMEMAKING—Since we were some of the first to be assigned to Zweibrucken Air Base, there was no waiting list for base housing, and we did not have to live on the economy. Base housing was not actually on base but a couple of miles away. The units were six-family units, two on each floor. We were the first family in our unit and chose the first floor. The rooms were tiny. Our boys slept in the same bedroom with bunk beds. The kitchen had no room for a table and chairs, but it had an open window to a very small dining room where we ate our meals. Property taxes in Germany are based on the number of doors in a dwelling. As a consequence, there are no closets. People used a huge piece of furniture called a shrunk to hang clothes.

As soon as we moved in just before Christmas, Verna scrambled to decorate it. She purchased yards and yards of German lace curtain and drapery material and zipped up window dressings on her newly purchased Singer. The tree was up by Christmas, and we went overboard with presents for the kids since they had been through so much turmoil for the last six months. It was also a trying time for Verna to be away from her family for the first time in seven years.

The Germans go out more for Christmas than we Americans. Frau Hipp invited us to their house in Sembach to see their tree. They had a custom of lighting sparklers on a live tree. She felt that David and Kevin would be amazed by it. They were; Verna and I were also amazed but for safety reasons.

Shortly after we moved into base housing, the Gorgas family took the apartment across the hall from us. Dan Gorgas was an army warrant officer who interpreted aerial photographs. His wife Erica was a German World War II refugee. Her German accent and local knowledge added more interest to our tour in Germany. They had three boys, Danny, Peter, and Roland, who were all relatively close in age to David and Kevin. They constantly ran back and forth across the hall, enjoying playtimes in our respective apartments. We kept in touch with the Gorgas's for the longest time after we all left Germany.

JAUNTS TO RAMSTEIN—Ramstein Air Base was less than an hour away. It had much larger shopping facilities and an Officers' Club. We had three routine family trips there. Saturdays took us there for shopping. The first stop was the cafeteria for burgers and milkshakes, then an afternoon of shopping. Before we headed home, we grabbed a pizza in a lower-level room in the Officers' Club. The ceiling had a cave-like finish imprinted with names, dates, and figures. They were created over the years by patrons taking the lighted candle in the Chianti wine bottle/basket on the table and holding it just close enough to the ceiling to cause smoke from the candle to leave its mark. By 1969, when we arrived, we had no space to add to this bit of historical documentation. Another little feature that added to the charm of enjoying a piece of pizza was the three musicians who strolled through it playing requests. David's request was always "Laura's Theme" from *Dr. Zhivago*. Kevin always requested a cute toon called *The Donkey Song* because one of the musicians mimicked a donkey braying as part of the vocal—home in the evening with the Volkswagen trunk packed with our treasures. And there was a once-a-month trip to the Officers's Club for Sunday afternoon brunch highlighting steamship round beef. For the kids' entertainment, there were cartoon films in a separate room and a bare tree about three feet high loaded with colorful little edible donuts hanging on the branches that the kids picked off on their way to the movies. Finally, every Monday evening was Lobster Night at the O'Club—a complete lobster-tail dinner from soup to dessert for $2.50. Although we did not go every Monday, we went often enough to make it a memorable event and create a longing taste for lobster for our boys.

BAZAARS—About every three months, vendors from all over Europe held a bazaar in a large building on the base. We used these to furnish our home when we returned to the States. We purchased numerous paintings, but since we had limited wall space, we had to store them under the beds in Germany. The list is too long to include, but some of the more significant items included a grandfather clock, an Italian marble coffee table, a Chinese sculptured rug, china, crystal, silverware, a Danish aria wool rug, and a crystal chandelier. Some of these items are still in our apartment, and every time they catch our eyes, we recall our buying experience and bargaining experience.

OTHER HIGHLIGHTS—About a year and a half after arriving in Germany, the Air Force changed the tour length from three to four years. That was a shocker. Imagine living out of your country for four years. Sure, there is the excitement, travel opportunities, and adventure, but three years would have been plenty. We returned to the States to visit Verna's family for the second Christmas (1970). That was a good "shot in the arm" for Verna.

The elementary school system for Air Force families used American teachers in schools on the bases. The quality of the teachers could have been better. Most saw the job as an opportunity to tour Europe and were not dedicated to teaching. David just started the third grade at the time and was bored. Verna brought this to the attention of the principal. He suggested she create a small group of advanced students to take accelerated math if Verna assisted the teacher. Verna took him up on his offer, but David was still bored. One teacher suggested we send David to a private school in Switzerland. We could not bring ourselves to do that. The principal then said they would test David's level of knowledge and see where he stood. They did and agreed that he was above the third-grade level. The principal said he would allow David to skip the third grade and go into the fourth, but if he did not do well, he would have to return to the third. David continued to get straight *A*'s. He eventually completed high school when he was sixteen years old.

David and Kevin always wanted a dog. Shouldn't every boy have a dog? But what kind of dog to get? The three main criteria were female, small, and not shed. A neighbor in base housing was breeding Yorkshire terriers. We put our bid in for one and got it. We named her "Princess."

While in Germany, David joined the Webelos (a branch of scouting between Cub Scouts and regular Scouts), and I became a Den Father. One day, when he wore his uniform, we took a picture of him in the front of our apartment. Forty years later, David was on a business trip to Germany and traveling past Zweibrucken. He went a little out of his way to stop at the apartment we had lived in and had someone take his picture in the same spot. David sent Verna that Mother's Day picture and a handwritten e-card card because he was still in Germany. Since they could write, David and Kevin always gave Verna and me a handwritten card on our birthdays, Mother's Day, and Father's Day.

The Air Force officers have a New Year's Eve tradition. There is a mandatory formal dinner and celebration at the Officers Club. While at Zweibrucken, I remember one of those occasions that we attended. We snuck home just before midnight to welcome the New Year with David and Kevin, who had a sitter. Then we went back to the club. As the festivities ended, a close friend of ours in charge of the dining hall suggested that our group mosey over to it for breakfast at about two a.m. Since he was in charge, the cooks and staff on duty welcomed us with open arms and whipped us up our breakfast orders: quite the picture, us sitting around the table in formal dinner attire, having a jolly old time. I wish we had a photo.

We made another trip to Verna's parents in the summer of 1972. That was when we would have completed our three-year tour had it not been extended. That helped ease the pain of that extra year somewhat. That was also the summer of Hurricane Agnes, which caused the Susquehanna River to flood the area near her parents' home, although they were not affected.

Six months before we were scheduled to return to the States, Verna's father died. He went into the hospital for gallbladder surgery and got a blood clot during recovery. We had to make a quick trip to the States, which was heartbreaking. So, while in Germany for four years, we made three round trips to the States.

One Sunday afternoon, we all jumped into our Volkswagen and went to a restaurant in the middle of the French woods. This was a dining experience unlike we ever had. The food is prepared from scratch on the spot and takes about an hour to prepare. We started with wine and an assortment of French cheese. We all ordered different authentic French entries and topped them off with French desserts and coffee(no American coffee was available, which was our only regret). The whole experience took over three hours. It became material for Kevin's "show and tell" school assignment when he returned to the States.

40. ZWEIBRUCKEN EXPERIENCES II

1969 - 1973

DEPARTING GESTURE—In addition to the three star German employees I mentioned in a previous story, two other German guys were working for me for a total of five civilian employees. It just occurred to me that all five were with me from day one and remained with me for three and a half years, which is somewhat of a testimonial that I treated them appropriately and they were satisfied with the working environment I created. One of the two other guys was Gunther Hirth. He was a good worker and pleasant gentleman, and although not a star performer, he did something that touched my heart, and I will never forget him. He had a marquetry(wood-inlay) hobby. One day, shortly before I left Germany, he walked into my office and gave me a wrapped package. Inside was a marquetry plague depicting the notable features of the city of Zweibrucken: a bridge with two rivers(*Zwei* for two and *brucken* for rivers), roses for a famous city landmark, and a horse which was another notable feature associated with Zweibrucken. It is one of my treasured keepsakes.

FROM STUDENT TO TEACHER—I completed my MBA in June 1971. When the Base Education Officer was notified of my accomplishment, he came to my office to congratulate me. While doing so, he asked if I might be interested in teaching college courses for the University of Maryland, which had an extension program on base. Ironically, this is the same university where I took my first college course in Iceland ten years earlier. Who would have ever imagined this happening? I jumped at the opportunity and taught a few introductory business courses in the evening for the next two years, as I had in Iceland. I knew an MBA would be useful someday, but not so soon. Furthermore, it continued to open other doors and opportunities for me when I returned to the

States, which was the beginning of a thirty-three-year evening career as an adjunct college instructor.

THE GRAND EUROPEAN TOUR—So, here we were in the heart of Europe for four years. Right off the bat, we intended to take advantage of the travel opportunities throughout our stay. We did everything from a one-day walking trip through the Black Forest to a two-week vacation to the island of Majorca in the Mediterranean. We took David and Kevin every time. Our friends said we should leave them home with the cleaning lady like they do. For one thing, we did not have a cleaning lady. They also said that they can come back when they get older. We told them we were taking them now, and they could still come back when they got older. As it turned out, they had occasions to go back and see some of Europe.

I constructed the following list of trips by going through our photo albums. They are in chronological order, but the dates are not necessary, and I spared you the details of each trip. However, they contain some comments to capture the highlights.

1969

- Four-day Labor Day weekend bus trip to Paris with Verna's parents, as mentioned in a previous story. A city tour took care of all of the famous Paris highlights. A side trip out to Versailles completed the package.

- During their visit, we took a one-day Rhine River cruise highlighting castles and cathedrals.

- On another occasion, we took a one-day train trip to Heidelberg, including a night river cruise to see the Heidelberg castle illuminated by fireworks. It was a wonderful experience that involved three generations of our family sharing quality time.

- We took a weekend bus trip to Garmisch in the Bavarian Alps that winter. The landscape and cute houses were very picturesque. A highlight was a cable car ride up the Zugspitz, the highest mountain in Germany. What a fantastic view!

1970

- With the tulips in full bloom in the spring, we ventured north to the Netherlands on a four-day bus trip. Included was an Amsterdam city tour that stopped at a cheese processing facility, a flower auction, and a wooden shoe-making demonstration where we bought the boys a pair of shoes that they never wore but still have. A side trip to a highly elaborate miniature village display at Volendam also occurred.

- We took a bus trip back to Bavaria during the summer with the Gorgas's. We then took another trip up the Zugspitz on a cog-wheeled train. A visit to King Ludwig's palace at Linderhof, which included his story, concluded that journey.

- Verna's mother came to see us during the summer. We took a twelve-day bus trip to Italy. Our boys were the only children on the bus, and the driver warned us they would have to behave and not disrupt the other travelers. When the trip concluded, the driver admitted that his warning was unnecessary; some fellow travelers even stated that the boys were less disruptive than some adult travelers. That trip had stops in Venice, Florence, Pisa, Milan, and Rome, which afforded a dip in the Mediterranean Sea. On the way home, we stopped in Lucerne, Switzerland, for a fondue dinner.

- During Christmas, we went on a one-day train trip to the famous Chriskindelmart in Nuremberg. Ironically, forty-nine years later, in 2019, Verna and I were on a Danube River cruise to the same spot. It was challenging to remember the scene without all the snow. Who would have thought?

1971

- A flight to Berlin for a long weekend included a view of the Berlin Wall and Checkpoint Charlie, which provided a "tale" that I will present in a future story. A memorable sight was a bombed-out church from World War II that is intentionally left in that state as a grim reminder and hope that something similar does not recur.

- Our longest trip (two weeks) was to the Spanish Island of Mallorca in the Mediterranean that summer. On the way to the airport in Luxembourg, we stopped at the World War II cemetery to pay our respects to those who gave all for us. This trip has got to be the best travel deal we ever had and will ever have. Two weeks in a five-star hotel, three meals a day, air travel there and back, two adults and two children, all for $1250! Highlights included visits to an artificial pearl factory and a monstrous cave. One Sunday afternoon, we went to the traditional weekly three p.m. bullfight. We all rooted for the bull, but he lost; at least we did not put any money on it.

- A third trip to Bavaria with stops in Salzburg for a salt mine tour, where we all got adorned in black salt-mining attire for a ride down into the mine in a little wagon on rails. Other memories included King Ludwig castle at Neuschwanstein, a bus trip to Hitler's headquarters called Eagles' Nest, and a terrifying trip down as the driver mentioned that the brakes on the bus don't last too long because of the extremely steep incline.

- We took a one-day walking tour through the local Black Forest that fall.

1972

- On Easter Sunday morning, we boarded a flight to London for a one-week stay in a Bed & Breakfast. Immediately upon arrival, a wonderful picturesque carriage parade was underway in Hyde Park. We settled into a daily routine of morning sightseeing and then going to matinee theaters in the afternoon. I don't think we missed any of the London hot spots, which included Tower Bridge, The Tower of London, Parliament, St. Paul Cathedral, Piccadilly Circus, Trafalgar Square, Westminster Abbey, The Old Curiosity Shop, Big Ben, Buckingham Palace, 10 Downing Street, and Harrods's Department Store. We went to Windsor Castle one day, but the Queen was unavailable. For about $2.50 each, we saw the following theatre performances: Showboat, Mousetrap, Canterbury Tales, a Minstrel, which is now a NoNo, and a Danny La Rue Review, including transvestites recommended for mature audiences. When we mentioned that to our son David (10 years old at the time), he responded, "Mommy, I'm mature"), so we went; there was nothing off-color.

- That summer, we took a flight to Athens for a week. Of course, we had to go to the Parthenon. One evening, a night music festival was on top of the Acropolis within walking distance of our hotel. When it was over, and we headed home, I lost our bearing coming off the hill and ended up in a bad part of the city and were lost. I had a city map with street names in English, but the street signs were Greek. I tried to find our location by counting the number of English letters on the map and comparing them with the number of Greek letters on the street sign. We finally found our way to the hotel at about midnight! Somedays, we took a bus ride to a nearby military base for lunch, then an afternoon at the beach. The over-packed-standing-room-only bus rides presented too much "close" contact with the local passengers. Jaunts to the flea market resulted in more home furnishings, including a three-foot-tall Grecian urn wrapped in burlap, which we carried with us on the plane placed under our feet (no longer allowed).

- Verna was in the market for a fur coat, and numerous shops were selling them. We stopped in one of them named "Nick The Greek's." There were no coats available on the racks to try on. The first thing they do is take you down into the basement to pick out the furs you want. Verna picked out an assortment of mink paws, primarily grey and beige. Then, they take your measurements, and you return the next day for a fitting. The coat is ready the next day. The final price is $250. Verna wore that coat for almost thirty years and received numerous compliments, and she could not refrain from bragging about her great purchases.

- Another trip that year, and our final one for our stay in Germany, was a weekend camping trip near Saarbrucken. It was a disaster, and no need to go into the details.

The above experiences are captured in about seven photo albums and hours of silent movies. Who knows what will become of them? But the memories are engrained in us, and hopefully, they will live on in the minds of our children.

MARQUETRY PLAQUE OF ZWEIBRUCKEN, GERMANY

41. CZECHOSLOVAKIA, WORLD WAR II, AND ME

This story may appear somewhat out of chronological sequence, but I could not tell it earlier because it contains a story within it that would have been out of place had I written it earlier. I'll get to that story within a story a little later. While becoming a radar operator in the Air Force, I had to get a Security clearance to obtain access to classified information. I had to complete this long "Statement of Personal History" form. I mentioned this form in Story 3. The address given for my father's family members is Baniske, Zupa, Kosicka, Czechoslovakia.

One of the few things I remember my father telling me about his background was that the family came to this country and returned to Czechoslovakia shortly after. This agrees that my father was born in Latrobe, Pennsylvania, near Pittsburg, but his mother lived in Czechoslovakia in 1956.

The city given above is most likely the city of Kosice because when I Googled the spelling, I got from the form that is what came up. Kosice is the second largest city in Slovakia, the largest being the capital city of Bratislava. It is located in southeast Slovakia, just north of the Hungarian border. I know from my extensive reading of history that that area was once called Moravia, and west of that was a country named Bohemia. Those two countries became part of the Austrian-Hungarian Empire under the Habsburg Dynasty. Then, after WW I, that empire was broken up into the nations of Austria, Hungary, and Czechoslovakia. Germany invaded Czechoslovakia in 1939 when I was one year old. So, during the first part of the 1940s, Czechoslovakia was dominated by Hitler. After WW II, the Soviets took over the country. More recently, after the break-up of the Soviet Union in 1989, Czechoslovakia was broken up into the Czech Republic in the West and Slovakia in the East.

Years ago, I was reading a book about the Crusades. I ran across a reference to King Kolman of Hungary around the year 1000. In the late

1980s, Verna and I were on a cruise in the Baltic Sea that stopped in Helsinki, Finland. During a city tour, we saw the name "Kolmen" in many stores and advertisements. Verna had a cold, so we stopped at a drugstore called an "Apoteket" in Europe. We purchased some medicine and pills and still have the bag from the store named "Kolmen Apoteket." Somewhere in my history reading, I learned that there is a similarity between the Finnish and Hungarian languages.

In 2007, our son Kevin was sent to Budapest, Hungary, on a six-month assignment with his company, General Electric. We visited him for three weeks, and while we were there, we took a tour of the Hungarian Parliament. During the tour, I noticed a painting of King Kalman. I pointed it out to the guide and told him my name was Kolman. He said that Kalman is a very common name in Hungary.

So, where do I come from? Slovakia, Czechoslovakia, Hungary, Moravia, Finland, possibly Vikings! Royalty (I doubt it). Who knows? And what does all of this have to do with me? Not much except for the following memories of relatives living in Czechoslovakia during the 1940s.

- My father received letters from them, but I don't know who answered them if anybody, because my father could not write. I'm not sure if my mother spoke Slovak, but her mother did, and I remember my grandmother and my father talking to each other in Slovak.

- My parents sent bundles of new clothes to Czechoslovakia. They wrapped the clothes in bedding ticking and sewed them up. They had this kit that included ink, a pen, and some devices to stretch the material so you could print the address on the bundle.

- I used to look through photo albums and see pictures of people. I had no idea who they were. There was one colored picture of a soldier in uniform that resembles current Russian military uniforms. Another of two soldiers holding a Japanese flag (Russian-Japanese War of

1904 or WW II)? A large colored postcard picture of an ocean liner named "Europa." It had to have been the one they crossed the Atlantic on.

It's a shame the pictures were not labeled or that no one ever explained them. I have no idea where that album is today.

There is another tidbit of information my father told me about his early years. He said he left Czechoslovakia when he was seventeen years old because he was told he had to go into the army (draft notice?). He did not want to go, so he returned to the States. I don't know how he managed that. I wish I had more details. Anyway, I incorporated that little story into one of my own. I was stationed in Zweibrucken, Germany, in the early seventies with the Air Force (previous stories). Our family took a trip to Berlin. We were on a city bus tour, and the next stop was the Berlin Wall. The bus stopped, and we could see "Checkpoint Charlie" with the Russian guards staring at the bus. The guide told us we could go into East Berlin, which the Soviet Union controlled, and there would be no problems. We debated. I had a Secret Security clearance then and was apprehensive about subjecting myself to Soviet control. Well, we decided to go for it. We approached the gate, and the armed Russian soldier asked for our passports. When he saw mine, he reviewed it for the longest time, then picked up a clipboard and started going through pages of listed names. He stopped, looked at me again, picked up the phone, and started talking to someone in Russian. He hung up the phone, grabbed my arm, and said, "Come with me. Your father, John Kolman, dodged the draft in 1934, and we have been looking for him. Now you have to serve his military time in the Soviet Army." I should have stayed on the bus. Okay, I made the last part up. We did not get off the bus, and I still felt uneasy about it. But I combined my father's true story with my partially embellished one and always got a good response whenever I told it. It's the kind of thing you see in movies, so I let my imagination do its thing.

Regarding World War II, I was three years old when the Japanese bombed Pearl Harbor and seven when the war ended. I have only a few memories associated with that war.

- Watching a parade of soldiers marching to the train station.
- A booklet of ration stamps for sugar is in our house.
- Seeing stickers on the rear windows of cars. Some were "A" and some "B" (gas rationing).
- An uncle visited our house in an army uniform.
- Hearing the phrase "Victory Gardens to help the war effort."
- Hearing sirens at night and turning all the lights off in the house (possible air raids).
- Although I was seven years old when the war ended, I don't recall the day it was announced. There was no television with 24/7 news.

42. COMING HOME TO NEW ROOTS

JULY - SEPTEMBER 1973

After putting in for an East Coast assignment and getting the West Coast on two previous occasions, I finally landed an East Coast assignment in Springfield, New Jersey, about two hours from Verna's parents' home in Pennsylvania.

To discourage the military in Europe from buying European-made cars at discount prices when they returned to the States, American car makers offered generous low prices on their vehicles. I have always wanted to own a Cadillac, so this was a good time to get that off my Bucket List. We bought a 1973 midnight blue Cadillac Seville for $6,000 without sales tax. The standard price was around $7000. We would fly to New York, pick up the car then drive to Pennsylvania. However, the timing could not have been worse. In July 1973, the price of gasoline was thirty-five cents a gallon. Then, the energy crisis hit in the autumn of that year, and gas prices went through the roof. Then, there were shortages with odd/even day rationing. The V8 Cadillac was getting ten miles per gallon. I was very out of step with the situation. Before we left Germany, we sold our Volkswagen to a fellow airman. We paid $1800 for it four years earlier and sold it for $1200. When we arrived in Germany in 1969, the mark/dollar exchange rate was four to one. It immediately started to drop; by the time we left four years later, it was two and a quarter to one. The VW held its value, and the exchange rate helped us get a good deal.

Furthermore, we needed two cars. Verna's brother Andy came through. He had a 1957 Nash Rambler he inherited from an older friend he took care of. Remember my Ambassador versus Rambler story? Now, I was eating crow because I had put down the name "Rambler."

Another bargain made available for returning military was American-built furniture. So, we purchased a French formal dining room set that would be delivered to us when we had a firm address. It was the one missing piece from other furniture placed in storage four years earlier, and we would soon get reacquainted with it.

After spending a week at Verna's parents' house, we left the boys and went to Springfield to report in and start house hunting. A fellow officer was assigned as our sponsor, and he put us up in his house for about five days until we found our place. We had $10,000 in cash and figured we could find a suitable house for $40,000. We arrived in Springfield on a Friday afternoon and were scheduled to meet our realtor on Saturday morning. After breakfast with our sponsor, he wanted us to see a development of new houses being constructed by his friend. The development was in a small town called Ironia, about thirty miles from Springfield and too far away for me to commute to work. But we went anyway, met the builder, and saw one house for $52,000 under construction. We then drove to the Springfield area to meet our realtor. We spent the remainder of Saturday and all day Sunday house-hunting with no success. The major problems were terrible neighborhoods, high prices, poor schools, and houses too small. We were disappointed. We kept comparing everything we saw to the brand new house in Ironia, which gave us more house for a dollar but beyond our budget and an hour's commute each way, which was not desirable but acceptable. An important criterion was good schools. So, on Monday morning, we visited the elementary school in Ironia. We were impressed and started to seriously consider living there.

We set up a meeting with the builder for Monday evening to discuss a deal. The house under construction was the first one being built on a fifteen-house cul-de-sac. It was about 75% complete and expected to be completed by September. The builder did have a realtor who had an exclusive on the development, but since she was not a part of our purchase, the builder had room to lower the price. To reduce the cost further, we asked how much he would drop it if we painted the interior and exterior of the house ourselves. We finally settled at $50,000. Another problem was that the bank wanted $15,000 down on an 8%, 30-year mortgage. We were $5,000 short on cash. Verna's mother offered to loan us the $5,000. We paid her back within five years, with the last payment one month before she died in 1978. We did all of the paperwork with a closing date of 1 September. So we had just purchased our first new home (without wheels).

All of the above happened in the middle of July. Verna and the boys stayed with Verna's mother and brother for the summer. I visited them on the weekends, leaving Springfield on Friday afternoon and returning on Sunday night. A fellow officer who had been at Springfield left but had not yet sold his house. He wanted someone to watch it, so I slept there on weekdays for about a month. After work each day, I drove to Ironia and painted the house. I painted outside until it got dark, then inside until about 11 p.m., then back to Springfield to sleep. Later in the summer, the builder let me spend the nights in our purchased house. He gave me a key, and there was hot water for a shower. I set up a cot in the empty house, which was somewhat of a weird lifestyle. When Verna and I look back at what I did, we realize how risky it was. There were no neighbors, and here I was, dangling off a 30-foot extension ladder as the sun set and darkness rolled in.

We planned to sell this house when I retired from the Air Force in four years and then move permanently to our original hometown in the Exeter, Pennsylvania, area. Looking back, it turned out that that extra year in Germany was a blessing in disguise. Had we returned to the States in 1972, I would have had five years to serve before retirement and subject to another assignment after three years at Springfield. I could have ended up on the West Coast again, and our lives would have taken us down a completely different road.

One winter morning, while driving to work in the Rambler, I hit a patch of black ice and bent a part of the front-end suspension on the car. I limped the car back home, called Andy, and he said he'd go to the junkyard, get a part and bring it out. He did the next day. The Rambler eventually died. Andy replaced it with a '75 Ford Pinto. That, too, eventually bit the dust. And once again, Andy came to the rescue with a '76 Capri. One day, the starter went on it. I called Andy, and he told me to take the starter off, and he would be out the next day, pick it up, take it to Pennsylvania to get it rebuilt, and then bring it back. I asked him what I would do without a second car. He reminded me that our driveway was downhill. All I had to do was back the car into the garage and to get to work in the morning, give it a nudge with my foot hanging out the door to start rolling down the driveway, and then "pop the clutch" to start the car (remember standard shifts). But what do I do when I get to work? The parking lot at work had a slight pitch to it, which would serve the same purpose. All I had to worry about was not getting stalled on a flat surface. I drove that car for a week with no starter and no stall-outs. Eventually, we bought a 1975 orange Datsun that got thirty miles per gallon. That was more in tune with the energy crisis times. Andy kept all three rescue vehicles registered in his name and paid for their registration and insurance. Now, that is what you call **"FAMILY."** I am pleased to note that his legacy of kindness and generosity was part of my story until he passed away in 2019. When we moved to New Jersey, it had been fifteen years since Verna and I got married, and except for three years when we lived with her parents and I was in Iceland, she was always too far away from her parents for frequent visits. To make up for it, we went to Pennsylvania every weekend or her family visited us on Sundays. Verna was happy, but sadly, that lasted only five years because her mother passed away in 1978. However, we still had frequent visits with her brothers Andy and Raymond. So we planted ourselves in New Jersey, and the roots grew well for the next thirty-one years.

43. DEFENSE CONTRACT ADMINISTRATION SERVICES

1973 - 1977

My assignment to Springfield, New Jersey, was an excellent way to wind up my Air Force career. I was not on a military base. I was assigned to the Defense Contract Administration Services (DCAS), which has offices throughout the US. The mission of DCAS was to monitor defense contractors. The office at Springfield had about one hundred civilian employees and only about a dozen military from the three main military branches: Army, Navy, and Air Force. We were responsible for defense contractors within about a fifty-mile radius of Springfield.

The office was divided into major functions: production and quality control specialists, government property managers, and contracting officers. The military did not have to wear a uniform unless we visited a contractor's facility. I had to add to my civilian wardrobe. Those were the years of wide ties and bell-bottom trousers. Then, there were the atrocious leisure suits that were just a fad.

My first job assignment was Special Emphasis Monitor. Specific contracts were critical to National Defense and required "Special Monitoring." I had to keep on top of those and ensure that the contractor did the same when it was urgently needed, required high quality, or both. Once a month, I had to brief a general in New York City responsible for all the DCAS offices in the greater New York area.

After a year as Special Emphasis Monitor, I asked for an Administrative Contracting Officer (ACO) position. Defense contracts are written at various military procuring agencies across the country. The person signing them for the government is called the Procuring Contracting Officer. Once the contract is consummated, the buying agency sends it to DCAS for administration. That is where and when the ACO comes into play. They become the primary conduit between the contractor and the requiring Defense Agency regarding problems, additions, deletions, or other changes to the contract.

This assignment gave me an insight into the big picture involved in the Department of Defense operation. During my four years at DCAS, I received an education you don't get from a book or school. Every time I visited a contractor's facility for the first time, I was given a tour of the entire operation. If the visit was to address a particular problem, I found myself getting into the intricacies of some manufacturing process. That four-year experience came in handy when I retired from the Air Force. It also somewhat rounded out my previous year's experiences in the Air Force. For example, as I had earlier in my career, sat in front of a radar set there was a nameplate on it citing the nomenclature of the set, various identification numbers, and the contractor's name and contract number. I had no idea what was behind that contract number and how it got from an identified need through a design phase, manufacturing, transportation, and setup right before me. Nor did I appreciate the role of an engineer from the contractor being assigned to the exact radar site as me to support that radar set. As a radar operator, I was on the first line of defense, although not in a gun-shooting-the-enemy role. On a radar site, the radar operators are the essential persons; the purpose of everyone else there, from the cooks to the radar maintenance people, is to support the radar operation function. As I outlined in a previous story, my office was no longer performing the base's primary mission when I moved from radar operator to Base Procurement. At Zweibrucken, the most essential functions were the pilots flying the planes, the aerial photographers, and the photo interpreters. I was close to the primary mission and could see the planes take off with my eyes. When I moved from Base Procurement to ACO, I was at the other end of the operator-support spectrum. Now I understood where the radar set came from and all the steps and issues that had to be resolved to get it to its intended purpose. My various assignments gave me an appreciation for the entire procurement cycle. I developed a respect for the engineer who first put paper to pencil (before computers) in the first design step, to a final user who needed that piece of equipment to do his job.

Having been bitten by the teaching bug in Zweibrucken, I began to scout the Springfield area for teaching possibilities. I landed a position as an adjunct instructor teaching business courses in the evening at Kean College near Springfield, New Jersey.

These four years became a significant transition point between my Air Force years, my second defense contracting civilian career, and a similar pattern regarding my secondary teaching journey.

44. KOLMAN KLAN HEADQUARTERS

1973 - 2004

ADDRESS:

2 Seneca Trail

Ironia NJ 07845

2 Seneca Trail is located in a small town called Ironia in the Northwest corner of New Jersey. It is so named for the large iron ore deposits. It is noteworthy that as a child, I grew up in a coal mining area of Pennsylvania, and here I am, almost forty years later, in another mining town. One day, while digging in the backyard, I hit a rock about the size of a softball with my shovel. I picked it up, and it was heavier than it should have been for a piece of rock that size; it was a chunk of iron ore. Near Ironia, an Army installation was established during the Revolutionary War. The base's mission is armament research and development, and a significant piece of armament at that time was canon and canon balls.

As scheduled, we closed on our new home on September 1, 1973. A few days later, our furniture and other possessions that had been in storage for four years arrived, and we were reacquainted. There was only minor damage to one headboard. Our new house was a bi-level, a unique style for us. As you entered the front door, there were seven steps up to the kitchen, living room, dining room, three bedrooms, and a bath and a half. As you went down seven steps, you entered a family room, den/family room, one-half bath, and attached two-car garage. Verna preferred a colonial style, but they were $10,000 above our budget. At this point, this would be home for only four years until I retired from the Air Force, and we planned to settle in our hometown of Exeter, Pennsylvania.

Even before I retired from the Air Force, we had decided to settle where we were in New Jersey. The primary reason for this decision was that David and Kevin were receiving a good education and were very happy. David was about to enter his senior year, and it would have been very upsetting to have him relocate at that time. Kevin was four years behind him and would be entering high school, and it would also have been difficult to relocate. Another reason for us staying there was job opportunities for me. My experience in government contracting and the many government contractors in the area were a perfect match. The decision was a no-brainer. It goes even further; our mindset then was that we would never move elsewhere. That held up for thirty-one years.

I referred to our home as "Family Headquarters" because, throughout those thirty-one years, all of our immediate family members would end up at our house whenever there was a family get-together for major holidays and other celebrations. There were no members from my immediate family. Between Verna's and our boys' families, the most we could gather around the table was nineteen for Christmas Eve dinner (Verna's favorite). And to get to nineteen, we included Verna's sister-in-law (Carol's) mother (Blanche), and an elderly lady friend of Verna's (Ruthie) whom we took under our wing. Carol and Raymond, who lived about five miles away, did Christmas-Day dinner. Christmas was the highlight of the year regarding family get-togethers. Verna's brother, Sonny, arrived during the afternoon with his mother until she passed away, then with his own family after he married. His pickup was loaded with presents (he loved to play Santa Claus), and most of the ingredients for the Christmas Eve dinner's main course to be prepared by Verna. When we were children, Christmas Eve dinner was much simpler and basic because the day was considered a day of fasting and abstinence from meat. Over the years, the meal evolved into a more elaborate combination of fish and seafood. The must-haves were herring, white fish, and smelts. Thanks to Sonny, the menu expanded to include shrimp and lobster tail. A traditional carry-over from our more austere years was homemade sauerkraut soup which Sonny started making about a month before Christmas.

Before dinner, there was a Polish/East European tradition that the head of the family was responsible for. The local catholic church provided (for a donation) something called "*Oplatki.*" It was a wafer about the size of a postcard with an image of The Nativity embossed. It was made from flour and water, the same ingredients as a Communion wafer distributed during a Catholic Mass. An *Oplatki*, along with a bit of honey, was placed on a small dish at each place setting. The head of the family says a prayer, breaks a piece of his *Oplatki* for himself, and then passes the remaining portion around the table for each person to break a piece and dip it in honey. When everyone has a piece, everyone consumes it at the same time.

After a leisurely but usually boisterous dinner (thanks to Sonny), some would linger at the table to finish the champagne and wine while others adjourned to more comfortable settings.

Back in the days of no meat on Christmas and Midnight Masses, another tradition developed in Verna's family: having a ham sandwich upon coming home after Midnight Mass. Sonny never gave up on that one. So immediately after Christmas Eve dinner, Verna had to have a ham prepared to pop into the oven and be sure it would be ready upon returning from midnight Mass. Of course, with the deletion of midnight Mass and the relaxation of the fasting requirements, the ham sandwich did not have to wait.

Another Christmas tradition developed during our New Jersey years. When Sonny and his wife (Georgia) returned to their home in Pennsylvania after the festivities, they left their children at our house until we went to their house to celebrate New Year's Eve. One of the activities that the kids got involved in with Verna was baking and cooking. Verna set up an assembly line to mass-produce all sorts of goodies. She was in her glory; some great lifelong memories were created for the kids.

Easter dinners included another "Old Country" tradition that needs to be documented for posterity. No, I am not talking about Easter Egg Hunts. Although we always had one for all the kids that were present using our wooded backyard for the hunting grounds. As the youngsters got older, we switched from candy to plastic eggs that contained anything from a few coins to a $5 bill. I think there is still one with five bucks in it somewhere in the old backyard! The Old Country tradition took place at the dinner table. I was unfamiliar with it in my Czech family, but Verna's Lithuanian heritage introduced me to it. Before dinner, everyone at the table gets a decorated hard-boiled egg. Each person taps their egg with a person on either side of them. Whosever egg does not crack as the eggs are banged against each other's wins. Bragging rights only!

Throughout the remainder of the years, Sonny brought his mother to our house every Sunday unless we happened to visit them in Pennsylvania for the weekend. As soon as they arrived on Sunday morning, we immediately went to the table for delicious homemade pancakes and sausage. Dinner was another culinary delight that everyone enjoyed. During the afternoon, Verna did her mother's hair. When her mother returned home, she bragged to her customers that every Sunday she goes to New Jersey for two gourmet meals and a hairdo by her daughter.

These pleasant occasions lasted five years until Verna's mother died in 1978. Verna had to make up for the years that the Air Force kept her from enjoying such family get-togethers. When Verna's other brother Raymond came home to live in Pennsylvania after leaving the Air Force, he and his family became part of the Sunday entourage. Sometime after Verna's mother died, Raymond relocated to New Jersey, leaving Sonny alone in Pennsylvania to run the family-owned tavern. He eventually married Georgia, and the Sunday/weekend rituals stayed intact with the visits to New Jersey, which took place either at our house or Raymond's. On top of that, Sonny showed up randomly in New Jersey on a weekday, usually to drop off and share some bargains he picked up on fresh fruit and vegetables. He liked to buy large quantities to get a better deal, and then he gave most of it away. If his trip were not a mission, he would admittedly say that he came to our or Raymond's house for a good meal. Carol, like Verna, is also a great cook and sets a fine table.

We all had a good thirty-one-year run of the above family "meetings." Those were good years for Verna; she could share meals with her two brothers and their families. And it gave our children an appreciation for solid family relations. Verna was happy, and when she was happy, I was too. Nevertheless, in my own right, I enjoyed those times, and they gave me a sense of family that I would never have experienced and made me a fuller person for it. I am not a talker; Verna and her brothers are, and whenever we get together, I cannot get a word in edgewise, so I soaked it all in, admired the relationship they shared, and was glad to be a part of it.

Occasionally, I secretly regretted that the same thing was not happening with my brothers.

That all ended in 2004, after thirty-one years, when we moved to The Villages in Florida. Of course, 2 Seneca Trail is still there, and if only those dining room walls could talk! But **THE MEMORIES** remain, and those thirty-one years (almost one-third of our lives) provided many happy get-togethers for all members who attended the Kolman Family "Korporate Meetings."

AIR FORCE RETIREMENT
Verna receiving appreciation certificate

CHRISTMAS - 2 SENECA TRAIL, NEW JERSEY

Children: Ellen (David and Anne's daughter) - Andrea (Andy and Georgia's daughter) - Thomas (David and Anne's son) - Adults left to right: Karen (Andy and Georgia's daughter) - Jack - Georgia (Andy's wife) - Blanche (Carol's mother) - Anne (David's wife) - Raymond (Verna's brother behind Anne) - Carol (Raymond's wife) - Andy "Sonny" (Verna's brother) - Verna - David (Jack and Verna's son behind Verna) - Michael (Raymond and Carol's son) - Andrea (Kevin's fiancée at the time) - Kevin (Jack and Verna's son).

HOLIDAY FAMILY GATHERING

Clockwise starting in lower left: Karen (Andy and Georgia's daughter) - Ellen (David's and Anne's daughter) - Anne (David's wife) - Trixie - Jack - David - Michael (Raymond and Carol's son) - Blanche (Carol's mother) - Ruth (Carol's aunt) - Raymond (Verna's brother).

45. 2 SENECA TRAIL - ITS OWN STORY

1973 - 2004

Owning our own home was a significantly new experience for us. Verna dove into furnishing it, and I had my eye on the garage, visualizing a workbench and the outside for landscaping possibilities. Our lot was about a third of an acre. There was a small lawn in the back, but most of the back was wooded with about one hundred (I made a rough count one day relaxing on the deck and admiring the fruits of my labor) trees of various species and sizes. There were rocks everywhere. My first reaction to the backyard was to have the builder cut down all the trees, level the area, and plant grass. I went so far as to ask him to do it. He said he would not, and we never even discussed the price. After I thought about it, I realized it would have been costly and a shame once you hear what I did with that wooded area.

A tiny stream ran down one side of our property; most of the time, there was just a trickle of water in it. Our property was on a hill, so there was no danger of flooding. The water table was very high, and I hit water if I dug a hole about two feet deep. We had no basement, and the builder graded the ground around the house so all the water flowed away from it.

The wooded area was virgin, so my first project was to clean and open it up by cutting out all of the scrub from the taller trees and rocks. Also, a cluster of four large trees near the rear of the house was too close for comfort. On his first visit to our home, Verna's brother, Sonny, brought me a chainsaw to do the job; that's him true to form. This led to my first experience with a chainsaw. Verna had to get into the act and check out the feel of the chainsaw. Years later, she happened to be a juror in a chainsaw case. When the judge asked if any jurors ever operated a chainsaw, Verna proudly raised her hand. Looking back, I can't believe I took it upon myself to cut those trees down. It was a stupid thing to do. Fortunately, there were no disasters. That experience was the first of many involving chainsaws in my life.

Shortly after we moved in, Kevin suggested using some of the rocks to make a path through the wooded area, and **HE** would build it. It sounded like a good idea, and I told him to start. Well, after about six feet, he abandoned the project. Of course, I picked up where he left off and ended up with a series of paths meandering through the entire area. That led to dividing the whole area into little mini-plots using rocks to separate them, each with its character and design consisting of a combination of ground cover, flowers, rocks, ferns, etc.

There were so many rocks, but they were in the wrong places. I'm pretty sure that a glacier had stopped there eons ago. They ranged from golf ball size to six feet in diameter. They were nicely rounded, weathered, crystalized, and decorative in their own right. I just had to find the right places for them. One way to use many was to build a rock wall down two sides of the property. The rocks were not optimally shaped for a wall because they did not have flat sides and were very irregular. But I built the walls anyway. I used the larger ones (about the size of a breadbox) for the first course and the smaller ones until I had a wall about two and a half feet high.

Some giant boulders were not in the right spots. Sonny gave me a large iron bar, about five feet in length, that was used in the construction of railways to set rails in place on the ties before they got spiked in. I used that bar to move the boulders (never more than three feet in diameter) inches at a time by placing the bar in one corner as a lever. It worked, but it was a slow, backbreaking process. And yes, I did injure my back doing it, and every so often, it went out on me, but that has not happened since we moved from New Jersey. If we still lived in New Jersey, that backyard would have gotten the best of me. I was constantly rearranging things. I'd look out over the property from the deck and see an area that got a little overgrown or did not look right, and all it needed was a little touch-up. The next thing I knew, the whole section had to be redone once I moved one small item.

Every so often, I had to split a rock with a sledgehammer or accidentally chipped it with my iron bar, and a very distinct odor reached my nostrils. It took me back millions of years when the Earth's atmosphere got encased in that rock's formation. I felt a strange connection with another era. I still remember that odor.

One year during those thirty years, our nephew Michael gave me a Father's Day present of about twenty little goldfish. He thought that I should have a fish pond in my wooded paradise. I immediately dug a little hole, lined it with plastic, and put the fish in. The following day, they were dead. What did I do wrong? Everything. But I liked the concept, so I started doing my homework on fish ponds. Well, one thing led to another. When we left New Jersey, I had two fish ponds with waterfalls and large koi that we sold before we left. One of the ponds was about two feet deep. It froze in the winter but was not solid. The fish survived, and I saw them through the ice, lethargically swimming at the bottom. I eventually felt sorry for them and built an indoor pond for them in the winter. "Fish" them out in November, then "Fish" them back in around April. One morning, I discovered some koi were missing and could not figure out what happened. Then, a little later, one morning, Verna looked out the back window and saw a blue heron at the edge of the pond swallowing a $25 breakfast! After that incident, I stretched a net over the pond.

The builder had seeded the small area in the back, but the grass was not doing well. The problem was that there were too many small stones in the soil. We decided to pay David and Kevin a penny for every stone they picked out of the soil. Before long, we were running out of pennies before they ran out of rocks so that joint venture ended.

Our township had a recycling center where you could go and get wood chips and mulch. They deliver it for a fee, or you could go there and take as much as you like. At some point during the thirty-one years, I convinced Verna that instead of having two cars, we should have one car and a truck. She finally agreed. I was a steady customer at the recycling center. I would like to have a nickel for every barrel of wood chips or mulch I lugged from the truck to the backyard.

I know I've moved some of those rocks twice, if not three times, from one place to another. Since that little stream was empty most of the time, I decided to fill it in with rocks, put a weed barrier down, and then put wood chips on top. After a few years, I did not like that look, so I pulled the rocks out. That is a pattern I developed over the years, and I am still stuck with it. I am forever changing things in our landscaping. Is it a curse or a blessing? I don't find projects, they find me. I will look at a piece of landscaping and see something that is not quite right. Others would see it every day and not notice a thing that should be done with it. A few years ago, I had surgery and could not play golf. Verna played with the couple we usually played with. I stayed home and took a walk through the neighborhood. I couldn't control myself. In every yard I came to, I had to evaluate and notice things (large and small) that needed to be done. Throughout my journey, I must have passed over a hundred yards, and 97% of them did not meet my standards. Curse or blessing?

Verna and I were in the front of the house one summer day. I had been working in the backyard earlier. For some reason, I went around to the back of the house, and at about the same time, I saw the guy who lived behind us running towards our house. Flames were shooting out of an attached shed. I quickly grabbed a hose a few feet away and doused the fire. There was minor scorch damage, but it could have been a disaster. What happened is that I left the door open in the shed. The door had a shelf where I had stored aerosol cans of bug spray. The open door was facing west, and the setting sun heated the cans enough to cause an explosion. Thank you, God!

One day, toward the end of our New Jersey residency, Verna suggested that she call the local newspaper to write a feature article on our wooded wonderland. I told her not yet, but when it's done, she knows better. It was scheduled. We played golf in the morning. When we got home, my back was bothering me. %#@*& ROCKS. Verna told me to take a pain pill. I took two (if one is good, two is better). The newspaper reporter showed up and started interviewing me. Verna noticed that I was talking funny. I told her what I did. She never let me forget it. Anyway, the interview went on. I pulled it off. The reporter captured my comments exactly as they were in my mind. We got the article laminated, and Verna has to tell that story (plus show the article) to everyone we have over our house.

Since we had so many nearby trees, our rain gutters needed an annual cleaning. I immediately eliminated that task after the following incident. I got the extension ladder, grabbed the hose, and went up on the roof to flush out the leaves. As I was walking around on the roof, I accidentally dropped the hose. As it slid down the roof, it knocked the ladder to the ground. Here I was stranded on the roof. Verna was at work, and no neighbors were nearby. I had a portable phone with me because I was expecting an important call (before we had an answering machine). I could call the fire department but was too ashamed to create a scene. I could call Verna, but I did not want to hear her wrath. It was about twenty feet to the ground but only ten feet to the deck. I inched myself down to the edge of the roof by the deck, and the longer I stared at the deck, the higher up I felt. I finally built up enough courage to jump. The deck was wet, and I slipped on my rear as I hit it. I guess I deserved that kick in the butt.

Where there are rocks, there are snakes. Sure enough, I ran across at least one a year. None longer than eighteen inches, probably harmless garter snakes or maybe a small copperhead or two. Once I spotted one, I had to get rid of it. People say that there are some "good" snakes. The only good snake is a "dead" snake. As I quickly learned, you cannot kill a snake by cutting it in half. After a few tries, I realized that to kill a snake, you had to smash its head or severe it. So whenever I spotted one, I quietly stepped away, went to my tool shed, and grabbed a flat-end shovel and a small spade. Then I quickly returned to where I spotted it, hoping it was still there. I quietly snuck up on it and used the flat-end shovel to pin it to the ground. After that, I took the smaller spade and beat the snake over the head until _____. All the while, the snake was trying to bite me but could not reach me. Don't try this with a large snake; if you pin it too near the tail, the creature may have enough room to reach your hand. I have a couple of classic snake stories. One spring day, I was cleaning up the winter debris from around one of my fish ponds and left a nice clear spot alongside it. I then went into the house to shower and looked out the bathroom window to admire my efforts. I spotted a stick about a yard long lying on the freshly exposed ground near the pond; it looked like a small branch that I assumed had fallen from an overhead tree. I knew it would be an eyesore until I picked it up. I went back downstairs and toward the area. It was not a stick. It was a snake almost two feet long, and it had the head of a frog in its mouth. It was trying to swallow it but could not get it down. I went to the tool shed and got my weapons. I approached the snake from the rear and slammed the flat-ended shovel in the middle of the snake. The frog went flying out into the pond. Frog, you owe me big time! On another occasion, I was working around the same pond and spotted a snake swimming. The flat-end shovel would not do the job. I was at a loss as to what to do. After some contemplation, I went to the tool shed and grabbed a rake, the flat-end shovel, and the spade. When I returned to the pond, I thought the snake had escaped my wrath. Then suddenly I spotted it still swimming. I watched it for a while, and to my amazement, I discovered that it could stay underwater for a long time. Eventually, it came up for air and in a position where I could scoop it out of the water with the rake. I did and threw it on the ground beside me, quickly dropped the rake, and picked up the shovel to pin it down. Success, one more "good" snake. Enough on the snakes.

Verna and I wanted a vegetable garden. I found a spot with the most sun during the day. We struggled to "grow our own" for the years we were there, but it was not economical. We also got into fruit trees that the deer enjoyed more than we did and strawberries on which the chipmunks gained weight. The deer eventually became too much when they started eating our flowers. To keep them out, I strung cables down the wooded property line from one tree to another and hung netting on them. I also had to put up a fence to separate the front yard from the back. That worked but created an incident. One evening, Verna and I were sitting on the deck when we noticed a baby deer running through our wooded sanctuary. It had gotten in but now could not get out. We didn't know what to do to help it. The mother was outside the fence and did not know what to do. I don't know how the baby deer got out but, the next thing we knew, they were reunited outside the fence where they belonged.

There is literally a lot of my blood and sweat in that backyard. Many a time, I would be back there moving rocks after it got dark (with a full moon providing some light), using just feeling to get it out of a hole. If a rock was partially buried and I wanted to move it someplace, I would pry a corner out of the hole a little, then kick a small rock under it to keep it there. Then go to the other corner and do the same thing. It would get a little tricky with one hand holding the bar, the other hand getting the other rock, and using my foot to wedge the smaller rock under the giant boulder. I'm lucky I never got my foot or hand crushed under the boulder. Although it might be dark, I had to get that rock out of that hole before I punched out for the night.

October is the time of year up north to plant tulips and other bulbs that bloom in the spring. I read somewhere that planting bulbs in the fall gives a person a sense of faith and hope that you will be there to see them resurrect after the dead of winter. My last chore for the season was to blow most of the fallen leaves to the right side and rear edge of the yard. It took about two weeks to complete that task. I could never get 100% of them where I wanted them, and the winter winds would do some rearranging of them. Around Thanksgiving, everything was tucked in. "Good Night, Yard; see you in the spring." The backyard was so picturesque after a heavy fresh snowfall. All that beauty and no maintenance, just look out the window and admire nature. As soon as winter started to release its grip, around March in northern New Jersey, I got antsy to get out there and start scratching around to wake up the yard. I felt a strong sense of satisfaction when I raked away a bunch of dried leaves and found the green tips of daffodils trying to break through. "Good Morning Yard."

That's enough about the yard; I'm exhausted. Let's go inside and talk about the house itself. The best way for the house to tell its story is to list and describe the major changes we made over thirty years. The following may not be in the exact correct chronological order, but most of it is.

Before we even moved in, Sonny had a pair of vintage stained glass windows that were sidelights for an old front door dwelling. Being the generous and kind-hearted person he was, he asked if we would like to have them. I visually sized them up and made a correlation with two similarly sized openings in the house we were purchasing. One was at the top of the wall that separated the two upstairs bathrooms, and the other was on a similar wall that separated the lower-level bathroom and the laundry room. The builder planned on putting a piece of colored plexiglass in those openings. I told him to leave the opening and that I would take care of the windows. Well, Sonny's windows were only about an inch too large, no problem. They added a bit of charm to our home and a nice little story when visitors admired them. Thank you, Sonny. Future owners will never appreciate where they came from.

Verna likes to fuss for a long time with her hair every day. The bathroom off of our bedroom was too small for a dressing table, and I wanted her to have a place to sit while she fussed. We decided to convert the shower in that bathroom to a closet and build a little dressing table with a slanted mirror behind her so she would not have to hold a mirror while doing her hair. Since, at that time, we did not intend to live in the house forever, our mindset was on resale value. So, to return that bathroom to its original configuration, I only cut the plumbing enough to make the closet, which had access only at the top half, and I lined it with cedar to store those clothing items we did not use regularly.

My next priority was to have a place to store all of my books. Since we did not use the lower level bedroom as a bedroom, we used it as a den. I built wall-to-wall shelving on two walls, and the problem was solved. A few years later, our son David was looking for something to do during one of his summer breaks from school. He got into model railroading since we had all those model buildings I built in Germany and a few trains. It was a nice father-son project. I don't remember Kevin being involved. I don't recall how long that setup remained in place, most likely until David went off to college. It's another pleasant memory.

Those early 70s were the first of the energy crisis, and everybody was looking for alternative ways to save energy. Fireplaces became the rage. We could not afford one. Sonny to the rescue. A year or so earlier, he gave us an old pot-belly stove that we did not know what to do with, so it went into the attic like everything else. We had all of that free wood from dead branches in the backyard. We could put it into use and save heating oil. I made a platform for the potbelly stove in the downstairs family room. Since there was no chimney, I Gerry-rigged one by placing the stove under a window, opening it halfway, sealing it, and running a metal stove pipe out the window and up the side of the house for about four feet. It worked. Then, one day, the Township Engineer who lived on our street noticed my Rube Goldberg setup, rang our doorbell and told me that what I did was illegal and did not meet building codes. I dismantled the entire arrangement. A few years later, we sprung for a real fireplace. I never had to pay money for any firewood. I just lived off of the fallen timber in the backyard. And old faithful Sonny constantly got us a supply from someplace or somebody in Pennsylvania. God bless him. The fireplace routine: chop the wood, lug it in, make the fire, remove the ashes, and clean the fireplace window. It got old after a while, so we converted it to a gas insert. Much better.

The fireplace presented another problem. A few years after it was built,

I noticed the chimney pulling away from the house at the top. I brought it to the attention of the builder, who said he would correct it if I tore down the chimney halfway, and he would rebuild that part, making it smaller, dig around the base, and pour some concrete around it. I agreed, but the same thing started to happen after a while. We threatened to take him to court but settled out of court. A few years later, while we were in the process of having the house resided, we had the brick chimney torn down and had an enclosed metal chimney built. Problem solved.

The house did not come with stairs to the attic. There was only an open panel, and you had to use a ladder to get into the attic. I installed pulled-down steps and put a floor in the attic. There was good storage space up there, and we used it well.

We wanted a deck to get a good view and enjoy the fruits of my labor in the backyard—the next major project. A neighbor across the street also wanted a deck, so we agreed to help each other. We drew up our plans and got the necessary permits. We used redwood (before the days of pressure-treated lumber). We did well and passed the township inspection. To provide access to the deck, I had to remove a double window in the dining room and install a sliding door. Luckily, they were both the same width. I only had to cut the window opening down to the floor and make space for the heating hot water line to run below the floor. No problem. We enjoyed the deck over the years. The redwood flooring did not hold up well, so I replaced it with composite decking.

Many areas in that part of New Jersey had radon problems, so we decided to have our home tested. It was borderline, and we had a system installed.

When our house was built, it had no storm windows or screens. The usual low-budget fix for that was to purchase something called "Triple Track Combination" windows from the local home improvement store. You screwed them in place from the outside. They helped. Eventually, we installed state-of-the-art double-pane vinyl-clad replacement windows, which were much better to maintain and more efficient.

After a while, our septic system had to be replaced for about $15,000. That was normal, even with getting it pumped out every two years as recommended.

Once we moved in, we started wallpapering all the rooms I had previously painted before we owned the house. We gave David and Kevin the liberty of decoupaging their closet doors with whatever they desired. I remember one of them choosing professional basketball players—I think that was Kevin. I'm unsure what David chose—hockey, golf, or baseball. At least neither one of them went with Playboy centerfolds! But we didn't check the inside half of the doors. HAHA!?

At the end of 1989, we made the most significant change. Verna always wanted a large bathroom off of the master bedroom. We added twelve feet to the end of the house, which was the master bedroom and another bedroom. At the lower level, we added a third garage. That was my reward for Verna getting her large bathroom, an indoor home for my '55 Chevy that I restored (future story). What was ironic about the decision to expand was that the boys had moved out, and it made no sense to make the house larger. We did not add any rooms; we just made the rooms there larger. The cost of that extension was about $60,000; we paid $50,000 for the entire house sixteen years earlier. The main elements in the extension included a larger bathroom with marble tile, a steam shower, and a jacuzzi tub with a view of our backyard as you sat in it (every Saturday night was couples bath night for one hour, with wine and cheese); converted the attached bathroom with the makeshift dressing table to a laundry room (no more lugging the laundry downstairs then upstairs); large walk-in closet for Verna that I cedar lined; two skylights in the main bedroom; new roof; conversion of oil furnace to natural gas; a foundation for a small greenhouse where the laundry room had been downstairs (I enclosed it with glass windows); new insulated garage doors.

About ten years later, in 1999, we gave the outside a major facelift at a cost of about $25,000. We replaced the previous siding with cream-colored seamless vinyl siding with black window shutters for accents on the front of the house. When we first moved in, the shutters were dark green; a little later, we switched to federal blue.

When I was working full-time, I had trouble keeping up with the property. When the boys were younger, there was always Little League, marching band, or other school activities that we did not want to miss. After they moved out, Verna and I started playing golf and became hooked. That was in 1988; we were fifty years old. I stopped working full-time in January of 1990, and keeping up with the house and property maintenance became easier. But the backyard was so demanding that I could have spent every waking hour caring for it and other things around the house. Verna and I went golfing six days a week between April and October. During those months, I worked in the yard for about four hours and then played eighteen holes of golf.

When it came time to sell 2 Seneca Trail and move to Florida, everyone said it would sell quickly and that there would be a bidding war. Wrong, Wrong, Wrong. We decided to relocate in December but did not put the house up for sale until spring when all the flowers and other foliage would bloom. We laid numerous photos of the property on the dining room table for potential buyers to view. Everyone who came to look admired the landscaping but got turned off by all the maintenance they foresaw. Eventually, someone from out of town fell in love with the place, and we settled at about 96% of our asking price. A year later, we received a phone call in Florida from him telling us he was selling. We asked him if he had put the same photos on the table, and he said no and that he was running into the same problem we had when we tried to sell. He finally sold it for much less than he paid for it. After a couple of years, those owners sold it again. What did they know that I did not that made them leave the place after a year or two? How long would we have stayed there had we not fallen in love with The Villages? Remember, we intended never to move from there. When we visit Verna's brother in New Jersey, we sometimes drive on 2 Seneca Trail. It is run down, but that doesn't bother me since I cannot do anything about it. I'm glad we moved when we did. I often think that the upkeep of the property would eventually kill me. I enjoyed it when I did it, and it was just another phase of my life that created many memories but no regrets. The upkeep on our Florida home was about 10% of what it was in New Jersey.

That is the end of the story. We paid $50,000 for the house in 1973, put a little over $100,000 into it, and sold it for $480,000 thirty-one years later. Financially, we did well, but we can't put a price tag on our quality of life and family memories created during those years. There are two distinct memories in my mind regarding 2 Seneca Trail. The first one was the Saturday morning Verna and I entered it while it was under construction and about 75% complete, somewhat naked with bare unpainted walls. The other corresponding memory is the morning we stepped out of it for the last time in August 2004. Empty house in the beginning, empty house at the end. But, Oh Boy, what took place in between? This story and some others in this collection, plus the memories of everyone who ever stepped through our front door, made 2 Seneca Trail proud. This story and the previous one about family get-togethers at 2 Seneca Trail pretty much capture the memories provided to me by nothing more than a building and a piece of land.

2 SENECA TRAIL, YOU DID GOOD!

NEW JERSEY BACK YARD

NEW JERSEY BACK YARD

46. A GENERATION OF CHANGES IN TECHNOLOGY

Since I elaborated on my early childhood experiences in writing my memoirs, I realized that there were many my children would never have. How were many of my everyday experiences during the 1940s different from those of my children going through their comparable ages about twenty to twenty-five years later in the 1960s? I am not talking about computers, iPhones, the Internet, or similar technical devices. I am thinking about more mundane and simpler everyday things. Here is a list of things that were a part of my life that will probably be difficult for our children and grandchildren to imagine or even believe. But as they say, "You can't make this stuff up!"

- Using an icebox instead of a refrigerator to preserve food. An iceman drove his truck through the neighborhood daily. Someone had to be home (most women did not have out-of-the-house careers in the 1940s) to stop the guy in the truck and have him bring in a twenty-five-cent piece of ice about one cubic foot in size. We ran out to the truck in the summer and asked him for a small chunk of ice to suck on; he always gave us one. A pipe was sticking out of the side of the house to drain the water from the icebox as the ice melted.

- Having a coal stove in the kitchen to cook food and heat water. It was about the size of a regular kitchen table. To keep the iron black top nice and shiny, I remember my grandmother using a wax paper wrapper that sliced bread came in. You had to use it when the stove was slightly warm. Roll the wrapper into a ball and rub it across the top of the stove; it makes it look brand new. Next to the stove was a large upright water tank about five feet tall and a foot in diameter. Water ran through a pipe into and out of the stove's firebox to heat the water, quite an eyesore in the kitchen.

- No ballpoint pens; get a fountain pen and a small bottle of ink.

- I experienced three ways to start a car aside from pushing it. The most basic was inserting a crank into a hole in the lower front end of the engine, turning the crank, and when the engine started, quickly take out the crank, or it would continue turning and break your arm. The first mechanical advance was a starter pedal about the diameter of a golf ball placed to the right of the gas pedal. You had to press the starter pedal with the toes of your right foot and the gas pedal with the heel of the same foot while keeping your left foot on the clutch. Take your toes off the starter pedal as soon as the vehicle starts. I experienced these archaic methods while working on a farm and driving a small old truck. Before a key in the ignition came into use, you pressed a starter button on the dash with your finger to start the vehicle after turning on the key.

- On a truck, there were two knobs on the dash, one labeled "C" and the other one "T." "C" was for the choke, which you pulled out before starting the vehicle when the engine was cold. The "T" meant throttle, which served the same purpose as the gas pedal. When you want to back up the truck, you start the vehicle, put it in reverse, and slowly give it enough gas with the gas pedal to get a slow speed going. Then, pull out the throttle lever to maintain that speed, take your foot off the gas pedal, open the door, stand on the running board with one hand on the steering wheel, and look toward the rear of the truck to guide it. Just before you got to where you wanted to stop, you had to jump back into the truck, push the throttle lever back in, and bring the truck to a stop. It takes a little practice to get the knack of it. Today, we use backup cameras!

- Reading ads in the newspaper for a used car and seeing "r/h" as part of the description. What did it mean? Radio and heater. Yes, there was a time when they were not built in.

- Draining the antifreeze from the car in the spring, filling the radiator with water, then draining that in the fall and replacing it with new antifreeze until spring. Eventually, permanent antifreeze became available.

- When it was going to be a frigid winter night, my father placed an old blanket over the grill of our car to keep the oil from getting too thick, which would make it difficult for the starter motor to start the engine. Of course, he did not realize that the blanket only retained any heat in the engine for a short period; after that, it served no purpose.

- No telephone in the house.

- Helped my father build a garage in our backyard and not use a single power tool.

- There is no shower in the house; there are only bathtubs.

- Having the following salesmen, deliveries, or trucks come to our house or street regularly: Fuller Brush man with an assortment of brushes; milkman; bakery truck in the morning with fresh bread and donuts; fruits and vegetable truck (the huckster); scissor and knife sharpener man carrying a large foot-operated grinding stone on his back; a peddler carrying a huge basket of small items such as thread, bandaids, soap, pencils, etc.; a ragman driving a very old truck and blowing a horn with his mouth. We called him the "Toot-a-toot-a man" and were somewhat afraid of him because of his unkept look. He gave you pennies for scrap rags, newspapers, and scrap iron (recycling before its time); Jewel Tea man selling cups, teapots, and other pieces of china.

- The Metropolitan Insurance salesman comes once a month to collect the monthly life insurance premiums. He always left pamphlets on nutrition, hygiene, and healthy living habits.

- Coal delivery truck. We had to make sure the cellar window to the coal bin was open. The driver used a chute to dump the coal through the window.

- The family doctor makes house calls with his little black bag and collection of pills and medicine.

- No garage door opener.

- Controlling the heat in the house by operating a chain in a room located directly above the monstrous furnace in the cellar. If the house was getting too cool, you pulled the chain in one direction. The chain was attached to a door at the bottom of the furnace and also to a door on the pipe running into the chimney. Opening the lower door caused more air to enter the fire, making it hotter. If the house is too hot, pull the chain in the opposite direction to reverse the above process. This manual operation was eventually replaced with an electric motor operated by a thermostat that used the same chain arrangement to control the heat.

- There is not a single electric clock in the house.

- A bathroom sink has separate hot and cold faucets. To get warm water (not just hot or cold water), turn on both faucets and swish your hand from one faucet to the other until the temperature is just right.

- Making toast by putting a slice of bread between a hand-held wire arrangement and holding it over the flame of the coal stove.

- No insulation in the house.

- Learning to type in school on a typewriter with the keys not labeled.

- Listening to a radio: *The Lone Ranger, The Shadow, and Jack Benny.* My father listened to the news every evening for a half hour at 9:00 p.m., presented by Gabriel Heater. It's not exactly CNN.

- Going to the following offices to pay the monthly bills in cash (no checking account nor credit cards): electric, water, gas, and mortgage ($27 per month!).

- My mother washed clothes every Monday. Then she sprinkled them with water from a soda bottle with a corked sprinkler top, rolled them up, and spent most of Tuesday ironing.

- Using a hot patch to fix a flat tire on my bike. Take the wheel off, then the tube out of the tire. Find the leak, clean the spot with a grater from the top of the repair kit, put the glue on the spot, light a match to the glue, and quickly stomp it with your foot to put it out, finally put the patch on and press it down, check it. It works every time.

- Joining the Christmas Club at the local bank. Having a book of weekly payment stubs. Take fifty cents to the bank every week. By Christmas time, you had $25. Where's the interest?

- Buying penny candy at the corner store. Pointing at it through the glass showcase. Having a nice variety for a nickel.

- Trick or Treat. There were no purchased costumes; all were homemade. Ring the doorbell and say, "Do you want any Halloweeners?" not "Trick or Treat." You had to sing a song, then get some pennies, not candy. The best deal was to go into the numerous local taverns, sing your way down the barstools, and get a much better payoff.

Well, there you have it. It's simpler and a little rougher than today. I wonder what our sons will say if and when they write a similar story comparing the differences in technology between them and their children's early years.

47. BROTHERS

I've mentioned my brothers a couple of times in my previous stories. And now, I need to explain them and the other brothers in my life. First, my brother Leonard was six years older than me and born in 1932. He was likely a half-brother, and my mother had him before she was married; his father is questionable. I imagine he lived in the same house as I did, but I don't remember him being around until I was in the second grade, and he was in the eighth at the same parochial school. There was a short period when we worked together on the same farm; I was about ten, and that would make him sixteen. I clearly remember one specific day and event: June 25, 1950, a Sunday. I was twelve, and he was eighteen. He caddied at a local country club and went to school with the caddie master (the person who selected kids from a group hanging around the clubhouse to be a caddie for a player). All the caddy did then was carry the bag; no advice was given to the golfer. My brother said he would introduce me to the caddying job and arranged with the caddy master to assign us to two golfers in the same foursome. This way, my brother would "show me the ropes." We both made $2.00. When we got home that day, there was an announcement on the radio that the Korean War had started. Later that summer, he joined the Navy. He ended up in Guam, and one Christmas, he sent me a maroon silk jacket with a map of Guam on the back. I remember him coming home on leave during high school and getting out of the Navy about the same time I left home to join the Air Force in 1956. We exchanged letters for about two years. I had been sending him money to hold for me. I don't know why I didn't put it in a bank. On my way home to get married, I stopped by his house to get my money, but I had difficulty getting it from him. I finally did, but our relationship has gone downhill and eventually completely vanished. I don't even know if he is still alive; it's a sad story.

When I was six years old, my second brother was born. I'm not sure, but he was either stillborn or died within a few days. They gave him the name Jerome. He was buried on a Sunday, which is unusual. I remember the funeral, but there was no Mass, even though we were Catholic. Pictures were taken of him in a small coffin, which is also unusual. I never heard any discussions about him.

My third brother, Ronnie, was born in 1947 when I was nine. The only thing I remember about him in my early years was having to babysit him. When I left home at age seventeen, he was eight years old. We reconnected a little when we both got older. He joined the Army and became a Green Beret, serving a couple of tours in Vietnam. Our relationship never developed. Should I have done more to establish it? There was no contact for ages, another sad story.

Brother number four, Richard, was born in 1950 when I was twelve. Once again, he was a chore for me because, like Ronnie, he was too young to play with but young enough to need a babysitter. When I left home, he was five years old. We never developed a relationship. He was the only one of us four who did not join the military. My father died in 1978, then a few years later, my mother died. Richard remained living in our house. After our mother died, he had to pay Leonard and Ronnie for their share of the house. I was not in the will to receive any of it; if I was, my brothers did not tell me. Because of the way my mother treated Verna and many other misgivings, I did not go to her funeral. I may have been in the will, but my brothers decided to eliminate me. After he owned the house for a couple of years, Verna and I got a phone call from Richard (after no contact for several years) asking us if we could loan him $1,000 to make the next mortgage payment. We agreed to loan him $1,500 so he could get on his feet a little. We never heard from him again, and a few years later, we heard that he had died. All of the above represent voids in my life that can never be filled.

When I married in 1958, at age nineteen, my family life changed dramatically. Verna came from a very tight-knit family with the same socio-economic background as mine. When I married her, I inherited a family I never had. Her maternal grandmother Baba (a Lithuanian name for grandma) lived in the household, plus Verna's parents and two brothers, Sonny and Raymond. There is a three-year difference between Sonny and me and eight years between Raymond and me.

After being married for one year, Verna and I lived in their house for two years. During those two years, Sonny, Raymond, and I did not have a close relationship. But as they matured, things began to happen, and our bonds grew stronger. Sonny took the initiative to refer to us as brothers, and Raymond followed suit. Numerous events, circumstances, and family get-togethers, especially holidays, provided me with the true meaning of family.

Over the years, Verna has always emphasized the value of family to our two sons, David and Kevin. She continually tells them to stay in contact and be a part of each other's lives. Once again, Verna and I want to share what I missed growing up with our children.

BROTHERS - EXPLAINED IN STORY

48. THE OTHER SIDE OF THE TABLE

MAY 1977 - NOVEMBER 1989

In previous stories, I alluded to my decision to join the Air Force as a life-changing event. To be more specific, there are three significant lifetime benefits that I received after a twenty-year career in the Air Force. The most practical one is financial. Immediately upon retiring from the Air Force in 1977 at age thirty-seven and a half, I started to receive a monthly check equivalent to 50% of my base pay at the time of my retirement. On top of that, the amount is adjusted annually for cost-of-living increases and has grown 400% in the past forty-seven years. Other minor financial benefits include shopping privileges at military establishments, 10% discounts at Lowes, Home Depot, and other retailers, and medical benefits.

The second major benefit I received was an education. I have previously covered the details of that entire experience and will mention more educational benefits in a future story.

In this story, I will detail the third significant benefit. I have already described my last four years in the Air Force, working with defense contractors in Northern New Jersey. Before leaving the Air Force, I put together the first resume of my life at age thirty-seven and went job hunting. There were a lot of defense contractors in the area; therefore, the job market was good, and I was very marketable, having sat across the table from them for the previous four years, plus having six years of government procurement experience before that. I had various options and ended up choosing a position as a Contract Administrator with Lockheed Electronics, an operating company of the Lockheed Corporation. I retired from the Air Force on a Friday, April 30, 1977, and started at Lockheed on Monday, May 3. I moved from the buying side of the table to the selling side. However, the table was not a Lockheed table. If Lockheed had been a contractor assigned to me while I was still in the Air

Force, I would have been prevented from accepting a position with them for several years.

The physical location of Lockheed was only a short distance from my last Air Force assignment, and my commute became a few miles shorter. Essentially, we referred generically to our products as "black boxes" (electronics) used in weapons systems for the Amy, Navy, and Air Force. Our engineers designed the product, and manufacturing made it. They were the direct employees, and they had no job unless we had a contract to produce something.

Each contract had a program manager responsible for coordinating the effort needed to fulfill the contract's requirements. The Program Manager could have more than one project to manage. However, they all tend to be from the same Defense Buying Agency. My assignments as a Contract Administrator were much more diversified. I worked hand-in-hand with Program Managers who had multiple contracts to contend with. In addition, I had more than one Program Manager to coordinate with. Therefore, my daily routine cuts across programs, defense agencies, product lines, people, and company functions. So there was no telling what each day would bring.

The cycle began whenever the company received a Request for Proposal (RFP) from a defense purchasing agency. My job was to review it to determine the requirements and necessary actions to submit a response to the RFP on time. I had to convert the contents of the RFP to an internal document distributed to various company functions and outline what they needed to do and by when. At this point, a Proposal Leader/Program Manager was assigned to the RFP, and we worked together. When the proposal was completed and reviewed by upper management, I was responsible for preparing and signing the transmittal letter and ensuring that it got to the customer on time. More than once, I ran through an airport to catch a flight and hand-carry the proposal. Had I still been in the Air Force, I could have been creating the RFP, mailing it to companies, and receiving their responses; now, I was on the other side of the table.

After the proposal was submitted, there was a series of meetings with the customer to discuss or clarify some areas and negotiate provisions and, of course, the final price. Once again, the Program Manager and I led that effort. I had to keep changing my return flight on more than one occasion because we "could not settle" on price or some troublesome issue.

Success was in the form of a signed contract being in our hands. The Program Manager anxiously waited for it to arrive. It was his bread and butter. I would still have a job, but he and a group of engineers and manufacturing personnel would not. Once again, I could easily have been the Air Force person signing that government contract. Let me tell you about a significant difference between working in purchasing/contracting for the government and working in industry. After completing my first negotiation for Lockheed, I asked my boss what documentation I needed to prepare and sign for the record. He asked me what I meant. I told him that whenever I completed a negotiation for the government, I had to write a "Memorandum of Negotiation" that described the negotiation process and how I determined the final price to be " fair and reasonable." He said, "No need for that here, as long as you end up with a price acceptable to management." Another example of documentation needed in the government was a "Sole Source Justification" that was required whenever there was no competition on a procurement involving a high dollar amount. The rationale behind the government's need for these types of documentation in the contract file was that public funds were being used, and they are always subject to audit by various agencies, primarily the GAO (Government Accounting Office).

Once the contract was received, my task was to convert the requirements to an internal working document called a Work Order that started the job. Three people signed the Work Order: me, the Program Manager, and someone from Finance (he had to make sure the money was available in the form of the funded contract). It was a mortal sin to start work without a contract. I had this one very aggressive Program Manager, and he always wanted to get a jump on the contract and have the work started before we had the contract in my hands. He pestered me and said he knew it was in the works. Just sign the Work Order, and then we'll both go to Finance and get them to sign off. That never happened!

After implementing the contract, I monitored it for compliance with the terms and conditions. The Program Manager was responsible for meeting the requirements regarding deliverables (actual products and supporting documents such as reports and manuals). And, of course, he had to be concerned with maintaining the budget. His performance evaluation depended entirely on how much profit was made on the contract. Throughout the contract's performance period, there were program reviews for the customers and, invariably, problems that could involve any of the numerous company functions. I was part of the program reviews and made presentations for specific areas. Regarding problem areas, I got engaged to the extent of "What does the contract say about that?" While I may get lost in some of the more technical engineering dialogs, I had to pay attention to be sure that the provisions of the contract and the specifications were not changed without a written contract amendment.

Back to my first days at Lockheed. I got in trouble on the second day. I didn't like the layout of my office. During lunchtime, I rearranged the furniture. When my boss returned from lunch, he said, "Kolman, what did you do?" I answered that I didn't like the layout, so I moved the furniture around. He chastised me and said, "We could get a union violation for you doing that." I asked him what he meant. He said the union contract designated tasks that union workers do. If anyone other than them does one of those tasks, it deprives them of their job and livelihood. My boss said it was good that a union member did not see me, and the next time I wanted furniture moved, I needed to call the appropriate people. A few months later, I got in trouble for a similar incident. The receiving department called me to say I had received a FedEx package. It was a contract I was expecting, so I went to the receiving department to pick it up. On my way back, I passed my boss in the hallway. He saw me carrying the package and again said, "Kolman, what are you doing?" I explained, and he said there are people whose job that is. You may say that I may be a slow learner, but I am also from the school, "If there is something that needs to be done, do it." There were no more such incidents.

Shortly after I arrived at Lockheed, I was asked to join LEMA. I wondered what LEMA was. LEMA was the Lockheed Electronics

Management Association, a National Management Association (NMA) chapter. The purpose was to create fellowship and professional development for managers and supervisors in the company. I agreed to sign up. I quickly learned that it was a program wherein courses developed by the NMA could be presented to company employees. The program was floundering and needed to be more organized and made more effective. Since I had an interest in and experience in teaching, I volunteered to take the program's reins and give it some new life. I had to select courses, design a form to announce the course, and process the registrations. Once there were enough candidates, I ordered the materials from NMA and facilitated the sessions conducted during lunchtime or after work. It was a structured program whereby a participant received a "Certified Manager" certificate from the NMA after completing a stated number of courses. I had to keep the appropriate records and coordinate with the local NMA representative. I performed that additional duty for about ten years and was awarded LEMA Member of the Year for my efforts at one of the annual LEMA banquets.

After about five years as a Contract Administrator, I was promoted to a Senior Contract Administrator with a salary increase. Shortly afterward, my boss left the company, and I expected to be promoted to be his replacement. The chemistry between my boss's boss and me was never good, and he chose someone else. I was disappointed and started looking for a position outside the company, but there was always a reason not to leave.

One day, while checking out internal job opportunities, I noticed an opening in the purchasing department for a Purchasing Manager who was one pay grade higher than me. I applied for it and got it. With my background in contracts, my new boss decided to reorganize the department and created a separate branch to handle large purchases and subcontracts and another branch to take care of more routine and smaller purchases. I became Manager of Subcontracts and had six people on my team. So now I am back on the "other side of the table." I felt more at home on the buying side than the selling side. Maybe it was because of my ten years of buying experience in the Air Force and my bad chemistry with the Contracts Director. However, I have to say that having been on both sides of the table when it comes to negotiation and making the deal, the seller has the advantage. The seller knows exactly what their costs are and how much they are making on each sale. The buyer never really knows how good of a deal they got. I was happy in my new position, and after a year, I was identified as the replacement for the Director of Purchasing in the succession plan.

But it would not come to pass. In 1989, after being with Lockheed for twelve and a half years, the company was acquired by an electronics company in New Hampshire. That company offered me the same position as Manager of Subcontracts, wherein I would be in charge of all current and future subcontracts. It meant relocating to New Hampshire and was a no-brainer decision. There was too much to leave in New Jersey, and I could not help but think that the New Hampshire company would only use me to help them get through the transition of current subcontracts and, after that, would let me go.

The Lockheed Electronics' closure announcement was made at 10 a.m. on November 30, 1989. The same morning, Verna called to say our first grandchild, Thomas, was born. What do I do now regarding a future job? What side of the table will I find myself on? Perhaps there would be no more tables in my life. I picked up the phone and started making calls. To be continued.

49. MY SECOND CAREER

1972 - 2003

In a previous story, I explained how I went from being a college student in Iceland in 1962 to a college adjunct instructor in 1972 while stationed at Zweibrucken Air Base in Germany. Having been bitten by the educator bug, I immediately sought teaching opportunities when I returned to the States in 1973.

Within a short period, I landed an adjunct instructor position at Kean College, a short distance from my assignment in Springfield, New Jersey. I was teaching evening classes in Production Management. That went on for a few years. After that, I taught a few non-credit evening courses in Supervision at Morris County Community College near home. The students, who were all adults in the working world, wanted me to come to their companies to teach similar courses during the day. I told them I had a full-time day job like them and could not go to their companies during the day.

That experience lasted a couple of years. Soon after I retired from the Air Force and went to work for Lockheed, another teaching opportunity presented itself. Let me insert a footnote in my stories at this time. For the twenty-plus years I spent in the Air Force, I always had a reference point for remembering important events. I used the months and years that were identified by various assignments. Once I left the Air Force and never had to relocate, I lost that handy time-marker. So, I don't recall what year (let alone month) this new teaching opportunity fell into my lap.

This is how it all played out. While working for Lockheed, I was in the habit of periodically checking educational/contract administration employment opportunities in the newspaper. One day, an ad caught my eye. It was from Fairleigh Dickinson University (FDU) in northern New Jersey, looking for someone with a teaching and government contracts background. I said to myself, "That's me!" The next day at work, I made a phone call responding to the ad. The person from FDU I spoke with was implementing an MBA program in Government Contracting. I briefly described my background, and he asked if we could meet for dinner that evening after work to discuss the situation. I called Verna and told her I would not be home for dinner and why. The FDU representatives suggested an upscale restaurant called Rod's Steakhouse. We met and had a delightful steak dinner. He outlined the program for me, and I fleshed out my teaching/government contracts background for him. As he picked up the pricy tab for dinner, he said, "The position is yours if you want it." Without hesitation and at the same time not appearing too anxious nor overwhelmed, I said, "Yes, and thank you." He then said he would call me to work out the details.

There were numerous defense contractors in the area, and FDU felt there was a market for such a program. The classes were conducted at the contractor's facility and began at five p.m. for fifteen weekly sessions, comprising a semester. The students never had to go to the campus. FDU went to the facility to register students and deliver the texts, and I showed up to teach the classes. It was my responsibility to select the textbook and design the course. I was paid $1800 for each class plus a stipend for mileage from Lockheed to the contractor's facility. That was the easiest money I ever made in my life. I had come a long way from making fifteen cents an hour working on a farm at age ten (previous Farm Boy story). More work was involved whenever I taught a course for the first time. However, once I went through the text and prepared my class notes and tests, the subsequent times I taught that course took minimal effort. Furthermore, I enjoyed the Three P's involved (Planning, Preparation, and Presentation). The subjects I was teaching were not complex, like math or science. The material was straightforward, as presented in the texts. I established my role as an educator to take the text material, pick out the essential information from the supporting details, and present it to the class in my own words that would be easy to retain and implement when needed. In addition, I related the text material to my experiences in the real working world to illustrate how the concepts and principles came into play. Another teaching technique of mine was to not burden the students with a requirement for extensive formal research papers and projects. However, since these were upper-level courses, I had to challenge the students to make some "extra" effort. I described my background and current job responsibilities during my first meeting with each class. I then explained that at various points in my life, I was also trying to balance my job, school, and family responsibilities simultaneously, just like they were doing. I had been in their shoes. So, instead of burdening them with research projects, I required the following from them. On a 3x5 card, I put the title of a topic that related to the course content along with a date. I then randomly passed out the cards, one to each student. They were responsible for preparing a PowerPoint presentation on that topic using an outside source and presenting it to the class on that designated date. This way, all students would reap the benefits of the information from the outside source. In addition, it would help the student develop their presentation skills. This technique was well-received by the students and always proved to be effective.

The MBA program in Government Contracting lasted only a short time. At some point, the FDU coordinator called me and said he was abandoning that program and creating an MBA Program in Pharmaceutical Studies, which would be presented at the pharmaceutical companies in the area. He asked if I would be interested in teaching some courses that would be a part of that program. I naturally responded in the affirmative. My course assignments included Marketing, International Business, International Marketing, Consumer Behavior, Business Law, and Ethics. FDU also had another MBA program in finance that was made available to other companies I had to be part of. As a result, I taught at the following companies over the years: Johnson & Johnson, Schering-Plough, Bristol-Meyers-Squibb, Dun & Bradstreet, and Prudential.

A first and unique experience for me in the pharmaceutical courses was occasionally having medical doctors as students who wanted to learn about the business world. They were excellent students and always the grade curve busters. Undoubtedly, it is a result of medical school's extensive and demanding rigors. My courses were a breeze for them. At the same time, everyone was generally a good student, and I enjoyed working with them. I liked that they were mature, motivated to learn, and in a working environment where they could relate text information to the real world.

My wardrobe at the time consisted of fourteen different suits/sport-coat combinations that I always wore with a shirt and tie to each class. Each week, I wore a different one. About halfway through the semester, the students commented that I always came dressed differently. But since there were fifteen sessions and I had only fourteen ensembles, I had to wear one of them twice. During the last class session, when final exams were given, the last question on the exam was, "Which suit did I wear twice?" I could always tell when a student came to that question because their eyes would leave the paper and stare at my suit. Nobody ever got the answer correctly. It was a zero-value point question.

On one occasion, I was on a business trip during the night of the final exam. I had Verna attend the class for me to proctor the exam. I told her that all she had to do was hand out the exams, collect them at the end of the session, and be sure not to give out any answers. She did well!

The routine I described above went on from around 1984 to 2003 (seventeen years). Toward the end of 2003, Verna and I made a weekend trip to The Villages in Florida and purchased a home (future story). I could have continued this second career if I wanted to. But I didn't give it a second thought. I have a recurring dream wherein I am assigned to teach a class. The following nightmare incidents occur: I don't show up for the first class; I show up for a class not prepared at all; I miss showing up for three or more classes in a row, and then I do show up completely unprepared. When we moved to The Villages, I did not want any more commitments like being sure I was well prepared for a class by a specific time or having to be at a particular place at a specific time to conduct a class. Furthermore, I did not want anything to interfere with and take away from spending remaining precious time with Verna. I do not miss the classroom environment and experience. It was a great and fulfilling part of my life while it lasted, but that **SECOND CAREER** ended in 2004 after a run of thirty-two years.

50. MY THIRD CAREER

1990 - 1993

In a previous story regarding my position at Lockheed and how that ended, I created some suspense as to "What do I do now?" On November 30, 1989, at precisely 10 a.m., all Lockheed Electronics employees were notified that the company would cease to exist shortly after the new year. Upon returning to my desk after that announcement, I immediately called Verna to inform her. Incidentally, within one hour of that phone call, Verna received a call from our son David, who said that his wife, Anne, had just given birth to our first grandchild, Thomas. I quickly gathered my thoughts and decided I would not seek full-time employment anywhere. Thanks to my Air Force retirement pay and general financial security (Verna was still working), we could get by if I could pick up a couple of bucks teaching something to somebody, someplace.

My first phone call was to Morris County Community College. No, they did not have any opportunities at the time. Next on the list was another local Community College in Sussex County. Pay-dirt! The school was getting off the ground and desperately needed someone to teach Accounting I and Introduction to Business. After outlining my background, the person in charge of hiring was relieved but told me they were day classes starting in January, which would conflict with my still being employed until February. I told him it was no problem and the deal was closed. Phew! I had about one month to be ready. I took vacation days on the days I had to teach until February when I would be finished at Lockheed. So, I had my foot in the door at the school and expressed my desire to make it a permanent arrangement.

That would not come to pass. I had a formal interview with the proper people, during which I explained my teaching experiences at four-year colleges and the MBA Program at Fairleigh Dickinson. That hurt me more than it helped. Another incident occurred that probably did not make me a good fit. The school required me to keep attendance records. One day, the person I reported to called me into his office to review the attendance records. He was concerned that attendance in my classes was poor and asked me if I called any of the absentees about it. I told him I did not think I should have to, but he disagreed. The motivation for learning I experienced at that school was way below what I saw when I had more mature students in my MBA classes. Toward the end of the semester, I received a phone call saying I had not gotten a permanent position at the school. I was disappointed. But I still had my Fairleigh Dickinson once-a-week sessions. Plus, another opportunity had fallen into my lap.

Before I get into that, I have to tell you about what turned out to be one of my life's fullest, most varied, and busiest days. I left home in the morning to teach my two classes, one in the morning and one in the afternoon. After that, I had an appointment for an MRI at the hospital for a medical condition. Then, I was scheduled for a six-o'clock Fairleigh Dickinson dinner honoring the recently graduating MBA class and I was the keynote speaker afterward. The school had a practice of doing that, and it was my turn to speak. I had to put together an appropriate after-dinner speech. As a token of appreciation for my effort, the school gave me a Fairleigh Dickinson sweatshirt.

In February, a week or two after I left Lockheed, I received a phone call in the morning from a woman who worked for me at Lockheed. She had gone to work in the Purchasing Department of another defense con-tractor in the area. She told me that the Purchasing Department was in deep trouble because they were about to be audited for compliance with government rules and regulations regarding procurement practices, and were concerned that they would not pass the audit. She recommended my assistance to the Purchasing Director, who asked me if I would be interested in helping them as a consultant. I immediately called him and set up a meeting for that afternoon. He explained the situation when we met and asked me when I could start and my fee. I had a quick answer for starting, which was right then. I did not have as fast an answer on my fee, but after a few seconds, I casually said, "Fifty dollars an hour" (as if I had been accustomed to such money). Once again, it was a long way from fifteen cents an hour working on the farm at age ten.

He then introduced me to his staff and explained my role. My first steps were to review their files on completed purchases to determine compliance with the requirements. Before that first day was over, I informed the Director that there were too many instances where the laws and regulations were not followed, and it wasn't the kind of thing you could go back and correct. We both accepted that they would fail the audit, but I consoled him that they would be given a reasonable time to "do things the right way," and then there would be a second chance to pass.

I told him I would continue my review of files to get a good grasp on all of the shortcomings and, in that process, point out the specific problems to his staff so that future procurements would "stand muster" when the auditors returned. It became a full-time job except for the days I had to teach. At one point, the Manager of their Contracts Department approached me and asked if I could write a Subcontract Management Manual for him. I told him yes and the same $50 per hour fee. I wrote the manual in longhand, and someone from his staff typed it. It took me exactly one week. It was the easiest $2000 bucks I had ever made.

Of course, the company passed the second audit, so I had worked myself out of a job, but that was the goal.

One last footnote. I was shocked at income tax time. Of course, all the money I had earned as a consultant was taxable. And unlike being on a company's payroll, nothing was withheld for the IRS. I periodically submitted an invoice for my hours with an attached activity report, and the company sent me a check. When the person doing our taxes for that first year became aware of the situation, he said I should have been paying an estimated tax. Since I did not, there could be a financial penalty plus interest for not giving the IRS their due during the year. He also informed me that since I was "self-employed," that made me both the employer and the employee, so I had a double whammy of a social security liability, half as an employer and half as an employee. The employer portion would be a tax-deductible expense. On top of that, I could reduce my tax liability if I contributed to an IRA, which would make some of the income tax-deferred. As a result, I had a sizable check to write at income tax time.

Fortunately, I never had to pay any penalty or interest. But I did learn my lesson for the following year.

My first consulting experience ended sometime in the early 1990s. What next?

51. MY FOURTH (AND LAST) CAREER

1993 - 1998

The defense contractor I was consulting with relocated to Florida in 1993. So, the only thing I had going for me was the weekly classes for Fairleigh Dickinson University. Then, one day, an ad in the newspaper caught my eye. It was a company selling management training courses and was looking for someone, but it was not specific regarding the position. I made the phone call and learned that a woman was selling management training courses developed by another larger company. She said she was looking for someone to sell and present the courses. I told her I was not interested in the selling, only the presentation. She said I had to sell a course before presenting it. I had nothing going on then, so I agreed to join her.

I had to make cold calls to prospective buyers from a list I had to create. There was a canned script I had to use verbatim. I hated that part! I hate trying to sell anything to anybody. I scraped up a couple of interviews but never made a sale. After a couple of months, I gave it up. I lost money because I had to purchase one of the courses myself and go through it. Plus, she had me buy costly business cards. So much for my selling career, never again!

A few months later, Verna and I were on a golf course in the middle of the week and the middle of the day. There were only two of us, and two guys were playing behind us. We asked them if they would like to join us, and they said yes. Walking down the next fairway, I talked to one of the guys and Verna to the other. The guy I was with asked me what I did for a living; I told him, and he asked if I was available to do some training in his company. I said to myself, "It's a weekday in the middle of the week; I am available." Verna had a similar conversation with the other fellow she was walking with. The person I was with asked if I could come to his company and present one of my topics to a group of his people. I told him I would be glad to. I put together a presentation for his purchasing staff on analyzing prices. He sat in on my presentation, and I had a job one day a week to present other topics. I kicked my hourly rate up to $60 an hour.

A short time later, I saw another ad in the paper. This small family-owned company had received a grant from the state of New Jersey for employee training and needed someone to administer it. The purpose of the grant was to improve the performance of the employees and thereby enable the company to grow and increase employment throughout the state. I figured administering a grant would be similar to administering a contract, so I answered the ad. We had an interview, and I had the position one day a week for sixty dollars an hour. My responsibilities were to schedule the training, keep the records, submit the paperwork to the state for reimbursement, and be sure that all of the terms and conditions of the grant were complied with. About every three months, someone from the state came to do an audit, and I had to satisfy him. While with that company, I noticed it was poorly managed and brought that to the owner's attention. I told him that one major problem was the need for more job descriptions for all employees. He asked if I could take care of that, and I said yes, and I did. Eventually, the grant was completed, and they no longer needed my services. I had prepared several job descriptions, but the company had so many other faults they weren't interested in correcting. I became frustrated with them and walked away.

Meanwhile, the first company I had been doing training for had received a similar grant submitted by one of their staff. When I told them I had experience administering grants, they gave me that assignment. When that grant was completed, we applied for another one and received it. One day, the governor of New Jersey came to the company to present a check to the company as a publicity gesture. There was a company across the street, and the president of that company happened to see the governor's car and entourage enter their neighbor company. The company's president called the president of my company and asked what was happening. When he explained and mentioned the grant and my name, the company's president across the way requested that I stop in to see him. I put together a presentation on the grant process, and he hired me to get a grant for his company. They got the grant, and now I had two companies to go to each one day a week, again $60 an hour. Don't forget, Fairleigh Dickinson is still going on one night a week.

Within about a year, there it was as I scanned the want ads again. Another small company was looking for someone to do some training—another family-owned small, well-run company. I made a phone call, had an interview, and, in addition to the training, I told the president about the grant process. We applied and received one—the same scenario at $60 an hour. Now I'm employed three days a week, I took Mondays and Fridays off. Be careful, or I'll be working full-time again. This all settled down gradually to a nice routine. Then, after a few rounds, each company had its share of grants, and my schedule incrementally dropped from three to two days a week, to one day a week, and finally to no days per week. Good timing because when I got down to no days a week, Verna had retired in 1998.

We started playing golf six days a week. We would have played seven, but the course was closed on Mondays. And no, this did not become a fourth career on the PGA. However, Verna was a better player than me, better in competition, having won numerous trophies and "Could Have Been A Contender," to borrow a line from Harry Belafonte in *On the Waterfront*. And I am finally retired!

CONSULTING CLIENT RECEIVING CHECK FROM NJ GOVERNOR

52. COAL MINER'S SON

According to the Continental Drift Theory, at one time, the Earth was one large land mass that began to break up into smaller pieces that drifted away from each other and formed the current continents. The northeast coast of the US was once attached to what became the west coast of Africa near the equator. Over time, all of the existing vegetation decayed became highly compressed and turned into anthracite coal (which has the highest carbon content of all types of coal). That coal became the primary means of earning a living in the small town of my childhood in Northeast Pennsylvania. That was the only type of job my father ever had other than carpentry work that he did on the side for extra income. His experiences, the landscape, and the peculiarities associated with coal mining have provided me with lifelong images and memories.

My wife's father was also a coal miner for his entire life, having started at age nine as a "breaker boy," whose job was to sort coal from other waste material as it came out of the mines and load it into small wheeled carts. I don't know how old my father was when he started to work in the mines.

Here are some of my memories gleaned from observations and overhearing my father's conversations:

- Every weekday at 5:00 a.m., sirens went off throughout the town, ensuring the miners did not sleep in. Occasionally, the sirens woke me up.

- There never was a time that my father was unemployed. But, there were a couple of periods when the miners went on strike.

- During one such strike, things got so bad for our family that my father and I went picking coal. There were gigantic piles of gray rocks that were dug out with the coal. But there were still pieces of coal mixed in with the debris.

My father told me to pick the shiny black pieces that were coal (the dull grey pieces were not). After filling the car trunk, we went home to crack the large pieces into smaller, usable ones. More than once, I smashed my fingers instead of the coal.

- A common joke among the coal miners was asking people if they wanted a job in the mines washing windows. Think about it for a second!

- The landscape in our area was dotted with large, tall, black buildings with covered chutes going down to the ground. These were breakers, where large chunks of coal were fed into the top, broken up with machinery, and gravity-fed into train cars or trucks for delivery. These became eyesores when the mines ceased to operate in the mid-50s.

- Miners were cautioned not to smoke in the mines because of flammable gas fumes. One of my father's co-workers lit a cigarette, and his face became covered with blue veins that never disappeared.

- My father earned a couple of extra dollars sharpening drill bits on the end of long rods powered with a jack-hammer to drill holes for dynamite. He used a special electric-powered grinding stone to sharpen the hard metal bits.

- One day, he brought home a dynamite detonator to repair. It was like a small box with a plunger on a handle. I remember seeing these devices in cowboy movies. When you pushed down on the handle, it produced a sight electrical charge connected with wires to the dynamite some distance away. I watched him work on it and was scared the whole time, thinking it might blow up our house.

- On Fridays, he brought home his dirty clothes wrapped in a towel with his belt to keep the bundle together. My mother washed the clothes on Saturday and bundled them up on Sunday night for Monday morning.

- There was a place in the mining area called the "Shifting Shanty." It was where the miners changed from their street clothes to mining clothes, took a shower at the end of their shift, and put their street clothes back on. Instead of lockers to store your clothes, there were hooks on a long rope attached to a pulley in the ceiling. They hung their clothes on the hook and raised it to the ceiling. This was to keep the rats from getting into the clothes. One day, my father came home dirty; his face was black and still in his mining clothes. There was no water at the shifting shanty to shower that day.

- Many times while sitting in school, we felt the building shake because of the blasts going on underground.

- Something called "Company Work" involved doing odd things around the mining area besides coal mining. Sometimes, my father came home complaining that he had to do "Company Work" that day. Usually, he was paid based on the number of cartloads of coal his crew mined for the day, which meant more money than "Company Work."

I often wondered why there were never any field trips to the mines for the kids in school. There is a coal museum in Scranton, Pennsylvania that conducts tours into an actual mine that is no longer in operation. The tour is available on YouTube. About five years ago, some family members went on the tour. It gave us great appreciation for what our fathers did to support us.

My father died in his 60s from "Black Lung," which was a collection of cold dust in the lungs. Smoking unfiltered Camel cigarettes his whole life did not help either. My wife's father also had "Black Lung."

My wife worked for a doctor a few years ago. He was highly opinionated, and one day, they got into a heated discussion about something.

The doctor told my wife, "What do you know? You're only a coal miner's daughter." My wife responded, "Who made it, doctor, who made it." She likes to tell that story. Of course, medicine is a more noble profession than mining, but he used the phrase in a derogatory and insulting way.

All of the memories listed above are more about my father than me. I was merely an observer and listener, but they are all a part of my life experiences. My wife and I are very proud of our accomplishments. Still, at the same time, the fact remains that children should have a sense of gratitude and appreciation for the efforts and sacrifices that their breadwinners put forth by going out into the working world, whatever the nature of that work. Not only are Verna and I proud of our accomplishments, but we are equally proud of and grateful to our fathers for going down into those mines to support us as their children.

53. TRIXIE

1980 - 1999

As I am about in the middle of my stories, I realize that they have become "Our Stories." I started including Verna in them with the story about us getting together in high school. That has to be when "My Stories" began to evolve into "Our Stories." However, there are still some after that point that are solely about me. Another way to look at it is that Verna's stories are mine, and mine are hers. We are so much a part of each other. For example, if it had not been for Verna, my life would have had no Trixie story.

Let me begin. During Verna's first job with Morris County Medical Services, there was another department on the upper floor of the building. Verna had to go upstairs whenever she needed to make copies of something. Before long, a little old lady named Ruthie caught her attention. Ruthie was sitting at her typewriter with her head buried in it, never looking up and never to be seen talking to anyone else in the office. Those kinds of scenes bother Verna because, to her, it's not normal for someone not to be engaged in conversation, not all of the time, but at least occasionally. She finally could not take it any longer and introduced herself to Ruthie. That was the beginning of a twenty-year relationship.

It was just a casual relationship between co-workers in the beginning. After a few years, Ruthie's husband passed away. Ruthie had no children and now lived alone. Verna took their relationship to another level. Ruthie had a dog that she was very fond of, but the dog died, and Ruthie became even more lonely. On the evening of the week I was teaching, Verna and she went to dinner. Verna also started talking to her on the phone, not every day, but regularly, mainly to check on her and see how she was doing.

Before long, we started including her at our Thanksgiving, Christmas, and Easter dinner table. She was never much of a conversationalist except in a one-on-one situation, so she just sat at the table((always next to Verna) enjoying her meal and took in all the family tales, squabbles, and banter. Verna gave her a doggie bag to take home. She lived about ten minutes from us. I picked her up and took her back to her house. She drove a car most of the time that we knew her but eventually had to give it up.

She had virtually never been to a doctor. She did have poor eyesight, and the time came when she needed cataract surgery. Verna took her for the pre-admission test to our family physician, and Ruthie was a basket case. After the cataract surgery, Verna went to her house at lunchtime, and before she went to bed, to put the medicine in her eyes.

The relationship was taken to a higher level about halfway through our twenty-year relationship. The company I worked for, Lockheed, relocated out of state, and we chose not to go with them. Since I was now unemployed, Ruthie offered me a job doing things around her house, like painting and yard work. I took her up on the offer and went there a couple of days a week. That lasted throughout the remainder of our relationship. When I arrived, she insisted that we have coffee and Danish. I worked for a few hours, then had lunch with her. Ruthie was not a cook, so it was always just sandwiches. I usually ended my day around three in the afternoon. Ruthie told me she liked our visits and looked forward to them. She started to play a motherly role toward me, and I also felt like a son she never had.

There came a time when Ruthie needed a new car. I took her shopping for one. We picked out a small, snappy one that was somewhat on the sporty side, painted red, with a red interior; it was not your typical "little old lady's sedan," but it was a good deal, and Ruthie liked it because of that. Our family got a kick from the mismatch, Ruthie, sports car, red, little old lady. I suggested a change in name for Ruthie, who became known as "Trixie" from then on. She went along with her new image, and it always brought a smile to her face when, at the dinner table, someone said, "Hey Trixie, how's it going?"

Toward the end of the 1990s, she started to fail. She probably should have moved into an assisted living facility. Verna knew she would have none of that, so we never suggested it. She loved her home and her privacy too much. She was now on pills for various reasons. Whenever she got a new prescription, I sorted them and placed them in her pill-box organizer. We also noticed she was mentally weaker. Trixie was an early riser, and she enjoyed reading her morning newspaper. She woke up before it arrived, and she was upset if it wasn't on time. We told her next-door neighbor that if her newspaper is not picked up by six a.m., she should call us because something is wrong.

In June 1999, Kevin's second son, Ryan, was born in upstate New York. We went there for a few days to help. After being there for a couple of days, I called our house in New Jersey to check my messages (before cell phones). I had a two-day-old message from our town's police department informing me to call regarding Trixie. I did and sadly learned that she had died a couple of days prior. One previous morning, her newspaper was thrown under a bush and out of sight by the neighbor, so there was no need for the neighbor to call us. The following day, the newspaper was not picked up. The neighbor called us but got no answer, so they called the local police. The police broke into the house and found Trixie dead in her bed. She had been so for a couple of days. Verna and I surmised that she probably forgot to take her meds or overdosed.

Before her death, Ruthie had a living trust prepared, and she designated Verna as the executrix. She made us aware of this. She showed me where it was in her house and told me that if anything ever happened to her, we should get it and follow its instructions. We left immediately for home, went to her house, and reviewed the document.

It gave Verna the responsibility of making funeral arrangements and sole and total control of Ruthie's assets. Ruthie had a brother who lived about three hours away. We never understood why she did not name him as executor.

As directed, we made the funeral arrangements. Verna selected the dress that Ruthie wore to our son Kevin's wedding for a dress to be buried in. Coincidentally, Verna unknowingly chose the identical casket Ruthie had selected for her husband. I don't know what possessed us, but we started removing things from Ruthie's house, including a giant TV. Ruthie's brother had a son living in California. We received a phone call from him challenging us on our interference. We explained the trust's provisions, and he said he and his father were on their way. We panicked;

they would wonder why the TV was missing, and we better get it back into the house. So, after it got dark the next night, like two cat burglars, we snuck the TV back. Whew!

The relatives arrived in time for the funeral, but there was no communication between us. Ruthie was not a church-going person. But Verna had our pastor say a few words at the funeral home service. There were only a handful of people there. One mutual friend, who drove the Senior Citizen bus, told a story about Ruthie being so impatient to get home that she got off the bus at one point in freezing weather and walked the rest of the way. I felt obligated to say something, so I commented on our imaginary mother-son relationship.

A couple of days after the funeral, we received a phone call from a lawyer representing Ruthie's relatives. He wanted a copy of the trust. I also sent him a copy of a log I had started of all of our actions, commencing with the phone call notifying us of her death. At the same time, I started accounting for all monetary transactions involving Ruthie's estate.

We had not returned to Ruthie's house while the relatives were still in town. Something we had done to the house caused them to conclude we were there. We locked the door between the garage and the house, which the relatives had to break into to get into the living quarters.

Within this same time frame, we were so impressed with how Ruthie's trust was designed and the ease of following it that we arranged to have a similar one prepared for us by the same legal office that did hers. A member of that legal practice happened to be at our house to discuss our trust. Suddenly, the doorbell rang, and a police officer informed us that we were arrested for breaking and entering. He explained that he had received a phone call from the relatives regarding our having been there. We panicked. The visiting attorney overheard the conversation and said. "Officer, just hold on a minute." She explained Ruthie's trust and our rights, authorities, and responsibilities. He asked if he could have a copy of the pages in the trust that she had quoted. We made him a copy. He apologized for the incident and said he was going right back to Ruthie's house to suggest that the relatives immediately leave the premises; they were the ones committing a crime, not us. Case closed.

Now, we had to get down to business. Fortunately, we were spared one major task. Ruthie had gotten an extension on filing her 1998 federal income taxes because she had extensive and numerous holdings in her portfolio with sparse records of their purchase prices. She had done a lot of selling and consolidating during the year, and her tax accountant did not have the time to work through the mess, so he put in for an extension. He had just completed and sent in her tax return the night before she died. The most significant order of business was to sell her house. Our first task was to empty it; what a mess. We had to go through every single item and decide what to do with it: sell, donate, or trash. We finally sold the house about four months later. Now that we had the estate's total value in liquid asset form, we had to file an estate tax return. As part of that process, the accountant asked Verna what her fee as executrix was. We had no idea what to say, so we asked him what was reasonable. He said the IRS allows a percentage of the estate value, so Verna agreed.

Ruthie had designated four beneficiaries in the trust: her brother, a brother-in-law, a long-time lady friend who had moved to North Carolina, and Verna. There was a special provision in the trust stating that under no circumstances was her nephew to receive any benefits from her estate. Ruthie told Verna she had loaned her nephew $25,000 some years back, but he never repaid it. She had a note and a copy of the cashed check in her files. We did not think of it then, but we could have taken legal action against him in the name of the trust. That would have been a nice turnabout.

Another stipulation in the trust was that Ruthie's friend and Verna were to receive their shares immediately. However, the benefits to her brother and brother-in-law were to be placed in an interest-bearing account and given to them over the rest of their life. We had to think of how we were going to handle this. We assumed that they each would live another ten years. So, we took the balance in the account every year, divided it by the number of years remaining, and sent them each a check. At one point, Ruthie's brother-in-law sent us a letter asking for the remainder of his share because he needed surgery. It was down to only a few thousand dollars by then, so we settled with him. Before the ten years were up, Ruthie's brother passed away.

We kept a large folder of all the documents relating to Ruthie's estate just in case there were issues that we needed to address in the future. After twenty years, we finally trashed it, but I did save the log we kept and the accounting of the funds.

The above story would not exist had it not been for Verna's concern for the lack of a personal relationship in a stranger's life. You never know where a simple gesture like, "Hello, my name is Verna, what's yours?" may lead. And as I said at the beginning of this story, this one is all about Verna and her big heart.

REST IN PEACE TRIXIE
LOVE, VERNA, AND JACK

THANKSGIVING DINNER
Anne (David's wife) - Karen (Andy and Georgia's daughter) - Trixie.

54. BOW! WOW! PRINCESS

1972 - 1984

Every boy wants a dog. I never had one, along with other things I never had when I was a boy. We had two boys, David and Kevin, who wanted a dog. We were stationed in Germany at the time. David was about ten and Kevin six. I was not keen on the idea, so we put it up for a family vote. Verna was the swing vote. You know who won; otherwise, you would not be reading this story.

My only condition was not a large dog. Verna agreed; she wanted a lap dog. If we get a dog, we may as well get a good one. What makes a "good" dog? I guess "pedigree" is a synonym for "good," which became a second requirement. We don't want one that sheds, and it has to look cute.

By coincidence, a couple in our neighborhood had a pedigree Yorkshire Terrier that they were breeding. It meets all our requirements; the selling price was about $200. Since this would be the kid's dog, they had to come up with the money. They were a little low on funds then, so we set up a payment plan. We made a house chores chart with dollar amounts associated with each. We hung the chart on a wall, and as chores were completed, the value was subtracted from the $200 starting amount. Verna's mother heard about the payment plan. She often slipped a couple of bucks into a letter to us to help the kids pay off their accounts.

Since she was an English dog, we called her "Princess." The day arrived for us to pick her up. However, an unfortunate event also took place on the same day. Princess was in our bedroom the first night because we didn't know how she would behave during her first night in a strange house. Soon after we got into bed, we received a phone call from Verna's mother. It could not be good news because we had never called each other from Germany because it was too expensive. Verna's father died. He was in the hospital recovering from gallbladder surgery and developed a blood clot. We were devastated. When we went back to bed, Verna naturally broke down and cried most of the night. Princess sensed the drama and became very upset herself. Ever since then, whenever Verna cried for one reason or another or sneezed, Princess ran to her and carried on.

It's time to return to the States. We did not like that Princess could not be in the aircraft cabin with us. Our close friends (the Steindels, he spoke German) gave us a ride to the airport. When we arrived, he gave the check-in attendant a sob story in German, and we were cleared to take Princess on board with us. But we had to put her under the seat in her cage during take-off and landing. We gave her a tranquilizer that the vet gave us in advance.

Shortly after we arrived at our new home, our boys wanted a return on their investment. I don't mean to make Princess sound like a commodity like oats on the futures market, but that was the plan. They paid for her and the associated expenses, such as AKC registration, shots, and tail clipping. They would breed her once at some future date, sell the pups, and keep the proceeds.

One time, we were playing whiffle ball. Princess joined in and got whacked by a bat, knocking out a couple of teeth. If the kids were tossing a football, she retrieved missed passes by grabbing the ball by a loose lace. Then she ran with it into a creek by our house to cool herself off. A few seconds later, she came back, she and the ball dripping water, waiting for the next missed pass.

Princess turned out to be a tomboy. We did not get her to be a show dog. We just wanted her to be herself. Of course, we had her groomed. David assumed the responsibility of brushing her hair. As he lay on the floor watching TV, he picked up her brush and banged it three times on the floor. Princess got the message and came by him for a hairdo. That all came to an end when David went off to college. Verna had to pick up the slack.

We told Verna's brother Raymond about our breeding plans. He was in the market for a dog, so he purchased a male Yorky and named him Chipper. When the time was right, Chipper and Princess "got together" literally. Shortly after, Princess ran off for a girl's night on the town one evening. We became worried that some stranger would become the father of the pups and not Chipper, so we had to sweat it out.

Finally, the big day was drawing near. Verna read up on midwifery for dogs. She learned that immediately after delivery, dogs like this particular gruel mixture. Verna made sure she had all of the ingredients on hand. By this time, Princess was in the habit of spending more time with her than anyone else. It was the night before Kevin's birthday, and it was time for delivery. David was away at college. We had put a box near our bed for her. Shortly after midnight, she delivered the first pup. Thank God it's Chippers! Verna went into Kevin's bedroom to wake him and tell him the good news. The first thing out of his mouth was, "Is it hers?"

That was only the beginning. About one hour later, she delivered another one. Then, just about every hour, they kept on coming out. By five a.m., there were five of them. Princess had to go outside, and when she returned, another came. She was exhausted and struggling. Verna had to help pull the last one out (canine midwifery). What an ordeal.

They were the cutest little things, just like a barrel of little monkeys all over the place. They quickly became trained and followed their mother whenever she had to go outside to do her business. Whenever we went to Pennsylvania for the weekend, they tagged along. One Sunday night, when we got home, Princess went into convulsions. We made an emergency call to the vet. He told us she was in shock from nursing six pups that had drained her of calcium. He said to bring her in for a calcium shot; I did and got light-headed from watching the procedure. We had to keep Princess separated from the pups so they did not drain her calcium again. To do this, we brought down the kid's playpen from the attic and kept them in it.

Princess turned out to be a negligent mother. Instead of caring for her children, she resumed her whiffle and football antics. We went through the registration process, shots, and tail-cutting and put them up for sale. We sold the pups quickly and were down to the last one. When it was gone, Verna broke down and cried because she had gotten attached to them. The phone rang while Verna was sobbing. The neighbor on the other end asked, "Did something happen to our mother?" Her mother had cancer at the time. Verna replied, "No, the last pup just left."

After paying all expenses including the stud fee for Chipper, the net profit was about $1200.

Here is a little side story about Princess. There was a lady where I worked who had a pedigree Dalmatian that she wanted to get rid of. We did not want it, but Verna's older brother, Sonny, said he would like it. It was the middle of winter in New Jersey. One day after work, I picked up the Dalmatian to bring home to take it to Sonny's the next day. I had on a cashmere overcoat. Dalmatians shed furiously. Here I am driving home, and the dog is all over me for almost an hour. My coat was loaded with white short hairs. The dog was emaciated. Verna made him a good hot meal, and he scarfed it down. Sonny named her "Sookie," a short version of the Lithuanian name for a young girl (Misook). Her spots were perfect, and Sonny was very proud and happy with her. She was a hit with his customers in the bar. Sookie had a special attachment for me, I think because I rescued her. She also had this thing for Verna because she gave Sookie her first good meal. Whenever we went to Sonny's, she jumped all over us. One day, we were at Sonny's, sitting on a sofa in the living room with Princess on Verna's lap. Suddenly, Sookie took a flying leap from the floor, landed on Princess, and popped her eyeball out. Sookie probably had a rush of jealousy. We were devastated and rushed Princess to the vet. He tried to save the eye but could not. It had to be removed and stitched over. That did not keep her off the ball field.

It was the spring of the year, and Princess was about twelve years old. Once again, Verna and I were at Sonny's for the weekend. It was a Saturday night. Sonny was tending the bar, and Verna and I were in the living room watching TV. Princess went outside to do her business. All of a sudden, this guy comes into the bar and says, "I don't know if it's your dog or not, but it's lying in the middle of the road." We jumped up from our chairs, and I ran outside; there she was, and I immediately began to sob as I picked her up from the road. Sonny buried her in the backyard that night.

That was a sad ending to a happy story. Princess had become one of the family. David and Kevin had "their dog." Verna had the daughter she never had, and I belatedly had my dog that every boy should have. This story covers twelve years of my life but expands my memoirs to another dimension and provides fond memories for all of us. Thank you, Princess. **GOOD GIRL!**

55. WHAT I DID IN THE COLD WAR

Most historians agree that the Cold War started with the Truman Doctrine in 1947 and ended with the dissolution of the Soviet Union in 1991. My years in the Air Force (1956 to 1977) are smack in the middle of that period. Furthermore, my employment as a civilian in the defense industry kept me in touch with weapons systems used by all branches of the military until 1990. That all adds up to thirty-four years and a major chunk of my adult life that needs to be documented. At the risk of being redundant, I will summarize "What I Did In The Cold War" just to be sure that the readers of this volume appreciate that slice of my life.

I will trace my military career and subsequent civilian positions concerning the Cold War. As you follow along, you will see the points in time, locations, and, in some cases, a reference (in quotations) to a previous story containing the details and a summary of my activities.

JULY TO SEPTEMBER 1956 - LACKLAND AIR FORCE BASE, SAN ANTONIO, TEXAS "INTO THE WILD BLUE YONDER"

Air Force basic training for an introduction and indoctrination into the physical and mental fundamentals of military life.

SEPTEMBER TO NOVEMBER 1956 - KEESLER AIR FORCE BASE, BILOXI, MISSISSIPPI, STUDENT, "SCOPE DOPE SCHOOL"

Continuation of Basic Training and Radar Operator School.

NOVEMBER 1956 TO JULY 1959 - JOELTON AIR FORCE STA-TION, JOELTON, TENNESSEE, RADAR OPERATOR/INTER-CEPT CONTROL TECHNICIAN

This was my first assignment as a radar operator. I was temporarily transferred to a smaller radar site in Kentucky for six months until Joelton became fully operational. I cycled through all of the functions associated with detecting, identifying, and destroying enemy air traffic and ended up specializing in the intercept (destroy if necessary) phase of that sequence.

JULY 1959 TO AUGUST 1961- BENTON AIR FORCE STATION, BENTON, PENNSYLVANIA, RADAR OPERATOR "WHERE'S THE PLOTTING BOARD?"

My introduction to the computer age of air defense. The primary function of the radar site was to provide radar input data to a huge concrete blockhouse housing massive computer hardware in Syracuse, New York, referred to as the SYRACUSE AIR DEFENSE SECTOR. The United States was divided into geographical sectors during this period. Their function was to do the Identifying and Destroying function of the NORAD (NORTH AMERICAN AIR DEFENSE) system using the radar inputs from various radar sites in the surrounding areas.

AUGUST 1961 TO JULY 1962 - ROCKVILLE AIR FORCE STATION, KEFLAVIK, ICELAND, INTERCEPT CONTROL TECHNICIAN "LAND OF FIRE AND ICE"

Back to the "Manual" system of Air Defense as it existed in Joelton, I picked up where I left off in 1959 as an "Intercept Control Technician." The significance of this assignment is that I now was on the first line of defense, geographically much closer to the Soviet Union. To make an analogy with football, I was now on the line as a tackle rather than ten feet back as a linebacker—much closer contact with the potential enemy. We had to keep our eyes open and pistols cocked!

JULY 1962 TO JULY 1963 - SAN FRANCISCO AIR DEFENSE SECTOR, BEALE AIR FORCE BASE, MARYSVILLE, CALIFORNIA, INTERCEPT CONTROL TECHNICIAN, "QUICK TURNAROUND"

Compared to my duties in the "Where's The Plotting Board" story, I was now on the receiving end of radar inputs. This became my first life experience with the wonders of computers. That remained my specialty since I had experience as an Intercept Control Technician. It was amazing how the computers "solved the intercept problem." Some of my tasks were more technical, such as pushing buttons and using a light gun. However, some stayed the same, such as monitoring ground-to-air voice transmissions, coordinating with the control tower at the interceptor base, and taking instructions from the officer sitting next to me.

JULY 1963 TO DECEMBER 1964 - CHICAGO AIR DEFENSE SECTOR, TRUAX FIELD, MADISON WISCONSIN, INTERCEPT CONTROL TECHNICIAN

NORAD consolidated the air defense sectors around the country and closed the one at Beale Air Force Base. I naturally picked up where I left off and stayed in the Intercept Control function.

JANUARY 1965 TO JANUARY 1967 - SYRACUSE UNIVERSITY, SYRACUSE, NEW YORK, STUDENT

This was during the peak of the Vietnam War, and here I was, going to Syracuse University full-time and never wearing a uniform, although I was still on active duty with the Air Force. Had I not found myself in this position, I would have been due for an overseas assignment at some remote radar site. Or worse, I could have ended up in Vietnam. In later years, I learned from other radar operators that people in that career field were finding themselves in the jungles of Southeast Asia as Forward Air Controllers directing aircraft to their targets.

JANUARY TO APRIL 1967- OFFICER TRAINING SCHOOL, LACKLAND AIR FORCE BASE, SAN ANTONIO, TEXAS

It was similar to Basic Training eleven years earlier but much more intense and at a much higher level of treatment.

MAY 1967 TO JULY 1969 - OXNARD AIR FORCE BASE, OXNARD, CALIFORNIA, BASE PROCUREMENT OFFICER INTERN

What a contrast, strait day shift and much more respect as I went about my duties learning the ins and outs of military procurement. I was no longer directly involved in Air Defense. However, by coincidence, Oxnard AFB was home to a squadron of fighter-interceptor aircraft. The same ones that I used to assist in controlling back in my Intercept Control Technician days. I had no contact with the aircraft, pilots, or their function. The base procurement function was to purchase supplies and services needed to support the base's people and facilities.

As I cycled through the various purchasing and contracting functions, I was responsible for overseeing a construction contract. The job involved renovating a building used to work on miniature electronic devices (avionics). It had to be converted to a "clean room," which, for example, meant that any ledges, such as window sills, had to be removed so that dust would not settle on them. It was a good experience that required me to visit the job site to monitor progress, interview workers to be sure they were paid the proper wages, submit reports to justify progress payments, and be part of the final inspection to certify that all contractual requirements were met.

As a side note and additional duty, I was made a commander of a Disaster Preparedness Shelter. A number of these were scattered throughout the base, and it was a good position for the lieutenants on the base to fill. If there was an actual disaster created by a natural event, terrorists, or an enemy, everyone on the base was assigned to go to a specific shelter. I ensured the shelter was always adequately stocked with food, water, etc. Also, I was the point of contact for that shelter and responsible for all its activities and personnel. There were periodic drills and inspections to ensure we were "Prepared." It reminds me of the Boy Scout motto, "Be Prepared."

JULY 1969 TO JULY 1973 - ZWEIBRUCKEN AIR BASE, ZWEIBRUCKEN, GERMANY, BASE PROCUREMENT OFFICER

My base procurement internship served its purpose, and the Air Force (to use a naval phrase) "gave me my own ship." However, I first had to build that ship, as explained in a previous story. That is, I was to be the Base Procurement Officer for a base in Germany and was responsible for the complete base procurement function with a staff of ten people. The base was home to tactical fighter aircraft (air-to-ground offensive operations) and reconnaissance aircraft that took aerial photographs of possible future targets. Being in Germany with the Soviet Union still in existence, this base was the first line of the NATO defense system. Once again, my proximity and relationship with the aircraft, pilots, and others who were more hands-on with them were a few steps removed.

JULY 1973 TO APRIL 1977 - DEFENSE CONTRACT ADMINISTRATION SERVICES, SPRINGFIELD, NEW JERSEY, ADMINISTRATIVE CONTRACTING OFFICER

This assignment brought me even more removed from Cold War action. It also broadened my perspective on the defense of our nation. As an Administrative Contracting Officer, I had extensive contact with designing and manufacturing defense equipment and supplies. Between meetings and plant visits at contractor's facilities, I became intimately familiar with the process and problems involved in converting a piece of paper (contractual document) to a piece of hardware out the back door to a service person, someone on the globe needing that item to fight the cold war. In addition, I became exposed to the varied needs of all three branches of the military: Army, Navy, and Air Force. One such example of this that became a recurring task was negotiating the price of spare boiler parts for ships that the Navy needed from the original equipment supplier. There were a dozen officers from the military branches in the office. Talking shop with them and socializing gave me an appreciation for the diversity and strength of our country's military horsepower.

MAY 1977 TO FEBRUARY 1990 - LOCKHEED ELECTRONICS COMPANY, PLAINFIELD, NEW JERSEY, CONTRACT ADMINISTRATOR AND MANAGER OF SUBCONTRACTS

This was a transition from the military to the civilian side of the industrial-military complex and from the purchasing to the selling side. On the other hand, it had one similarity with my last Air Force assignment: I dealt with all branches of the military's need for supplies and equipment. To mention a few during my thirteen years at Lockheed: electronic test equipment for missiles on nuclear submarines; fire control systems on destroyers;

fuzes for army mortars; black boxes for cargo planes; circuit boards for army nuclear surface-to-surface missiles; and designs for the stealth bomber, for which I had to get a top-secret clearance that was higher than the clearance I needed during my twenty-year Air Force career.

This wraps up my series of war stories. They extend from sitting in front of a radar scope that had a nameplate and a contract number in 1956 at age eighteen to understanding and appreciating what was behind that contract number thirty-four years later in 1990. These are not the kind of war stories that make a good movie but the kind that never get told—until now!

Well, there you have it: no battlefield heroics, blood and guts, or Purple Heart Medals. What I did in the war was to learn, train, and prepare for a war we hoped would never be fought. And it didn't, so I guess we won!

56. THE VILLAGES - OUR STORY

2003 - 2023

If I had to condense the description of The Villages into one and only one word, that word would be "**CHOICES**." Everything is a choice, and there are so many choices. To begin with, you have a choice to live here or not. Then the choices present themselves: exactly where in The Villages to live; in what type of house; which restaurant to go to tonight; what golf course to play today; what clubs do I want to join, if any; what part-time job do I want, if any; and the list goes on and on.

Everybody in The Villages has their story about The Villages. Their story entails how they got here. The fact is that nobody was born there. Everybody is from someplace else, and something or someone had to spur them on to decide to move from where they were at the time to where they are now. Granted, some Villagers have not permanently moved here. They may own a home here and another someplace else. Nevertheless, they still have their story.

Our story begins with good friends Jim and Peg O'Donnell, whom we knew in New Jersey and who moved to The Villages a little over a year earlier than us. They invited us down for a weekend, and we took advantage of The Villages' promotion package. The package included a Villages limo with drinks, picking us up at the airport. That was our first good impression. We called Peg from the limo and told her we were impressed. Peg said, "Impressed, you haven't even seen anything yet."

Our first stop was the Sales Office. As we entered, we saw a large board that indicated that on that day, there were about 100 people on the promotion package. When we arrived, we had to give them $400 in cash, and they gave us $300 back in funny money that could be used in restaurants and golf courses within The Villages. Our living quarters were within walking distance of the Sales Office, where a continental breakfast was served every morning. Jim had made arrangements with our salesperson, Jerry, to loan us his golf cart to get around, but we could not get it until the following day. After we finished checking in, Jim came to get us to have dinner at their house. When we arrived there, we were again impressed with their home and their great view of a golf course.

We arrived on a Friday. Jim had scheduled us to play golf on a nine-hole executive course Saturday. Verna's comment was, "Oh, a crappy pitch and putt." When we got to the course and finished the first hole, Verna had to eat her words. The course was very challenging, and Jim never let Verna forget her remarks.

We were both impressed again as we traveled around The Villages on Saturday. It was early December, and everything was green, with no bare trees and flowers in full bloom everywhere. The grounds were so neat and clean. Everything looked fresh, new, clean, and tidy. I never saw one eyesore. Nothing needed repair, painting, or clean up, not a bit of litter. And everybody was so cheerful and friendly. Invariably, they waved as you passed someone walking or in a golf cart. Verna said she felt like the Pope as we rode along in the golf cart with her waving at everyone.

We all went out for dinner Saturday evening and picked up the tab using some of our funny money. The restaurant, food, and prices were great. The founder of The Village, Mr. Schwartz, had a policy regarding restaurant owners that they would not gouge seniors with unreasonable prices since they were on a fixed income.

Sunday morning, we went to their church with Peg and Jim. They introduced us to four couples they were friendly with. After Mass, we all ate breakfast at one of the country clubs. It was just like our Sunday morning routine in New Jersey.

The plan for Sunday was to spend the day with Peg and Jim. Another couple we both were friends with in New Jersey had purchased a home outside of The Villages because they wanted more space. They joined us at the O'Donnells for dinner. We hung around the house in the afternoon, and Peg was preparing dinner. All of a sudden, Jim said he was going to take us on a little tour to see his next house. We didn't know what he meant. When they sold their house in New Jersey and purchased their current home, they had about $100,000 left over. At that time in The Villages, some people bought small houses for about $100,000, completely furnishing them, then selling them as "turnkey" dwellings for $110,000 to $120,000. Jim had done that three times. That practice came to an end when one person purchased thirty of them. The Villages did not want the place to become a resort with no full-time residents. They started adding provisions in their sales contract that ended it.

As part of our tour, Jim took us to see the next house he had intended to turn over once it was up for sale. It happened to be near a golf course. As we rode along, a spectacular view caught Verna's and my eyes, so we told Jim to stop. It was a gorgeous panoramic view of three holes of a golf course with a large body of water and a huge, perfectly shaped oak tree on the edge of it. We were impressed. There were a few empty lots where we stood, and I noted the street address so I could check it out with Jerry, our real estate agent, in the morning. When we returned to the house, Verna shouted as we entered, "Peg, we found our lot!" She responded, "You did what? You did not come down here to buy." We said, yes, we knew that. The place sells itself. The management knows that all they have to do is get the people here, and the rest will take care of itself. Before we came down, we told the O'Donnells that we were not interested in purchasing a home, and Jim relayed that to Jerry. You can imagine what dominated the dinner conversation that evening.

We had no intention of relocating to The Villages, and our mindset upon arrival was that as long as we were here, we might as well get some information for possible future use; you never know. We were sold on the place by Sunday, so we went to our Monday morning meeting with the Sales Office. The first order of business was to take a trolley ride tour of The Villages with a narration and a few stops for a "look and see." After about an hour, we returned to the Sales Office, where Jerry was supposed to meet us and make his pitch. He was not there. After a while, as we were the only couple in the lobby, the Sales Manager walked up to us and inquired about the problem. He immediately made a phone call, and our salesperson was there within minutes. Perhaps he took Jim's comment about us not being interested at heart.

Our first interest was to get some information on pre-owned homes.

After seeing the prices on a few, we changed our minds. Purchasing something new was a better deal. We had done a little homework looking at various house descriptions, floor plans, and prices, plus picking the O'Donnell's brains over the weekend. We knew exactly what house plan we wanted. We also told Jerry about the empty lots we saw on Sunday. He took us to see them. Although there were four empty lots, only one was available, but it was too close to a tee box. Jerry pulled out a set of drawings, opened them up, and then told us to look out to the right at this stretch of at least twenty-five lots that ran down along a par-four fairway. He looked at his notes and informed us that all those lots had just been put on the market that morning. He said we could have any one of them. WOW! Talk about a kid in a candy store. He said let's walk down the golf cart path and as we came to each one, we stopped, took in the view, read off the price, and moved on to the next one. We were in $100,000 territory. We were somewhere in the vicinity of the tee boxes for the par-four hole. We had to choose this point because further down the fairway or near the green would be "golf-ball-in-the-yard-territory." We had the choices narrowed down to three or four. We evaluated the panorama that provided the best view of the course, the water, and the tree while not being too close to any of the tee boxes. "This one," we told Jerry. He checked the price list: $105,000, "We'll take it." Some of the lots were more and some less, but the view was always wrong. We had no problem with the price. As we learned in subsequent years, there are a limited number of lots with good views in The Villages. The ones with good views go at a premium price. We knew that every time we looked out the window at that view, we would get a good return on our money. I also subsequently developed my pricing formula for the lot. Golf course view $30,000; water view $30,000; oak tree view $30,000; total $90,000; the land itself; $15,000, total price $105,000. I can't help but imagine that The Villages considered all of those features when they set the prices for lots.

Back to the Sales Office. Jerry said he would need to draw up the paperwork all day and meet us at a restaurant at nine p.m. to sign off. We spent the rest of the day with Jim and Peg looking over the lot we chose to see if there were any negative issues, such as compass orientation, fire hydrants, lights flashing into windows, utility boxes, etc. We passed their inspection. We also arranged to spend a few hours in a model home identical to our floor plan to start visualizing furnishings and furniture arrangements and getting used to the overall feeling. While we were there, a few potential buyers stopped by. I think Verna made three sales as she spoke about our impressions of The Villages. She never did get her commission check! HAHA!

We closed the deal that night as scheduled. "Sign here _____, and that will be $2,500 to start the process, credit card please." "What did we just do?" we asked ourselves as we sipped our after-dinner wine and digested what just happened. Jerry told us that we would have to return in February for "Home Order" and sign the contract. We went back to our room. We could not sleep and had a four a.m. limo pickup for the airport. A thousand questions needed to be dealt with, and numerous issues raced through our minds.

When we arrived at the airport the next morning, we were so early that we were able to catch an earlier flight home. Once we settled on the plane, we continued to struggle with our decision. To give us peace of mind, I suggested to Verna that we imagine that we did not make the commitment and see how that made us feel. We had to force ourselves to do that. We both agreed that when we landed and our friend, Al, picked us up, we would not say anything about what we did—okay, agreed. Since we had arrived earlier, we had to wait about an hour for Al. We sat near our suitcases when Verna said, "Show me the floor plans again." Oh no, so much for imagining we did not buy. Al arrives. We get into the car, and Verna immediately blurts out, "Al, we bought a house!"

We have to call the kids as soon as we get in our house. We called David first because he was older. His response was unfavorable; he was concerned that he had done something wrong and said we had not told him we were planning to move. We were disappointed in his reaction and told him we were not planning on moving; it just happened. Then we called Kevin. He was much more positive, even happy for us. We started to have second thoughts. Things got so intense that before the day was over, we decided to call Jerry the next day to cancel the deal. No problem; he said he would cancel our credit card deposit and that The Villages will always be available whenever we're ready. We were sad that our dream vanished as quickly as it was created. The next day, we got a call from David. He had settled down some, and perhaps the shock effect subsided. We started to have second thoughts about our second thoughts. As we were mulling it over, I told Verna that we would always be only a short plane ride away from our family up north. That realization pushed us over the edge. We'll call Jerry in the morning. We hope and pray that nobody else bought our perfect lot. Jerry answered and said he'd have to check and would call us back. We anxiously stayed near the phone all day. Ring, "This is Jerry; the lot is still yours; let me have your credit card number again." Thank you, God!

We went back to The Villages in February as scheduled. Home Order is a process where you have to make numerous decisions regarding the house plan you selected and the countless decisions that go into designing a house. We were told to allow at least five days for it. The house we chose had a basic floor plan. The first series of choices were any changes you wanted to make to the overall dimensions of the house or any internal modifications to the size of rooms. The house was large enough, so we kept the square footage the same. One thing we should have done was to have the kitchen made larger by expanding one side of the house a few feet. Another item we missed is that we were unaware we could have had the lanai sliding glass doors changed to pocket doors that would give us an uninterrupted view outside. We did make minor changes and additions, such as eliminating two of four windows in the master bedroom and eliminating shelving in all of the closets because we wanted to lay them out ourselves. We also had to tell them where to place two outlets in the dining room for two crystal wall sconces that matched the chandelier we would bring from New Jersey. And not to put in fans because we would purchase our own, and I would install them. We also had to add a lanai because it did not come with the house, and we wanted a two-car garage plus a space for a golf cart and workbench. I do not like St. Augustine grass, which is typical in Florida, so we asked how much of the front yard has to be grass so that I could maximize the size of the concrete driveway. We ended up with a circular driveway.

Then, on to the details, we had to decide on everything that goes into the finishing touches. They are too numerous to list. But to give you an idea, they ranged from door hinges and hardware to appliances, floor coverings, paint colors, cabinetry, toilet handles, etc. They had a good system. There was a showroom loaded with samples. As you made some choices, samples were put in a shopping cart to match future selections. A running tab was kept as decisions were made. Some couples going through the process had difficulty, as we overheard them having a heated disagreement about something in an adjoining room or the samples room. Verna and I had no such problem. We always tended to have the same tastes on such matters. We enjoyed the process as we mentally built our dream home. Here's the final bill. Lot - $105,000; house - $178,000; additions/changes/deletions - $60,000; total - $343,000. Twenty-five thousand dollars down to start construction, closing date July 1, 2004. Sign here _____. In our lifetime, this was the third house we purchased. All three were brand new, and we had never lived in a house that somebody else had lived in. Remember our mobile home, on wheels, but still, a house no one had lived in before? The house in New Jersey was new. We will never own a house that somebody had previously lived in and never have that experience of wondering what went on inside these walls before us.

The closing went as scheduled, and construction was completed on time. We moved in on August 18, 2004, and were pleasantly surprised with the finished product. That's our "Villages Story."

57. THINGS I DID FOR MONEY (MY OTHER RESUME)

Starting at age eight, when I became an altar boy and had to serve Mass in addition to attending school, I never did just one thing until I was about age sixty-five. I never <u>just</u> went to school or <u>just</u> went to work. It was always either school plus a job, a job plus school, or a job plus a second job.

Here is a list and some stories of various things I did throughout my life, in addition to attending school and my regular job as an adult. I did these to make a couple of extra dollars and sometimes a couple of cents for myself.

- When I was about nine, a few of us kids became friends with the mailman who delivered the mail to our area. During one summer, we followed him around. He handed us the mail for a particular house as we approached it. One of us walked up the sidewalk to the door and put the mail in the mail slot or box. The route took about an hour. At the end of it, he gave us ten cents each. What he and we did was probably illegal!

- Shoveling snow for a neighbor while I was in high school.

- Working on a farm (a previous story).

- Caddying - There are two parts to this. At ages twelve through fifteen, going to the local country club and hoped to get picked for a job. Most of the time, I did. I made $2 for the day, summer only. More recently, at about age seventy-five, the senior members of the LPGA (Ladies Professional Group Association), known as the Legends, came to The Villages in Florida for a tournament. A friend, Bev, whom Verna and I played golf with, volunteered for the event and happened to be working on registering the players for the tournament. She overheard one of the ladies, Elaine Cosby, saying that she needed a caddie because her regular one had a death in the family and could not make it. Bev knew that I caddied as a kid and said that she would call me if it were okay with Elaine; she said, "Yes." Verna took the call. I was working in the yard, and she came out and **told** me I would be a caddy for a professional golfer. It was a three-day event. It went well, and Elaine won $3000. When it was over, and I walked with her to the car to put the clubs away, she asked me if I would mind if she paid me. I was a little taken aback and said I did not expect any payment and that it was an interesting experience and an honor to have done it. She took out her checkbook and asked how I spelled my last name. I told her, and she wrote me a check for $300—much more than I had ever made during my amateur caddy career.

- There was a miniature golf course near where I grew up. One evening, when I was about twelve, I sat on a bench by the first hole to watch the players. A group of six guys came to play, and they could not decide who would keep score, so they said to me, "Hey kid, would you keep score for us?" I said, "OK." When they got done, they each gave me fifteen cents for a total of ninety cents. I was elated. I thought I had a permanent job for the summer, so I went there the next evening and asked a few people if they wanted me to keep their scores, but no takers—a one-day career on my resume.

- Throughout the five years of my altar boy career (previous story), I occasionally got assigned to serve a wedding Mass with other boys on a Saturday morning. At the end of the Mass, the groom, best man, ushers, or all gave us some money. I usually received a few dollars, but never more than $5.

- Paperboy (previous story).

- Working on a soda delivery truck during the winters of my high school years. I worked on a farm during the summer. On Saturdays, an older neighbor friend (the best man at our wedding) and I delivered soda to private houses in our town. He drove the truck, and I was the helper. We had to load the truck for the day first thing in the morning. Then, we start our route. We had a list of regular customers. One of us went to the house and asked if they wanted any soda that week and what kind. We always stopped for lunch at the same diner and had soup and a burger; he paid. At the end of the day, we had to unload all of the wooden cases of empty bottles and fill the truck up for the next day. I made $5 a day. I did the other part of this job during the days off from school during the Christmas break. This time, I worked with one of the family owners of the distribution business. During my high school years, I also had a morning paper route (previous story), and I usually got up at 5:00 a.m. to deliver the papers before I went to school. But during the Christmas break, when I had this other extra job, I had to get up at 3:30 a.m. to deliver the papers because every morning at 5:00 a.m., we had to be on our way to the bottling plant one hour away to get a load of soda for the day. When we got to the plant, my job was to help unload the cases of empty bottles and help load the truck with cases of full bottles. Then, the one-hour ride back and grab some breakfast at home, one block from the truck's location. Back into the truck to "Start" the day's work at about 8:00 a.m. I had already been awake for four and a half hours. Our route was a nearby town where we delivered the soda to small "MOM & POP" stores. My boss, Evo, drove up to the store and went inside to take the order. I went into the dark and dingy cellar to search for our bottles and took them out to the truck. Evo sent me hand signals from the store about what flavor and how many of each the store owner wanted. I then took them into the cellar, went back to the truck, and waited for him. Then, on to the next store. The best part of the day was lunch on him. We were done at about 6:00 p.m. and loaded the truck for the next morning's 5:00 a.m. trip. I made $5.00 a day. Merry Christmas!

- During the first six years of my Air Force career, there was this duty called "KP," meaning Kitchen Police. About once per month, you were assigned to do it on one of your regular work days. It involved reporting to the Dining Hall at 6:00 a.m. with three other guys. There were four jobs. The first guy there got their first choice, and so on. Two of the jobs were to do the dishes and tableware, which involved cleaning the scraps off the plates and then putting them and the tableware in a tray to be sent through a huge dishwashing machine called a "Clipper." The third job was washing all of the pots and pans. The fourth was sweeping, mopping, and buffing the dining room floor. No one job was better than the others. Some guys disliked doing KP, so they paid others and took the day off. The going rate was $12 for a twelve-hour day. I was stationed on radar sites with only about 200 guys during those years, so making permanent arrangements for taking care of business was easy. About ten of us did this regularly so we could accommodate our clients. Of course, I could only do this on my regular days off.

- During my second year in the Air Force, I was at this radar site that had an NCO (Non-Commissioned Officers) Club, which was a place to get a drink and snacks. A sergeant at the site who took me under his wing was on the

Board of Directors for the club. They needed someone to clean the place, and he asked me if I wanted the job. It paid $55 a month. I said OK. It took about two hours a day but had to be done daily and only while it was closed. I was working shifts at the time. There was no problem on my days off. I did it before or after my shift on the days I worked. I did that job for two years, the second year being the first year Verna and I were married. Then we got transferred to another place (previous story).

- During my first couple of years in the Air Force, before I got married, I was living in the barracks. I didn't smoke or drink and was one of the few guys who did not run out of money before the next payday. A few of my buddies played cards for money, and when they were losing and out of money but wanted to continue playing, they came to me to borrow a few bucks. I loaned them $2 for $3, payable on the next payday. We got paid every two weeks in cash. We had to stand in line, present ourselves to an officer, salute, give our name, rank, and serial number, and say, "Sir, Airman Second Class John J. Kolman reporting for pay!" An airman from the finance office beside him looked at a list and told the officer how much cash to give me. I saluted and went out the back door. I always made sure I was in line before anyone who owed me money. I waited outside with my little book and collected my loans plus interest from my clients. I never got stuck. Our older son tells me I could have been arrested for loan-sharking!

- The first year my wife and I married, we struggled financially. I was making $200 a month with a car payment of $50 and rent of $55. Verna had experience sewing in a pants factory in Pennsylvania, so she tried to find a similar or any other job where we were stationed in Tennessee. She could not find any because they would not hire someone who would likely be transferred at any time (now illegal). As mentioned above, I was making extra money by pulling KP and cleaning the NCO Club, but we were still short at the end of the month. Our apartment was owned by someone who also rented trailers for people to live in. One day, he approached us and asked if we would like to do odd jobs and clean vacant trailers for him for twenty-five cents an hour for each of us. We said yes and did that for a year before we got transferred.

- When I was stationed in Iceland, in addition to my regular shift work, I took correspondence courses, attended evening college (previous story), and pulled KP for money. One day, the officer in charge of our radar operators crew responsible for the library came to me and asked if I was interested in working during my free time in the library and checking out books. He had a staff to do this and needed one more person. Of course, I said, "Yes," an easy job plus a good time to study and do my homework. It paid $2 an hour.

- When we lived in New Jersey, Verna worked with a widow who needed help maintaining her house and yard (previous story). I did that for several years before she passed away. She paid me $15 an hour.

- I had an extensive flower garden in New Jersey. There came a time when my perennials became so prolific that I had no place to plant them. One day, we had a garage sale, and Verna said to dig some out and put them up for sale. I did, and they went like hotcakes. I developed a lot of repeat customers. I toyed with the idea of telling the federal government I was now a farmer and would like to be part of their program, where they paid farmers not to plant anymore. HAHA! Verna said, "Don't push it."

- One day, a lady came to our garage sale and admired my landscaping. She said she would pay me to look at her yard and give her some suggestions on improving it. I did, and she paid me $20. This is another one-time career experience on my resume.
- University Adjunct Professor (previous story)
- Consultant (previous stories)

So when people ask me what I do for a living, what should I say? And if I were to convert the above to an actual resume and go job hunting with it, what would the reaction be?

58. BEST FRIENDS

2000 - PRESENT

Peg and Jim O'Donnell are their names, and they are both Irish. Our first contact with them was at our church in New Jersey. They sat behind us, and the extent of our contact was a casual "Good Morning" and "Peace Be With You" during that part of the Catholic Mass. We knew just one thing about Jim for the longest time. That is, after Mass, he always visited his mother in a nursing home. He was such a good Irish son to his Mom.

At some point, our relationship expanded to asking him if he would like to join us for a round of golf at the Army base country club we belonged to. I don't remember exactly how we learned of Jim's interest in golf. It must have been Verna's knack for getting people to divulge themselves to her and Jim's tendency to be very talkative (being Irish and having been in sales his whole career). Peg did not golf at the time.

The next thing we knew, we were walking down the first fairway one day, and Jim, out of the clear blue, mentioned an upcoming trip to Ireland. For several years, he and Peg were involved in Project Children. That was a program wherein about three hundred Catholic and Protestant children from Northern Ireland came to the states and were dispersed to various families across the country for six weeks. The objective was to have them enjoy the experience of living in an environment where families and children all get along with each other, unlike the strife in Northern Ireland that they were experiencing at the time. Peg's and Jim's roles involved them in planning and making a trip to Belfast with others from the States to escort them here. They had children living with them every time.

Back to the golf course. Jim commented that they would be making the trip sometime soon. For some unknown reason, I commented that we'd join them on one trip when Verna retires. It must have been an inner desire to visit Ireland sometime in my life. Verna's comment was, "Why wait until I retire?" Sometime between that scene and the actual trip, Peg started to golf.

So here we were, going on a ten-day trip with a couple we had never been out with or been in each other's homes. We did have an occasion or two to go to their house to plan the trip. How would it play out? The plan was to fly to Shannon, then hit the B&Bs around the southern tip of Ireland, ending up in Dublin. We would fly home from there, and Peg and Jim would scoot up to Belfast to pick up the plane load of kids.

Our first B&B was at "Cousin Anna's." Jim has a story about this one. While making arrangements for a previous trip to Ireland, Peg and Jim ran across a B&B owned by Anna O'Donnell (same last name as Jim and Peg). They booked it. When they arrived at the door, Jim introduced himself as a "Long-lost cousin from America." That was not the case, but Jim was so convincing in his greeting that it stuck. Cousin Anna did not treat us as regular guests; we were "Family" and had our meals at their kitchen table. Jim loves that sort of thing.

After a day or two and some golf, we hit the road. We rented a van. Peg did all of the driving. She amazed us, driving on the left side of the road and down some very narrow country roads with only inches to spare when two vehicles approached each other.

As we were ready to leave one B&B, Peg found one for the next day. Our routine was to get up in the morning, play golf, have lunch, then move on to the next B&B. We were there for ten days and played golf eleven times. One day, we played twice.

Ireland, like The Villages, is a golfers' paradise. The beauty of the countryside blew us away, so picturesque. We were so distracted by the beautiful landscape that golf scores became secondary. One day, on one of the tees, Verna and I were so enthralled by the view that we purposely hit a golf ball into the Irish Sea just because it was there. Here we were on mountainous terrain (no golf cart) with the Irish Sea splashing its fury and the mist hitting our faces, giving the inner sensation of being blessed with holy water. Ireland is such a beautiful country. One of the first impressions is the freshness and all of that green. Ireland is the first country in Europe that you reach after three thousand miles across the ocean from New York. All the pollution in the atmosphere has a long time to dissipate before reaching Ireland. Verna's mother had a saying to her children when they were small,

"Go outside and get the stink blown off you." Do you see the connection? Another thing I like about Ireland is that there are no snakes; I hate them.

One day, as we were on our way to the following B&B, we approached a Waterford Crystal factory. Peg asked if we were interested in stopping. Verna responded, "No, we are here to play golf," as we zoomed by.

During the trip, we had dinner with two of Jim's legitimate cousins. That was a good way to learn more about a country and its people, and it added a nice touch to the entire trip.

There was another day when we made a stop near the shore. Verna said she would like to go down and touch the Irish Sea. Peg did not want to go down, so I stayed with her. Jim agreed to go with Verna. There were about one hundred wooden steps to get to the shore. When Verna and Jim returned, Verna was huffing and puffing, carrying a load of stones in her shirt pulled up, exposing her belly. They were some of the nicest stones I ever saw, about three inches, well-smoothed from tumbling in the sea for eons, and some with very intricate veining. A whole cove was covered with them, and I told Verna she should have brought more. Her response is not fit to print!

The following day, Peg and Jim had to take care of some business in town before we went to golf. They arranged to drop us off near the cove so I could get some more stones, and then they would pick us up. Peg got us a couple of plastic shopping bags and we went treasure gathering. We went down the one hundred steps, loaded the bags, and I found two larger beauties, about six inches in size, that I picked up to make into book ends when we returned home. Then, the hard part of lugging them up the one hundred steps.

Now to get them home. We decided to disperse them throughout our golf bag carriers and suitcases. When we arrived at the airport to depart, we were somewhat apprehensive when we put our bags on the scale to be weighed. No problem; the attendant was very friendly, like most Irish people, and started to chat about our trip; we talked about everything except our bags, and so far, so good.

When we got home, I emptied the stones into a five-gallon bucket and weighed them: eighty pounds. Now, where do I place them in my yard? I found the perfect spot as an accent feature near one of my koi fish ponds. Guess what happened when I dumped them out of the bucket to arrange them? All the snakes in our backyard slithered out from underneath all the other rocks in the yard and headed for the neighbors' yards. Thank You, St. Patrick! Just kidding! According to legend, during the 400s, when St. Patrick arrived in Ireland, all of the snakes vanished. St. Patrick went to Ireland then, but there were never any snakes in Ireland. It makes such a good story that I can't resist telling it.

When we moved from New Jersey to The Villages in Florida, I had to bring the stones. But I treasured them so much, and they provided the literal material for my tale that I could not risk losing them during the move. They came with us in the car. While unpacking, I had to find the perfect place for them again. I arranged them into an imaginary short river near the entrance of our house. There is a saying in Florida, "You are never more than three feet away from a snake." Okay, St. Patrick, this is a second chance to be a hero. Guess what? Nothing happened. I know, "Fool me once, shame on you, fool me twice, shame on me." When we sold our house in Florida (future story), we were at a loss as to what to do with the stones. The new homeowner would have no idea of the story behind them. We decided to give them to Peg and Jim, who would appreciate them. They were elated.

Having had such a great time on the Ireland trip, we all agreed to go on another golf trip. We all went to Myrtle Beach, North Carolina, on a golf package the following year. Once again, it all went well. So, where to next year? Well, guess what? Peg and Jim moved to The Villages, dang it. Shortly after they moved, we checked out The Villages by receiving their promotion package and CD. Our reaction was, "It's not for us." After more than a year and numerous invites from Peg and Jim, we agreed to go down to see them and take advantage of the promotion package as long as we were going. That was in December 2003 (previous story). Being the great friends that they are, Peg and Jim monitored our house as it was being constructed and took pictures of the progress. Jim even mowed our grass once it was completed until we moved in. They put us up for the night we arrived until our furniture arrived the next day. They introduced us to some of their friends who are still our friends after twenty years. Soon after we settled in, we started golfing with Jim and Peg. No one ever said anything, but Verna and I sensed an unspoken competition between her and Jim for the best round. We played every Friday for many years, but that ended. We kept in touch throughout the years. We don't see each other frequently, but we know they are there, and we are here if either of us needs each other. We eventually resumed golfing with them, but only for nine holes; COVID-19 put a damper on that. Verna and Peg got into mahjong, which was interrupted for the same reason. We owe Peg and Jim big time. Not only for the great Ireland trip but had it not been for them, we would not have lived some of the best years of our lives in The Villages. Being in the Air Force for twenty years, we never had the opportunity to develop Best Friends. For the thirty-one years we lived in New Jersey, we had a lot of friends but never developed a lasting relationship with any of them. Jim is a lot like Verna, and I am like Peg. We have this joke between us. If feisty Verna and feisty Jim lived together, they would quickly kill each other. If Peg and I lived together, one of us would be dead for a week before the other knew it because we would both have our noses buried in a book. We make a good package that is neatly wrapped and labeled "Best Friends!"

God Bless!

P.S. Jim passed away unexpectedly in June 2024. We have frequent phone calls with Peg. In the back of our minds, we still have great memories. Thank you, O'Donnells!

JACK VERNA PEG JIM

59. THE PHOENIX ('55 CHEVY)

The Phoenix is an immortal bird associated with Greek mythology that cyclically regenerates or is otherwise born again. Associated with the sun, a phoenix obtains new life by rising from the ashes of its predecessor.

The cars of the 1950s are in a class by themselves. For example, compared to earlier cars, they were more colorful. No color was off limits, including pink. They had a lot of chrome. A bumper was a "bumper" then, unlike future cars where the bumper was made of plastic, and you couldn't tell where the bumper ended and where the remainder of the car started. Those cars were jazzy with some extreme designs. You could tell them apart, not only between manufacturers but between years. I could tell you the difference between a 1952 Chevy and a 1953 Chevy as far away as I could see them. The following year's models always came out in September or October, and it was a great "unveiling event" that created a lot of excitement regarding next year's look.

My first car was "our" first car. Verna and I got married on June 21, 1958. We needed a car to get back to Tennessee and set up housekeeping where I was stationed with the Air Force. We went to the Chevrolet dealer from whom Verna's parents purchased their cars. We could not afford a brand-new one. A '55 Chevy four-door turquoise and white sedan caught our eye. Its only shortcoming was the lack of a radio, which did not make sense. We purchased it for $1,250 with a few dollars down and $50 a month for two years. We couldn't afford a custom radio, but Verna's brother, Sonny, came to the rescue as usual. He found us a radio for a couple of bucks. The only problem was that it was six volts instead of twelve and quite clumsy because the speaker was built in. It was about a twelve-inch cube in dimension. The only place we could put it was on the floor of the front passenger side. I had to install a voltage reducer (resistor) to hook it up to the car because it was a six-volt radio in a twelve-volt car. Verna became the radio operator. It never worked well, and the volume was always too low. Not knowing much about electric circuitry, I bypassed the reducer to give it more power. When I did that, the radio had a lot of volume for a few seconds, then gasped its last breath. Sometime later, I put in the "correct" radio.

We kept the car for about two years, then upgraded it to a '59 Chevy. Sometime around 1980, I became interested in vintage cars from the fifties. There was a place in my heart for a '55 Chevy. I kept my eyes on the Want Ads. Eventually, one caught my eye. "For Sale, 1955 Chevy $250." WOW! Such a deal. I couldn't believe the price, so I called to confirm it and got the particulars. The price was correct, and the car was in running condition, but those were the only two good things about it. It was on a farm near us in New Jersey. Verna went with me to take a look, all the time wondering what I was doing. Sure enough, the car started and was drivable. "I'll take it." Chickens had been living in the trunk. It was far from a shinny turquoise and white Bel-air. It was a 150 Model, the lowest in the line of three models. The middle model was a 210 Del Ray, and the Bel Air was the top-of-the-line. It was an ugly sea green with a white top, four-door sedan—a real rust bucket with a large gaping hole in the driver's floorboard. As Verna followed me home, she kept waiting for my feet to drop through the floor and start peddling—shades of *The Flintstones*. I had my project car.

I enrolled in an evening auto-body class at the local vocational school to learn the fundamentals of auto-body repair. I also joined the local chapter of a Vintage Car Club to share new experiences and pick up a few tips. After a few years, I quit the club because I wasn't into it as much as the other guys.

I planned to upgrade the 150 model to a Bel-Air. The biggest part was finding all the trim pieces that "dressed up" the vehicle. Then, I had to figure out where to drill the holes in the body of the car to attach them. I found a lot of what I needed from a local junkyard. Also, a Classic Chevy Club in Orlando sold parts, plus a mail-order company, J. C. Whitney, selling car parts and accessories.

My first concern was safety, so I had a fellow club member replace the entire brake and front-end suspension systems. The engine was a six-cylinder, not a V-8 like our first Chevy. Also, it was a stick shift, not an automatic.

I started a record of all of the expenses. I never did keep track of the hours I put into it. It needed a lot of work. The correct way to restore such a car is to remove everything off the frame. Yes, the body does come off the frame. After you remove the doors, fenders, hood, and trunk door, what is left is the engine, steering column, and the body, which is called the "Clip," which is only attached to the frame with nuts and bolts. Of course, the engine, steering column, wheels, and drive train are all a matter of nuts and bolts. Take out all that; the only remaining thing is the frame without a single part, nut, or bolt. The pure way to start the restoration process is to take the frame to a place where it is dipped into a large container of solvent to remove all dirt, grime, and rust. The frame is then painted and coated with an under-seal substance. Finally, clean up everything you took off and start reassembling the vehicle.

I cheated. I was not a purist about my restoration. My finished product was a "Road Car," not a "Show Car." Show cars are entered into competitions where expert judges evaluate them and reward points for originality and authenticity. They get into details, and you lose points if a nut and bolt are not the same as when the car comes off the assembly line. That I changed my vehicle from a 150 to a Bel-Air would not qualify me to enter it in such a show. My Chevy was "bastardized." I'll give you an idea as to how low-end-of-the-line it was. When you open the door of a vehicle, you expect the interior light to come on. My 150 did not do that because there were no button switches on the door frames to activate the dome light. To turn the dome light on, you had to turn the headlight control knob to the left. So I had to drill holes for the switches and run wires to the dome light.

Getting back to my cheating, I did take off the doors and front fenders, but that was it. The engine ran, so there was no need to mess with it. I took off the bumpers and had them sent out to be re-chromed. I removed all of the paint inside and out.

I bought an air compressor and spray gun to paint it. That turned out to be a disaster. First, I had to make my garage as dust-free as possible.

The day I was set up to paint, it turned out to be rainy all day. I did have a proper mask. I had to add urethane to the paint as a hardener. That night, I had trouble breathing and had to go to the ER the next day. My lungs cleared up in a couple of days. On top of all that, the paint job turned out poorly. It was called "orange peel," not smooth and glossy. I had to rub it smooth with rubbing compound. A couple of years later, I had it repainted by a professional. I used an airbrush to paint the dash, which turned out well. I bought vinyl seat covers (not the original design nor fabric, more points lost). I also purchased a new turquoise headliner, which was tricky to install. I bought matching material to make the door panels, but Verna had to sew the covers for the armrests using the old ones as patterns. I purchased a shop manual that gave good instructions for replacing every part of the vehicle. I made good use of it at various stages of the process.

I don't recall how many years I worked on the car. I do remember completing it in 1984. I know I had worked on it for at least four years. It always ran. As it set outside, I made it a point to start it up and take it for a drive regularly. In the extreme winter months, it was sometimes covered with snow. After I dug it out, I had to pump the gas pedal about one hundred times to get gas to the carburetor. Eventually, it turned over. I let it run for a while and then let it go back into hibernation.

During nice weather, I took it to church and ran some errands. I would get a few "thumbs up" from admirers along the way. It had Historic license plates that had no expiration date, and the car was excluded from annual inspections by the state. As a consequence, it was illegal to use it regularly. If I ever got stopped and was challenged for not complying with the restriction, my story was that I was taking it for repairs someplace. I never was stopped. I had to use it in a few emergencies to get to work.

Around 1990, Verna and I decided to expand twelve feet to one side of our house. We did not add any rooms but did make the two end bedrooms and the master bath larger. Verna always wanted a larger master bath. The lower level space under the addition was just the right size for an attached garage next to the double garage that was already there. After all those years fighting the elements, my baby was nice and cozy.

When I bought the car, the odometer read 14,000 miles. The owner was not the original owner nor familiar with the car's history. Did it have 14,000 or 114,000 miles on it? Back then, odometers only went up to 99,000 miles, and there were no requirements certifying odometer readings. The engine could have been old from age but not from use. Anyway, there was no need to do anything with the engine except a tune-up. If the engine ever went, I would put a V-8 in it.

When it came time for us to relocate to The Villages, I did not want to lug it down there. It had served a purpose in my life, and I had scratched that "Rust Bucket off my Bucket List." We put it up for sale and had a few nibbles. Then, this guy and his teenage son showed up. The kid was interested in it, and his father said it would be a good bonding vehicle for them. We sold it for $7,000, and I had put about $4,000 into it.

I gave them the car's history plus a set of before, during, and after restoration snapshots. I wish I had kept a copy. There is still a place in my heart for those '50s Classics, but I have moved on to other interests. But my Phoenix did provide a good story that describes a slice of my life.

RESTORED '55 CHEVY AT 2 SENECA TRAIL

60. EDUCATIONAL PAYOFF

1981 - 1983

Although I already had undergraduate and graduate degrees, I only took four liberal arts courses (Fine Arts, Cultural Anthropology, Western Civilization, and Judaism/Christianity). I wanted to learn more about history, literature, philosophy, etc.. So, one day, I went to a nearby community college to enroll in an evening history class. The registrar asked me if I was a veteran, and I answered yes. She said if I take one course at a time, the VA would pay for it. She went on to ask me if I had any dependents. I told her I had three. She said, "Well, if you take two courses at a time, the VA will send you a monthly check. I answered, "Okay, I'll take two courses." I did this for a while, taking courses in history, literature, philosophy, etc.

While chatting with the younger students during class breaks, they told me I was crazy for going to school when I already had an advanced degree. They never understood my simple explanation, "I just wanted to learn."

After taking a few courses, I received a letter from the registrar asking me to come in and see her. I did, and she said, "You have to matriculate and select the degree you want to pursue." I replied, "I don't want a degree; I just want to take the courses." She adamantly responded, "You have to commit to a degree." I reluctantly replied, "Okay, give me the catalog of courses, and I'll pick something out." I selected a degree that gave me the most electives. I continued my learning adventure and did well compared to the other students. I was more eager and had a different motivation.

The most interesting course I took was one on Russian history. One night in class, the professor took us to the campus library for an assignment to look up any topic in the Soviet Encyclopedia and report on it to the class. I was interested in management then, so I looked that up. What did I find? Nothing! The Communistic Soviets had no concept of management as we know it. Their government makes all the decisions customarily performed by managers in a capitalistic economy. They decide what products to make, whom to sell them to, and at what price. I presented my findings to the class with a little of Marx and Engles thrown in. Another interesting incident from that class was that the professor suggested we attend a Sunday Eastern Orthodox Mass in a nearby church. Verna and I went. It was much longer than a Roman Catholic Mass, heavy on incense, and more ritualistic. At that time, who would have known that twenty-five years later, Verna and I would be on a river cruise in Russia and visiting numerous Russian churches? You never know!

I eventually completed the degree requirements and received my diploma for an Associate of Arts Degree. Seeing my name on a piece of paper associated with the arts seemed strange. I am not an art student. I appreciate an excellent painting, but that is as far as my interests in arts go.

The following semester, I went to register for more classes, but I was refused. I went to see the registrar for an explanation. She curtly told me, "You're finished, and the VA will not pay for any more courses." I could have audited more courses and paid for them myself, but I didn't pursue that. I did have more VA educational benefits coming, but the only way I could use them was if I went on to obtain a doctorate. I thought about that possibility for a while but decided against it because it had no value in the business world that I was working in then; doing it part-time would take too many years.

By the way, the monthly checks I received totaled $12,000 (tax-free). When I started taking college courses years ago, I tracked how much they cost me. My first thirty credits cost me $250. The Air Force paid for my undergraduate degree, and the MBA and Associate Degrees were VA benefits. So, if I subtract the $250 from the $12,000 I received from the VA, I am $11,750 ahead, which is not bad. Furthermore, the learning and doors that those classroom hours opened up for me in the future are priceless.

61. GOLF, A DOZEN SLICES
(PARDON THE PUN) OF LIFE 1988 - PRESENT

When Verna and I were fifty years old we started playing golf regularly. The primary reason at that time was Verna's doctor's suggestion that she get some physical activity.

We purchased a set of golf clubs, brand name Shamrock, generally referred to as a "Starter Set." Mistake number one. It's a common mistake similar to the one that a homeowner makes when the guy buys cheap tools to take care of minor DIY (Do It Yourself) projects. As compared to a professional, the DIYer does not have the skill level of the professional, then to make matters worse, he goes out and buys inferior tools to further diminish the results of his efforts. There's a saying in golf, "It's not the arrow, it's the Indian." I used to subscribe to that philosophy until Verna eventually persuaded me to upgrade our clubs (tools). I have to agree with her; it's a combination of the arrow and the Indian.

We joined a golf course on an Army base about twenty minutes from our home in New Jersey. Being a military retiree, we were eligible to play there, and it was the best deal in town. We immediately signed up for lessons and purchased a package deal. Mistake number two: too much information. We were saturated with new terminology, body positions, body movements, and body-mind coordination, let alone the mental dynamics of the game itself. Another saying in golf is, "It's ninety percent mental and the remaining ten percent is in your head."

Our course was in a wooded area and a few holes had very narrow fairways plus there was a large creek about thirty feet wide that meandered through six of the holes. On more than one occasion, we saw bears on the fairways. I had trouble hitting my drives on those narrow fairways. My drives tended to be long but not straight. Verna's were shorter but straighter. One day, I hit a ball deep into the woods, went in to find it (wearing shorts), and came out empty-handed but with a bad case of poison oak.

We made it a habit of playing when the course was not busy, and the better golfers were not on it. We were often the last ones on the course and driving home in the dark. If there were golfers behind us, we got off the fairway, hid behind a tree, and let them play through. We took some liberties with the rules, and we were not very concerned about our scores. After a while, when we got a little more comfortable on the course, we set our first goal of breaking one hundred for eighteen holes. Somewhere, I read that only ten percent of amateur golfers break one hundred. Verna broke a hundred before me. She was then, and still is, a much more consistent golfer.

She joined the Women's League at our course and won six trophies. One time she won the championship by beating someone twenty years younger than her. She became a legend there. She also won a County Championship. I entered one tournament and it was a disaster. Our club had an annual Couples Scramble that we participated in and that was another disaster. The way it works is that you alternate shots. I tee off first and wherever my ball went, Verna had to hit it from there; then wherever her shot went, I hit it, and so on until we got the ball in the cup and recorded our score. The very first time we participated, I hit my first drive into the Club's swimming pool. That was a penalty so now Verna had to hit from the men's tee which is further back than the women's. As I said earlier I had trouble keeping my shots in the fairway so Verna found herself hitting from places she had never been. She would hit a good shot then I messed it up on my turn. The event became known as "The Divorce Open." Of course, we never won it, but we came in third place one year. To ease the pain, there was always a nice dinner and wine afterward during the awards presentation. After a couple of wines, all is well until next year.

This golfing part of our lives lasted sixteen years until we moved to The Villages in Florida. We became addicted to the game, Verna more than me. In New Jersey, there was a stretch of time when we were playing six days a week (the course was closed on Mondays for maintenance). During the week when Verna was working, I took off early if I was consulting. When Verna came home from work, she quickly changed clothes, threw them on the bed, grabbed a sandwich that I had prepared, jumped in the car, and we were on the first tee in twenty minutes.

The golfing season in northern New Jersey is from April to October. We were averaging a hundred rounds a year. At times it felt like a job.

Of course, we resumed playing golf when we moved to The Villages. It's a golfers' paradise with so many courses. Our golfing routine in New Jersey was limited to only one course. And I knew that course like the back of my hand. Verna only saw the short grass in the fairways (except for the Divorce Open).

Golf has significantly impacted my thinking about life. We like to play with other couples and make it a social event. Over the years, I've made some observations, established some attitudes, and identified some peculiarities about golf.

- When we first started playing, I was very nervous for the first few holes, but then I settled down. I am no longer nervous about the first few holes.

- I also had the bad habit of letting a bad shot or bad hole ruin the rest of the round. That no longer happens. My golf game comes and goes, so I just patiently let it run its course. The same thing happens to the pros. You never see the same names on the first page of the leaderboards all season. Even Tiger Woods has his ups and downs.

- I don't let a bad round ruin my day. I paid hard-earned money to play and gave up four-plus hours of my precious time.

- It helps me emphasize positive thinking. If you're facing a shot that you have to carry the ball over a body of water or a sand trap and say to yourself, "I'm going to put it in the water or the sand," more often than not, that's exactly what will happen. The same thing occurs as you stand over a three-foot makable putt.

- Every so often, you come to a hole that is "Risk/Reward."

You can play the hole conservatively and avoid the risk, or you can "Go for it." I like to go for it. It's only a game. A couple of years ago, our son David visited us, and when he did, we played as much golf as possible with him. One day, we approached this up-sloping par four hole that was a little shorter than normal but had numerous sand traps in front of the green. The higher elevation of the green and all of the sand traps presented a beautiful panorama. If you hit a really good shot with your driver, you could fly the ball over all of the traps and hit the green. But if you did not hit a good shot, chances were pretty good that you'd end up in one of the traps. Alternatively, you could aim for the fairway, which made the hole longer, but no sand traps were on it. I drove first. I did not hit a perfect shot but was lucky and landed between some traps. David got up to the tee and said he was going to take less club and go for someplace short of the traps. I told him no. Use your driver. Here's an opportunity to go for it, and I talked him into it. He cranked up a good swing, hit a perfect shot, and the ball landed on the green. He was elated. We took his picture, and it became a treasured memory; if only I had taken a video of the shot. "You never know."

- A hole-in-one is an overrated sign of an excellent player. My take on it is that hitting the green is a skill, but getting the ball in the hole is luck. You don't expect to hit the ball into the cup off the tee; you may aim for a certain portion of the green, and if you hit it, you feel good, but you are never disappointed that the ball did not go in the hole. Verna has had five holes in one. I have never had any. She is more accurate than me, so she hits the green more often, and this gives her more opportunities to get it in the cup.

- A favorite golf saying of mine is, "You never know what's going to happen." It may apply to me more than some other golfers because I am so inconsistent. On numerous occasions, I would hit a perfect shot, and the very next one would be a disaster, and vice versa. The same thing applies to a good hole followed by a poor one. Or even to a good round when you start thinking that you have mastered the game only to go out the next time and do poorly. Standing on the first tee or standing over the next shot is like waking up in the morning, not knowing what the day will bring. "You never know."

- Practice does not work for me. After a bad round, Verna would say, "You have to go to the driving range." We'd go, and I'd feel like I had accomplished something. Then, in the next round, there would be no improvement. For some reason, the effort on the practice range does not carry over to the course. Practicing even makes me feel worse because I feel like I wasted time and money.

- Golf is a game of honor. It is easy to cheat and stretch the rules. I see this as an opportunity to test my character and see what I am made of. I feel better about myself when I could have easily and surreptitiously improved my lie but did not and hit the ball where it lay just like you are supposed to.

- Amateur Golf is usually not a team sport. There is just you and the ball. There is nobody to blame if you don't do well, and if you do well, you get all of the credit. This simplifies things. When we play with other couples or even just Verna and me, I don't begrudge the other person doing well. I feel that the only competition going on is with myself. One of my goals for each round is to improve my average score.

- Golf brings balance and fulfillment to my life: physical, mental, emotional, and social.

- Golf is addictive. Some time ago, I came across this saying: "I hate this game, but I can't wait to play it again."

So, there you have it. A tidy dozen quips of life that have been a part of me for many years and hopefully many, many more.

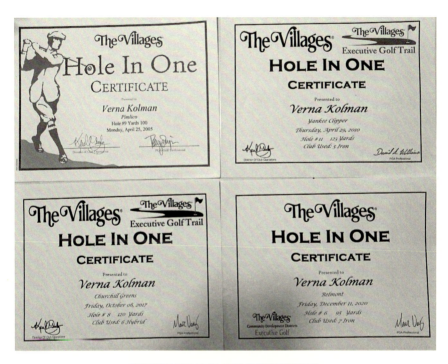

VERNA'S HOLE-IN-ONE CERTIFICATES

VERNA'S USGA HANDICAP CARD

62. PERFECT IS THE ENEMY OF GOOD

About three years ago, I was involved in a month-long woodworking project. As I was working on it, I had a lot of ideas that would make a good story. Before I get into the story, let me say a few words about the title. About five years ago, I was helping our son, David, construct a flower bed using heavy-duty landscaping wooden ties. We were cutting two pieces to fit together, which were not matching perfectly. I suggested we recut them, and then David said, "Perfect is the enemy of good." It took me a few seconds to process his philosophical but practical comment. Then, it hit me, so I applied the concept and considered the job done. It was a wise comment, and I have used it more than once on various projects since then. A fine example of a dad learning something from a son!

Back to the project. It all started about four years ago when I converted a section of our backyard into a Japanese garden effect. As a finishing touch, I wanted a small Chinese bridge to be placed over an imaginary river. I could not find one I liked, so I made one. I created a design and purchased some cedar wood and a jigsaw. The first problem was laying out an arc. I knew there was a way to do it mathematically, but I was unaware of it, so I free-handed one. The second problem was cutting it perfectly. There were guides on the jig saw for cutting perfectly straight lines but no guides for curves. However, I'm sure a device can be used with a router to let the machine do the work. I did not take the trouble to investigate that, nor did I want to invest money into something I would probably never use again. So I cut the curves without a guide and sanded them, and although I was as careful as possible, I found that they were not perfect. A third problem with the bridge surfaced when I noticed some of the wood rotting. I purposely chose cedar wood because it is not supposed to rot. What I am pretty sure happened is that on the top of each post (there were ten of them), I attached golf balls by using a screw threaded on both sides to fasten them to each post. Water must have seeped into the posts around the screws and started the rotting process. It is moisture that causes wood to rot. If a piece of wood gets wet and dries out quickly, it will not rot. Painting a piece of wood exposed to the elements protects the outside surface, but if moisture gets inside, the paint prevents the wood from completely drying, and it rots. If you build a wooden fence, don't paint it, and be sure that no part of the wood touches the ground; it will not rot. That is why you see a lot of farm barns not painted, even with gaps between the siding boards. The boards may get wet, but they quickly dry out. After a while, the barn boards become weather-beaten and take on a patina that makes them attractive to some artisans who purchase them "as is" to make various artifacts with the weathered boards.

Having explained the cause of the rotting problem, I put "repair bridge" on my "To Do" list. I planned to replace the rotted pieces, but the only way to prevent the replaced pieces from rotting again was to leave them unpainted. However, that would not match the rest of the painted red bridge. That option was out. I decided to use vinyl pieces instead of wood. Vinyl has become a popular replacement for wood exposed to the elements. It comes in various shapes and types of molding and plain boards. And there is paint that will adhere to it. I cannot have a white Chinese bridge; it has to be red.

As is usually the case, once I removed the rotted pieces, I discovered that the rot was more extensive than I first realized. I may replace the entire side (five posts and two rails). But how long will it be before the other side rots? I may as well replace both sides. But then again, it is only a matter of time before the supporting pieces and planks rot, and I will have to replace them. You see where this is going: replace the entire bridge. While at it, I decided to change the bridge's design. The original one was too steep. Although it was merely a miniature replica of an actual bridge, walking over a real one with the same design would have been impossible. It's funny that for all of the people who saw it, no one ever made that criticism. My new design will use a more realistic elongated arc. My second revision will be in cutting the rails. On the first bridge, I could not make the rails with one piece of wood because no pieces of cedar were available wide enough to accommodate the sharp arc. I had to make the rails in pieces and splice them at the posts. My revised design will allow me to make the rails in one piece.

Before I get into the construction, here are a few thoughts on carpentry that crept into my mind during the project. As I mentioned in a previous story, my father was a coal miner, but he did carpentry on the side, and until I left home, I was always at his side, watching or helping. I guess working with wood is in my blood. I like the smell of wood and sawdust as I cut it or drill a hole in the wood. However, I missed that since I was working on this project with vinyl, not wood.

Speaking of carpentry, I have, over the years, dabbled in minor plumbing and electrical DIY tasks. But I was never comfortable with them. During this project, I came up with a comparison between the three primary trades: plumbing, electrical, and carpentry. With plumbing, there is a major frustration factor of being unable to stop a leak. The frustration with electrical is being unable to determine the cause of a circuit breaker flipping off. There are no such frustrations with carpentry. You have more control over things. It's strictly up to you to correctly measure and cut or drill the piece of wood. No big mysteries are involved. If it's not right, it's strictly your fault; do it again until you get it right. However, you must deal with additional effort, time, and costs. There is an adage in carpentry, "Measure twice, cut once!" Do you get my point?

Another of my thoughts on carpentry concerns various skill levels. If I were an instructor in a woodworking class, my first assignment would be to build a twelve-inch by twelve-inch by twelve-inch wooden box. It seems very simple: what can go wrong? Any one of the six pieces may not be correctly measured, cut, or fastened together. Try building such a simple, perfect box and see how "Simple" it could be.

Let's kick it up a notch. Now, make a pyramid with a twelve-inch base and twelve inches high, with no wood edges showing. So, we went from simple straight edges to angles, which were somewhat more complicated regarding measurements and cutting skills.

A third skill level is going from straight cuts to curves. This project is a round game table. Years ago, my brother-in-law, Andy, gave me an old wooden barrel. I did not know what to do with it, so I made a game table. When our boys were younger, Friday night was game night, and our favorites were "Careers" and "Life." I cut the barrel to the proper table height and made a circular top with a four-foot diameter piece of plywood. I quickly learned that drawing a perfect circle is relatively easy but impossible to cut it perfectly without some guide. So, I used a two-foot narrow board attached to the center of the piece for the tabletop. I attached it so it would rotate. At the end of that board, I held a router and rotated the router around the circle to cut the tabletop. We created a lot of good memories around my created circular project.

Moving on to the next level involves arcs, which are more difficult because they are only a part of a circle. A circle has a consistent shape. An arc has inconsistency in it. I discovered that in making the bridge. The first step in constructing the bridge was to draw the arc for the two supports. I wanted it to be about thirty-two inches long and six inches high. It was easy to draw it roughly, but to make it symmetrical was a problem. In the back of my mind, I knew there was a mathematical way to draw a perfect arc, but I still needed to get to that chapter in my algebra/geometry/trigonometry lessons (another story). I tried some techniques but could not develop a good one, so I researched and discovered numerous ways to draw an arc. I found a straightforward method on YouTube. Put two nails in a board thirty inches apart. Then, take a piece of something flexible like a metal yardstick or molding. Place it on one side of the nails, then with the other hand, push the middle up to the desired height of the arc and draw the curve along the edge of the yardstick. Perfect arc! Now I have the pattern for the supports and the rails. Not so! When I laid out the supporting piece and the two rails, the proper distance above them and between all three could have been more consistent. I was puzzled. What changed? I realized the rails would all have a different arc because the radius (distance from the circle's center) would differ. To maintain an equal distance between all three pieces, I used a scribe set at two and a half inches and followed the curve of the support for the first rail and the curve of the first rail for the second rail. You see how the measurement process at this level has intensified. I'll get to the cutting phase a little later. I still have one more skill level to discuss.

We went from straight edges to angles, to circles, to arcs. What's left? How about a combination of angles and curves? A few years ago, I was in a lumber yard picking up some lumber. On the shop floor, I saw these guys building a spiral staircase. I couldn't help but admire the skills required to create such a complex woodworking piece. That has to be the epitome of master craftsmanship. You have to have dabbled in woodworking to appreciate it.

Okay, back to the actual construction of my new replacement bridge. I purchased the vinyl pieces I needed and cut out the two supporting pieces. I had to make each support in two pieces because the available boards were not wide enough to cover the thirty-two-inch length and the six-inch width. So, I had four pieces and spliced them together at the center post. I cut them out on the jigsaw without a guide. The curves turned out relatively smooth. Only the lower curve would be visible because the upper curve would be concealed with the planks. Moving along, I used vinyl lattice strips eight inches long for the planks and brass (won't rust) screws to hold everything together. At this point, I noticed that one of the four edges of the supports was about a half inch in the air, but I thought that after I attached the posts and rails, their weight would force them down evenly with the other three. The next step was to cut the posts, five for each side, space them, and screw them into the supports. The final pieces were the rails. I cut the lower rail but had trouble making a perfectly smooth cut by hand, even after meticulously sanding it. Oh well, good enough! (Perfect is the Enemy of Good). I mounted the rail to the five supports using notches in the post to accommodate the rail. I then jumped over to the other side of the bridge to attach the lower rail. Problem! The posts were not lining up with the posts on the other side. What's wrong? I discovered that one of the four pieces used for the supports did not match the other three, and therefore, the arc on one side of the bridge did not mirror the other. I had to remove all of the twenty screws on one side, then make a new fourth support piece that matched the other three and reassemble everything back to where I was. It turned out the bridge was not setting on all four corner posts.

I was still not satisfied with the shape of the first rail. I wondered if I could find a piece of vinyl to bend into an arc and use it for the rails rather than cutting one out. Off to Lowes and Home Depot. I found a piece of vinyl a little over one-half inch square and eight feet long. It would be narrower than my original design, but I could live with that. I bent the piece in the store at about the thirty-two-inch point and could get a six-inch arc out of it without snapping it. I rushed home and couldn't wait to try it. It worked. The rail problem is solved.

The finished bridge looks good white, but as I said above, it had to be red. I knew this right along. The vinyl pieces had a glossy finish, so as I made each piece, I sanded it to help the paint adhere to it.

There you have it. When I was done, I examined the finished product from all angles to see if it looked right. It did. I took some measurements here and there to confirm my eyeball inspection. There are a lot of possible measurements and room for error. I was not off by more than one-eighth of an inch in some places, which was unnoticeable to a glance with the naked eye. Back to the title of this story, "Perfect is the Enemy of Good." Good (enough) wins!!!

JACK BUILDING THE BRIDGE

63. WE GOT MAIL

1956 - 1958

Based on the above dates, this story and the next three may appear out of sequence. However, you will understand by the end of this story.

As I was on the train taking me from my home in Exeter, Pennsylvania, to Lackland Air Force Base in San Antonio, Texas for basic training, I wrote my first letter to my high school sweetheart, Verna. It was a three-day trip, and as I wrote letters to her, I mailed them from various railway stops. This was the beginning of what became, for the most part, a daily ritual for Verna and me. With very few exceptions, we wrote to each other daily. I used a flashlight after "Lights Out" in the barracks on more than one occasion, finishing my daily letter. In basic training, we did not get our mail directly from the post office. Once a day, our drill sergeant picked up all the mail for us and then conducted a "Mail Call." We gathered around him, and he shouted our name if we had a letter. If we had one, he tossed it to us or handed it down from one guy to another. You were disappointed if you did not get a letter. Getting a letter from Verna was the highlight of my day and made everything about basic training bearable. My second highlight was writing her a letter, and the third was mealtime.

At the beginning of our letter-writing campaign, we used airmail stamps costing six cents each. Regular mail was three cents. After a while, Verna suggested we experiment with regular mail to see the time difference. We discovered that it was just as fast as airmail, so there were savings of three cents on a letter. Sixty-eight years later, we still find ourselves watching the pennies! One peculiarity about daily writing is that it wasn't a simple question-answer procedure. There were questions, comments, answers, and comments on previous comments in various stages of transition.

During my first months in the Air Force, I bought high-quality boxed stationery embossed with the Air Force Base logo and wrote on only one side of the sheets, as we learned in high school business classes. I did away with the fancy, expensive stationery at Verna's suggestion. She also said we should start using both sides of the paper.

Neither of us wrote very mushy love letters; we were and still are (to a fault) too practical. We tended to explain and describe what we did that day and other mundane tidbits of information. A typical example of this was one letter Verna wrote describing her day. She went to work in a pants factory where she sewed the back pockets on Gary Player golf wear. She was swift and paid for piecework. Then she came home, painted the stairs in her parents' house, and made a chocolate cake for her family to top off the day. In a lot of my letters, I told her what I had to eat that day and the various work and daily experiences. Eventually, we started getting ahead of ourselves in our relationship and began using the phrase, "When we get married . . . ." and so on.

I saved all of Verna's letters and kept them in my locker. Whenever I opened it and other guys saw the stacks of letters, they asked if I was running a post office. I kept them in sequence and tied them up in little bundles. Verna did the same thing.

We got married twenty-three months after I joined the Air Force. What became of those letters? Well, that's a story within a story. When I left barracks life to get married, I took my collection of letters to Verna's parents' house and stored them in their attic with her letters from me. That was in 1958. They stayed in that attic for fifteen years until 1973, when we were stationed in New Jersey and had our first house. We transferred the letters from Verna's parents' attic to ours. Thirty-one years later, we purchased a home in The Villages, Florida, and felt it was a good time to go through everything in our attic and decide what to weed out. We both agreed to get rid of the letters but read them first. So we started from the beginning every morning, before we got into the day, still in our pajamas with the coffee flowing. One of us read a letter we wrote aloud, and the other read their letter using the postmark dates to keep them in order and try to make sense of the dialog. Sometimes, this lasted three to four hours (we were both retired). We got addicted to them, and the process became somewhat of an adventure. At times, it felt as if we were reading about somebody else's life and did not know how it all turned out between these two. We found ourselves laughing at this absurdity.

As we opened each envelope, we threw the envelopes into a separate pile for trash. After reading a letter, we threw the pages of our respective letters into two piles, his and hers. I wish I had a picture of that scene. When we finally finished weeks later, we gathered the scrambled and separated pages and put the whole pile in a cardboard box.

After reliving those two years of our documented courtship, we realized that we did not run across a letter where I asked Verna to marry me. However, numerous times at the end, we discussed our wedding plans. Over the years, as I looked back upon our love-letter relationship, it appears that our decision to marry each other was, as they say, "a foregone conclusion." It was a given. I went home on leave the Christmas before our June wedding. I bought Verna an engagement ring; the most I could afford was $250. It has been upgraded a few times since then. I purchased the ring as her Christmas present. I am ashamed to say I was so naive that I don't remember asking Verna's father for her hand, as you should. It is one of my greatest regrets. I also regret that I did nothing romantic but merely gave Verna a ring wrapped in a box, as I would any mundane Christmas present. I did not get on my knee and never even popped the question. There is this saying, "If you may not be able to live with the answer, don't even ask the question." But I wasn't aware of that warning then, so that is not my excuse. However, after being married to Verna for sixty-six years, I have realized that I would not have been able to live if she said no. I referred to the above scenario to a group of about seventy friends when we celebrated our fiftieth wedding anniversary. So, in front of all of those people, I somewhat proposed after the fact, but Verna said I was still not off the hook. I am sorry that I blew the whole proposal scene and deprived Verna of a more romantic memory.

Back to the letters, we planned to trash them in New Jersey after reading them, but we could not bring ourselves to do so then. So we brought the jumbled box of letters to Florida in our car because we did not want them to get lost in the move. They had been in our closet there for fifteen years, and we decided to get rid of them. We offered them to our boys, but they felt the letters were too personal to read. Plus, they were in such disarray that sorting and arranging them into any usable form would be nearly impossible. So what did we do? These are the options we considered.

- Leave them where they are and let our kids deal with them. Not fair.
- Put them back together and make a book out of them. Impossible and highly impractical.
- Burn them. Where? How? There would be nothing left of us.
- Put them out with the trash. I don't like the image of us being in a landfill.
- Recycled paper. We live on, who knows where or in what form, but we are together. So, we **"STILL"** GOT MAIL!!!

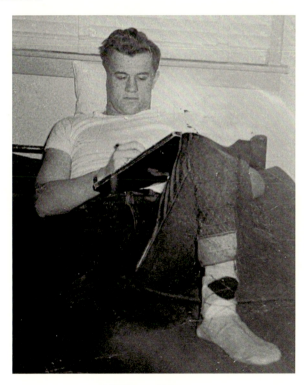

"DEAREST VERNA,"....

64. SOUL MATES

1956 - ???

At the end of the previous story, "We Got Mail," I listed the options we considered for disposing of the letters Verna and I had written during our courtship. However, I never stated which one we selected. As a matter of routine, when I finish writing a story, I email it to our sons, grandchildren, Verna's brother and his wife, one nephew, and one niece for comments, suggestions, and questions. As I mentioned, when our sons and grandchildren received that story, nobody wanted us to save the letters for them. Our oldest grandson, Thomas, suggested another option: shred one of mine and one of Verna's and have them encapsulated in a clear acrylic paperweight figurine or Christmas tree ornament; it's not a bad idea. David also offered another idea, which was to plant a tree in our yard and bury them in the soil of that tree, another possibility.

We went with David's suggestion with a slight variation. I was in the process of redoing the landscaping around our house. Two pyramid-shaped holly trees about five feet high are on each corner of our lanai. I was planning on refreshing a bed of stones under them, so I pulled them away from underneath the trees to replace the weed barrier, and then I would wash and replace the rocks. I suggested to Verna that we put some of our combined letters on the soil under the weed barrier, where they would eventually decompose and integrate into the soil. She agreed.

While spreading them lovingly on the soil, I felt somewhat sad and said to myself, at least save one of each of our letters for posterity. One of my letters caught my eye as they lay before me because it had a colorful Lackland Air Force Base logo on the first page. I picked it up. Then, I randomly picked up one from Verna. When I took them into the house to show Verna, we could not resist the temptation to read them to each other. My letter from Lackland started, "Dearest Verna, Well, I made it . . . . ." It was a letter explaining my bivouac experience when I went through basic training, lived in a tent in the Texas desert for a few days, went through the obstacle course, and so on. In my twenty-plus years in the Air Force, those few days were the only ones I felt like I was in the military. It contains many details and provides a first-hand tidbit of personal military history. I typed that letter verbatim and did the same with one of Verna's letters to me (following stories). Incidentally, I forgot in my last story that although Verna and I wrote to each other for the year I was alone in Iceland, we did not save any of those letters. By then, we had been married for three years and were an old couple whose romance had faded (just kidding about that last comment). However, when our first child, David, was born and I was in Iceland, I wrote Verna a very emotional twelve-page thank-you letter that we saved, but that letter was destroyed in a fire.

Back to this story. After reading the salvaged letters, we both started to have second thoughts about what we were in the process of doing. It's not too late to run outside, scoop them up, put them back in the box, and let them live another day. But we overcame the temptation. I went outside to resume the burial. I also picked up one envelope with a three-cent stamp and one with an airmail stamp. Does anyone remember the practice of putting the stamps upside down on the envelope? The meaning is "I love you."

As the letters lay there waiting to be covered with the weed barrier fabric, the wind kicked up, and a few pages started to blow away to escape their fate. Oh No! I envisioned our love life flying down the sixth fairway of Palmer's golf course directly adjacent to our house. What to do? I quickly grabbed the nearby garden hose and wet them to prevent their escape. As I did that, the hose water dissolved the ink (we did not use ballpoint pens), and the words vanished from the pages, and we were goners! Oh No! But then, an inspiration struck me. Our words, with all of our thoughts and love for each other, only changed form. They were now co-mingled and became chemically integrated into the soil. Over time, the ingredients of that soil would be absorbed into the roots of the trees, then the trunk, then the branches, then the leaves, and finally, the bright red holly berries. Our love for each other lives on!

As I contemplated this story, my imagination started to run away with me. The two holly trees, in all of their magnificence, represent each of our sons, one for David and one for Kevin. Over future years, some of their berries will be consumed by a bird, digested, and eventually excreted into some little niche of Mother Earth, who knows where and become a subsequent generation of our holly trees, and so on, and so on. So the words on the letters represent our souls, and as they were combined in the soil (mated), the trees live on through future ages, just like Verna and I will through our children, their children, their children, and so on (take a second look at the title of this story). Have I gone too far? But this is only a story. Or is it more than that?

Incidentally, a few years later, we were in upstate New York. One day, Verna and I were walking near a wooded area, and we noticed a small holly tree about three feet tall vibrating as we walked by it! Just kidding!

65. HI HON (MAY 16, 1958, FRIDAY)

Here is a letter from Verna that I pulled out of the pile. It is verbatim as she wrote it.

Hi Hon,

Well, here I am. I didn't wash clothes today. I didn't have time. I cleaned out the rest of the cupboards and straightened out the kitchen. I made supper. I made baked macaroni, fried fish, and shrimp and bought a crab. It was terrible. It was a giant one. I didn't care for it. It was from the Food Fair. That is the last time I'll buy those from there. They all said it was good. I tried out the cookbook Mrs. Krasinsky gave me for the baked macaroni. It's a good cookbook.

Aunt Bertha was over today. She still feels bad about it. Her eyes are all red from crying. Hon, we will give her that lighter even though she isn't standing for us. Is that okay with you? I think it will be. We'll give it to her before the wedding. I guess we'll go down and tell your Uncle George on Sunday. It's better to talk to him in person than on the telephone.

I will write all the names and addresses on a tablet if I have time tomorrow. My mother has all of them, but I want a space to put what they gave us.

I received your letter today and was very glad to hear from you. If I didn't get any mail from you like I do, I think I'd be more miserable than I am now. Letters keep us together. If we didn't write often, we probably wouldn't be planning on getting married and wouldn't be serious about each other.

I better answer yesterday's letter first. I thought today was Saturday, but it seems that way because I am not working today. I was going to save one letter for Sunday.

I'm going to put the clipping from the Echo in it. They made a mistake. Instead of bridal, they have Friday. They couldn't put all the names in and left a lot out. You could save it for me. You can also save the pictures until you come home.

Bobby should have written you a few lines saying he wants to be your best man. It's funny he didn't. He could find time. He hangs out at the gas station and has time for that. Even if it's just a postal card, it's better than nothing at all.

It's hard for a guy to be away from his girl or wife, but if he really and truly loves her, he'll stick it out, no matter what. I know there's a lot of temptation. So does the girl. It's not easy for either one of them. When a guy cheats on a girl, he'll always do it even after they're married. There's a lot of guys like that. I could see it. There are a lot of cases that come to our place. I can't stand people who cheat on each other. They shouldn't get married if they aren't settled down yet. I know you aren't like that. I hope you always stay just the way you are. I don't want you to change in any way.

Aunt Bertha wouldn't drown you. She wouldn't dare. She's a lot of fun. No matter where she goes, they all like her. I can't see why your mother doesn't like her. She gets along with everybody. She's the life of the party.

I know you love your mother. It would be best if you didn't hate her. After all, she's still your mother no matter what she does. My mother always used to tell me that.

Yes, I'd have to go to school to become a beautician. If I stay here until September, I could work during the day and go to school at night. The money I'd make at the factory would pay my way there. I think it would be a good idea. Sewing is hard on the nerves. I don't think being a beautician is very hard on the nerves. Even if it is, I'd get more money.

Your father was over with Mr. O'Malley today. I was watching the bar. I also played 500 rummy with Pepo because there wasn't anybody in there until we started playing. My father went to bed, and nobody could watch the bar, so I had to. My father gets me mad.

He's supposed to be sick, so he comes downstairs when he can be in bed. Then he said he could die, and we wouldn't care. He never asks my mother how she feels. He doesn't care. He tells everybody that she puts on an act. I know you could never act like that. My mother isn't like that. She acts as if there's nothing wrong with her. This is about the fourth time I heard my mother cry because she couldn't stand the pain. Jerry Lewis was just on. He's good. I wish he were on every week.

What a dream I had last night. I dreamt that we got our invitations ordered, and we had to get married a week before we even got the invitations. So we got married in a Russian church. I was late for the ceremony. I was crying because my hair wasn't fixed right, and my father couldn't give me away, so my Uncle Steve would give me away. So when we got to church, your mother yelled to the priest that he was Protestant. So he wasn't even going to marry us. We were both crying and pleading with the priest. He married us in the back of the church. I was mad, and I started hollering at your mother, and she started laughing. What a dream that was. After we married, you went home or someplace, and I went home. That was the end of it.

My Aunt didn't tell my Uncle why she couldn't stand for me. She told him she would tell me she couldn't afford it. He started to holler at her. He said he would come over and tell me that she could. I don't know what he said when she told him she lied. I have to find out.

It was a nice day today for a change. Tomorrow, we have to wash our clothes. It will be hard because either my mother or I will have to tend the bar, too. We'll find a way.

Well, Hon, I'd better start closing. It's getting late. I wish you were home now. I wouldn't say it's getting late, would I? I miss you so much, Hon. It's awful how we have to be apart, and I'd better close. Goodnight, Hon. I love you, X. I love you, X. I love you, X.

Love Always,

    Verna

    XXXXXXX

P.S. I love and miss you very much.

66. DEAREST VERNA (AUGUST 8, 1956, WEDNESDAY)

And this is one of my letters to Verna that I randomly pulled out of the pile. It is verbatim.

Dearest Verna,

Well, I made it, and here I am back in the barracks, still in pretty good shape except for a few scratches, aches, and sore feet. That's what everybody has right now. We got back about 2 o'clock this afternoon.

Maybe you won't want to know, but I'll tell you what it was like anyway. We arrived early Monday morning after carrying our 50 lb. pack and nine lb. helmet. We went on the firing range for 2 hours. There we had "Dry Fire," by dry fire, I mean, there was no ammunition; we were practicing. After that, we had a couple of classes until dinner. After that, we got our "weapon," our carbine, in other words, but we had to call it a weapon. Then we put our tents up. I shared a tent with a colored guy who slept in the barracks beside me. He sure is a nice guy. He's from Massachusetts. He's one of the few guys around here who writes only to one girl. After putting our tents up, we laid around and went to supper. After supper, we got ready for our "night march." Boy, was that rough. We started at about 7 o'clock and marched with our packs and weapon for about an hour or more. Then we came to this building, which we thought was burning, but we found out we had to run through it. After that, we started to come back and finally went to sleep at about 10:30. Tuesday morning, we got up at 3:15 for revelry. Oh! I forgot to tell you I got two of your letters Monday before we left for our march, so I was sitting in a field with dust all over the place reading your letters. Boy, that sure made me feel good. Well, to return to Tuesday, at 6 a.m., we had to go through the obstacle course. To start it off, we had to lie on the side of a road with our heads down for about 15 minutes. Boy, it seemed like an hour. Then somebody yelled, "Let's go." Then we took off running across a field, dodging and hitting the dirt, getting up and running again. Then we came to a pond. We had to swing across it on a rope. Some of the other things we did were jumping from one foxhole to another, crawling under barbed wire on our backs, that's where I got scratched, crawling down a cliff with a rope, climbing up a cliff with a rope, climbing over a wooden wall, jumping off a wall, going through a house full of smoke, and then came the roughest part, crawling through a minefield under barbed wire, and every-time any part of you touched the wire a mine went off next to you in your ear. A couple of guys passed out here and just laid there. Afterward, we crawled down gullies on a cliff and crossed a small river on two cables. A couple of guys fell in there. That was the end. Boy, you should have seen us after that. We were muddy, dusty, sweaty, and all bruised up. We could just about walk. Then we went to dinner. After dinner, we had to go through the gas chamber. First, we went in with gas masks, and then we had to take them off. Boy, does that tear gas burn your eyes. We were in there for about 5 or 7 minutes without the masks. If we had ever touched our eyes, we would have burned them out. After that, we had the rest of the day to ourselves from about 4 o'clock on. I forgot to tell you, in the morning after we finished the obstacle course, we had some more "dry fire" until dinner time. This morning, we got up at three again. I also got a letter from you last night. I read it while I was lying in the tent. About 6 o'clock this morning, we left for the firing range. This time, we used ammunition. We fired 100 shots; half were for practicing, and the other half were for our record. It sure was a lot of fun. Out of a possible 200 points, we had to score 129 to qualify. Out of our flight, 76.1% qualified. We came in second among five flights; the top flight had 77.2% who qualified. About 11 o'clock, we started the long march home. It's about 6 or 7 miles back and forth, up and down hills. After dinner, we handed in our stuff and left for the barracks. Boy, did it feel good to be back and go to the chow hall to eat and not be in the field.

I still don't know how I made it. I felt good Monday all day. When we were on the night march, it rained slowly for about half an hour, but it didn't even wet the ground. Now and then, when we were marching, we would see some guys lying on the side. Then, the ambulance would come and pick them up.

When I got up Tuesday, boy, I couldn't even stand. I thought I wouldn't even be able to walk. My feet felt a little better after I took a few steps, but they still hurt. I never thought I'd make it through that obstacle course. Even before we started, the instructor asked us if we wanted to drop out and not run it. I was going to tell him, but I didn't. You know me, I'm nuts. But once I ran, I felt OK; they didn't bother me. The only time they bothered me was when I would do some extra marching, and then when I would get up in the morning or after sitting for a while, they would hurt until I walked for about 5 or 10 minutes. Don't tell my mother about this; my feet hurt like that last week. Make sure you don't tell her. It was something like a miracle that I made it through Bivwack. I guess the hardest part of Basic Training is over. It feels good to go around scaring all these guys like they did to us. They were telling us about rattlesnakes and scorpions, but they weren't fooling because there are rattlesnakes and scorpions out there. Our instructor even showed us how to kill them with our shovel or weapon, and they told us when we go to bed to keep both of them by our side and when we get up to bang our shoes and make sure there are no scorpions in them.

Our "TI" told us you'll find out where we will go on Tuesday or Thursday when we ship out. If I get that radar school, I'll most likely go to Keesler Air Force Base, Mississippi; that's where Alex and Eddie were. I'll let you know when I write on Tuesday.

I received your letter today, so I have four to answer. I read the letter, and you're right; it was calls, not cries. If you still have one of those pictures of you in the gown, you could send it without getting it made into a wallet size. You know which one I want, and I hope you send it.

Someone told me that Jeanie got a "Dear John" letter from Eddie, but I didn't pay any attention to them. Maybe it was true. That sure is a nice poem; I read it about ten times.

You're right about the bets; Angie was always like that. You're right she does have a lot of nerve. She isn't exactly a good girl for my brother. I wonder if they'll ever get together. Thanks for sending the clippings from the paper.

That's not true about Carl, but he's still the same guy. Do you mean that you cried all day Monday? I'll never forget when you started that Sunday at the Drive-In. I thought you would start from then on, but it's a good thing you stopped because I didn't want to leave you crying. Yes, George still goes with Jema. She came to the station with his mother and father the night we left. I was sorry to hear about that guy in the hospital. It sure gives you a funny feeling. I don't know whether or not I gained any weight. I only know that when I first came here, I weighed 135 pounds. Last week, I weighed 147 pounds with my clothes on. About the discharge, I hope you win.

You're right about 13 being my lucky number. I think 3-4 children would make a nice family. No, I didn't get sick from the needles.

You told me to tell you if I ever find someone else, well I know I won't have to tell you, so don't worry about it. Remember what you said about "Love is Trust and Trust is Love," so keep thinking about it like I am, and everything will be okay. I trust you because I love you, so I'm not worried about you going out. I always hear you saying, "No, I have a boyfriend." Don't worry. I'll be home; everything will be the best we can do when I get home. OKAY? I think I told you everything I had to, so I guess I'll close and maybe write my mother a letter before I go to sleep.

With All My Love,
Jackie XXXXXX
XXXXX
P.S. Remember, don't tell my mother.

67. MY BETTER HALF

This collection of stories is about me, but many of them include my wife, Verna. Nevertheless, Verna has her own collection of stories and many things about her need to be documented. She has told her stories numerous times. As our nephew, Michael, nudged me to write my stories, he told his Aunt Verna that she should write hers or record them verbally. That's not going to happen. Verna is not a writer like me; she is a good talker, but at the moment, she has a lot on her plate with pain and health issues. So, I have taken it upon myself to write this story. As I have done with all of my stories, she will have been the first to see this one, proofread it for errors, and make suggestions for additions, deletions, or changes in content. Therefore, she will have "signed off" on this one, which is "Her Story." I will divide this story into **GENEALOGY, VERNA'S STORIES, AND VERNA'S STORY.**

GENEALOGY

Unfortunately, there is not much for me to work with regarding this subject. We have photos but no clues to tell who they are. We also have a collection of various certificates. The certificates are certificates of some event taking place at some time in the past, a certificate of a certificate, not an actual birth or marriage certificate. I was able to piece together some bits of information from them to at least create the following skeleton of Verna's ancestry.

According to one certificate, Veronica Bartnick (Verna's maternal grandmother) was born in 1883 in Russia. However, another certificate indicates that she was born in Lithuania in 1894. Lithuania was part of Russia until 1922 but was once a significant East European power and a much larger country.

At age twenty-four or thirteen, we believe that the correct birth date is 1894 because Verna remembers Baba (the Slavic name for grandmother) telling her that she was only thirteen when she married). In 1907, Veronica Bartnick married Dominick Wisnowski(Wisnoski), born in Russia in 1882. He was twenty-five years old when they got married. He resided in Edwardsville, Pennsylvania. He was a laborer, a term given to a person working in the coal mines, but he did not have the skill level of a miner; he was more of a helper to a miner. At that time, Veronica lived in Stermerville, Pennsylvania. Dominick died in July 1933 after having been married for twenty-six years.

One and a half years later, on November 28, 1934, Veronica married William Shonk, who was thirty-seven years old and born in Luzerne, Pennsylvania. Veronica would have been forty years old. Both lived in Exeter, Pennsylvania, at the time of the marriage. William was a fireman on the railroad. He served in the Navy from 1918 until 1921 and was honorably discharged. He died in 1943. Baba died in 1961.

Our oldest son, David, was born twenty-four days later. Had she lived a little longer or he been born a little earlier, there would have been four generations in the Shonk, Klapal, and Kolman families.

Verna's father, Andrew Klapal (Clapald), was born in Shoemaker, Pennsylvania, on November 30, 1894. His father's name was Anthony, and his mother's was Frances (maiden name Hanushka). Anthony was a miner, and they lived in Kingston Township, Pennsylvania. Verna's father died in 1972 at age seventy-eight as a result of a blood clot after gallbladder surgery. We were stationed in Germany at the time, and this was a shock to us. Verna had a great admiration for her father. At age nine, he had to go to work in the coal mines to help support his many siblings. His mother died when he was young.

Verna's mother, Martha Wisnouskas (these are not my misspellings; they are the various ways the name was listed on the certificates), was born in 1915. She married Andrew in 1937 and died from cancer in 1978 at age sixty-three. Like her father, Verna had a lot of love and respect for her. After being separated from her family for eighteen years while I was in the Air Force, she relished her mother's Sunday visits to our home in New Jersey when Verna did her hair and treated her to a great breakfast and grand dinner. Unfortunately, that lasted only five years.

Although not genealogy, this is an excellent place to document one of Verna's brother's life. Andrew Jr. was born in 1941. The family called him "Sonny." He was a big guy with a big heart. The most generous and kind person I have ever met. I have mentioned him in some previous stories. He played on the Exeter High School football team the same year as I did. I was in the eleventh grade, and he was in the eighth. At age sixteen, he was in a terrible car accident in which one boy was killed. He felt so guilty about it, and the town was so down on him because he was driving the car, that he never went back to school. We all know that he would have had a great football career.

After breast cancer, Sonny's physical condition began to deteriorate even further. He was in and out of health care and nursing facilities. In the later part of 2018, he found himself in a deplorable nursing home. Verna and I visited him for an extended period, and she pleaded with the staff to move him to more pleasant surroundings in that facility, but to no avail. One day, we took him out for a day to change scenery, drove him around the area, and then stopped at Wendy's for a treat he was craving. It was a Friday, and he wanted to watch some high school football on TV, so we took him to his home. We had to return him to the nursing home that night. We felt good that we had given him a day out.

Early in 2019, he was back in his own house. But he was rapidly getting worse, and hospice was brought on board. He said he wanted to die in his own home and not in a strange place. Verna and I flew up to "help" care for him and be with him until the end. It all turned out to be a nightmare. On the day of the flight, we had to get up at three AM for a flight to upstate New York, where our son David lived. He picked us up at the airport and drove us three hours to Sonny's. That evening, as we were both sitting on a sofa in Sonny's room, his daughter, Karen, walked in. We were surprised to see her because we had been estranged for some time. We quickly jumped up from the sofa and heard a loud snap coming from Verna's left shoulder. I thought she had dislocated her shoulder, so she started to rotate it. The pain was excruciating. It was approaching midnight. We had no car, so we called Sonny's other daughter, Andrea, to take us to the ER. It turns out that Verna had broken her clavicle. We finally got back to Sonny's about one AM. At this point, we had been on the road and awake for twenty-two hours. That entire incident marked the beginning of a very sad time in our lives that is still going on. It includes Sonny dying, Verna falling on a cruise, breaking a disk, Verna developing multiple myeloma, and living in constant excruciating pain that is still persistent.

Back to Sonny, the sleeping arrangements in his house were poor. To be close to Sonny during our vigil, Verna slept on a broken, worn recliner and me on a sofa. Whenever Sonny stirred, Verna jumped up to see what was wrong and tried to comfort him. After the ER, we saw an orthopedic the next day, who put her arm in a sling.

The hospice put Sonny on oxygen and prescribed morphine to be injected for severe pain. We thought a hospice nurse would be at the house 24/7, but that was not so. They popped in now and then, but only during the day. We were given instructions on maintaining the oxygen and administering the morphine.

During the first night we were "on duty," the shocking realization hit me that we were not trained or qualified to do this. We had gone there to "help," not to "do." When we woke the following day, I told Georgia, Sonny's wife, that she had to call someone ASAP and make arrangements for a professional caregiver to be on-site 24/7. That day, someone came to the house to discuss the matter. But it would be a matter of time before arrangements and a determination on out-of-pocket costs could be made. Without financial coverage, I would suggest we share the costs with Sonny's two daughters and his brother Raymond. If they refused, we were willing to pay for it ourselves. While waiting for professional help to start, things got worse. We explained to all family members that, once again, we were there to help, not do.

Nevertheless, the next day, everybody was available during the day, but as the day ended, everyone picked themselves up and went back to their own home. Here we were, Georgia and us for the night. I panicked, had it, and blew my top. Georgia and her daughters got the message, and arrangements were made to have one of them on duty full-time. At this point, Sonny's family stopped talking to us, and the atmosphere became strained. The next day, we called Verna's brother in New Jersey to ask him to please come and get us to stay at his house. He said he could not. We called our son David, and he drove three hours to pick us up and then three hours back to his house.

After a day or two, he drove us back to Sonny's, but we stayed in a motel this time. Our son, Kevin, flew from South Carolina during this ordeal. Shortly after he walked into the room, a spark of energy hit Sonny as he jumped out of bed and gingerly made it to the bathroom. Kevin had his moments with Sonny and was happy he had made the effort to be there. Sonny continued to fail, and we thought it was over on more than one occasion. David's son, Thomas, and daughter, Ellen, arrived on a Friday. Sonny was very fond of them and they of him. Verna sensed that he wanted to see and speak with them one last time. They both had their moments with him Friday night. They had to leave on Saturday and had come just in time. Sometime late on Saturday, Sonny went into a comma. It was touch and go again. We went back to our motel on Saturday night. On Sunday night, we decided to stay at the house. We felt the end was near. He survived the night. Sonny had been moved to a recliner that was set up in another room that previously had been the barroom. Monday evening, we were all chatting. As usual, I listened more than I talked. All of a sudden, I heard nothing. I mean that we could all hear Sonny's heavy breathing (as usual) coming from the other room, but now I did not hear it. I suddenly told everyone to be quiet and gave a "Time Out" signal as I pointed to Sonny's room and announced that he stopped breathing. We all (Verna in her sling) jumped up and dashed into the old barroom. It was over! I noted that Sonny's recliner was exactly where the cash register would have been. How appropriate! Goodbye, Dear Brother!

Over the years, he developed such a good reputation and became so loved by the community that over four hundred people attended his memorial service. Many were adults who had been on the Little League Team he sponsored. Sonny is a strong part of Verna's story as well as mine.

Before moving on to Verna's stories, let me explain the tavern scene alluded to above and set the stage for her stories and story. Unfortunately, we do not know how Baba became an entrepreneur owning a tavern in northeast Pennsylvania. Since her first husband died in 1933, and she married Bill Shonk shortly after that, and since prohibition ended in 1933, I will surmise there is a connection between all three events. Perhaps the first husband, Dominick, gave Baba a livelihood as a mine laborer. But now that he was gone, Baba needed to make a living alone, so she opened a tavern, and her second husband, Bill, was a customer. Or perhaps Baba and Bill met someplace, got married, and then opened the tavern together, but since Bill had a job on the railroad, he would be gone quite often, and Baba took care of the business on her own. That does not matter. During the thirties and forties, the mining industry in that area was booming. Stories told by Baba indicated that miners stopped in at five AM for their "shot and a beer" before heading underground. I can't blame them. For many, it was also their first stop on the way home. Plus, there were the weekend nights. To give you an idea of how successful Baba was, by 1953, she had accumulated $25,000 in cash to build a new home next to the tavern to house six people with two rooms dedicated to the tavern. Verna's father's earnings as a coal miner also contributed.

VERNA'S STORIES

These stories are short; they are more of a collection of memories, but collectively, they make a nice package that Verna cherishes. They are also in no particular sequence, but that is how Verna remembers them and tells them randomly.

- As a child in Lithuania (Russia), Baba remembered having to eat cooked potato peelings because things were so bad.

- As Baba's family migrated to America, they told her to throw away her old ratty dolls because she could get much nicer ones there. Not so.

- As a youngster in America, Baba was taken out of kindergarten to babysit someone with the last name Friday. In subsequent years, Miss Friday became the principal of Verna's mother's and her elementary school in Exeter. So Baba never learned to read or write.

- Verna remembers seeing Dominic sitting in a fur coat on the front porch in the middle of the summer. He suffered from a severe case of rheumatism.

- At one time, when Baba was giving birth at home, Dominic was in another room of the house, making out with another woman. The baby turned out to be stillborn.

- A family rented a part of the original barroom while living there. The father of that family tried to steal money that Baba was carrying in her bosom, as she had a habit of doing.

- When Baba was a toddler, they had a Charlie Brown Christmas tree decorated with popcorn balls because they could not afford regular ornaments.

- In addition to Verna's mother, Baba had a son named Tony. He was a couple of years older than his sister Martha. He had Parkinson's since he was nineteen years old. He married, and his family moved to Connecticut.

- Verna's mother married Andrew when she was twenty-two, and he was forty-three. They met in a tavern. Verna's father had just lost a finger in the mines, and his mother had just passed away. Verna's mother felt sorry for him. His sisters resented the marriage because he was supporting many siblings at the time.

- When Verna was living in Swoyersville, one of her father's brothers, Uncle Steve, lived in the basement. Her father helped pay his way at a seminary to become a priest, but he dropped out before finishing. Her father bought him a car and loaned him a lot of machinery that he never returned.

- Verna's mother once had to go to the hospital for something. Baba had diabetes and had to get a daily injection of insulin. Verna had to give Baba the needle while her mother was in the hospital. Verna's mother had her practice inserting the needle into an orange. When her mother returned from the hospital, Verna kept on giving Baba her needle because she liked the way she gave it more than Verna's mother did.

- When the family moved from Swoyersville to Exeter, Verna was in the second grade. She had to go to school alone on her first day at her new school. Why by herself?

- Baba's children were not allowed to talk at the dinner table. If they did, Dominic whacked them with a large wooden spoon. Once, he was getting ready to hit Baba with a large cast iron frying pan.

- Verna's fondest memory as a child was her father frolicking with her and Sonny on the floor of their house before they moved to live with Baba. Once they moved, those joyous moments came to an end. The new living environment was not a scene from *Ozzie and Harriet*. After working a shift in the mines, Verna's father had to tend the bar. It was not fair. Quality family time was a thing of the past.

- On numerous occasions, Verna's father told her how unhappy he became after they moved to Exeter. He even said that he wished he had never married. Verna responded by telling him that he would never have had her as a daughter. He was sorry he said what he did and never repeated that statement.

- One of Verna's favorite stories is about Baba and her mother, who were in the business of making and selling moonshine during prohibition. On one occasion, they were making a delivery, carrying the booze in a satchel and hitchhiking. They were picked up by the Pennsylvania State Police, who nonchalantly drove them and their stash to their "Customer" (Speakeasy).

- Verna's early years were spent in a town called Swoyersville, not too far from Exeter, Pennsylvania, where Baba was running the tavern. It came to Verna's mother's attention that some of Baba's customers were ripping her off. They ordered drinks and then "Markie Bookie." Baba allowed them to record the transaction themselves for what they had to pay on payday. Baba could not read or write. You see what was happening. That's when Verna's mother decided to have her family move into the tavern(large enough to accommodate them all) and end the illegal and unfair practice.

- The only free family day was Sunday when the tavern was not allowed to be open. One memorable way to spend it was the family piling into the 1947 green Chevrolet, packing a lunch, and driving through the countryside of northeast Pennsylvania to see if they "could get lost." They never did. Verna remembers how her father sped up the car going down a hill and told Verna, "Get ready to feel your belly tickle."

- Whenever they had bacon, Verna remembers how her father cut a slab into small pieces, stuck them on the tip of an iron poker, opened the coal-burning furnace door, and made the bacon nice and crispy. Then they chatted and munched.

- Baba had a son who lived in Connecticut. During the forties and early 1950s, Verna's family visited them for a day at the beach. One year, Verna wanted to go there for Trick or Treat because the kids got candy instead of cash as they did in Pennsylvania.

- Baba had friends or a distant cousin who lived in New York City. They happened to visit Baba in Pennsylvania, and the woman was distraught about losing her husband. Verna's mother "volunteered" Verna to go back with the woman for a few days to console her. Verna remembers how the woman cried the whole time, and she asked herself what she was doing there. It's not a good memory.

- While in her early teens, Verna and Baba would have a "Girls' Day Out." They dressed in their Sunday Best, jumped on the city bus to Wilkes-Barre, went to a movie, had lunch, and then went shopping. Baba bought Verna the nicest dresses. Upon returning home, Verna put on a fashion show and sashayed down the stairs and through the house—shades of *The Loretta Young Show*. Verna also prided herself on balancing a book on her head at the same time.

- Verna was a sickly child. She was taken to the hospital for an appendectomy. While lying on the hospital bed, she noticed a twelve-inch tapeworm that had crawled out of her. What a fright!

- Sometimes, when she was five or six years old, she had convulsions. The doctors could not figure out why. Maybe she was "possessed by the devil," was suggested by elderly neighborhood women! Arrangements were made to have her receive First Holy Communion before the traditional age of seven, "Satan Begone!"

- Verna had two girl playmates her approximate age. One was Anna, and the other was Ann. Verna's middle name is Ann. The other would be jealous whenever Verna visited or played with only Anna or Ann. Anna was born with a disease that affected her ability to walk. As they walked to school together, Anna hung on to Verna's arm, and Verna became annoyed. Later, when Anna was confined to a wheelchair, Verna felt guilty about being annoyed with her earlier. Anna became our first son's godmother. Ann was Verna's maid of honor.

- As a child, Verna had aches in her knees. As a remedy, she slept with an electric heating pad on them. Something went wrong once, and she got a burn on her shin, and she still has the scar.

- Verna also had boy playmates and was somewhat of a tomboy. One day, she was riding one of the boy's bikes and flipped over the handlebars—another scar on her body, this time under her chin.

- There was an abandoned chicken coop in the backyard. Next door lived a boy named Bernie, who was a couple of years older than Verna. He and Verna converted the hen house into a play house, curtains and all. His area was decorated much nicer than Verna's and made Verna jealous. When Bernie was seventeen, he joined the Navy. When he was home on leave one time, he told Verna that the Navy asked him if he liked boys or girls. She doesn't recall his answer. It turns out that Bernie was gay. He became a very successful owner of a florist shop. Going back to the chicken coup, she should have known!

- In addition to the chickens, there were also pigs in the backyard. Verna recalls a scene where Baba falls into the mud in the pig sty.

- When Verna was three-plus years old, her brother Sonny was born. When her mother brought him home from the hospital, Verna cried and said, "You did not bring home a baby; you brought home a boy!" Sonny weighed twelve pounds.

- Baba had a brother named Joseph Bartnick, who became blind in his later years. He was called Uncle Joe. He had a daughter named Bertha. Somewhere along the line, Uncle Joe's wife left him as she drove off with a fellow on a motorcycle. Uncle Joe ran off with another woman, and Baba helped raise his two sons, Thomas and Eddie, plus a daughter, Bertha, who became like a sister to Verna's mother. Verna referred to Bertha as Aunt Bertha, and it was her favorite aunt. There were times when Verna's mother resented the fact that Baba was raising all three of them because she had to share things with them, and at times, they received more attention from Baba than Verna's mother did. For example, Verna's mother told her she remembered having to wear boys' hightop shoes called clod hoppers because the family could not afford a pair of girl shoes for her. Baba went so far as to tell Verna to treat Aunt Bertha as her second mother.

- When she was sixteen, Aunt Bertha married a rich man from New York City. She visited Verna and the family and was always dressed to the nines. When Verna was young, she gave her jewelry and a charm bracelet, which she has kept all these years.

VERNA'S STORY

- Verna was named after Baba Veronica, but her name was changed to Verna while in high school. She was born on July 15, 1938, four months or 121 days before me. Whenever people ask us our age, Verna comments that since I am younger than her, she always tells me, "You go get it; you are younger." I did and still do. My comment to any questions about our age is, "She was an older woman who took advantage of me. What did I know?" Both of our comments always earn a chuckle from others.

- We both belong to The Silent Generation, and one characteristic of that generation is frugality. Verna fits the profile as neatly as I do, being frugal, thrifty, etc.

Hopefully, her stories outlined above give you the flavor of her early years. I will pick up from when she entered my high school life. My objective will be to fill in the gaps that describe her but have yet to come through in my previous stories.

- Like me, she was not popular in high school. She was not involved in any extracurricular activities. She was not a cheerleader nor a majorette. She did suffer a major disappointment in high school. She tried out to be a majorette. It came down to her and another girl. She was the better twirler; the other girl dropped her baton during the audition, but Verna never did. The other girl was chosen. Her father was on the School Board. Baba consoled her by telling her that her knees would hurt her too much when she would have to march in the cold weather.

- During high school, she went home for lunch. On her way back, she stopped at the church next to the school to say a few prayers.

- At one time (before we got married, thank God), she considered becoming a nun. Baba talked her out of that, saying it would be too hard on her knees with all that kneeling. Thank you, Baba.

- Also, like me, Verna was not studious. Her best subject was Home Economics, and she liked Biology. She hated Algebra, and she was not doing well at it. Her teacher told her that if she played a part in a school play that she was directing, she would give her a passing grade in Algebra. Verna took the deal. We still have the script from the play. It was called *Mother's Vacation*, and Verna played the part of Mrs. Thompson.

- She had learned to sew from Baba. As a teenager, she made shirts for Sonny because his large sizes were too expensive. For their first class in sewing, the Home Economics teacher told the girls to keep it simple. Verna brought in plaid material. That's my wife, the overachiever. The teacher wanted her to take a test for a scholarship in Home Economics Studies, but Verna did not like the idea of taking tests. In later years, Verna applied her seamstress skills to make clothes for herself and our boys, upholster, and make draperies for our home. She also had a job in a pants factory. The pay was for piecework, and Verna was the curve buster, always making more money than the other sewers.

- Verna is as happy in the kitchen as I am in the garage or the yard. While working in the New Jersey yard or The Villages, I could smell the aroma of something brewing from the stove vent. My mouth started to water.

- When Verna graduated high school, her parents asked her if she would like to go to college or get a new car. She said, "I don't have to go to college because I'll be getting married," and chose a '57 Chevy. In later years, she picked up a few college credits, completed a Lasalle University Correspondence course on Interior Decorating, and earned a Certificate in Medical Administration from a Business School.

- She is more into technology than I am. I am a pencil and paper person. If there is a problem with the computer, iPad, or iPhone, that's a challenge for her to fix, and she has the perseverance to do it. I have to call someone for the simplest things.

- Verna loves words, and I love numbers. She plays Scrabble and word games, and I solve math problems.

- She follows a movie on TV better than I do. I have trouble keeping track of who's who. She will also remember, sooner than I, that we already saw a movie.

- Family is a big thing for her. It was never for me until I became her family, and they became mine. She promised her mother on her deathbed that she would keep the family together, and she has. She is the matriarch of our family and plays the role well. It makes her sad to see a person alone and looking like they want someone to talk to. She gets concerned when our sons don't call each other for a long time and we don't hear from them or our grandchildren. Many times when we are out shopping, I may go down an aisle for something and then come back to find her chatting with someone. I ask where she knows them from. She responds, "No place, we just met." She could get a person's life history in a matter of minutes.

- Verna is a better golfer than me. That's because she is more consistent in her game.

- She is meticulous about her hair and appearance. She can't stand a hair out of place or a spot on her clothing. Whenever she comes home from the beauty shop, she heads right for her dressing table to look over the hairdo with maybe a little snip here and a little tuck there.

- Verna has had health issues all of her life. She handles pain like a trooper. There is never just one medical issue she is coping with. If I am not 100%, I am not well. Compared to Verna, I'm a wimp. I also feel guilty because I am helpless to make her feel better and that I cannot take on some of her aches and pains.

- She is most creative in the kitchen. She can make something out of nothing. Verna will start with the recipe, then halfway through it, close the book, and start tasting and improvising. Her meatloaf and soups always turn out differently (but always good each time), depending on what is available in the kitchen.

- Verna keeps me in line with my eating habits. I would be twenty pounds heavier.

- She says what she thinks. What you see is what you get. I think too much before I speak.

- Worrying is a vital part of her nature. She tends to worry about everything and everybody. If she is not worrying about something, she worries about what she misses. HaHa!

- Verna's heart is bigger than mine. She is more compassionate and giving.

- She's a hugger. A handshake or peck on the cheek doesn't hack it. COVID-19 cramped her style.

- One of my favorite scenes involves us sitting in our recliners, having a glass of wine, and enjoying a movie. If the film presents a nice moment, Verna will get a half-smile and half-grin on her face, which tells me she's happy for that split second or two. When I quickly and nonchalantly glance toward her and see it, I feel great that she is having that moment.

- There are two kinds of people. One has a glass of wine, and the other has milk and cookies. Sometimes, after the first glass or two of wine. Verna will say, "I'll have another." I will go for the milk and cookies. YMMM! Homemade, of course. To each their own.

CAREER WOMAN - After Verna's mother passed away, she became very distraught. Our oldest son, David, had just completed high school and would be off to college in two months. His younger brother, Kevin, was entering high school. Verna decided to go to Business School full-time and become a Medical Administrator. It was a two-year program.

Before she finished, she was offered a job in the Medical Records Department of a local hospital. She took the position and was able to complete her education at the same time. Her position at the hospital got her involved in processing medical records as they were requested by attorneys representing malpractice claims against the hospital. Once in a while, she came home with interesting stories.

After about a year or so, she became aware of a position available in our County Medical Facility as an administrative assistant to the County Physician. She enjoyed the nature of the work because it involved health issues and helping people. The physician and his staff left something to be desired, and on more than one occasion, Verna found herself "practicing medicine without a license." Once again, she came home with bizarre stories which cannot be told here. While there, a position became available as the Administrative Assistant to the County Administrator. Another woman who was a single mom struggling to make ends meet applied for the position. Verna was offered the job but turned it down so the other woman could get it.

After a few years, she had had enough and took a position in the County Youth Shelter. Her main tasks were processing Counselors' notes on troubled children under eighteen as their cases came up for legal/placement review. The counselors were all younger than Verna and had a bad habit of using foul language. After a short time, Verna broke them off that habit, and they developed a respect for her. Eventually, she became a "counselor to the counselors," again doing more than was expected and caring for others. One danger that presented itself was her tendency to get too personally concerned about the troubled youngsters. And again, some interesting "take-home stories."

The Shelter became privatized—the next stop, the Alcohol Recover Center/Women's Shelter, processing intakes. More stories, there's a good juicy book in the making if Verna was so inclined. I told her, "Don't go there." That facility also became privatized. By this time, Verna was developing a reputation as an "Albatross."

The final stop was the Human Services Department. The position included processing requests for assistance from "down and out" county residents seeking aid from the government. She did not care for the working environment or the too many bogus claims she observed. There were more bizarre stories around our dinner table. She could have retired at this point in her career, but she stuck it out for a few more years to retire with a great medical benefits package. That turned out to be worth thousands of dollars since then. Looking back on her career, the people she met daily constituted an element of society far removed from a more pleasant work environment.

That is it for describing my better half. But before I wrap it up, there is one more input to add. Since they were youngsters, our sons wrote us birthday, Mother's Day, and Father's Day cards instead of purchased cards. They all contain good words that we treasure. But one year, Kevin outdid himself and came up with words that hit home. First, he videoed us and read his card word for word. Verna and I broke down after that sincere and touching presentation. Then he mailed the card to us. I will plagiarize and copy them here because they need to be saved for posterity. They say so much about his mother that it adds to her story.

> *"Dear Mom,*
>
> *You, indeed, are a one and only. What makes you unique are your characteristics. I'll highlight a few: Adventurous to try almost anything and go in whole-heartedly like when we went through sports phases (fishing, tennis, and now golf). You are extremely diverse in taking on and excelling in all sorts of endeavors, such as cooking, baking, sewing, and other crafts. You have a strong sense of helping others, especially those who are less fortunate than most. You've been a go-getter in not being shy about stepping up when needed (serving in the Church, being a Cub Scouts den leader, tutoring me and other children in Germany).*
>
> *Sometimes, this shows up as you being one of the first on a dance floor to break the ice. You have also appreciated the finer things in this world, like food, wine, and decor. You are so resourceful in finding ways to give us more by making the dollar stretch and splurging on us and others as you've done throughout your life.*
>
> *Though other people may have some of these characteristics, this unique blend makes you truly a one-and-only. I truly love you for who you are.*
>
> *Happy Birthday Mom!*
>
> *I love you! Kevin!"*

It is difficult to describe what the past sixty-six years with Verna have meant to me. Hopefully, this collection of my stories will tell future generations who we were and what we were like. I always liked the concept of **SYNERGY**. Two plus two equals five. The sum is more than the total of the parts. A synonym is **TEAMWORK.** Verna's half and my half make more than a whole. We are both better than ourselves individually for having been a part of each other. God bless us both and those who follow us.

VERNA'S GRANDMOTHER
(BABA)

GROUND BREAKING FOR NEW HOUSE & BAR
724 TUNK. AVE.   1953-54

GROUND BREAKING FOR 724 TUNK. AVE.

Front row: Raymond (Verna's brother) - unknown

Middle row: Jenny (Verna's cousin) - Verna - unknown baroom customer - Butchy (Verna's cousin) - Andy "Sonny" (Verna's brother)

Top row: Verna's, Uncle Tony - contractor - Baba (Verna's grandmother) - Verna's mother - Verna's Aunt Mary (Uncle Tony's wife) - Verna's Aunt Bertha - Verna's Uncle Steve (Aunt Bertha's husband) - unknown baroom customer - Verna's father.

VERNA'S FIRST COMMUNION

VERNA (WORLD WAR II VETERAN) HAHA!

She lied about her age haha! Verna's grandmother (Baba) made the uniform out of Verna's Uncle Steve's uniform.

VERNA – 5TH OR 6TH GRADE

VERNA – 10TH OR 11TH GRADE

MEDICAL ADMINISTRATIVE ASSISTANT

VERNA'S "THREE" SONS

Left To Right: Nephew Michael (Verna's brother Raymond's son, Verna helped raise him and became very attached to him. She liked to refer to him as her son and loved this photo) - Kevin - David.

68. LOST AND FOUND

This story contains nothing personal about Verna or me. It is three stories that are just dying to be told and pleading to be saved.

When we returned from one of our cruises some years ago, Verna discovered she had lost a studded diamond earring. We filed an insurance claim and were reimbursed for the value. We took the remaining earring to a jeweler and added the diamond to a pendant necklace Verna had.

A few years later, we were packing our luggage to leave the ship on another cruise. I opened one of our black, huge suitcases on the bed. There it was, the lost earring lying in the middle of the black bottom of the suitcase, staring me in the eye as if to say, " Here I am, where have you been?"

Almost a year later, as Verna was going through her jewelry box, she found only one studded diamond earring. She exclaimed, "Oh my God, I'm missing an earring!" We searched all over the house before we went to bed. Then it hit me while I was still awake, and Verna had already fallen asleep. There is no other earring. We lost one on our last cruise, added the remaining one to your necklace, and then found the missing one. The "lost" earring is now on your necklace. So what do we do now with the found earring? We added it to the necklace. Now, both earrings are on the necklace. I hope you followed this strange sequence of events—end of story one.

Story two. Verna had just gone to work, and I was home. The phone rang, and it was Verna in a panic, stating that she was typing and noticed that the diamond in her ring was missing. She was working at the Alcohol Recovery Center at the time. All of the inmates and staff were searching for the diamond. One of the staff members whispered to Verna, "If one of those alcoholics finds it, do you think they'll tell you?" Verna said, "Yes." I hung up the phone and told Verna I would look around the house on the floor to see if I could find it. Within a minute, I spotted the diamond lying on the floor between the bedroom and the bathroom. I quickly picked up the phone and called Verna—end of story two.

Story three. About sixteen years later, during a visit with our son David in upstate New York, we went with him for a medical appointment. When we arrived home, Verna discovered she lost a diamond earring. We had purchased another pair of earrings to replace the diamonds from the lost pair that were now on the necklace. The first thing we did was call the doctor's office. They had not found it but would keep an eye open.

We stopped at a grocery store on the way home from the doctor's. I went back to the store to inquire and trace my steps up and down the aisles. Nobody found anything. Then I remembered that as we left the store, Verna had pulled off her COVID-19 mask and thrown it in a trash barrel outside its entrance. I rummaged through that. I looked like a homeless person looking for something to eat. But nobody gave me the proverbial "dime for a cup of coffee." There had just been a drizzle of frozen rain, and the ground was covered with crushed ice crystals. And here I was, looking for a diamond among them. I thought I found it a thousand times because all the ice crystals looked like diamonds. I gave up and went home.

All the while, I couldn't help but feel that sooner or later, I was going to find the earring. After all, my batting average was two for two, 100%. We started to consider other possibilities. Verna had been sleeping on a recliner. We had just purchased a sleeping sofa that replaced the recliner. The recliner was on the back porch waiting to be picked up for donation. We went through the recliner and traced our path from the room to the porch. And then, we searched the floor on the porch, but there was nothing.

Then, I thought of another possibility. We had vacuumed the floor of the room we had been sleeping in after removing all the furniture. The next place to look was inside the vacuum cleaner bag. I emptied the bag's contents onto a newspaper on the kitchen table and went through the debris inch by inch. Alas, I found the back of the earring stud. I'm on the right trail. Within seconds, there it was! This is getting weird.

What is it about lost diamonds and me? It makes one wonder. Anyway, if you ever lose a diamond, call Jack. The finder's fee is 10% of the assessed value. You can't make this stuff up!

69. COMPASS ROSE

2019

I was our neighborhood's "Go-to Guy" for minor DIY projects when we lived in The Villages. Plus, I had a reputation for good landscaping. One day, our next-door neighbors, the McCrackens, asked if I could give them some suggestions for landscaping a 10'x10' area at the front entrance of their house. Of course, we both knew it would end up with more than a suggestion.

Naturally, the first thing that entered my mind was rocks. I came up with a bed of small brown pebbles and a compass rose with small white stones in the center. The compass rose measured about three feet. I made a base from composite decking material that would not rot. I put plastic edging along the eight points to create a tray to hold the stones. The McCrackens bought a sundial with a pedestal to put in the center of the compass rose. They also purchased black plastic letters to designate the four major points of the compass. They were pleased with the final creation and received many compliments as guests entered their front door.

I was very pleased with my creation and wanted one for our front yard. But where to put it? We had a circular driveway with a perfect spot near the edge of the road. I enhanced the design by installing aluminum angle iron as dividers in the eight compost points and used small black and white stones for added contrast. A pedestal sundial would not work because I had other features in the area that would detract from it. So, I purchased a twelve-inch sundial plate embossed with a bit of philosophy that read, "Come and Grow Old With Me. The Best is Yet to Come."

Our homes had a perfect North-South orientation. I could easily give passersby an approximation of the current time within ten minutes as they stopped to admire my handiwork, which was right along the edge of the road.

To receive recognition for my efforts, Verna submitted the project to The Villages newspaper, which took a picture and wrote an excellent article about it.

NEIGHBOR TOM ON RIGHT AND MY COMPASS ROSE

70. MENTAL GYMNASTICS - A PART OF ME TODAY

BOOKS

To set the stage for this story, I have to go back to 2004 when we moved to The Villages and entered a new lifestyle. While downsizing in New Jersey, we went through all our "stuff." I had a collection of about 1,200 books. I am addicted to books and reading. My collection consisted of fiction and non-fiction. My favorite type of fiction is historical, and currently, it is the only type of fiction (other than the classics) that I read.

A part of my fiction collection included a large number of *Readers' Digest* condensed books. Our church sponsored a rummage sale one time. Verna and I were part of the committee running it. A large stack of those condensed books was not sold when it was over. Rather than trash them, I took them home and eventually got the idea to try to collect all of them in print. I kept a list of the ones I had in my billfold, and whenever we ran across a garage sale, I was on the hunt for those I was missing. Eventually, as my collection increased, I changed my list from what I had to what I was missing and crossed them out as I "bagged" the prey. The series started in the early 1950s; about four are published annually. I never paid more than twenty-five cents when I found one. By the time we were downsizing, I had all of them through the 1980s. You are probably wondering if I ever read them. My reading plan back then was to read one fiction, one nonfiction, and one professional book and then cycle through that sequence again. I had read all of them up to the early 1960s. They were good, wholesome reads.

But what to do with my collection? I bit the bullet and decided that they had to go. That became a problem. We tried our garage sale, but no takers. I could not bring myself to put them in the trash. I finally called the local Salvation Army, and they agreed to take a few. They said to bring them to their facility and leave a "few," but not all at the back door. I must have taken about fifty and surreptitiously dumped them there. I couldn't help feeling like a mother abandoning her newborn baby on the church steps.

My Classics comprised a very handsome and expensive collection of leather-bound books published by Easton Press. I also had about a dozen nice hardbound Greatest Historical Novels published by Bantam and twenty-one hardbound editions from The Classics Club. All of these made the cut to take to Florida. While in Florida, I added twenty-one Barnes & Noble paperback classics to my Classic collection. They are not very handsome as they sit on the bookshelves, but for under $10, I could not resist adding them to my collection. Plus, it's still something to hunt for at Goodwill and garage sales. My nonfiction was and still is mostly history. However, I did have every conceivable subject covered in my library.

I brought about five hundred books to The Villages. I have interesting stories about three sets of books in my library and how I acquired them. I have forty-eight hard-bound books on US History published by Yale University Press. There are fifty in the series. The complete set is available on Amazon, but nobody wants to break it up. I picked this collection up at a church rummage sale for $15. Used books have got to be the best deal going. These books are hardbound; the first in the set were published in the early 1900s, and the last were published before 1920. What I found remarkable about them is that while I was reading them, I occasionally came to two pages that I had to cut at the outer edge to read. So here were these books sitting on someone's shelf for over 100 years and never been read. What a shame! When I see shelves full of books in someone's house or a movie on TV, I wonder how many have they read. I will comment on this in my next section.

Here is the second story about my literary treasures. Some years ago, my brother-in-law Andy was good friends with a black fellow in the next town. His parents had passed away, and he was going through their house to dispose of their belongings. He was selling some of the stuff and invited Andy over if he wanted to buy anything. Andy asked Verna and me if we wanted to come along, and we jumped at the opportunity. We both like garage and rummage sales. We bought a vintage solid oak legal bookcase with glass doors, a very handsome piece of furniture. The family was the only black family within a radius of at least twenty miles of our hometown in Exeter, Pennsylvania. They were a well-respected and popular family. They had a collection of books I scarfed up for a few dollars (I feel like I stole them). One set is entitled *Six Thousand Years of History*, published over one hundred years ago. So here was this black family that was so far ahead of me in literary pursuits. I grew up in a family that did not have one single book in the house.

My third story is an eleven-volume set of *The Story of Civilization*. Will Durant wrote the first six volumes. His wife, Ariel, co-authored the remaining five volumes with him. Do you remember the Doubleday Book Club? The deal was like buying one book now, committing to purchase so many in the future, and receiving four additional books free now. I signed up sometime in the late 1960s. One of my free book choices was the ten volumes of *The Story of Civilization*. That's right, the entire set counted as one free book! Some years later, they wrote an eleventh volume I picked up at a bargain someplace. I checked some prices for these books on Amazon and found a price range of $20 to $100 for one new one, but of course, the prices were all over the place for used ones.

While downsizing in preparation for our relocation to upstate New York, I struggled with what to do with all of my books. I had a collection of about 500 and had read over 90% of them. We would be cramped for space, so I had to get rid of some of them. My first attempt was to offer them to our sons. David wanted about three dozen, and Kevin only a handful. All of our grandchildren were living in apartments and had no space for them. I also have concluded that their generation values books differently than I do. I also tried to sell the handsome glass bookcase but could not get a reasonable price. David said he would take it, and it ended up with his daughter Ellen. I am glad it is still in the family. I tried selling the remaining books but only got rid of a handful.

Shortly after we were settled in our current residence, I put my collection up for sale. But once again, there was a lack of interest. I finally found a local bookseller who took most of the paperbacks off my hands at a meager price. I then put the remaining books on Marketplace at giveaway prices. Then, one day, I received a phone call from someone interested in the older history books. Their teenage son was interested in history, and they wanted him to read history written in the past. They came to our apartment to check out the books they were interested in. While they were here, I showed them my list, and suddenly, they became interested in the entire lot. They also had a daughter who was interested in some of the collection. Even the parents indicated they would like many to read themselves. I offered them a reasonable price for my entire library, and they accepted. Since they now had so many books, I suggested they would need my two handsome bookcases, and they agreed. What made me feel good about the transaction was that a young boy about thirteen years old could not wait to get his nose into my treasures. Since I signed my name on the inside cover of each book (which is a habit of mine after I read it), there will be a loving connection between him and me over future years. I miss my books but am happy they found sincere and dedicated new readers.

READING

So much for my books themselves, but now how about reading them? As a child, I was nowhere near a bookworm. However, after graduating from college in 1967, I started reading and collecting books. Since that time (fifty-seven years), there has not been a time when I have not been reading a book. I pick another one up from my collection as soon as I complete one. I always had a system of alternating between types of books to keep things in balance. The only kind of book I don't read is poetry. I never developed an appreciation for it. Getting back to all of those houses with shelves of books unread. My goal is to read all of the books in my collection. So far, of the approximately five hundred, I have read about 90%. I might make it!

Throughout all of these years of reading, I felt deeply unsatisfied. Every so often, as I completed a book, put it back on the shelf, and began searching for the next one, I would look at the title and ask myself if I read it. I have a practice of signing my name in the upper right-hand corner of the very first page of a book once I read it. But then, after I saw my signature, I tried to recall something from the book and drew a blank. It did not make me feel good. So when we got to The Villages and had these five hundred books to plow through, I started to think of what I should do to make my reading more effective. I remembered that in New Jersey, as I glanced at my bookshelves, my eye would catch a book that I had used during my teaching career, and immediately, my mind recalled the contents of that book. So I asked myself, what was different about the textbooks and the other books in my library? Two things hit me: I went through that textbook more than once and read it actively because I had to present it to the class. I had to understand it and put it in my own words, not just read it to the class. Those two things, repetition, and active reading, were the keys to recalling what I read. Now I started reading with a pencil. When I came across some information I should remember, I put a slight pencil mark in the margin next to it. When I finished the book, I returned to the beginning. Where there was a pencil mark, I reread that area and wrote an objective question (multiple choice, True or False, fill in the blank, or matching) that captured the point.

Over the years, I have a collection of about 20,000 questions from two hundred and twenty books. That takes care of the active versus passive part, but what about repetition? Once I had a few books in question form, I devised a plan to handle repetition. Once a week, I go through one hundred questions and test myself with an honest percentage grade. When I cycle through all the questions, I return to question one and plow through again. I have been through the earliest question numerous times. I record and track my level of retention in two ways. I compute a cumulative average for each one hundred questions. Over the years, I have achieved 66.7%. That may not be a passing grade, but it tells me I retain two-thirds of my reading. Before I started this program, my retention was zero. I carry my cumulative average out to one decimal place, and my goal is to improve that average if only by one-tenth of a point each time I take a test. For each block of one hundred questions, I track how I am doing compared to the last time I went through those same questions. My other goal is to improve each time I go through that block. Sometimes, I do poorer than the previous time, which upsets me.

Since my 20,000-plus questions include a lot of trivia and details regarding history, I need to adjust my history reading slightly. I want to step back from the details, focus on the big picture, and combine it by concentrating on the big picture. I have a book called *The Greatest One Hundred Events in World History* that should be a good resource. I have also picked up a few others in a genre called "Big History" that show historical trends.

My 20,000-plus questions are handwritten in cursive and currently fill four loose-leaf binders. Over the years, after many handlings, the sheets have gotten ratty, and I have eliminated some insignificant questions. About three years ago, I started a clean-up campaign. Instead of doing a hundred per week, I started typing the questions using Pages on an Apple computer. I am about halfway through my cleanup project. The ones done are much neater and can be accessed for future use. Our son, Kevin, suggested that I put my collection on a website and sell them, but I am not interested in that. I hope David, Kevin, or our grandchildren don't destroy my collection.

LITERATURE (THE CLASSICS)

Mark Twain defined a classic as "a book people praise and don't read." These are heavy-duty readings. I have read every one of the Classics in my collection. Of course, I want to retain as much as possible, so I apply my active/repetition program. Once again, I use questions to identify significant points such as the setting, historical context, and themes. Once a month, I go through about 100 questions. Literature is not one of my strongest areas. My cumulative average is 52.1%. I cycle through all of the books and try to get a better grade each time I do a book.

GEOGRAPHY

I recently read a few history books emphasizing a correlation between history and geography. I am interested in both subjects, and their connection makes them all the more valuable. I like maps; seeing a map or globe of all those countries and their differences fascinates me.

There are about two hundred countries in the world. Between my military career and cruising, we have been in over thirty of them. And that will be the extent of it. Age, health, a bad experience on our last cruise, and COVID-19 have closed that chapter in our lives. When I was teaching International Business courses, I was amazed that so many adults were unfamiliar with the names and locations of the countries in the world. A few years ago, I asked myself if someone had laid a map of the world before me with no names of any of the countries, how many could I identify? I have blank maps of all of the continents and their respective countries. Antarctica is a continent but is not divided into countries. Did you know that fifty-four of the two hundred or so countries are in Africa? Once a month, I do a continent. My cumulative average is 96.0%.

By the way, I covered the walls of one of our garages in New Jersey and our garage walls in The Villages with maps from my collection of old *National Geographic* maps. Sometimes, when waiting for Verna to go somewhere in the car or golf cart, I would review some of the countries I had trouble locating. I am currently making an encyclopedia of all of the countries in the world consisting of a handful of questions about each one that will capture something significant about it. Of course, when it is completed, it will become part of my monthly routine.

ENCYCLOPEDIA

About thirteen years ago, our son Kevin was assigned by GE to work in Budapest for six months. While he was there, Verna and I visited him and his family for almost three weeks. While sitting around the apartment one day, a book on an end table caught my eye: a one-volume *Phillip's Encyclopedia*. I could not control myself and had to pick it up. As I glanced through it, I said, "WOW, what a wealth of information it contains." The book was published in the United Kingdom and sold for about $90. It was worth it, and I planned on ordering a copy once we returned home. I asked our daughter-in-law, who was homeschooling her children, where she got it, and she said at a bookstore around the corner for $15. I asked her if she remembered seeing any more there. She said she did not remember but would take me there if I wanted to. I jumped up off the sofa and said. "Let's go." We got to the bookstore and headed immediately to the corner in a back room where she found her copy. Another copy was set on the shelf, waiting for me to arrive. I grabbed it!

Now, we all know that encyclopedias are obsolete. But if I were stranded on an isolated island, wouldn't having a copy of that book be great? That is what I like about a book. The words on the pages are always there, waiting for me to devour. I don't have to worry about the battery on my iPhone going dead or some other technical glitch that prevents me from getting into Google or Wikipedia. Or, if I had to give up all of my books except one, that one would be that Encyclopedia.

Now, how will I handle the wealth of knowledge in that book? I can't possibly start on page one and start writing questions. I have to be a little more selective and focused. So, I periodically opened the book randomly and browsed the contents of those two pages facing me. If there was something that I wanted to put in my memory bank, I made a question out of it. As I did those two pages, I circled the page numbers, and eventually, I completed all of the pages and had a collection of about eight hundred questions that I put on 3x5 cards with the answers on the back. Once a month, I go through about an inch of cards. My cumulative average is 71.8%.

SCIENCE

I never took a science course during my eight years at a parochial school. In high school, in the ninth grade, I took a General Science course and Biology in the tenth grade. In the eleventh grade, I had two DAYS of Chemistry. Remember that story (High School, I Got Nothing Out of It)? I took a correspondence course in Chemistry before the Air Force sent me to college. In college, I had to take two science courses. I chose Astronomy and Physics For Non-Science Majors. So, after twenty years of classroom education, I had no grasp of the scientific world. This was a gap in my overall learning that needed to be closed. Furthermore, for the longest time, all of my reading consisted of subjective matter. History is not a science. I've learned that it depends on who writes it. I've come across gaps, inconsistencies, and different points of emphasis. I was ready to break into a new field of learning, the sciences. I went to Barnes &

Noble and found a series of books called Homework Helpers. I picked up four: Earth Science, Biology, Chemistry, and Physics. I went through the first two with the following grades: Earth Science-89% and Biology-78%. Before I got to the others, I picked up some books our daughter-in-law was using to homeschool her children. I completed those: Earth Science-88%; Biology-91%; Chemistry-84%; and Physics-82%. After those two rounds, I still felt short in the sciences.

A few years later, once again browsing through homeschool books at Kevin's, a series by Wiley caught my eye. They impressed me in that there were a lot of exercises, problems, and tests that would require me to go through them **ACTIVELY**. I bought five of them: Physical Science, Biology, Chemistry, Physics, and The Human Body (everyone should know something about their body). I completed the first four; Physical Science-90%; Biology-77%; Chemistry-86%; Physics-82%. I enjoyed Physical Science, Chemistry, and Physics more than Biology. Those three required me to solve problems, and I like to develop algorithms to solve them so that when a similar problem pops up again, I don't have to "reinvent the wheel." I had trouble with Biology because there are many uncommon words to remember. But I did develop an appreciation for this "Science of Life."

As I said earlier, I am following the active part of my learning by doing all the exercises. My plan for the repetition part is to go through a Barron series for the same subjects and then go through Wiley's five books again to reinforce the knowledge and try to get better grades.

A few years ago, I picked up a book on Oceanography. I went through it and, of course, condensed everything into questions and answers. Now, I have to go through those and test myself. Geology is another science that interests me, but that's further down the road.

CULTURAL LITERACY

About twenty years ago, I picked up a book entitled *The Dictionary of Cultural Literacy: What Every American Needs to Know*; it's encyclopedic, covering twenty-one topics. It also would be a good companion on a deserted island. Somewhere along the line, I saw it recommended for anyone planning on going on the TV show *Jeopardy*. I "read" the book once many years ago. Again, the problem was, "What did I retain?" Relatively nothing. So, I applied my learning plan, eliminated the information I had retained, and ended up with 1770 questions for things I "Should Know." Once a month, I go through a topic. My cumulative average is 63.8%. Strong in some areas and weak in others.

CHRONOLOGY OF THE WORLD

Putting events in sequence is important and interesting to me. Put the following in their proper order: Charlemagne, the Thirty Years' War, Napoleon, the Magna Carta, the Russian Revolution, Caesar, and the Crusades. That may be an easy one, but you get my point. There are a lot of published chronologies nicely arranged with time frames down one axis and topics/person's names across the other. They make a good reference resource but are not meant to be read. Without a photographic memory, absorbing and retaining so much information crammed on single pages is impossible. As I searched for a comprehensive worldwide chronology, I ran across Asimov's *Chronology of the World-History of the World From the Big Bang to Modern Times*. It contains the times, events, and reading material to flesh out the skeleton. I started creating a timeline chart, but it got too unwieldy and ineffective for repetition. I tried different arrangements, but nothing worked until I returned to using questions to capture the main events and names. It took me a couple of years to plow through the book. I have 2,900 questions broken up into twenty-nine time periods. No, it is not exactly one hundred questions per period; it just happened to work out that way. Partway through the project, I started a list of names of people as they appeared in history. That's another project to be discussed later. In addition to my questions, I needed another visual, so I created my simplified list with the time period at the top and the significant events and people associated with that period. Breaking the big picture into these smaller ones is easier to digest and lock in my memory bank. So, once a month, I went through the questions for a time period; my cumulative average was 58.3%. After I did the questions for that period, I stared at my simplified chart for a few minutes and tried to burn the events and names into my brain. As another combination active/repetitive tool, I took the significant events and people's names and put them on one side of a 3x5 card, and on the reverse of the card, I had the appropriate time period. The stack of cards ended up being twelve inches high. Once a month, I went through about an inch, looked at the event or person's name on one side, and tried to answer with the correct time period. This was a challenging task; my cumulative average was 43%. Something is wrong with my program. I'm not getting that much out of all my effort. I think I will lighten up a little, and instead of trying to get the exact date for each event, I will concentrate on the sequence. I will randomly select ten cards, arrange them in their correct chronological order, and test myself on that. I'll go through ten stacks a month. I still have to do something with the 2,900 questions. Or do I? As much as I hate to trash them, I have enough similar information captured in other formats. So, I may have to "Bite The Bullet" and write that effort off. I'm putting that decision on the back burner for now.

BIOGRAPHIES

There are so many significant personal and group names in history. Who were they? What are they noted for? When did they live? What is the first individual name that pops up in recorded history? Menes (also known as Narmer), who, in about 3100 BCE, is noted for combining Upper and Lower Egypt. However, there is a variety of possibilities. Imagine having that as your legacy!

I like to read biographies. You can learn a lot of history by reading them. I would like to have a nice set of biographies. *Readers' Digest* published some at one time. I had nine of them. They look like their condensed books and would make a nice collection. But they must have canceled that effort. Like I tend to do when I can't find an available source for something I desire, **I DO IT MYSELF**. So, off the top of my head, I created a list of all the names I ran across in my extensive reading of history over the last twenty-some years. As I mentioned above, I had already started such a list chronologically.

Furthermore, in addition to individuals, I added groups of people such as the Celts, Anglo-Saxons, Cossacks, etc. I ended up with about 300 names. I had a publication of the 100 most influential people in the world. I reviewed it and created a 200-question matching test (some names are used more than once). I have to take that test myself and see how much I remember. I still have to research the 300 names and put my findings in a question-and-answer format. That project is patiently waiting for me, along with a few others.

AMERICAN HISTORY

A few years ago, our son David was involved in an upstate New York program helping Syrian refugees assimilate into our country. He became a tutor and mentor and undertook a program to help them learn American History. When he mentioned that to me, I immediately thought of my collection of questions and suggested using them to help David. That would not work because of the language barrier and the reading level at which I wrote the questions. I offered to develop something simpler, create a collection of questions written to their reading level, and still provide the essential elements of American History. I found an excellent source with just the right amount of information written at the appropriate reading level. So I put pen to paper, and after about six months, I had a collection of 1300 questions. By the time I was done, David had already set up a website to help them. So here I am with this resource setting unused. If anyone wants a crash course on American History, make an offer. I am going through 100 questions monthly to see how much I know about our country. After nine months, my average score is 84%.

WORLD HISTORY

It's the same scenario as American History above, except what spurred this on has a different twist. As David was getting involved with helping the Syrians, he came up with a scheme to help them earn some money. Since it was spring, he suggested that they do yard work for private households. Verna and I were visiting him, and he had a crew of guys on a cleanup project. They happened to return to David's for a coffee break. We were all chatting, and one young fellow showed a sincere and impressive desire to learn World history. No pun intended, but the "rest is history." By the time I did my research and prepared something useful, we lost contact with the interested and anxious fellow. I now have 825 World History questions in mint condition. Once again, after nine months, my average is 84%.

GREAT CIVILIZATIONS

One thing leads to another, and the more you learn, the more you find out you don't know. While searching for basic elementary American and World History books to help the Syrians, I ran across an interesting book on the Great Civilizations. This reminds me of when you are looking for a book on Amazon, and they have this section: "People who bought this are also interested in _____." Here was this handy book. What I liked about it is that it presented the material differently. It covers nineteen civilizations and follows their development from beginning to end. I could not resist myself. I've been through the book and have many questions in cursive waiting to be typed. My inventory is growing, so I may have to have a clearance sale.

GED

Having missed out on a solid high school education (you must read that story to understand), I wondered how I would fare if I took a GED. So, about fourteen years ago, I purchased a GED book from Barnes & Noble (one of my three favorite stores, the others being Lowes and Home Depot). I make it a habit of not going into Barnes & Noble anymore; it's too tempting. Plus, used books are a better deal. I took the sample GED.

Here is how I did:

US History-83	Earth & Space-81	
World History-93	Physical Science-87	
Civics-89	Social Science-84	
Economics-98	Science-92	
Geography-89	Algebra-94	
Life Science-74	Geometry-91	Average-88

The above topics represent a comprehensive collection of subjects that would make a good benchmark for evaluating one's level of education after twelve years of school. I should retake these tests and compare my scores.

MATH

This is the biggie. It started with asking, "Can I teach myself calculus?" At the end of eight years in a parochial school, I never heard of Algebra. I think today's kids are introduced to it in some of their first few years of elementary school. Ninth grade, Exeter High School, and I'm taking Algebra I. I admit I was not a good student, but the Algebra teacher was poor. I don't remember her making the subject interesting. I remember her coming to class, bringing the latest monthly issue of the *Readers' Digest*, and writing the vocabulary test on the blackboard for us to take. What did that have to do with Algebra? When I look back at her practice of doing that, it should have been brought to the principal's attention. But that was another era in a low-income socioeconomic environment.

I didn't encounter the word "Algebra" again until eight years later, in 1960. I decided to make the Air Force a career and began to take correspondence courses in the subjects I missed in high school. I did well because the courses were well-designed, and I could proceed at my rate. I worked myself up through Geometry. Later, while taking night college courses, I enrolled in a community college Algebra course. I did okay, but the school did not give me the three credits for it; they said since I did not have two years of Algebra on my high school transcript, they used that course to fill in that gap. I already told you about my experience taking a math course at the University of Wisconsin and how I struggled with "x times 0 = 0, prove it." When I went to Syracuse University, I had to take one Algebra course, and I did okay. That was the end of my independent and classroom education in math.

About the same time I got interested in learning science independently, I felt the same itch to go back to math. I remember glancing at our son's high school texts on Trigonometry and Calculus, saying WOW!

Wouldn't it be great to discover what those subjects are all about? Another trip to Barnes & Noble. I found a series of math books in the "Homework Helpers" series, like the science ones I mentioned earlier. I picked up Algebra, Geometry, Trigonometry, Pre-Calculus, and Calculus. I made it through Algebra and Geometry, 95% and 89%, respectively. But that series was not doing it for me. There were too many obvious mistakes in the books, and although there was an answer key for the problems, the steps in the solution were not available, and they could have been helpful in better understanding the concepts. I did not go on to Trigonometry in that series. I went to Barnes & Noble again to find a better source for learning trigonometry. I asked the clerk for help. He selected a book. I imagined him going home that night and saying to his wife, " You won't believe this. An old fart walks into the store today looking for a book on Trigonometry!" Only in The Villages.

Well, I went through that book and got a little taste of Trigonometry (87%). However, I needed help with the mechanics of algebra in applying trigonometry concepts. I then realized that I needed a solid background in math fundamentals if I ever wanted to make it through Calculus. While visiting Kevin in South Carolina, I browsed through the kids' homeschooling math books. They grabbed me. There is nothing colorful about them; there are no pictures, just problems, many, many problems. They are created by Saxon and use an incremental approach. Once you learn a new concept, you never leave it.

There are four books involved. Book one is Algebra I and has 120 chapters. At the end of each chapter, there are thirty problems; about five are on the newly learned concept, and the remaining twenty-five are on something you learned earlier. There's the repetition technique being applied. And, of course, you don't passively read an algebra book; you have to do the problems to learn it. So, after 120 chapters with thirty problems each, I completed 3600 problems continually and randomly, covering the book's entire contents. It took me over a year to complete that course. My cumulative average grade for all 3600 problems is 95.55%. By the way, I bought the solution manual, which proved very helpful. This is my grading scheme. I do not deduct any points if I get a problem wrong because of a simple arithmetic error. If I get a problem wrong, I take off one point. But if I finally see how to get the correct answer, I give myself back half of that point.

Book 2 is Algebra II, which I completed. It has one hundred and thirty lessons with the usual thirty problems per chapter for 3,900 problems. I misplaced my final average, but up to lesson 80, I had a cumulative average of 80%. In addition to more advanced concepts, this book was more complex. In Algebra I, the previously covered end-of-chapter problems and the chapter number that introduced that concept were noted. So, if I looked at a problem and didn't know what to do with it, I got a good clue from the point covered in the indicated earlier chapter. The previous chapter that should be applied in Algebra II is not noted. I have to stare at the problem and determine what lesson comes into play and how to start the solution process. Word problems are much more challenging than the other exercises. The key to the word problems is setting up the correct equation.

Book 3 is Advanced Algebra. I have 20 years of classroom education but have never taken an advanced course. After a gap of almost a year because of our relocation, I started this course about a year ago. I worried I would have forgotten so much that I may have had to return to Algebra II. However, I was pleasantly surprised that it all came back to me. I progressed at a pretty good pace, with a cumulative average of 82% after 32 lessons. About nine months ago, I had to put it on the shelf because we were overcome with severe health issues regarding our son David. Currently, my priority is to concentrate on completing this memoir project. Then, I will pick up where I left off and hopefully not have to go back to page one. Book four is Calculus with Trigonometry and Analytic Geometry, but that is one to two years down the road. If I ever make it through Calculus, I would like to learn Statistics.

Now, there you have it. That's all there is. It may sound like I spend every waking moment with my nose in a book, but that is not so. Until five years ago, when Verna had severe back problems, we played golf, on average, three times weekly. I did my yard work and helped Verna around the house. We socialized, and every evening, Verna and I watched TV together (movies and taped golf). I like to think that my life is balanced. As much as I like to read, I never sit all day and do just that. However, our new lifestyle presents a significantly different daily routine. For one reason or another, as you will discover in future stories, we have not quite yet found our new routine. A significant difference is much less time spent playing golf, doing yard work, house maintenance, and helping Verna with housework. A large part of our time is taken up with medical appointments. Another chunk is dinner itself, which can be a two-hour ordeal, which we look forward to because it provides valuable socializing.

I look at all of my mental gyrations as a hobby—something to fill the moments when I'm not doing something else. There is no schedule or pressure involved. To pass the time, some people do crossword puzzles, Sudoku, scrabble, other word games, Candy Crush, or whatever. For me, it's researching information, creating learning devices through questions and answers, solving math problems, and challenging myself to improve.

When I selected the title for this story, it was tentative. But as I got to the end of it, I got to thinking about "gymnastics," and a series of words came to mind that seemed to apply to gymnastics and my mental projects: concentration—practice—drive—balance—repetition—constant— strength (mental)—improvement—variety—discipline—dedication—challenge—movement—active—goals—satisfaction.

That sums up a part of me that should be documented for posterity. After putting it all together in this story, it occurred to me that when it comes time for David and Kevin to go through my stuff, this information will help them understand my collection of books, numerous binders of questions, and stacks of 3 x 5 cards.

REPORT CARD

20,000+ Questions 66.7

Literature 52.1

Maps 96.0

Encyclopedia 71.8

Earth Science (Homework Helpers) 89.0

Biology 78.0
Earth Science (Andrea's). 88.0
Biology 91.0
Chemistry 84.0
Physics 82.0
Physical Science (Wiley). 90.0
Biology 77.0
Chemistry 86.0
Physics. 81.5
Cultural Literacy 63.8
Chronology Questions 58.3
Chronology Cards 43.0
American History. 84.0
World History. 84.0
GED Average. 87.9
Algebra (Homework Helpers) 95.0
Geometry 89.0
Trigonometry (Barnes&Noble) 87.0
Algebra I (Saxon) 95.6
Algebra II 80.0
GRAND AVERAGE 80.03
(THE NUMBER TO BEAT IN THE FUTURE)

71. THE SILENT GENERATION (1928 TO 1945)

While writing these stories and describing myself, I realized there is another dimension to whom I am. How did what was happening in the world during my formative years contribute to my making? This got me thinking about the different labels that are attached to generations, starting with the "Lost Generation" (1883 to 1900) up to Generation Alpha(2010 to mid-2020s).

My generation is comparatively small because the Great Depression and WWII caused people to have fewer children. The years that denote the Silent Generation are 1928 to 1945, a span of 17 years. I was born in 1938. I am about in the middle of that span, so I represent that generation well. Furthermore, Verna and I were born four months apart, which makes us a good match, just like we are in many other ways.

These are the characteristics that define us:

SILENT

FOLLOW THE RULES

WORK HARD AND KEEP OUR HEADS DOWN

DON'T TAKE RISKS

FRUGAL

DON'T WASTE ANYTHING

LOVE A BARGAIN

MAKE THINGS LAST

MARRY YOUNG AND HAVE CHILDREN YOUNG

SAVE MONEY BY WATCHING THE PENNIES

AND THEY ARE RIGHT ON!

72. AROUND THE WORLD CRUISE (ALMOST AND IN SEGMENTS)

1983 - 2019

My wife, Verna, and I celebrated our twenty-fifth wedding anniversary in 1983. We decided to do something special and memorable, so we took our first cruise.

The purpose of this story is to document all of our cruises. We have volumes of photos capturing all the cruises we've been on, but the pictures do not entirely describe some of our most remarkable experiences and memories. I did, however, use the albums to determine the years and sequence of all of them. Please don't stop reading because I will not bore you with endless details about each one. I will limit my comments to the highlights of each one and will try to control myself. Since they cover many years of our lives, I felt they should be documented in my memoirs. "Fasten your seatbelt," or I should say, "Put on your life preserver." Here we go.

1. 1983 - EASTERN CARIBBEAN - PRINCESS CRUISE LINE - 7 DAYS

Our first one was to the Eastern Caribbean. It was an easy choice because it was a popular place to go. It was a small ship featured in the TV series *The Love Boat*. The most remarkable memory of that cruise was how impressed we were with the entire cruising experience. Unlike today's cruises, they still had the midnight buffet, and everyone dressed up. And every meal was a special occasion. There was no need for "specialty dining" highlighted in current cruise brochures. Verna won a $400 Bingo Jackpot. We were hooked on cruising, and before the cruise ended, we decided it was the only way to vacation.

2. 1984 - THE WESTERN CARIBBEAN - THE *VERA CRUZ* - 7 DAYS

After our first cruise, it occurred to us that if we were going to do that regularly, we should find the most economical way to do it. We chose a less popular (and less expensive) ship called *Vera Cruz* for our second cruise. Our objective was to compare and see what, if any, differences there were in what you paid for a cruise. And there were significant differences. In everything from meals, which were mediocre, to entertainment, which was audience participation. Even the little daily ship's newspaper was nothing more than a one-page Xeroxed sheet compared to a more professional four to six-page publication on the *Princess*. Lesson learned: you get what you pay for. We'll stick to the mainstream ships. Where are we off to next?

3. 1986 - THE HAWAIIAN ISLANDS - THE *S.S.CONSTI-TUTION* - 7 DAYS

Everyone wants to go to Hawaii. Most people fly there and see only one island. We took another approach. Fly there and take a seven-day cruise visiting all of the islands. An added feature on this cruise was that Verna's brother, Ray, his wife, Carol, and their son, Michael, joined us. That in itself provided extra enjoyment and quality time. The highlight has to be the helicopter ride in Maui. It felt like you could reach out and touch the waterfalls as the helicopter swirled inside the canyon. I get motion sickness when I ride backward on a train, so Verna gave up her forward-facing seat for me. AH! What you do for love!

4. 1987 - THE PANAMA CANAL - CUNARD CRUISE LINES - 10 DAYS

We thought it would be interesting to go through the Panama Canal. And it was a great experience that lasted an entire day. However, as a highlight, I have to tell you a more sinister experience regarding a table-mate of ours. It just so happened that two other couples and we ended up at the Captain's table for dinner every evening. Although it is called the "Captain's" table, he rarely sits at it. But every evening, one of his officers joined us. It was a nice touch that added to dinner conversations. During the first dinner, this guy suggested to the other couple and us that at the end of the cruise, we should all give him our customary cash gratuities for the wait staff, and he would combine it with his and give it to our waiter as a group thing. We all thought it was a little out of line, but no further comments were made. Since I will refer to this guy quite a bit, and I don't remember his name, I will call him "Louie." The other couple and we hit it off and became good friends during the cruise. We started to notice some peculiarities about Louie. One was that he always wore a plain white shirt and black trousers whenever we saw him around the ship. Secondly, on a few occasions, we arrived at the dinner table, and there was an open bottle of wine, which was a compliment from the officer joining us. Louie had the audacity to help himself with the wine before the officer arrived. That did not seem appropriate. Louie always had bizarre stories to tell, one being how he survived an airplane crash and similar braggadocio. Louie's wife was a travel agent, and one of the officers said something about her that made the hair on the back of his neck stand up. Louie was in the jewelry business.

One of our ports was in Colombia, South America. The ship warned us about pickpocketing if we went ashore. We went into town as usual with the other couple at our table. As we were strolling the streets, we noticed Louie across the way standing on a corner in his white shirt, black trousers, a red baseball cap, and a briefcase. He stood out.

Toward the end of the cruise, we all started to be frightened by him. On the very last night, Louie showed up at dinner with the black briefcase. After dinner, as we wandered around the ship, we bumped into him occasionally, and he was always carrying the briefcase. Our imagination started to get the best of us. We created this scenario in which Louie, being in the jewelry business, was a bagman for jewelry stolen from tourists. Our imagination went further, and the other couple and I admitted that there probably was a phone call that went something like: "I'll be the guy in a white shirt, black trousers, and a red baseball cap." Our last dinner was somewhat uncomfortable; by that time, our conversation with Louie had become strained, and inside, we were praying that he did not think that we were on to his "jewelry business" and that he would have to do something to keep us quiet and not blow his cover. By this time, we had him all figured out, and the matter of us giving him our cash to give to our waiter was a dead issue. That adventure on the high seas certainly could have ended with us overboard!

5. 1988 - ALASKA - PRINCESS LINE - 12 DAYS

This one has much less to write about than the previous cruise. The memorable experience was the day we spent in Glacier Bay. Here is the scene. The ship parks in the bay among icebergs of various sizes, with an occasional seal napping on one of them. It's a beautiful, sunny but cool day. The ship is intentionally quiet. Distractions are held to a minimum. The conversation is in whispers, and there is an air of solemnity aboard. All eyes are focused on the edge of a glacier so as not to miss the calving (when a junk of ice breaks away and hits the water). There is a few-second delay from when you see it happen to when you hear the thunder made by the splash. The larger the chunk (calf), the louder the noise and the louder the applause from the audience. Larger chunks create a larger ripple effect, and as you follow the ripple, it causes floating icebergs to bounce off the ship's hull. I hope they do not get too big! Dinner that evening took on a different tone. We were at a table of eight. Usually, different couples go off on shore excursions, and a variety of "Show and Tell" stories are shared at dinner. Tonight, we all had the same awesome daytime experiences, and each cherished it within themselves. There was no need for words.

6. 1989 - THE BALTIC SEA - PRINCESS LINE - 12 DAYS

In a previous story, I outlined our trips across Europe while stationed with the Air Force in Germany. None of those excursions took us to any of the Scandinavian countries. We had to close that gap. Just like Alaska, the ships only go there during the summer. I have a deep admiration for the Scandinavian people, and this was confirmed during this trip. We hit all Scandinavian countries: Denmark, Norway, Sweden, and Finland.

However, our highlight does not come from any of those countries, but I did have a few words to say about Helsinki, Finland, in a previous story. In addition to the Scandinavian capitals, we had a two-day visit to Leningrad, Russia, which was changed to St. Petersburg in 1991. I am fascinated with the history, geography, and culture of Russia. In 1989, it was the Soviet Union, not Russia. Before we embarked, the ship's staff warned us to be careful on shore. Be careful what you say, do, and where you go. Leningrad is overflowing with history; you can see it rolling down the streets! Home-place of the czars and the Revolution. We sucked in the grandeur of the palaces and, at the other extreme, the oppressed people in the downtrodden city with empty stores.

Here is a story that includes a lesson in economics and a comparison between capitalism and communism. Before we arrived in Leningrad, we were told not to purchase anything from any Russian. Foreigners could only buy from a "Dollar Store." Sure enough, as soon as we got off the bus on our first excursion, locals were selling popular Russian items like caviar, nesting Russian dolls, and T-shirts. And sure enough, some of our fellow travelers made some purchases. On that particular day, we had a trip to the Summer Palace, about an hour outside Leningrad. On the way there, we passed a Dollar Store, and all the ladies shouted, "Stop the bus!" We zoomed right past it. When we arrived at our destination, we all asked the tour guide to have the driver stop on the way back. Some passengers even offered money to have him stop. On the way back, he did stop, but we had only about fifteen minutes to shop. Verna bought a pair of unique Russian earrings and wanted a necklace to match them, but there was not enough time. Everyone was disappointed that we couldn't stay longer and do more purchasing.

The next day, we had a city tour, including lunch at a hotel. We all noticed a Dollar Store in the lobby as soon as we entered the hotel. We all headed for it, but as soon as we arrived at the entrance, the clerk put up a sign that read "Closed for Lunch." During lunch, everyone anxiously discussed and compared their shopping list for the Dollar Store. About an hour later, we all rushed downstairs to the Dollar Store. To our dismay, it was still closed. The tour guide sternly commanded, "Okay, everybody, back on the bus." We could have made history by creating a Second Bolshevik Revolution. Do you get the point? Can you imagine how much the Soviet Union economy could have reaped in those two days from a few thousand tourists anxious to leave their dollars in their country? That became the main topic of discussion back on the ship at the dinner table as we departed Leningrad.

7. 2000 - SOUTH AMERICA - PRINCESS LINE - 12 DAYS

This cruise started halfway down South America in Chile, around the southern tip, and then up to the other side of South America to Argentina. It was January, the middle of winter for us in New Jersey, but summer below the equator. No specific highlights during this cruise lend themselves to a story. So, I will list a few sights we saw and experiences we felt that created lasting images in our minds.

- We spent two days viewing glaciers as we sailed down the coast of Chile.
- Numerous half-sunken and abandoned seagoing vessels lie left to rust, victims of the "Roaring Forties" (the most treacherous waters in the world at the South 40s latitude).
- Snow flurries and extremely high wind as we took our midsummer morning stroll on the Promenade Deck.
- One day in Ushuaia (the southernmost city in the world).
- Docked next to a Russian research vessel as it embarked and headed south to Antarctica.
- Penguins and ostriches.
- Twenty-two-foot waves one night. It felt like the ship was going to break in half.
- We had the greatest dinner partners we ever had. We were a group of four couples and a pair of sisters with the last name "Andrew." They were not the famous Andrew Sisters of the 1940s. We stayed in touch with some of

the couples for the longest time. We did learn from our waiter that the ship uses your demographics to decide who sits at what table. We were very compatible.

When people ask us what our favorite cruises were, this one makes the top three because it varied in its interests.

8. 2001 - CANADA - PRINCESS LINE - 7 DAYS

We took this trip in October 2001 and were still a little shell-shocked from 9-11. The remarkable thing about this cruise is that nothing was outstanding. We enjoyed it, but we did not bring anything home with us. We sailed through the Maritime Provinces, bouncing off all the islands, then down the St. Lawrence to Quebec. I refer to this cruise as our "Warmup" cruise for a three-week vacation we were booked for in a couple of months to Australia on New Year's Eve 2001.

9. 2002 - AUSTRALIA & NEW ZEALAND - NORWEGIAN LINE - 14 DAYS

Now, here was a trip to write home about. It was a three-week trip, starting with a few days in Sydney, then two weeks on the ship, ending up in Auckland for a few days. Once again, the memories, sites, and experiences are too numerous to mention. The most memorable thing about the trip was the actual location. Look at a world map; you see this relatively small continent with an island (New Zealand) off to one side. So far away from home. What is it doing there? Who would ever think that in my lifetime, I would set my feet in such a remote place? It is so far off the beaten track, yet so much the same in many ways. You don't even feel you are in a foreign country and about as far to another side of the world as you can. When I was a kid, there was a saying that if you dig a hole deep enough in northeast Pennsylvania, you end up in China. That's wrong. If you take the latitude and longitudes of our home in northern New Jersey, where we lived at the time of this cruise, change the North latitude numbers to South latitude and add 180 degrees (half the circumference of the 360 degrees of the world) to the longitude numbers, you find yourself a little off the southwest coast of Australia. Everybody should visit Australia at least once for the overall experience.

10. 2002 - ICELAND & THE BRITISH ISLES - PRINCESS LINE - 14 DAYS

This was an excellent way to cover the British Isles with a detour thrown around Iceland and then back to London. Of course, it hit all of the significant points within the British Isles except the little country of Wales. Poor, little-forgotten Wales; I have never seen a cruise ship that stops there.

We got a certificate for crossing the Arctic Circle at the Northeast tip of Iceland. As we approached Reykjavik, I started to ask myself if the radar site I was stationed at exactly forty years ago was still there. While at breakfast, I spotted a couple of Icelandic customs agents before we exited the ship. I approached them and asked about the radar site about an hour outside the city. He said it is physically there but is being used as a drug rehabilitation center. I told him why I was interested, and he suggested we go into town and hire a cab to take us there. We thanked him and went ashore. The young cab driver wanted $100 to take us there, wait for us, and return us to the ship. Verna offered him $80, and he said okay. While riding there, he commented that he had never been out of the city and said he could never have lived in such a lonely place. I told him of the four radar sites in Iceland and that the one we were going to was the least isolated. The other three were on the other three corners of the island.

When we approached the radar site, it looked the same as when I left it; the domes covering the radar antennas and buildings were still there. I explained to the guard why I was there as we approached the gate. He called the facility's director, who invited us to come in and chat with him. I first asked him if I could go and see my barracks. He said they were renovating it, but we could walk down and look in the window. We did, then went back to his office, where we had some coffee, and he appreciated what I could tell him about the place. His office was in the same building that included our mailboxes. Each little mailbox had a three-letter combination. I remembered my box number and noticed a letter still in it. After several tries, I remembered my combination and took out the letter. It was from Verna, which had been sitting there for forty years. I couldn't resist, so I opened it and read it. Oh My God, it was a "Dear John" letter! Just kidding! I like to embellish this story with that added bit of drama. It gets a lot of laughs whenever I tell it. The story is true until I reached the point of remembering my mailbox number.

That night, back on the ship, at the dinner table, I was the keynote speaker as I told my story and then "fessed" up with the truth. One final comment: Who would have ever thought that as I left that place in 1962, I would ever return?

11. 2003 - DISNEY CRUISE - 7 DAYS

In 2002, Verna and I decided to give our children an advance on their inheritance by taking them and their children on a Disney Cruise (all expenses $20,000 paid). We scheduled it for a few days after Christmas for one week (the most expensive week of the year).

The most remarkable feature of the cruise was the quality family time that it provided. Pure enjoyment and relaxation. No preparation, cooking, cleaning up, making beds, washing dishes, picking up, etc. Shades of *Downton Abby,* get dressed for dinner, go to dinner, be waited on, pick up and leave the table when you're done, and off to fun, relaxation, entertainment, or whatever—money well spent. Maybe we should do it again?

12. 2003 - FRENCH POLYNESIA (TAHITI) - PRINCESS LINE - 7 DAYS

By this time, we were collecting significant perks from Princess Cruises for having been on several cruises with them. One day in 2003, we received a two-for-one deal with extremely low airfares. We could not pass it up, so we booked it for January 2004 (a good time to leave New Jersey for a few weeks). It wasn't a cruise that included famous cultural, historical, or exciting vistas. It was a R&R package. What is there to do on a mini island in the middle of the Pacific? It was noteworthy to see how the lifestyle of the natives on these small islands differed so much from our lives. Shades of Robinson Crusoe living off the land (and sea). That's the image we brought back.

13. 2016 - THE NORTH ATLANTIC - PRINCESS LINE - 29 DAYS

In late 2003, we purchased a home in The Villages, Florida. There were no more cruises in our sights after we moved there in mid-2004. We were so enamored and satisfied with the lifestyle that we closed the book on any more cruises. Cruise brochures continued appearing in the mail, but I immediately trashed them.

Fast forward twelve years to 2016. We're getting up in age, and if we want to do any more cruising, we should start now. Many of our previous sailings had taken us to places the ships go to in the winter. That is no problem. Being in Florida, the time to escape is summer, not winter. So we started looking for a summer voyage. Enter Princess, once again, because of our history of sailing with them, they gave us some excellent perks. We thought we would try something different that would alleviate lengthy airplane flights. We could eliminate one long flight if we could find a repositioning cruise that crossed the ocean. Fly to the starting point, then take the ship back. We also decided to go for a more extended trip as long as we "were already there." Here is one. Nice and long (twenty-nine days; our previous record was twenty-one days). Fly to Amsterdam, up to a bit of Norway, bounce around some British Isles, then start heading home up north around Iceland and finally five more sea days to Boston.

This would be our second cruise that stopped in Iceland. However, this one included a stop that the previous one did not. The one word that describes this cruise is "disappointment." It hit us the first night as we sat down for dinner and read the menu. The choices did not grab us. I was more disappointed when the dishes arrived; something was missing. Our disappointment in the quality of food continued each day. We expressed it up the line through our waiter and his captain, and eventually, a meeting was arranged with the head chef and hotel manager. Nothing they said satisfied us. It was a "that's just the way it is." It was not only us; other people on the ship had the same sentiment. The consensus was that if you wanted higher quality food, you had to go on a more expensive ship. The Princess Line was always in that group, but during our twelve-year hiatus, things changed, and to us, it had a shocking effect because we did not experience it gradually.

We started to gather a list of more upscale ships for future reference. Another disappointment was the "fly-one-way-sail-back" experiment. It was five long days from Iceland to Boston. The weather was cold, and the large ship was too crowded inside. We sailed just off the tip of Greenland and near Newfoundland. Stopping at each place to break the trip up would have been nice. Oh Well! It's time to start shopping for our next cruise and "kick it up a notch."

14. 2017 - THE MEDITERRANEAN - OCEANIA LINE

We did kick it up a notch, all the way up to the top. We booked a cruise on an Oceania ship. A suite with a butler and a good itinerary that covered the highlights of the Mediterranean, the former Yugoslavian countries, plus a stop in Morocco. Now we can say that we've been to Africa. But, it was not to be. One week before we were due to sail, I developed a heart problem. I had to wear a defibrillator for three months that was being monitored and could not leave the country. Given the circumstances, we would not have been comfortable away from home anyway. A note from the doctor got us a full refund from the trip insurance we always purchase.

15. 2018 - THE WATERWAY OF THE CZARS (RUSSIAN RIVER CRUSE) VIKING LINE AND THE MEDITERRANEAN - AZAMARA LINE - 29 DAYS

One year later, we're still kicking it up a notch. We could not find the Oceania cruise we had to cancel last year. We did find a similar one for the summer. After we booked it, I wondered if I could combine it with something else, as long as we were already across the pond. We bounced it off our travel agent, and she said it was a good idea. I started shopping for something in Europe with a schedule compatible with our Mediterranean cruise.

I stumbled across a two-week Viking River cruise from St. Petersburg to Moscow. There was a four-day gap between cruises that we had to fill. We traveled with another couple and agreed to see Paris during that gap. The complete trip was twenty-nine days.

After we booked both cruises, our oldest son, David, said he would like to join us for the Viking one. He checked, and it was fully booked, but he could get on the Azamara and share our room at a meager price. It was no problem, and it added a nice touch.

Now for the highlight of each cruise. The first one was Viking. As you previously read, we had been in Leningrad twenty-nine years ago when it was part of the Soviet Union. Now it was called St. Petersburg. And there was a significant difference; it was not the downtrodden place it used to be. It was much more modern and alive. We saw the same sights and enjoyed the few days there. The following comments will capture the highlight of the cruise:

- The subdued atmosphere of the smaller Viking ship reflects their motto, "The thinking person's cruise, not the drinking person's cruise."

- The opportunity to see more of the country with daily stops along the river.

- Daily lectures on Russian history. It was like going to school each day (no quizzes).

- A visit to a Russian family's home for drinks and snacks.

- Hearing a group of five musicians playing the "Star-Spangled Banner" as we went ashore at one stop.

- One of the tour guides commented, "We Russian people are not that much different from you all. It's the government officials who tend to alienate us." This was followed by a round of applause from everybody on the bus.

- Moscow is the cleanest city we have ever seen. There was not a cigarette butt or piece of paper on the ground and not one bit of graffiti.

- Taking photos of St. Basil's Cathedral and Red Square. These are the same scenes you see on TV whenever Russia is mentioned on a news channel. How many people can say they have been there?

In summary, this cruise would also be one of our top three.

THE MEDITERRANEAN - 14 DAYS

There's no question about it: what made this cruise significant was having David with us and seeing him enjoy the ship, meals, excursions, and the entire experience. He created a professional short video capturing highlights that greatly outshines my numerous amateurish photos. And yes, the Azamara turned out to be upscale regarding the food quality, and we were back cruising as we knew and liked it.

16. 2019 - THE DANUBE RIVER - VIKING LINE - 21 DAYS

Having had such a great experience on last year's Viking Russian cruise, we booked another with them. The itinerary took us through much of Europe, which we had already seen while stationed with the Air Force in Germany. Once a year, Viking extends this cruise to include some of the countries that were once part of the Soviet Union and those that went their separate ways after the break up of Yugoslavia in the early 1990s. It goes all the way from the Black Sea to the Baltic Sea. But this was such a popular cruise. What could go wrong? Alas, wait and see, and let me count the ways!

On the day of our flight to Europe, Verna woke up with a bladder infection. Our driver was going to pick us up at 10 AM. At 6:30, we were in the ER. Verna has a recurring history of bladder infections, and the medication always takes care of it without any problem. We had a legitimate reason to cancel the trip and get our money back, but we decided not to. Mistake.

- The quality of the food on the Viking ship could have been better.

- The sight-seeing in the first few countries was depressing. They were former communist countries that had not yet recovered from that failed system.

- We immediately learned that we would have to change ships in Budapest.

- Verna's bladder infection flared up within a couple of days on the ship. It was the first time the meds did not work. Plus, I felt a case of bronchitis coming on. No doctor was on board, so we had to take a cab to see a doctor.

- My bronchitis was getting worse, and Verna started to develop a case of it. Fortunately, the ship arranged for a doctor to visit us on board.

- That same night, Verna slipped in the shower. We had trouble getting her to the bed. She did not appear to have broken any bones but was in severe pain. We brought some extra painkillers with us from a previous injury. They enabled her to get around, but she was still struggling. We erroneously concluded that she did not break anything since she could walk. We considered leaving the ship in Budapest and flying back to the States, but the arrangements were not suitable, and Verna said she would tough it out. We were also reluctant to go to a European doctor, afraid she would end up in a hospital and who knows what else. When we returned to the States, we found out that she had crushed one of her vertebrates.

- Shipmates on board and even one of the cooks offered various remedies to ease the pain, but Verna continued to struggle. She then became severely constipated from all of the painkillers. Another trip to some city to go to an ER for relief. They tried various remedies, but none were effective. We were running out of time before the ship would depart. They gave us some kind of mixture similar to the preparation before a colonoscopy to take back to the ship. When we returned to the ship, we had to get a crew member to translate the directions on the bottle. Success. Back to "normal" except still with back pain and bronchitis lingering. I started to worry about the back pain, so we made another unplanned excursion to an ER in Koblenz, Germany. We struggled with the language, and they misdiagnosed it as a "Bad bruise." Verna still had a black and blue bump on her rear.

- We had to change ships again but have yet to find out why.

- The closest we had to one good day was a Sunday when we cruised the Rhine River and viewed the picturesque castles.

That was our last cruise, and it may be our final one. We will not go to a foreign country if we ever do another. Some possibilities are the Mississippi River, Great Lakes, Alaska, and a Lobster Feast Cruise off New England. China and Japan were on our list at one time. But even before our last disastrous experience, we had scrubbed those. It is too far, and we don't relate to Far East culture. Our roots are in Europe, someplace. Southeast Asia, India, Africa, and the Middle East were never on our list.

SUMMARY

Here are a few statistics that summarize what overall was an enjoyable chunk of our life experience:

1. Total cruises - 16

2. Total days on board - 194

3. Countries visited via cruises - 30 - Argentina, Australia, Barbados, Bulgaria, Canada, Chile, Colombia, Croatia, Denmark, Finland, Jamaica, Martinique, Mexico, Monaco, Montenegro, New Zealand, Northern Ireland, Norway, Panama, Puerto

Rico, Romania, Russia. St. Barts. St. Maarten, Scotland, Serbia, Slovenia, Spain, Sweden, Uruguay.

An additional 16 countries were visited via other travel: Austria, Bahamas, Belgium, Bermuda, Czech Republic, England, France, Germany, Greece, Hungary, Italy, Ireland, Luxembourg, Netherlands, Switzerland, and Vatican City.

The total number of countries is 46, which is about 25% of the world's total number of countries.

4. Crossed the Equator.

5. Crossed the International Date Line.

6. Farthest distance traveled north: 66 degrees of the 90 degrees of latitude to the top of the world.

7. The farthest distance traveled south: 55 degrees of 90 degrees of latitude to the bottom of the world.

8. Farthest distance traveled east: 115 degrees of longitude to Moscow.

9. Farthest distance traveled west: 135 degrees of longitude to Sydney.

10. Given the 360 degrees for the circumference of the Earth, we covered 250 degrees, which is about two-thirds of the way around the world. We almost made it! It was a good run!

OUR FIRST CRUISE (NO FRILLS!)

Taken at our senior class outing.

FIRST PRINCESS CRUISE

Meeting the captain

73. HOME FOR THE HOLIDAYS (SOMETIMES)

CHRISTMAS 2021

I was not attending Memoir Writing meetings because of the risks associated with COVID-19. However, I occasionally got e-mails from the leader of our group. Around Christmas time, she gave the group an assignment to write a "Christmas Memoir." I did not have to because I'm not attending the meetings to read it. Nevertheless, I thought about the assignment a little. Although I referenced Christmas in a few of my earlier stories, that would not have satisfied the assignment. The assignment did create a spark that inspired me to think about my Christmases past. The more I thought about it, the more I began to develop a story that traces my Christmas experiences over the last eighty-plus years. I will naturally start at the beginning. In some instances, I will describe a specific Christmas; in others, I will group a series of them into a common memory. Here they are.

EARLIEST MEMORY

I must have been about age four. It was Christmas Eve at my grandmother's house. I have a very faint image in my mind. We were gathered in the formal dining room, used only for special occasions. It was dimly lit. My only other memory is the words coming from my older brother saying, "Tommy got the tie." There was an exchange of gifts. Tommy was a border in my grandmother's house. He had his bedroom, made his meals, and ate them in a finished basement with a coal stove, refrigerator, sink, etc. I guess on this special occasion, he was treated as a family member.

ELEMENTARY SCHOOL YEARS

There is one particular memory. I can't pinpoint my age, probably seven or eight. It was a few weeks before Christmas. My older brother wanted to attend a high school basketball game but did not have the twenty-five cents to get in. He told me that if I gave him a quarter, he would show me where my Christmas presents were. I gave him the quarter (I have no idea how I happened to have a quarter). He showed me where the presents were. It was not the "telling moment" for shattering my belief in Santa Claus. I don't recall ever having that moment. The presents (not wrapped) included an erector set, a Flash Gordon space pistol, Lincoln Logs, and a "President Game." I don't recall how I faked my surprise on Christmas morning.

A second specific memory covering every Christmas Eve meal was eating "*Babalki*." These were little dough balls about the size of a large grape. They were baked as bread, boiled in water, and mixed with poppy seed or cottage cheese. I liked them. The other part of the meal was mushroom soup, which I also liked.

One more specific memory concerns an Eastern European (Czech) tradition. Very early on Christmas Eve morning, young men walked through the neighborhood. If they saw a light on in a kitchen, it could very well be the woman of the house preparing the baked goods for the Christmas Eve meal. The young man knocked on the door, and when it was opened, he recited this Christmas Greeting in the Slovak language called "Vinchea." That's the word that sticks in my mind. I researched and discovered that " Merry Christmas" in Slovak is "*Vesele Vianoce*," which is close enough. The little old lady gives the young man a few coins and then goes to the next house with a light in the kitchen. I never did that, but my older brother did. He would come home with a couple of bucks.

A favorite treat of mine during those early years was homemade nut rolls and nut fingers, generically called "*kolacki*." I remember the feeling of coming in from sledding and scarfing down a few. My wife, Verna, keeps that baking tradition alive. Her Lithuanian family made kolacki. Our niece, Andrea, is picking up that baton and will carry the tradition for another generation on the Klapal side of the family. There are no takers yet on the Kolman side.

A final Christmas memory from my elementary school years was the Altar Boy experiences that I described in detail in that story.

HIGH SCHOOL YEARS

As mentioned in a few previous stories, my high school days were dominated by work and not learning. First, I somehow assumed the responsibility of decorating our tree and doing the outside decorations. Secondly, Christmas morning was no longer running downstairs to check under the tree (that was only a one-time experience). Christmas morning now consisted of getting up at five, jumping on my bike, and delivering the morning paper. I do specifically remember the first Christmas morning I did that. It was clear but bitterly cold. The papers were extra thick that day with all of the "After-Christmas sales." I had trouble folding them. I did a little research and discovered that Christmas that year was on a Thursday; the following year, it was on a Friday; and the third year, it was on a Saturday. Christmas 1955, the last Christmas of my four-year paperboy career, was a Sunday. I could sleep in on Christmas morning (there was no morning paper on Sundays). Merry Christmas. One final note: during my last two high school years, I had this extra job working on a 7-UP soda delivery truck on Saturdays and the Christmas season, so I had to get up at three-thirty in the morning, not five during those pre-Christmas days.

1956 AIR FORCE - TENNESSEE

This was my first Christmas away from home and alone. I was stationed at a radar site in the hills of Tennessee. I was working shift work, but I remember not being at work on Christmas Eve. I called my parents from a pay phone (costly) to wish them a Merry Christmas. Verna and I had been going steady for about a year, and I missed her more than my family.

1957 - PENNSYLVANIA

I was still stationed in Tennessee. I was going home for Christmas. One of my friends had a car, so a few of us who lived between Tennessee and Pennsylvania chipped in for gas and made the trip. I had to take a bus from where the guy with the car lived to my house. The major event of that Christmas was my "botched-up" proposal to Verna to marry me (previous story).

1958 - PENNSYLVANIA

From this point on, my stories became Verna's and my stories. Verna and I got married in June 1958. Verna's older brother, Sonny, had a bad car accident in July, and her parents were having a difficult time with other problems. As Christmas approached, Verna was highly distraught. This would be her first Christmas away from her family. We had to get home. We were financially strapped. We rounded up a couple of guys who wanted to go north for Christmas. We charged them way too little for door-to-door service. I drove nineteen hours from Tennessee to Pennsylvania (old US Route 11, now I-81). The trip was well worth it. Details are in a previous story.

1959 AND 1960 - PENNSYLVANIA

I had gotten a transfer from Tennessee to Pennsylvania, and we were living with Verna's family. These were pleasant Christmas memories. There was a problem with getting the barroom customers to leave so we all could sit down for the traditional extended family Christmas Eve dinner. The bar being closed on Christmas Day was a welcomed break for her family. I was still in the Air Force, working shifts at a radar site. I could only get Christmas or New Year's off and had to work twelve-hour shifts for the other days. I was lucky to get Christmas off for both of those years.

1961 - ICELAND/PENNSYLVANIA

In August 1961, I was transferred to a radar site in Iceland. Verna was pregnant, and our first child was to be born in November. David was born on November 26. I put in for leave from the middle of December to after New Year's. David was Christened before Christmas. He was the best present we received that Christmas.

1962 - BEALE AFB CALIFORNIA

David was a little over one year old. We could not afford to fly home, and a car trip across the country would take too much time. Plus, we were shell-shocked for the harrowing trip we had just made that summer (previous story). It was Verna's first Christmas away from her family. I don't remember the details of how badly she felt. Her mother flew out to see us, but it was after Christmas Day. Perhaps knowing that her mother would be coming soon helped ease her pain and sadness.

1963 - TRUAX AFB WISCONSIN/PENNSYLVANIA

In July of 1963, I was transferred from California to Wisconsin. We were much closer to Verna's home, so we drove there for Christmas. Once again, I had to be back to work the twelve-hour shifts during New Year's. Ironically, the distance was within ten miles, the same as the Tennessee trip was. I don't remember us stopping on the way to Pennsylvania, but on the return trip, we had to pull over on the side of the road in the middle of the night for me to catch a few winks.

1964, 65, & 66 - SYRACUSE/PENNSYLVANIA

I was scheduled to start attending classes at Syracuse University in January 1965. Perfect timing! We left Wisconsin a couple of days before Christmas for Pennsylvania. Our mobile home would arrive in Syracuse a few days later. Verna's younger brother Raymond and I scooted up there to make the arrangements regarding its relocation. We had planned on returning to Pennsylvania on the same day, but there were complications, and we had to spend the night in a motel there. After spending the holidays with Verna's family, she, her father, and I went to Syracuse to set up our mobile home (water, electricity, heat, etc.) We had three good Christmas's in a row. There was no school during Christmas, so we made it to Verna's house, which was only about three hours away.

1967 AND 1968 - OXNARD AFB/PENNSYLVANIA

I graduated from Syracuse University in January 1967. My next assignment was Oxnard AFB in southern California. We were now in a much better financial situation and could afford to fly home with our two boys for Christmas. I am drawing a blank because I do not recall any specifics of these two Christmases. I do remember us flying home for one of them, and I don't recall putting up a Christmas tree in our mobile home in December '67. I went to our photo albums, and there are pictures of Christmas '67 at Verna's parents' house. One picture shows David and Kevin standing by the Christmas tree with a train layout. By Christmas '68, we had sold our mobile home and lived in base housing. I don't remember putting up a tree in that house, but at the same time, there are no photos, only videos, of Christmas at Verna's parents' home in 1968. In conclusion, we had to have been there. I surmise that being there had become the new norm; otherwise, there would have been some "out-of-the-ordinary" circumstances that I would have remembered. All of this brings us to a new situation.

1969 - ZWEIBRUCKEN, GERMANY

In the summer of 1969, we were transferred to Germany. About two weeks before Christmas, we had to move from one base to another in Zweibrucken. There was no "Home for the Holidays" this year. We had to get settled, and I was under a lot of pressure to create a Procurement Office out of nothing (previous story). Plus, Verna had her hands full setting up our new living quarters. A great deal of activity kept us busy, and I guess that took some of the sting out of not being home. Verna had the apartment all set up, we had our Christmas tree, and we overwhelmed the boys with presents.

1970 - PENNSYLVANIA

Flew "Home for the Holidays." You get the picture.

1971 - ZWEIBRUCKEN

We bit the bullet for this one and stayed in Germany. We would be returning to the States within six months anyway.

1972 - STILL IN GERMANY

To our dismay, in early 1972, the Air Force added another year to our tour in Germany. We planned to go to Verna's parents' home for this Christmas. But her father passed away in November. We flew home but had to return to Germany for Christmas. It was a sad Christmas for all.

1973 - 2003 - BACK HOME NEW JERSEY

It is our best assignment yet. I am approaching the end of a twenty-plus career in the Air Force. We are in a good financial position, living in our first brand-new home (without wheels) and ninety minutes from Verna's parents. Life is good! This was the beginning of a thirty-year run of "Home for the Holidays" that generated plenty of good memories for everyone. As I mentioned at the beginning of this story, my purpose is not to dive into the details of each Christmas. I only want to trace the circumstances associated with each and show the various scenarios each presented.

2004 - 2021 - THE VILLAGES FLORIDA

The beginning of another new run of Christmas's with a different twist. We arrived in The Village in the summer of 2004. This was our first Christmas in thirty years without the rest of the family. It was too much to swallow. So, we traveled to New Jersey for the 2004 Christmas season. However, after that, Christmas took on a different feeling. We are somewhat ashamed to say that we began to dread the season. We found ourselves in a "survivor" mode. Make it through Christmas Eve and the next day, and then we will be home-free for the remainder of the year. It had come to that. Somewhere along the line, we did go up north for one Christmas. More recently, the COVID-19 and Verna's health situation further dampened the spirit, and we are becoming more bummed out. One bright spot is our dear friend, "Alexa," and FaceTime helps us see and talk to family members. Our oldest son, David, sends us unusual gifts each Christmas. This year, to get the most out of the experience, we got Alexa to bring us together as we opened our presents. Suddenly, something hit me: "What goes around comes around." I told David that when he and Kevin were toddlers, we made their Christmas by getting them presents and enjoying their joy. Now, fifty-plus years later, one is getting joy from giving us joy and excitement at Christmas. I broke down and shed a tear or two.

2022 - THE VILLAGES FLORIDA

A significant development occurred during the summer of 2022. I explained it in a future story. It amounts to us being in the process of selling our home in The Villages during the Christmas season. Christmas 2022 would be our last one in The Villages and our final one to spend without family members after a long time.

2023 - BEVERWYCK INDEPENDENT LIVING, UPSTATE NEW YORK

I have to get ahead of myself for a bit. I want to continue the theme of this story and bring it up to date. In the following stories, I outlined our relocation. For this story, I just want to focus on Christmas 2023. Our son, David, was in a Boston hospital during the Christmas season being treated for cancer. This was not what we expected when we relocated. We had visions of a long-awaited family Christmas. However, our first Christmas in our new lifestyles was shared with residents in our independent living facility. Total strangers, we had not met until March of 2023, but now an integral part of our daily routine. Although we had relatives nearby in New Jersey and Pennsylvania, we used the Christmas season to visit David and spend time with his children (Thomas and Ellen, our grandchildren) as we all visited David in the hospital along with Thomas and his wife Maggie, and Ellen and her fiance Jose. Thomas prepared a great five-course dinner for the six of us during that visit. We did have a family gathering, if not on Christmas Eve and Christmas Day, but at least during the season. However, a large cloud was hanging over the occasion because of David's situation and his significant other, Donna, not being at the table. In the back of our minds was, "Christmas 2024?"

2024 - SOUTH CAROLINA

Once again, you will have to hold off until you get to some of the following stories to understand Christmas 2024. We had somewhat lost the spirit of Christmas during 2024 because of what happened to David and Verna's cancer taking a turn for the worse. In the summer of that year, our son Kevin suggested we visit South Carolina to spend Christmas with his family. We mentally noted the invitation but did not commit. As the season approached and the deadline for making travel plans was near, we decided to go for four nights. A couple of weeks before our departure date, Verna had a bad bronchial condition and a case of urinary tract infection, so it was a "touch and go" situation. Fortunately, she recovered, and we made the trip.

We had not been to South Carolina and seen one of Kevin's sons, Ryan, for seven years. We had seen the remainder of Kevin's family during the last year and a half.

It was a "Christmas with Family," and we caught up on what was going on with Kevin, Andrea, and our grandchildren. We enjoyed the meals, snacks, and drinks. Trevor (Kevin and Andrea's oldest child) suggested starting an annual tradition of everyone painting a Christmas ornament, which was a good idea. We played a few hands of a new card game. Verna and I received gifts from Kevin, Andrea, and their children, which we did not expect. One gift was a golf-putting game. The night before we left, we had a putting contest that everyone participated in. Kevin and I tied for first place and had to play an extra round, which Kevin won. Perhaps another annual Christmas tradition. I am writing his story the day after our return home. Although Verna had no physical health episodes, she was physically and emotionally drained from the trip.

It was a good trip, and after a twenty-year run of "Home Alone for Christmas," it was a good shot in the arm. But once again, we can't help but ask, "Christmas 2025?"

FIRST CHRISTMAS MARRIED - 1958

HOME FOR CHRISTMAS - 1964

CHRISTMAS 2024

Left to right: Kevin (our son) - Andrea (Kevin's wife) - Verna - Jack - Trevor (Kevin and Andrea's son) - Ryan (Kevin and Andrea's son) - Anna (Ryan's girlfriend) - Olivia (Kevin and Andrea's daughter).

74. HER BALL AND CHAIN AND MY ACHILLES' HEEL

Let me say a few words about the title to set the stage for this story. A ball and chain limits one's freedom to move or do things. We are all familiar with the image of a ball and chain attached to prisoners. Achilles' Heel is a weakness or a soft spot despite overall strength, which can lead to downfall.

Now, on to our stories; they would be more accurate and complete if I had better records. We are both eighty-six years old. Suppose we had a record of every time we went to a doctor or a hospital. How old were we at the time, and what was the purpose of the visit? It would make interesting reading by itself. I will not try to construct such a record; it's unnecessary to make my point, which is in the title of this story.

I will discuss Verna first and then tell you about myself. Our stories have a different pattern. Her story will have two parts: the past and the present. The best I can do about the past is to list the health issues Verna dealt with starting from as far back as she can remember the experience. As you know, we started going together in high school and married just before we turned twenty. So that's only one-fourth of the eighty-six years we have been alive. This means that I have first-hand experience with her health issues for three-fourths of her life. The list is not in correct chronological order and does not have to be.

tonsillectomy

appendectomy

upset stomach-mostly during her teenage years

convulsions

knee pain - started in childhood and continues today

heart murmur

mononucleosis

bronchitis - almost an annual event

hysterectomy

"female" problems

thyroidectomy

bladder infection - recurring

food poisoning - more than once

cold urticaria - allergic to cold weather and cold water

Dupuytren - one or more fingers stay bent toward the palm

skin cancer- an ongoing battle, she finds the suspicious spot herself

swollen ankles

migraine headaches

blood clots

trouble breathing

osteoporosis

foot spurs

blood disorders

in-grown toenails

multiple myeloma

partial knee-replacement

laminectomy

breast cancer

mastectomy

That is quite a list! One of Verna's recurring comments about her well-being is, "I never just have one thing wrong." Another one is, "I never get anything normal." And a third, "I wish I had just one day without a health issue." When Verna tells someone about one of her health issues, the usual response is, "But you look great." She always does because she is meticulous about her hair, never has spotted or wrinkled clothes, and doesn't overdue the makeup. She hardly has any wrinkles. I tell people if she only felt half as good as she looks, she would be great.

Now for the present part of her story. The present starts in March

2019. That's when things started to go downhill. Not that she was the picture of health before that. We were in Pennsylvania visiting Verna's brother, Sonny, who was failing and died during that visit. We were sitting on a sofa, and when we both got up, we heard a loud snap from Verna's left shoulder. I thought it got out of place, so she started to rotate it, but her pain was excruciating. A visit to the ER disclosed that she had broken her clavicle. Nothing to do about it but keep it immobile and let it heal on its own. As soon as we arrived home, we made an appointment with an orthopedic, Dr. Tangston, who confirmed that the best thing to do is to let it heal on its own. He then referred us to another orthopedic, Dr. Thomas, who specializes in osteoporosis, to find out why her clavicle broke for no apparent reason. That led to a series of other tests and office visits to find out why Verna was suffering from knee and back pain.

We were on a Danube River cruise about four months after the broken clavicle. During that cruise, Verna had four medical mishaps requiring doctor/hospital visits: bronchitis, bladder infection, constipation, and broken vertebrae. The broken vertebrae began the prolonged problem. Verna fell in the shower, and although she was in excruciating pain, we erroneously assumed that nothing had been broken. So she lived on pain pills we brought with us. There was no doctor on the ship, and we were afraid to see a doctor along the way because we did not want to end up in a hospital in a foreign country. Verna toughed it out but finally could not take it anymore, so we went to an urgent care facility. The diagnosis was a "bad bruise." No x-rays were taken. We finally made it home and immediately made an appointment to see Dr. Thomas. Vertebrae L4 (lower back) was shattered. No wonder there was so much pain and not subsiding. Verna had to get an injection of an epoxy substance into the cavity of the vertebrae to repair, seal, and stabilize it. The pain in her back did not go away.

The doctor who injected suggested a chiropractor, but that did not relieve the pain. At one of the subsequent visits to Dr. Thomas, after Verna gave up on the chiropractor, the doctor asked if Verna had fallen because an X-ray showed damage to vertebrae L5 just below L4. We highly suspect that the chiropractor did it. She got another injection of epoxy to stabilize L5. We dare not tell Dr. Thomas that Verna went to a chiropractor; she would have fired us. During this period, Verna also underwent physical therapy for her knee. Also, she felt a lump on the side of her temple at about the same time frame. She always finds those things. The dermatologist said it was a cyst. All of the above brings us to the end of 2019.

Shortly into 2020, our son, David, in upstate New York, was diagnosed with lymphoma and was in the hospital. We immediately went up to be there for him. Verna was scheduled for a bone density test in February. We scooted home for the test, and Verna was concerned about the cyst on her temple. Once again, the dermatologist said to keep an eye on it. Verna had the bone density test and another MRI of her back. Then we flew back to be with David.

We returned home in early March to get the results of the bone density test and the MRI, plus see the dermatologist. When we picked up the phone to call Dr. Thomas, we received a message that she was out of the office until the end of March. We tried to contact someone else in the practice, but nobody answered. We surmised that the facility was shut down because of COVID-19, so we were dead in the water. We finally got our primary care physician, Dr. Cheema, to obtain a copy of the tests. Verna did not have full-blown osteoporosis, but because of the issues with her lower spine, Dr. Cheema referred Verna to a rheumatologist, who in turn referred us to an endocrinologist. We never did understand the reason for that. Verna got even more worried about the "cyst" and wanted the dermatologist, Dr. Tran, to remove it. He said it was considered elective surgery, and because of COVID-19, he could not do it. A few weeks later, Verna insisted that he look at it. She had an appointment on Monday, April 20. I remember the date well because it turned out to be a disaster.

Verna went to the dermatologist by herself because we assumed it would be a minor cut to obtain a sample to send out for a biopsy. At about one PM, I received a frantic call from Dr. Tran's office that I had to come immediately and take Verna to the ER because they could not stop the bleeding. It was not a cyst; it was a cancerous tumor. We don't know why they did not call an ambulance for her. I picked Verna up, and she had to hold a large wad of gauze on her temple; the blood was gushing out. It took about eight minutes to get to the ER. They rushed her in, but I could not get past the main entrance because of COVID-19. I sat on a bench at the entrance of the hospital and then decided to come home. At about six PM, I received a call from the hospital. They were able to stop the bleeding but were going to evacuate Verna by helicopter to a hospital in Gainesville. They said they did this because although they stopped the bleeding, they were afraid that if it started up again, they would not be able to control it. There was nothing for me to do except hope and pray. They told me to go there in the morning and that I would probably be able to take Verna home. I did, and we were back home on Tuesday.

Now, I need to digest the bad news and obtain more information. We had already received the shock that it was cancer. Dr. Tran immediately knew that from the way it bled. He even made a preliminary diagnosis that it was in the blood and bones. He expedited the biopsy, and within a day, it was diagnosed as multiple myeloma. Myeloma means in the bones and multiple, indicating more than one place. It is not curable but treatable. Dr. Tran referred Verna to a hematologist/oncologist, Dr. Reyes. By coincidence, Verna had seen him years prior for blood/bone marrow concerns.

Dr. Reyes started treatment in early May. It was a three-part plan: weekly injections, daily heavy-duty chemo pills, and steroids. The steroids became a problem; they were ten a day for four days every week. Verna was getting too wired from them, so we asked why they could not be spread out; Dr. Reyes said he'd go one better and stop them altogether. Verna had a PET scan before the treatment started, and it showed lesions in three parts of her body. About two months into the treatment plan, Dr. Reyes had a blood test conducted, which showed that she had improved by 90%. He performed that test every few months, and Verna held that line on the chart. Her routine had been going on for a little over a year. Every week, she got blood work and an injection of chemo for three weeks, then skipped a week. She took the heavy-duty chemo pill every day for three weeks, then skipped a week. At the end of one year of treatment, Verna had a follow-up PET scan. The good news was that the lesions were no longer there. Dr. Reyes was delighted, and so were we. She no longer needed the injection nor the chemo pills and was in remission.

Back to the knee and back problems. Since we could not put our finger on what was causing the pain, we concluded that the cancer was causing it. We bounced that off Dr. Reyes, and he said it was not based on the good blood tests and the PET scan. He referred us to an orthopedic specialist who specializes in cancer patients. He had the same conclusion: the pains are not being caused by the cancer. We asked Dr. Reyes what we do now. He referred Verna to a pain management specialist. She gave Verna an epidural and prescribed some painkillers. After a few weeks and no results, we had another visit to her, but she did not give us any satisfaction, so we found another pain management specialist, Dr. Deluca. He gave Verna a couple of epidurals and prescribed different painkillers. Since no progress was made, Dr. Deluca's office referred her to a neurosurgeon, Dr. Reddy.

An MRI disclosed that Verna had pinched nerves in her spinal column. The procedure (laminectomy) was performed, and Dr. Reddy claimed that the problem in her back was solved, which should also help the knees. Verna did get some relief but still had pain in her lower back and knees. Dr. Reddy said that it would take six months to a year for the results of his surgery to take full effect. Verna did not find that acceptable; her knees were still painful, especially the right one. We went back to Dr. Deluca's office, and they prescribed other painkiller meds and physical therapy. After ten therapy sessions, the pains were getting worse instead of better. Verna had it with the therapy and made an appointment with an orthopedic surgeon, Dr. Williams, to concentrate on her right knee. Verna had a partial knee replacement on that knee about eight years ago. Dr. Williams had an X-ray taken, and the diagnosis was that a total knee replacement was necessary. He advised us to think about it. Nothing is urgent, but it is the only solution to the right knee problem. The left knee is not as bad. He did suggest that since Verna had major surgery only three months ago, she should hold off for a bit longer. That brings us to September 9, 2021. I will continue this grim tale in a future story.

As I reconstructed the above information covering a little over two years, I realized that all of the painful episodes, endurances, surgeries, medical appointments, medications, etc., have dominated our lifestyle the entire period. Let alone the limitations laid on us by COVID-19. Just for the heck of it, I went through the previous year's calendar to see how many medical appointments Verna had in 2020. There were one hundred and ten, which did not include dental or eye-related ones—no wonder we are overwhelmed. At one point, Verna and I had eight medical appointments in one week.

I'll follow the same pattern for my story by summarizing my health history and then going into more detail regarding my current condition. Here is a list of health issues in my past:

- As a baby, I had a severe illness and almost died. That is what my father told me when I was a young adult. It is the only fatherly thing he ever said to me. I was so shocked to hear him be so fatherly that I failed to ask him for more information about his meaning.

- tonsillectomy

- measles

- scarlet fever

- With pains in my legs, I remember my parents taking me to a doctor by the name of Robinhold, I used to call him Robinhood. He also made house calls with his little black bag and left a tiny envelope with pills in it. That must have been when I had scarlet fever and measles.

- rheumatic fever twice

- prostate cancer, in remission after forty-two radiation treatments, still gets checked every three months

- removal of a small section of my large intestine because of polyps

- borderline diabetic

Although it is nowhere near as extensive as Verna's, you already know how different we are in this category of our lives. That's a bit ironic because we are more similar than different in many other ways.

My "current" story covers a much more extended period than Verna's current situation. While I elaborated on two years for her, mine is stretched over about twenty-eight years. I don't have any record of an exact date, but the best estimate I can come up with is me at age sixty-five (2003). I happened to have an appointment with our family physician, Dr. Miller, in New Jersey for routine blood work. At the time of my visit to his office, I had back pain from moving rocks. As the nurse called my name in the waiting room, I struggled to get up from the chair. Dr. Miller noticed this and asked what the problem was; I told him my back was bothering me. He gave me some sample Vioxx pills. I took some that night. I had an awful night; something strange was going on in my body. I prayed to God that I wouldn't have to call 911. I got out of bed and sat in a chair for a while, then got back in bed and made it through the night. It was a Monday night. In the morning, Verna went to play golf (Tuesday is ladies' day). She told me to go and see Dr. Miller. I had a nine AM appointment. I don't remember how it all came about, but he gave me an EKG, and the next thing I knew, he said I had a silent heart attack. I never understood that phrase. He also said my heart was racing way too fast and I should go to the ER. I felt okay. I don't recall if he said anything about an ambulance, but I drove to the ER. To save a few bucks, I did not park in the hospital parking lot but on a side street within walking distance of the hospital. When I walked into the ER and told them why I was there, they were all over me: no name, paperwork, nothing. They plopped me on a bed and said I'd be okay. Shortly after they completed their routine, they asked if there was anybody I'd like them to call. I asked them what time it was. They told me, and I mentally calculated what hole of the golf course Verna would be on. I estimated she would not be finished yet, so I told the nurse no.

A little later, when I figured Verna would be finished with her round of golf, I told the nurse how to contact Verna. It turns out that Verna was only on the sixteenth hole. She got the message, rushed home, and had her brother Raymond's wife, Carol, drive her to the hospital. When she got to the hospital and saw me, she chewed me out for interrupting her round of golf. Just kidding! She cried when she saw me. It turns out the Vioxx was subsequently found to cause cardiovascular problems and was eventually taken off the market. Was it just a coincidence with the Vioxx and me, or was I having heart issues anyway? We don't know. From that episode on, I've been under the care of a cardiologist. There are two more episodes in my story.

Sometime around 2012, while I was being seen regularly by a cardiologist, something triggered my need to wear a heart monitor. It must have been the result of a stress test. One morning, Verna and I sat on our lanai, watching the golfers go by. A friend of ours was a marshal (ambassador in The Villages). As he drove by on duty, he pulled up to say hello. He asked about the gadget I was wearing. As I explained it to him, Verna and I noticed it was not working. We checked all of the connections, and nothing seemed wrong. I called the company as indicated if there's a problem with the monitor. The answer I received was that Dr. Upadia had it turned off. I did not recognize the name, and they could not tell me anymore. We immediately hung up and called my cardiologist's office. There was no answer, and I had to leave a message, but there was no response that day. The next day, I was laying some cinder landscape blocks around our house. I was cutting them with a saw and covered in dust. Suddenly, Verna came out with the phone and said my cardiologist's office was on the line. The message was that my heart rate was dangerously low (in the thirties at night), and I had to get to the ER ASAP. I asked Tom, our next-door neighbor, to put my tools away and clean the driveway. I took a shower, and Verna drove me to the ER. While in the ER, the alarm they had hooked up to me kept going off. They finally got me admitted with a crash cart alongside the bed. They said I needed a pacemaker but could not operate on me until my blood thickens (I was on a blood thinner). A nurse walked in with a piece of paper during the few days I was waiting. She said, "Let me show you this." It was a printout of my heartbeat. She explained that I would have four somewhat regular beats, then my heart would stop for four and a half seconds, then kick in. She said I was about one-half second away from it not starting again. I still shutter every time I tell that story.

Dr. Upadia saw another patient in the same room as I was being discharged. He recognized my name and said, "So you are the guy who kept waking me at night." He was the doctor in the practice assigned to take such alarms the night he had my device turned off. I wish I had responded, "And you are the doctor who almost let me die." After that incident, I lost all faith and respect for that office and found another one. I could have sued them, but no pain or suffering was involved. However, had I died, Verna would have had a strong malpractice case.

Episode three, five years later, it's 2017. I was working in the yard on a Saturday morning. It was early summer and, of course, hot. I was getting short of breath and didn't feel normal. We called my cardiologist's office for whoever was on call; the doctor who answered told me to take an extra heart med, not to do anything strenuous, and to come into the office Monday morning. When we saw my cardiologist Monday morning, he scheduled an angiogram for a few days later that week. He also said not to do anything strenuous, but if I had any chest pain or sensation in my left arm, to call 911. I did as I was told. Tuesday evening at about ten, we were watching TV in our recliners. I started feeling sweaty, a sensation in my left arm, and slightly chest pain. Verna called 911. They said they were on their way and for me to take aspirin but chew it and swallow it, so it dissolves faster. I changed clothes, Verna did the same, and called our neighbor to drive her to the ER. The ambulance arrived in minutes. They rang the doorbell, and I answered. They asked if I was the patient, but said the patient usually lies on the floor. I said, "Wait a second, I'll get on the floor." They didn't think that was funny. I remember they asked me many questions as they did their routine. They gave me the customary nitro pill to put under my tongue. As they drove away from the house, I told them I felt fine and to take me back home. They did not listen.

After I was admitted, they said that they were going to do the angiogram and, if necessary, an angioplasty at the same time. It turns out that I had 90% blockage in a main artery, so they inserted a stent. Then, they sent me home with an external defibrillator to wear for ninety days. After ninety days, they would determine if I needed one internally. The device consisted of a vest with a pocket for a battery and a series of sensors placed on my upper torso. If the sensors indicated that I was going into cardiac arrest, the unit would shock me, and I would be okay. A technician gave us detailed instructions on the procedures before we left the hospital.

The first thing I did when we got home was take a shower. I was allowed to remove the device while I took a shower. We messed up and forgot to disconnect the battery while it was off, and the alarm went off while it was lying on the bed. We panicked but then remembered that little step. Of course, I had to wear it while I slept, and the battery lying between Verna and me became a nuisance. If I felt a vibration on my back, I had about seven seconds to push a button to cancel the shock. They said you don't want to be shocked if you don't need it because it would be painful. If you feel the vibration, it's a false alarm, and you don't need to be shocked. You only need it if you don't feel it because you would have already passed out. If you need it, it will do its thing, and you will recover on the floor or ground and ask what happened after you recovered. A few times in bed, I got false alarms and had to push the button quickly.

I was also told not to let anyone pat me on the back or stand in a store doorway with a theft-sensing device because these two things would trigger a false alarm. Another warning was not for anybody to touch me while I was being knocked down because they would feel the same jolt. One time, I was just a second or two from disarming the device and heard this message from the unit. "Passersby, do not interfere." It was a long, hot summer. I had numerous false alarms, and that in itself was enough to give me a heart attack. I had a spare vest, so we had to launder one by hand occasionally. I also had to clean the sensors with an alcohol wipe and put a cream on them. The company sent me a smaller vest to help alleviate the false alarms because the vest is designed to press the sensors tightly against your body. I continued to do my yard work and play golf. Verna helped me mix cement and carry it for a stepping-stone project I was working on. We worked in the early morning. If the vest got too wet from sweat, it would trigger a false alarm. I never really needed to be shocked for the ninety days, but my cardiologist said it would be better to have the defibrillator installed permanently. It has been in me since then. It's programmed into my iPhone and is downloaded every night with info going to my cardiologist. Once a year, I go to a technician who checks a few things to ensure everything is okay. My previous pacemaker was set at sixty heartbeats a minute. This one is cranked up to seventy. I periodically get an ultrasound of my heart. My ejection fraction in the beginning was thirty to thirty-five percent, which was too low. It's a measure of the efficiency of your heart as a pump. After a year or so, my fraction went up to forty to forty-five, so that's an improvement. A normal reading is fifty to fifty-five. The device is its own continuous EKG. I had a stress test a few months ago and passed that. I have no adverse symptoms like dizziness, chest pain, or shortness of breath. Thank you, God. Pacemakers came into use in 1960. Where would I be without technology?

So, there you have it. Verna with her ball and chain, "something that limits one's freedom" (golfing, cooking, baking, simply walking without pain). She constantly struggles dragging the ball and chain around. And I, with my Achilles heel, "weakness despite overall strength." I can physically do anything I need or want to, but the old ticker is on my mind as I go my merry ole way. Please don't stop yet. Talk about life experiences; we are having them, and they are not good, especially for Verna!

75. LIFESTYLE

2004 - 2023

"Lifestyle" is a theme The Villages developers incorporate into everything they do and say. For example, they say, "You're not buying a house, you're buying a lifestyle." As I draw near the completion of my memoirs, it occurs to me that except for a few stories, I have not said much about the nineteen years we enjoyed the Villages Lifestyle. The term is one I have never used much before. But I guess you can say that the twenty-plus years Verna and I spent in the Air Force and the thirty-plus years we lived in New Jersey constituted two distinct lifestyles. But even within those two time periods, the lifestyles were not constant. This story will be somewhat of an assortment of activities, routines, experiences, events, etc. I guess you can say that those are elements of a lifestyle.

WELCOME — On August 18, 2004, we put the key in the door and took our first step into our new home (lifestyle). We were so excited and pleased with how it all came together from the home-order process and all those choices. We did well. We headed straight for the lanai and the $105,000 view (lifestyle) we purchased. The second time we looked, the cost was down to $52,500. After nineteen years, the price per peek is probably pennies, which is money well spent.

As we admired the view, our next-door neighbors on the right side, Mary Kay and Tom McCracken, introduced themselves through the screen on their lanai. They said they were anxiously waiting for us to move in. We are within months of the same age. Mary Kay said she was not the Mary Kay of cosmetic fame. When we got into our house, Verna said she (Mary Kay) had a facelift. After we got to know them better, Mary Kay said that she said the same thing about Verna, "She had a facelift." For the record, neither of them did.

BUNCO — We never heard of it until we moved to The Villages. Bunco is a dice game generally played with twelve or more players divided into groups of four, trying to score points while taking turns rolling three dice in a series of six rounds. A bunco is achieved when a person rolls three-of-a-kind, and all three numbers match the round number. It's a stupid game with absolutely zero skill and 100% chance. However, it lends itself to socializing. Everybody chips in $5, distributed based on most buncos and other criteria. Our bunco group comprised the friends we met when we first arrived in The Villages. We played once a month on Sunday evenings and rotated at each other's house. Dessert is served at the end with coffee (no alcohol). It was a fun thing that lasted a few years but petered out. It transitioned to just going out for dinner once a month.

GOLF — We came here to play golf and jumped right in. Eighteen holes on Fridays with the O'Donnells (who were instrumental in getting us there). Eighteen holes on Saturday with our left-side neighbors, Long Island Jack and his wife, Katherine. We gave him that nickname to distinguish him from me (Jack). We always went out for dinner at the country club where we played. Verna's recurring comment at dinner was, "We are so blessed," and it became the neighborhood slogan. Long Island Jack passed away. He had a great voice and did karaoke regularly. Verna jokingly became his manager. He made us a CD of his songs, which sound very professional. Finally, we played eighteen holes on Sunday with Pen and Judy. Pen had been a minister. We also ate out with them after golf. Pen passed away before Long Island Jack.

That run of Friday, Saturday, and Sunday came to an end one at a time because of the two deaths. In addition to those three weekly rounds, Verna and I played a nine-hole Executive course some other days. Also, Verna played a Lady's Day scramble every Wednesday morning. She chipped in $3 for a lowest-score prize and "closest to the pin" prize on a designated hole. I kept records of her winnings until she stopped (for health reasons). She was $744 ahead. One day, she came home with $80.

After the Friday, Saturday, and Sunday routine petered out, we had to find other couples to play with. Verna had met Bev on Lady's Day. She and Verna paired up on a Lady's Executive Tournament and won, thanks to Verna sinking a thirty-plus foot put on the last hole. We started playing eighteen holes with Bev and her husband, Mike, once or twice weekly. They had a part-time side career of marshaling at PGA and LPGA events. They received free rounds at championship courses in the Orlando area and invited us to join them as a reward. That series of golf with them ended. They were friendly, but other than golf, we had nothing in common with them.

Verna joined a neighborhood lady's Friday morning golf and lunch event somewhere along the way. Again, because of COVID-19 and health issues, she gave that up.

For a while, a few neighborhood couples would play twilight golf in the summer at five PM and then grab a burger as part of the package. We would have liked to play until it got dark, but everyone else wanted to quit after only nine holes. "Nine and Dine" was their motto. That pattern also petered out.

Verna and I had to find a more steady arrangement. Except for Verna's Wednesday and Friday routine, we only golfed as a couple with other couples. We got into the practice of waiting until the tee times were published, then picked one with another couple playing alone. We eventually found two couples that way, Bill and Karen from upstate New York and Todd and Lori from Wisconsin. It's usually one round a week with each. The only problem is that they are snowbirds, so we became "golf orphans" in the summer. Until a couple of years ago (health issues and COVID-19), Verna and I played eighteen holes in the summer evenings. We have been very "absent" from golf for about two years. We had a little run of weekly nine-hole Executive rounds with the O'Donnells, but that stopped after about six months because of Verna's pain and hot weather.

FLAG NITE — Our neighbors moved to The Villages within weeks of each other. As you would expect, we were all eager to meet each other and socialize. That led to various types of get-togethers. One of the couples, Sandy and Royce, moved here from another Village location. They brought up an idea called "Flag Nite." The concept was that, more than likely, around five PM, a couple in the neighborhood was having a glass of wine while, at the same time, you were. If you want some company, stick a flag in your front yard. The rules were to bring your drinks and glasses and come on over. We'll serve a light snack, and there is a two-hour limit. We ran the idea "up the flag pole" (no pun intended) to see what the neighbors thought. We all went for it. Verna and I decided to try it first. We purchased a piece of material with an Air Force symbol, and Verna made a flag. We stuck it in the front lawn and asked ourselves, what if nobody saw it? We'd look like fools. Verna said we should make some phone calls, so we did and notified the neighbors. We're already breaking the rules. It was a hit; at least five couples showed up, and some lingered until eight PM. So, the variation on the theme was to plan the event and inform the neighbors. We cycled through that for a while. Then, it evolved into something larger. Instead of just a light snack, it became appetizers. Then we combined it with nine holes of golf, including a game and a little kitty of cash for prizes. One couple was responsible for making the golf arrangements and running the game, and another for hosting the get-together at their house. Everybody brought an appetizer, their drinks, and glasses. We tried going to a restaurant, but sometimes we had twenty people, and it was too difficult to make arrangements. That whole scenario gradually came to an end.

THREE CHURCHES PLUS ONE — As I said in a previous story, Peg and Jim O'Donnell introduced us to their church friends on our first visit to The Villages. We went to that church for a while but did not care for the priest. The only other local one was in The Villages, so we tried it. It was way too large and impersonal. None of our original church friends changed to go there. We did not know anyone there. It was not friendly. Everybody just went, ran to their cars after Mass, and took off. We were not getting anything out of it. At about the same time, we heard of a new parish being established nearby but out of The Villages. We decided to give it a try. We liked both priests, and some of our original church friends started going there. They had a building fund to build a church, and we pledged our fair share. Soon after the pledges were in, both priests got transferred. We did not care for the replacements. When they gave a sermon, they read it and spoke in broken English. When a deacon gave the sermon, he mostly just read it. Once again, we were not getting anything out of it. That, plus all of the news about child molestation by priests, the uselessness of the Roman Catholic hierarchy, and the archaic rituals of the Catholic Church, were just too much.

Some of our neighbors belonged to a Methodist church and seemed to be getting more out of their religion than we were. We decided to go shopping for another church. We said we would not go to their church merely because they did. We did say we would go there once to check it out and then sample others. The first Sunday we went, there was a shocker. As soon as we walked through the main door, there was a large area for mingling, coffee, and cookies. There was a whole lot of socializing going on. Then, it was time to go inside. It was more like an auditorium than a Catholic church. There was still a lot of chattering and socializing. Finally, the pastor entered. We did not know what to expect. Going to church on Sunday was always going to a Mass. A series of songs by a large and excellent choir followed a few introductory and opening remarks. Then, the pastor began his presentation. I was immediately impressed. He instantly grabbed my attention. I was waiting for him to pick up a piece of paper to read from or at least some notes. His words were flowing. I had to turn around a couple of times to see if there was a prompt he was following, but there was none. His content and presentation skills were excellent. More lingering and socializing on the way out. Okay, next week we'll try an Episcopalian church in The Villages. It was very small and dead, with no energy in the air, no socializing, and very unfriendly. Similar to a Catholic Mass. It didn't grab us.

We returned to the Methodist the next week to confirm our first impressions. But we returned to the Episcopalian the next week to give it a second chance. No better than the first visit. That's it; there's no sense in looking any further. We signed up for the Methodist. I had less of a problem with the change than Verna. We were getting more out of our religious life than we ever had. I characterized the pastor as being entertaining, informative, and inspiring. Because of COVID-19, we have not been to church since Christmas 2019. We're disappointed some of our pew partners did not contact us regarding our prolonged absence. We don't know where we are right now in our spirituality. One big thing we missed about a Catholic Mass is their concept of Holy Communion. The Methodist theology and presentation of it leaves something wanting. There is still a catholic spark in us, "Once a Catholic, always a Catholic." I don't know what we are going to do. Nothing is pulling us one way or another right now.

HAPPY ANNIVERSARY — In 2008, we celebrated our 50th wedding anniversary. Sandy and Royce, who introduced us to Flag Nite, happened to be married on the same day. When we found that out, we said when the time comes, we'll celebrate together. I wanted to make it a significant affair. Verna had been cheated out of a lovely wedding day (previous story) that can never be replaced. This was a little opportunity to make up a piece of it. We decided to have a reception in a country club and sent out invitations. The guests included exclusive friends of Sandy and Royce, exclusive friends of ours, and mutual friends of both of us. We offered three dinner choices: wine, beer, and soft drinks; other drinks were on a cash-bar basis. About seventy people attended. We had a cake, set up some photos, and a head table. Our guests at the head table were the O'Donnells and the McCrackens. Sandy and Royce had their daughter, who lived nearby as their guest. The evening went well. I told how I messed up my proposal to Verna (previous story). A few weeks before the big event, Verna came down with a severe case of food poisoning, and she had not eaten much for many days. She could eat for the first time at our celebration as a few guests watched and commented, "Verna is eating." A bit of a footnote: we went north that summer and our boys set up a second great event in a restaurant. They took care of everything. Verna's families from New Jersey and Pennsylvania, plus a few Jersey friends, were the guests. They put together a creative slide show based on a series of questions with audience participation for the answers regarding our history together. Fast forward ten years to 2018. We would be married sixty years and both be eighty years old. I wanted to do something special again. I had a theme already in mind, "140 YEARS" (80+60). It was a major milestone in our lives. We planned it for the Christmas season to enable our sons and their families to make it. As time approached, one excuse led to another, dwindling to something much less than we had hoped. We were disappointed; those two milestones came and went, not duly celebrated.

BOOK CLUB—A few years ago, the neighborhood ladies formed a Book Club, meeting once a month. Verna joined and enjoyed the idea of getting together. They all got together for a nice Christmas lunch some-place. Occasionally, they had lunch with a theme related to the book they discussed. I was glad that Verna had those opportunities. She had to bow out for a while; they made her an honorary member.

HELPING HANDS — The Methodist church we were going to has a program for helping the needy. They identify families that are struggling economically and have inadequate housing. It seems that all of the cases are single black moms living in squalor. Somehow, they owned a piece of property (shades of Forty Acres and a Mule from Civil War days). A requirement to be part of the program is to own a piece of property. The deal is that this group called "Helping Hands" purchases a mobile home, locates it on their property, reconditions and furnishes it, and makes it a turnkey transaction. The recipient signs an agreement to repay a portion of the total cost over some time. There is no penalty if not repaid; various fund-raising events cover the upfront expenses.

I teamed up with a guy, Kris, who was in charge of landscaping, and we worked well together. I was initially interested in the program, but then I lost interest. It all began one day when Kris did follow-ups on completed homes. We pulled up to this one where we had recently planted forty azaleas, but none were there. Had they been stolen or perhaps sold for cash? It was very disappointing to both of us. We went to other properties and found the flower beds dead, missing, or full of weeds.

On another occasion, we were working on this project when I glanced across the street and saw a yard full of black men drinking and playing cards. Something did not set well with me. Why would they not come over and help us? One final incident was the last straw. A neighbor of ours was one of the leaders of the program. One day, while working in my front yard, he pulled up and asked if I could go with them to repair some damage to a previous project. I said okay. There was a water leak in the bathroom that had damaged the floor. As we walked into the place, the woman was lying on the sofa watching *Jerry Springe*r. The place was a mess. We did the repair and started to clean up, assuming that the lady would say she'd take care of that, but she did not get up from the sofa as we asked her for the vacuum given to her as part of the turnkey package. She said she no longer had it. That's it; I bowed out of the program. My heart was no longer in it. The leaders prided themselves on how many projects they completed, but they did not evaluate the long-term effects. Part of the program included mentoring the property owners on how to maintain their property, live on a budget, and improve the quality of their life. Before I "resigned," I suggested that the leaders measure the program's effectiveness. Why not contact one of the local universities and find a socio-economic student who needs a project for a dissertation? Explain the project's goals and give them the names and addresses of the forty-plus projects completed. Then, have them follow up with a good sampling and do a before-and-after analysis. Then, write the whole thing with goals, findings, conclusions, and recommendations. Finally, use that to make decisions regarding the continuation of the program. It is a noble program with good intentions. I did not see evidence of positive results.

MEN'S BREAKFAST — After being invited by a neighbor and "encouraged" by Verna numerous times to start going to Men's Breakfast, I finally gave in. It's a Tuesday morning event that begins at 7:30 and is usually over by nine. It is well-attended by about 200 men. The program consists of pertinent announcements, a little levity in the form of a funny internet story always provided by one guy, a prayer list where attendees add names and reasons for adding the names (these names are given to a church prayer group as part of their ministry), and finally a keynote speaker from the group with an inspirational message. Of course, there is a fellowship of six to eight guys around a table sharing stories. The cost is a reasonable $4. Once again, that all came to an end in January 2020 because of

COVID-19. I missed going. They resumed in September 2021, but I did not attend because Verna and I limited our social contacts because of her compromised immune system.

MILITARY BALL—There are numerous veterans in The Villages, probably the most densely veteran-populated area in the country. When we first got there, we joined a Military Families Group. We went with another couple who invited us to join, but we were disappointed in what they had to offer. Plus, as is often the case, people only socialize with those they already know.

One nice thing the club does is an annual formal Veterans Day affair. To begin the evening, there is a solemn ceremony honoring deceased veterans. As an added touch, they identified the oldest and youngest living veterans in attendance. Then, the younger feeds the oldest a piece of cake. There's dinner, dancing, and formal attire. We went a few times but then bowed out.

ENTERTAINMENT—The Villages has a Performing Arts Center, and there are always many attractions. We've been to a number of them. They are very professional, reasonably priced, and very convenient to get to. There is also a Little Theatre that has quality performances. Night live entertainment and line dancing are staples in the three town squares that attract many regulars. It's not our thing; we only strolled through them when we had guests, which was not too often.

DINING OUT— This is a BIG thing in The Villages. In my estimation, 75% of the people eat out 75% of the time. A couple of our original friends, Dennis and Rosemary, eat out every day. When we had our trolley tour of The Villages, the escort made the jest, "Guys, if you want to hide something from your wife, put it in the oven." There are a lot of restaurants, but there are not enough fine dining establishments. We like it to be a special event with extraordinary food and a pleasant atmosphere when we eat out.

PHYSICAL FITNESS — We joined the Wellness Center shortly after arriving here. They had strength training machines, aerobic devices, an indoor pool, a hot tub, and a sauna. We regularly went at least two or three times a week. It was a two-plus hour ordeal, and we felt physically great afterward. After a while, the facility closed. New ownership took over in another building. We continued to belong, but there was no longer a pool. One major shortcoming of The Villages is the need for an indoor pool. There are a lot of public outdoor pools, but there is too much sun in the summer and too cold in the winter. We continued our program until 2016 when we went on a cruise. We put a hold on our membership but never resumed that part of our lives for one reason or another. After a spell, we searched for another facility and found one. We gave that a shot for a while, then stopped a couple of years ago when Verna's problems started. Returning to it was out of the question because of Verna's pains and COVID-19.

M & M (MAHJONG AND MEMOIRS) — Verna was looking for mental stimulation. She chose mahjong, learned it, and started a Tuesday morning session with three other ladies. Coincidentally, it was about the same time that I joined the Memoirs writing group. So we had this nice little Tuesday routine. Men's breakfast, Mahjong, and Memoirs (now 3 M's). These activities came to an end in January 2020. We resumed memoirs via ZOOM, but Verna never went back to Mahjong.

I HAVE ROCKS - PHASE I — Verna's family planned to visit us shortly after we moved into The Villages. Verna said we must upgrade the landscaping, and "You're not doing it yourself; moving rocks and yard work is no longer part of your lifestyle." I responded, "Yes, dear," but whispered, "Rats."

Our next-door neighbor had hired Rick to do their landscaping, and they recommended him. He gave us a design and a price. We hired him, and it was a big mistake. We should have gotten more proposals. We overpaid; there was something shady about Rick, and his crew changed every few days; plus, it was the first time that some of them did any landscaping.

The only thing worth anything was a lot of lugging rocks and boulders that I would have had to do myself. Rick had this idea of a "waterless pond" for a water feature. I didn't understand it. He buried a fifty-five-gallon iron drum in the ground. That was stupid to begin with because it would immediately begin to rust. He then filled it with water, put a pump in it, had it run into a little pond area, and returned to the barrel; there was never any water that stayed in the pond. I felt as if I suddenly regressed mentally and physically and had to depend on and watch people do something that I could have done so much better myself. After a while, we stopped him on the job and never paid him the total amount. As I said above, there was something shady about Rick. A neighbor down the street hired him about a month after we fired him. Turns out that they paid him a chunk of money in advance for rocks. The supplier delivered the rocks, but Rick did not pay the supplier. The supplier put a lien on the couple's house, and he had to pay the supplier to release the lien. At least we lucked out in that respect and did not have to pay twice for our rocks. Soon after Rick left, I dug out the partially rusted barrel and rebuilt the pond the way it should have been in the first place.

I HAVE ROCKS - PHASE II — Rick used steel edging around the house to separate the rocks from the lawn. After a while, it began to rust and become an eyesore. We had concrete curbing installed to correct that, which was a big improvement. I do not like the St. Augustine grass, which is common in Florida. It's like ryegrass up north that the farmers sow to keep their soil in place over the winter. I talked Verna into replacing our lawn with a much nicer Zoysia grass. Even The Villages started using it soon after we moved in. We had a landscaper come in to give us a price on the lawn. While he was in the process of measuring, he noticed our extensive landscaping and suggested a further enhancement, such as replacing the grass in the backyard with hardscape (rocks, stones, and landscape blocks). We liked the idea. It would be much more interesting, and less grass would be cut. He laid out a design and gave us a price. Then he turned into a "Used Car salesman," if we signed up now, he would give us a good discount. We went for it. When the truckload of the rocks arrived and were dumped at the front of the house, they were all coated in mud. I should have stopped the job right then and there. I knew that all of the mud on the rocks would be a breeding ground for weeds. As the crew moved the rocks to the backyard, I frantically tried to hose some mud off them. We had other issues with the landscaper. He appeared to be bipolar, and we had words. A few months later, we returned from a trip up north and found the backyard bed of rocks loaded with weeds. We had words again with the landscaper, but no satisfaction. I couldn't stand the weeds. The only solution was to wash them and place a new weed barrier on the old one. I got a thirty-gallon plastic trash barrel and put a few holes near the top to drain water as it filled the barrel. I worked on a three-foot-wide section at a time. I filled a screen with about four shovels of stone, picked up the hose, and, with the other hand, swished the rocks around in the sieve as I washed them. Then, I dumped them to one side. When I reached the end of the three-foot path, I laid the new weed barrier and replaced it with clean stone. Then, on to the next three-foot path. The area I had to work through was about sixty by twenty feet. It took over a month to do it. It was a hot August, but the splashing cooled me off.

I discovered another problem in the yard. The concrete curbing was not high enough, and rocks kept sliding into the lawn. I had myself another project. I laid landscape blocks on top of the curbing. First, I had to lay a cement bed on the curbing to make it flat. I got about twenty blocks from Lowes at a time in our car. Each block weighed about twenty-two pounds, about four hundred pounds in the car. I ended up laying about eleven hundred blocks around the house. One thing led to another, but eventually, I was "done" with the landscaping.

I HAVE ROCKS - PHASE III — About four years ago, we got a phone call from our son Kevin in South Carolina. He said there was a section of his yard that he wanted to dress up a little, and did I have any suggestions? He gave me the particulars, and I said I'd consider it. Of course, the first thing that comes into my mind is rocks. That led to a Japanese Garden possibility. Although we call them Japanese Gardens, Japanese merchants witnessed the gardens built in China in the sixth century. They brought many of the Chinese gardening techniques and styles back home. Three elements in Japanese Gardening are rocks, water, and greenery. I went to the computer for inspiration and started getting jealous that I had no similar nice arrangements in our backyard. I asked myself, why not? I had a water feature, and this large expanse was mainly covered with rocks. It looked boring when I compared that expanse to some of the layouts I saw on the computer. I had this huge space to work with. I threw around a couple of layouts in my head and devised a plan. Lay a path of stepping stones through the area. Create an imaginary parallel river bed alongside it to give a Yin-Yang effect. Yin-yang is an ancient symbol of harmony and balance and is an objective in creating a Japanese Garden—a couple of pagodas and a bridge complete the effect. We were able to find two pagodas but not a bridge. So I decided to make my own. The project became complicated because I was not starting with a blank canvas (empty space). I had to remove what was there, get it out of the way, then get some rocks of a different color from another section to put in the new layout. It finally all came together, and I was satisfied with the finished product. However, I must admit that the entire backyard does not represent a purely correct Japanese concept. I have the three elements: rock, water, and green. But I have a fourth element that does not belong: color. I have colored flowers. That's okay, I can live with that. I like the variety and change that the flowers bring throughout the year. Confucius, please forgive me. By the way, our son never got his Japanese garden nor anything done to that section of his landscaping. He never followed up on his request. I got mine and am still available to give him some ideas.

I HAVE ROCKS - PHASE IV— About two years ago, as the cooler winter months of Florida approached, I was looking for an outdoor project. After bearing the heat of the summer months and coming into the house drenched in sweat, I owed it to myself to do something outside in the winter when it's so pleasant and comfortable that you don't even "feel the weather." What to do? I went through the entire yard and tried to make it more maintenance-free since I was getting up in age. A big maintenance chore in Florida is weeding, a weekly task in the summer. There were about thirty shrubs around our house that weeds liked to grow under. Plus, the clippings from trimmings got lodged under the shrubs. I came up with the idea of making octagon-shaped enclosures around the shrubs and filling them with small stones. Also, weeds tend to pop up along the edges of the rock beds and landscape blocks. I put aluminum flashing there by using concrete screws into the landscape cinder blocks and large staples in the weed barrier. While at it, I removed all the stones I laid out in Phase III, laid down the best weed barrier I could find, and replaced them. Once again, I had to work in piece-meal steps to remove and replace. One thing led to another, as it usually does when I get involved, and the whole project took two years. I **THINK** I'm done! One last thought: every time I was working on these landscape projects, I kept praying and hoping that nothing would happen to me before I finished it. Verna would have to hire someone to complete it, and they would have no idea what my plans were because I never had anything on paper; it was always only in my head. I tend to design as I go along. Verna does the same thing when she cooks; it's all in her head or taste buds because she tastes as she goes along.

I HAVE ROCKS - PHASE V — The weeds are winning. After putting down the best weed barrier I could find and going through a lot of detail in sealing the edges, I still had weeds. I concluded that the weeds were not growing through the barrier. They were growing "on" the barrier. The weed barrier material is a type of fabric. As careful as I was in sealing the edges, seeds would sprout in them. If you don't pull a weed out before it goes to seed, the wind will blow the seeds into other places. As this happened, some seeds found their way on top of the weed barrier and began to sprout.

My layout had two corners where the stones were about one foot deep. There were never weeds in those sections. I wondered why this was and concluded that although weed seeds probably did blow there, they never grew for two reasons. One is that they never made their way down to the fabric of the weed barrier. And secondly, if they did reach the barrier, there was not enough sunlight for them to germinate. The big difference between these sections and the other main section was that the stones were only about three inches deep in the problem section compared to twelve inches deep in the corner sections. I could not have added another nine inches of stone in the main section because that would have disrupted the height of the edging around the stones.

I had to devise a way to keep the weed seeds away from the barrier. In one of the previous phases, I removed the stones from a dry river bed, laid a thick piece of plastic on top of the weed barrier, and then replaced the stones. I then noticed that no weeds were growing there as they were before, so that's the solution. Pull the stones away from the problem area, lay heavy-duty plastic, then replace the stones. I was about to begin that project but was concerned that the plastic would disintegrate over time. Yes, plastic does not last forever. I discovered this in other sections where I had used it. I needed something more durable. I considered aluminum, concrete wonder board, 4'x8' sheets of plastic formica, and tar paper. For one reason or another, each of the above had limitations. The only viable one was the tarpaper, but I was afraid that heat would melt it, and as I walked on the stones, they would get all messed up, and I'd be walking in the house with tar on my shoes; no way.

I had one little 8'x8' section that I decided to experiment with. I went with the tar paper idea but used roofing shingles instead. The tiny granules on their upper side would prevent tar from sticking to the stones. Plus, the small size of the shingles would be easier to work with where fitting and cutting were needed. One concern I had was creating a pool of water that would not drain and breed mosquitos. I counted on a slope, imperfect seals at the edges, and hairline gaps between each shingle to provide drainage. Here goes. But first, let me check the price of shingles. Quite expensive. However, I noticed at Lowes that they sell what's left at a discount whenever a bundle is busted and some are missing. So I went down that route.

The process went well. I kept an eye on the area, and guess what? There were no weeds and no standing water. All of the above occurred during the winter, so I took advantage of the cool weather and tackled the main area. Am I done, or will there be a PHASE VI? There was no Phase VI. And maybe only because we relocated to upstate New York and had no yard to play with rocks!

DOWNTIME — All of the above plus some related stories hopefully give you an idea of the " STYLE OF OUR LIFE" (LIFESTYLE) during our stay in The Villages. There was a lot of variety and coming and going, but there was one constant. We always ended up together at the end of the day. It was time for our first glass of wine at about five PM. Then, we had dinner and settled in our recliners for a second glass. We started watching a movie or golf. Verna's brother, Raymond, and his wife, Carol, checked in at about eight PM via Alexa, and we (mostly Verna) shared our day's events for about an hour, back to our movie or golf plus a nightcap. David usually checked in on the phone for a few minutes, which added a nice wrap-up of the day. Then off to bed around 10:30. Thank God for the day and our lifestyle.

"IT WAS THE BEST OF TIMES, IT WAS THE WORST OF TIMES"—This is the opening line in Charles Dickens's classic *The Tale of Two Cities*. I have always liked that line because it can be applied to many situations in life.

When we first arrived in The Villages in 2004, we were sixty-five years old. One of my first comments about our new lifestyle was, "It's like we died and went to heaven, but we are still in contact with our living families; we can call them whenever we want and even take a trip up north to see them."

That sensation lasted nineteen years; we will probably record it as the best years of our lives. The various topics presented in this story gave you a taste of what I mean. In addition to The Village's lifestyle, another thing that makes these years so enjoyable is that we are retired and financially comfortable. You also read how the flavor of those activities changed so drastically about two years ago.

At least once a year during the hot summer months here, we headed north. The circuit included our oldest son, David, and his family in upstate New York; our younger son, Kevin, and his family in South Carolina; Verna's older brother, Sonny, and his family in our hometown of Exeter, Pennsylvania; and Verna's younger brother, Raymond, and his family in New Jersey (our residence for thirty-one years before we moved to The Villages).

The biggest drawback was missing Christmas with all of them. We did go up for Christmas one year, but missing all of the other Christmases was the price we paid for the other 364 days.

Sometime during 2019, we entered a "holding pattern." Two things had to happen for us to get out of that slump. First, COVID-19 had to go away, and it eventually did. Secondly, Verna had to get relief from her physical pain. And there were two parts to that. Her neurosurgeon claimed that a laminectomy would solve her back problem but could take up to a year to become fully effective. Verna had the surgery, and it did relieve her sciatica pain. The pain in her knee required a total knee replacement to resolve. We were hoping to be back to normal by May 2022. There is still her multiple myeloma to deal with, but that is already part of her routine and is not going to go away. The best we can hope for there is to keep it under control. Regarding our nineteen years in The Villages, we had "The Best of Times" for fifteen years and "The Worst of Times for three years. We'll take it and pray for another good lifestyle run after that. We shall see what tomorrow brings!

AERIAL VIEW OF VILLAGES HOME

AERIAL VIEW OF VILLAGES HOME

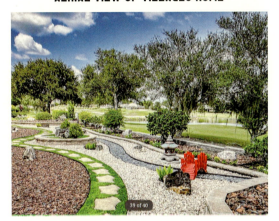

BACK YARD OF VILLAGES HOME

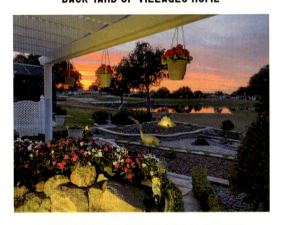

VIEW FROM RECLINER IN VILLAGES HOME

76. WE'RE BACK (WITH A NEW LIFESTYLE)

It is now the spring of 2024. Verna and I reside in an independent living facility in upstate New York. Why are we here? It has been a few years since I did anything active regarding these stories. The last memoir activity I remember is meeting via ZOOM with other members of the Memoir Writing Club in The Villages, Florida, because of the COVID-19 epidemic, which began in early 2020. Even those meetings petered out, but eventually, the group met in person once the epidemic subsided. However, I chose not to attend the meetings because of Verna's compromised immune system resulting from her multiple myeloma.

A great deal has happened to us in the last few years, preventing me from finalizing this project. But now it's time to update everyone and put the finishing touches on my epic journey.

I am unsure where to start covering this gap in our developments. If you were reading a book but were interrupted for an extended period, when you returned to the book, you likely skimmed a few pages of what you had already read to get back into it. When I picked up my pen to resume my stories, I was at a loss as to the missing pieces. I was also concerned about being redundant and providing continuity. To accomplish this, I did go back to some of my recent stories to see where I left off. I also had to refer to our 2021-22 calendar (we have a habit of saving old calendars for reference) to identify significant events that I already wrote or did not write about.

It turns out it was the autumn of 2021, and I commented in story 75 (Lifestyles), "We shall see what tomorrow brings." Hence, I appropriately used the word "Lifestyle" in the title of this story.

77. AN EYE OPENER

After waiting for a reasonable time to recover from Verna's Laminectomy surgery, as recommended by her orthopedic, Dr. Williams performed a total right knee replacement on her in February 2022. Aside from the fact that she did have pain in that knee, we also hoped that the damaged knee was contributing to her back problem and that the knee surgery would bring some relief. The surgery "went well," as they customarily say. However, Dr. Williams recommended physical therapy as part of the recovery process. After a couple of sessions of therapy, Verna began to experience excruciating pain, so she stopped the therapy and went back to see Dr. Williams. The severe pain was caused by a detached ligament in her knee that most likely happened during therapy. Dr. Williams had to "go back in" and attach the ligament. The bottom line is that the knee pain disappeared, but the back pain remained. Subsequent routine follow-up appointments with Dr. Reddy (Laminectomy) and Dr. Williams ended with a phrase, "It takes time" for the surgery's final effects to occur. Back to pain management and physical therapy. Neither brought relief, plus additional pain from the physical therapy.

Moving on to the summer of 2022. My prostate raised its ugly head in the form of an increased PSA level and a subsequent unfavorable biopsy. A surgical procedure involving freezing my prostate was performed on July 15 (Verna's birthday. Blah!). Since Verna was still recovering from her second knee surgery and on painkillers, we had to have a neighbor drive us to the hospital and bring us back home (outpatient procedure). This was the first time Verna and I were incapacitated at the same time. Every other time one of us needed surgery, the other could take care of the other.

Coincidently, around the same time the above occurred, we received an unexpected invitation from our neighbors, May Kay and Tom Mc Cracken, to share a glass of wine in their house. We had been cautious about socializing because COVID-19 was still rampant. Tom and Mary Kay had a severe case earlier in the year. As it turns out, the reason for the unexpected invite was to inform us of their decision to sell their house and move next to their daughter and son-in-law in North Carolina. Mary Kay and Tom had been two of our closest friends since we moved to The Villages eighteen years earlier. We were surprised at their decision but understood when they explained that their terrible bout with COVID-19 made them realize how helpless they quickly became. They stated that despite how much they did not want to leave their enjoyable lifestyle, they would feel more secure and comfortable near their family should something similar happen in the future.

Very quickly after we left their home and on our way to our house, Verna and I had the same thought, "That could happen to us." Just like we both became helpless and needed assistance a short time earlier, we had an **EYE OPENER!**

78. GOOD NEWS/BAD NEWS

In an earlier story, I referred to our son, David, being diagnosed with cancer (lymphoma) in early 2020. Although these stories started as my stories and evolved into "our" (Verna's and my) stories, I need to start including David because so much has happened to him in the last two years that has dominated our lives.

David received chemotherapy for his lymphoma and enjoyed about a year of relatively good health. However, sometime around the middle of 2022, the lymphoma flared up again, and he had to undergo stem cell therapy. The treatment went well, and David was doing well towards the end of 2022.

Before I leave 2022, I need to document one piece of good news to balance the Good-Bad scale. Verna's multi-myeloma went into remission in October of that year. We know it is only temporary, but we will take a reprieve for now.

79. PUSH/PULL

Having had our Eye Opener (two stories ago), what do we do now? Our Village Lifestyle was changing. Some factors to consider:

- Only a handful of couples who had constituted our network of friends for the last eighteen years were still around. They had passed on or left The Villages to be closer to family.

- New arrivals in the neighborhood were a generation younger, transients, or both. We had little in common with them.

- As much as I liked or did not hate keeping up with house and yard maintenance, I "had enough" and needed some more-carefree living.

- We need to be near good medical facilities, given Verna's cancer and my heart issues.

- We want to be within driving distance of at least some family members.

- I don't know about Verna, but I missed four seasons and more weather variety. Growing up in Pennsylvania and spending most of my adult life in northern climates, I felt out of place in Florida. I like evergreen trees more than palm trees, and I don't have a problem with an all-day rain.

- Culture Wars. Relocating to South Carolina to be near our son Kevin and his family would satisfy the family requirement. But it was not far enough north, and new friends would primarily be locals. We would have different backgrounds and values. Plus, we would not feel secure or comfortable with the medical facilities.

So, you see, it's a combination of **PUSHING** us out of The Villages and **PULLING** us someplace else. And as much as we enjoyed our Villages Lifestyle, it was time to turn the pages and move on to the next chapter in our lives.

80. FIND A NEW HOME

One firm requirement-not another house! That leaves apartment living of some form. We are not ready for a nursing home (assisted living), so the current buzzword is "Independent Living" with no maintenance and meal plans optional.

Toward the end of the summer of 2022, I went online to check out Independent Living. I checked out South Carolina first to avoid omitting any possibilities. I mentally noted one acceptable place within driving distance of Kevin and his family. We mentioned our plans to relocate to Kevin and Andrea, and Andrea graciously offered to have us move in with them. They have a large home that would be comfortable, but we gratefully declined.

Our other son, David, lived in a small town near Albany in upstate New York. I started browsing the area for possibilities, and one caught my eye. It was called Beverwyck and was part of a national chain of such facilities. It included three levels of care: Independent, Assisted, and Nursing Home. The amenities were appealing. I glanced at a few others for comparison, but this one made the cut. The next step was to pick up the phone and take the process to the next level. It immediately became evident that the person on the other end of the line was interviewing us as much as we were attempting to obtain more information about their facility. One of their immediate concerns was our current health condition. It became evident that we had to be healthy enough for independent living because the next two levels were restricted to residents already in the first level (independent living). We signed up after a few more calls and a virtual Beverwyck tour. We were told it would be two to four years before getting the type of apartment we wanted. As a point of interest, the Beverwyck representative told us that if we were in a hurry, we could apply for a smaller place and expect to get it within six months. I made a mental note of that.

81. DOWNSIZING

Immediately after we committed to relocate, we started to downsize. Our new living space will be half the size of our current one. We had to get rid of a lot of stuff. We considered going the garage sale route but decided against it. We used "Marketplace" on Facebook and did well. It broke our hearts to get rid of a lot of our treasures. I'll give you a couple of examples. We had a formal dining room set, and nobody wanted it. It appears that they are out of style. Eventually, one woman became interested in it and had plans to use it regularly. It went for $600 and was the highest ticket item we sold. We had the set for almost fifty years, and it was well-used. When our boys were still living at home, we sat at it every night for dinner. It also was well-used for family holidays and Sunday extended family dinners. So many memories. If those chairs could talk, the stories they could tell!

On more than one occasion, the person purchasing an item told us their plans and even sent us photos of where they placed it. We are still in touch with some customers.

Another touching moment took place regarding my tools. I was selling them individually and doing reasonably well, but I never would sell out at that rate. I kept a small collection for some possible future DIY projects. I also had a collection of about twenty-five containers of nuts, bolts, screws, etc. I decided to advertise the whole lot for one price. Sure enough, a guy showed up, we negotiated, and he wiped me out. After we loaded everything on his truck and he drove away, I broke down and cried. I went into the house and told Verna that those tools were like an extension of my hands. When I was fifteen, I purchased an adjustable wrench to fix my bicycle. That was 70 years ago. One set of sockets I had for sixty years. I used those tools for many large and small projects in many different locations and situations. Once again, "If those tools could talk!"

We "gave" items to a good customer on multiple occasions. We didn't sell out and did not expect to. I kept a record of business, and we sold about 150 items and picked up $8,000. A few days before the moving van showed up, I went to Goodwill to complete our Downsizing. Here comes the moving van; I have to load up the treasures that made the cut.

82. HOUSE FOR SALE

Having committed to relocate, we found ourselves in a transitory frame of mind. Our lifestyle in The Villages took on a different flavor, and we were filled with anxiety about what our new lifestyle would be like. We decided to go for a smaller apartment to break this spell and hoped to "move in" in a few months instead of years.

We called Beverwyck, did the necessary paperwork, and were told we could expect something within three months. One month later, we had a place that would be ready by mid-December, so we had about three months to sell our house.

No problem! It had been a sellers' market in The Villages. Within the last six months, two neighbors sold their homes quickly and got their asking price. An immediate neighbor had their house on the market for a couple of months but no action, even after lowering the price more than once. What happened? We missed the bubble and were disappointed. We started with an asking price of about three times our purchase price. But by the end of the year, we were approaching twice our purchase price. Our greatest upward price driver was the location with a great view. Lowering the value were things we did not expect, such as the age of the house, rug floors, white appliances, blue house (most homes in The Villages were Builders' Beige), and finally, to my chagrin, most lookers did not appreciate my extensive landscaping. That was the second time that happened to me. When we tried to sell our previous house in New Jersey, my landscaping masterpiece became a liability, not an asset.

By January 1, we had yet to receive a single offer. Our realtor had two suggestions: paint the house a more neutral color and move up North, leaving the house empty to give it more appeal as a new home than a used one. We did have the house painted and made arrangements with a mover and flight reservations to move out. (We had our car transported rather than drive it up North).

It must have been late January or early February when, early in the day, this eighty-six-year-old single man walked in with his daughter and a realtor. He loved the place "as is." He had just started shopping and had a list of other possibilities. We were a little hopeful. Towards the end of the day, he returned and said that he had not found anything he liked more and that a much more expensive house he had seen did not appeal to him at all.

We had a good nibble and thought we would hook him with an offer. Our realtor called us within an hour or two with a reasonable offer. After several counteroffers, we landed him at twice our purchase price and 90% of our then-asking price. **SOLD!** Better yet, he wanted a quick closing, and that was set for February 21. We had to firm up the movers and re-schedule our airline ticket. We're out of here! By the way, he would have bought the house blue. RATS! We could have saved $2000.

83. HERE WE ARE AND A TURNABOUT EVENT

The closing on our house took place as scheduled. We spent our final few days in The Villages in the home of our best friends, Peg and Jim O'Donnell (see previous story). How appropriate because they were the couple with whom we spent our very first days in The Villages nineteen years earlier.

The next day, we jumped on the plane and landed at the Albany airport. David picked us up, and as he drove us to his home, we were welcomed by a cloudy day with a few snow flurries beginning to fall. I finally got my first dose of some different weather patterns.

We spent a few days with David until our furniture arrived. It had been three years since we had seen David because of COVID-19. We enjoyed each other's company as we sat around the roaring fireplace and watched the gently falling snowflakes rekindle my love of seasonal weather.

We arranged to move into our new abode on March 1, when the moving van arrived. On the day before, the Beverwyck management staff invited David and us for a welcome lunch. It created a turnabout event. Verna had a flashback of David on his first day of school. As we waited for him at the school bus stop, Verna spotted a little boy also waiting for the bus. Being the great and worried mother that she is, she was concerned about sending her son out and alone into a new, unknown world. She would feel more secure if he had someone to share the dramatic experience with. So she made a point of introducing the two boys to each other (the other boy was with his father). The boys became friends and stayed in touch for several years after we were reassigned to another location.

Fast forward a few years to David's leaving home for his first day at college. In a similar scene, we were waiting to get David settled in his dorm, and Mom spotted another lonely soul of a boy standing by himself. Her motherly instinct kicked in, and, yes, you got it, she introduced them to each other. And, as the pattern repeats itself, they remained friends during college and up to the present.

So here we are; David drives us to Beverwyck for our initial entry to a new, unknown world. Verna and I have visions of the two scenarios, but the roles are reversed. We express this vision to David and describe the previous experiences and the irony that perhaps he is as concerned about our new situation as his Mom was so many years ago. Are we going to like our new world? Will we have friends? Will we be happy?

84. 40 AUTUMN DRIVE APT. 212

When we married sixty-plus years ago, our first home was a small apartment. Throughout those years, we lived chronologically in an apartment, Verna's parent's home, a mobile home, a military duplex, a small apartment above a German house, a military six-unit apartment dwelling, a brand new house, another brand new house, and finally, a small apartment (about the same size as our first apartment).

There is an interesting and significant fact regarding our first and last apartment. The rent for our first apartment was $52 a month. Sixty-five years later, we are paying not ten times as much but one hundred times as much. Yes, $5,000 per month (but it includes meals). Talk about a quantum leap!

Back to the apartment. It is cozy, adequate, and temporary. It will do for a couple of years. More significant than our actual living space is the new lifestyle. One of our first reactions and observations caused us to question, "What are we doing here?" There are so many people with walkers or wheelchairs and relatively little activity during the daytime hours. We knew that the average age is eighty-six compared to sixty-five at The Villages. Oh Well! That could be us someday.

We were assigned a greeter couple who invited us to dinner the first night along with another couple. That was a pleasant surprise and a harbinger of things to come. The place comes alive at five pm. The dining room seats about 150 people. Tables accommodating up to seven people are nicely set with linen tablecloths, centerpieces, and place settings.

As we walked into the dining room for the first time, all eyes were on us. We were the "new kids on the block." Seating arrangements are based on reservation or open seating. We do a combination of both. The female-to-male ratio is about three to one, so you tend to see more women gathered around a table than couples. We quickly found our network of couples and a few single women and men to share our dining experience.

I have no problem sitting at a table with four women. I can hold my own.

Most residents are from the local area, and many knew each other before moving to Beverwyck. Dinner conversations are fascinating and varied as everyone shares their backgrounds and experiences. Sometimes, dinner is a two-hour event. Residents tend to be upper-middle class and highly educated. Verna has developed a reputation for being a social butterfly. When our meal is completed, she "works the room" by stopping by other tables to say hello and spread some cheer.

I use our dining experience as an example of how drastically our lives have changed. I'll explain this using a "Who, Where, What, When, and Why" analysis.

- **WHO do we eat with?** - More than just Verna and I every night. But sometimes we do. Now, it's a mixed bag.

- **WHERE do we eat?** - In The Villages, we drifted into the poor habit of eating in our recliners. Now, we sit more properly and comfortably.

- **WHAT do we eat?** - More variety, more balanced, and smaller portions. Much more fruits and vegetables.

- **WHEN do we eat?** - The same time every day (give or take a few minutes). Previously, we sometimes put off dinner until too late, and if we were not too hungry, we just picked on snacks.

- **WHY do we eat?** - Because we paid for it! Or, more seriously, because it's a big part of our social life. Some residents always eat alone in their apartments. There may be a good reason, but that routine does not appeal to us.

One final word about the quality of the food. It is our only disappointment with Beverwyck, but it is a major one. We are going to have to pursue the problem. One option is to change our meal plan to half the days we eat in the dining room. After not having them for one year, we miss too many of Verna's delicious dishes. We are not yet ready to make that change; the jury is still out.

To finish more positively, the dining staff goes out of their way to put on special events such as monthly men's breakfasts and women's lunches with guest speakers, holiday special venues, ice-cream socials, theme dinners, etc.

To wrap up my description of our new lifestyle, I'll list a few amenities that attracted us.

- A fitness room and programs, an indoor swimming pool, and a hot tub exist. We have not settled into those because of Verna's health issues.
- Bus trips to nearby entertainment programs and other attractions.
- Bus transportation to shopping, banking, and other facilities.
- Free transportation to medical facilities, airports, and train stations.
- Library, book clubs, and discussion groups.
- On-site entertainment.
- Bridge, cards, and mahjong (Verna plays twice a week).
- A residents' council to present problems and concerns to management.

To conclude, I will summarize our first year. Immediately after we moved in, two major power outages were caused by heavy, wet snowfalls. Be careful what you wish for! Also, right after we moved in, they started the renovation, which was supposed to be completed in three months and took one year. Other personal issues developed, which I will elaborate on in my next story. After one year, we have not settled down to a pleasant and enjoyable routine. Nevertheless, the bottom line remains positive: we made the right decision to call 40 Autumn Drive our new address at the right time.

85. CAN'T CATCH OUR BREATH

This story will highlight various events that have taken place since our move into Beverwyck. To a large extent, they will be in chronological order and again will be a mixed bag of good, bad, and neither (just like the story of life itself).

- **MEDICAL** - Two days after our arrival, while we stayed with David, Verna had an appointment with Dr. Raval. He was David's oncologist, and we had personally met him when we were taking David for his lymphoma chemo treatments at the beginning of 2020. When David told him about us moving here, he said he wanted Verna with her multiple myeloma as his patient. We jumped at the offer. As a side note, in the back of our minds, we were hoping that this relocation would find some medical relief from Verna's persistent pain. We had trouble finding a primary care physician. Dr. Raval landed one for us and referred us to a pain management specialist. After jumping through all the hoops of getting records from Florida and cycling through various specialists, procedures, and meds, Verna continues to drag her ball and chain (see story 74).

- **SON JOINS PARENTS IN RETIREMENT** - The chemo David was receiving during 2020 gave him some relief. However, the cancer flared up again in 2021, and he underwent stem-cell therapy. As part of the recovery process, he was placed on extended disability leave from work. When that ended, he decided to go back to work on a part-time basis. Having had a taste of what retirement would be like, he decided to completely retire on June 1, 2023.

- **DONNA** - Sometime during the last couple of years, a mutual friend introduced David to Donna. When David told us that he had "Met Someone," we were ecstatic; we had been hoping for that for a long time. David had been alone way too long. Donna's husband died from cancer about ten years ago. David told Donna he had built too many walls around him. Donna told us he was "The sweetest guy she ever knew." That's our son. Donna did wonders for David. He became so much happier and developed a great smile. Donna is from the professional art world and was the Director at a local sculptor museum. David is from the technical world and now was introduced to a new network of friends, topics, places, etc. In his own words, "I can hold my own." And he could because he is very rounded, has a curious mind, and has an outgoing personality.

- **SELL HOUSE, MOVE TO BOSTON** - No, not us, David. Donna resides in Lenox, Massachusetts, which is between here and Boston. She also retired within months of David. To maximize their retirement, David decided to sell the house he lived in for about thirty years. He and Donna planned on renting an apartment in Boston for one year, effective July 1, 2023. Donna would keep her apartment in Lenox for one year; then they would find something more permanent between here and Boston. They wanted to take advantage of everything Boston offered and figured a year would do it. We were somewhat disappointed that David was moving away since his location was one of the reasons we selected Beverwyck. But we did not express our disappointment nor let it interfere with his retirement plans or the enjoyment of our new lifestyle.

- **WEDDING BELLS AND A FAMILY REUNION** - No, not David and Donna; David's son, Thomas, our first grandchild, married Maggie Duthaler on June 1, 2023, in Chicago, where Maggie was from. It was a long time coming; they had been going together for eight years, and David longed for a grandchild. Maybe soon! The wedding presented an opportunity for a reunion on our side of the family. We had not seen our son Kevin and his family, Verna's brother Raymond and his family in New Jersey, Verna's sister-in-law Georgia, and her two daughters Karen and Andrea from Pennsylvania in three years.

- **HAPPY ANNIVERSARY** - Sixty-five years! WOW! June 21 was our anniversary. I considered a surprise dinner with Verna, David, and Donna at a nice restaurant. I quickly expanded on the theme to make it a more significant event. I secretly had David invite other family members, his in-laws, a couple we knew from Florida that come north for the summers, and another couple who were David's friends and now ours. We ended up with an entourage of sixteen, and Verna was completely surprised.

- **HAPPY FATHER'S DAY** - David drove us to New Jersey to see Verna's brother's family for the day in his brand-new Audi—a retirement gift he gave to himself. On the way home, a stone hit the windshield and cracked it. A bad omen?

- **MEDICAL SETBACK** - While preparing his house for sale, downsizing, etc., David began to experience pains in his back. Verna and I pitched in to help. David attributed the pains to physical movement. He went to his primary care physician, and an MRI revealed a tumor pressing against his lower spinal column (lymphoma raising its ugly head again). The next thing we knew was that David was in the hospital with Dr. Raval and other specialists, deciding on a treatment plan. By coincidence, I was in the same hospital for a one-day procedure to have my defibrillator replaced because the existing one's battery had expired. It was a day in August. The short-range plan was to give David chemo to shrink the tumor and relieve the pressure on his spine. The long-term plan was a clinical trial known as CAR-T therapy to be performed at the Dana Faber Cancer Institute in Boston. As arrangements were being made, a PET scan disclosed that the chemo administered in August had been so effective that it reduced the tumor to a size not eligible for the trial treatment. The plan now was to keep an eye on the situation.

- **BAD NEWS** - We had been searching for a year for relief from Verna's pain and had exhausted all possibilities. Dr. Raval then suggested a PET scan to see if her multiple myeloma was the cause. Nothing suspicious showed up in her lower back, but the scan indicated a tumor in her left breast. That led to a mammogram, which disclosed malignancy. A mastectomy was performed on March 6, and all went well. In addition to the breast cancer, routine bloodwork on Verna disclosed that her multiple myeloma was no longer in remission, and she had to resume her chemo medication. Plus, images taken during her mastectomy disclosed potential cancer near her right breast. She now has to take preventive medicines for that.

- **MORE BAD NEWS** - David's reprieve regarding his lymphoma lasted only a few months. Tests revealed it was returning, and the tumor was now large enough to make him eligible for CAR-T therapy. He entered the hospital just before Thanksgiving. However, during the January-February 2024 timeframe, there were indications that the treatment was ineffective. Sometime during February, David and his immediate family decided to stop treatment, which had been deteriorating his quality of life.

- **MORE WEDDING BELLS** - David's daughter Ellen was scheduled to be married to Jose Monsanto on June 3 in New Jersey. David wanted so much to see her get married. When it appeared that David would not last that long, arrangements were made to have a marriage ceremony performed before June. A ceremony was conducted in a Boston church with immediate family members present. David was able to attend and managed to make it down the aisle with Ellen at his side as his son, Thomas, pushed him in a wheelchair. Everyone present and those viewing it on FaceTime claimed that they had never witnessed such a beautiful wedding ceremony. After the ceremony, there was a reception in a local restaurant. David could not make that so Verna and I returned with him to the hospital. The day before the wedding, our son, Kevin, received a call from his wife, Andrea, informing him that she was experiencing heart problems. Kevin made arrangements to fly home to South Carolina immediately after the church ceremony the next day.

- **GOOD NEWS/MORE BAD NEWS** - Around March, David indicated that he would like to return to his apartment and perhaps be a little more comfortable. Arrangements were made for round-the-clock caregivers. One day, as we were visiting him and listening to music, I suggested we make a change and listen to Big Band music. Suddenly, as David was sitting in his wheelchair, his feet began moving automatically to the beat of the music. We noticed it and brought it to his attention. He then started to get into the rhythm and consciously started moving his feet all the more. That began a series of improvements in his mobility and the reopening of his right eye. We could not believe it! David started walking with the aid of a walker. Things were improving so much that plans began to formulate to have him attend Ellen's wedding in June and perhaps even see David walking her down the aisle. Sometime around May, the doctors resumed treatment in the hospital because David was feeling better physically. However, before that happened, his progress reversed, and he had to be admitted to the hospital for care. Because of this, he never received the chemo or returned home. The June 3 wedding date was quickly approaching, and we all struggled with the decision regarding David's attendance. We finally decided against it, and Donna remained in Boston with David; everybody else went to the wedding.

DONNA AND DAVID

This was taken at a Boston Pops summer concert in Tanglewood Music Center in Massachusetts on one of their first dates.

86. AN ULTIMATE LIFE-CHANGING EVENT

Verna and I had planned to visit her brother Raymond and his family in New Jersey for a few days after the wedding. Just as we were about to leave the hotel for his house, we received a call from Thomas saying that David was failing and that it would be better to be prepared to go to Boston instead of New Jersey. We returned to our apartment on Sunday. On Tuesday morning, we were notified by Thomas that David was in hospice. We made hotel arrangements and headed for Boston. This would be our eleventh trip to Boston in the last six months. Kevin, Andrea, and their daughter, Olivia, arrived the next day. David was lucid for the first couple of days. But for the last three days, he was utterly unresponsive to words or actions. It was agony to see our child slowly drifting away over seven days. It was the most difficult thing I experienced in my entire life. Verna had witnessed her grandmother, mother, and older brother pass away. I was there for her mother and brother. On the sixth night at a hospice, the nurse told us that it would happen within the next sixteen hours. We were all there at the sixteenth hour on Tuesday, June 11, around 10 a.m. (Thomas, Ellen, Donna, Verna, and me, Kevin, and family had to leave on Friday). Thomas was sitting closest to the bed, and when it appeared that breathing had stopped, he reached over and placed his hand on David's heart, then gave us the sign that it was over! The viewing was held on June 21, our sixty-sixth wedding anniversary. A funeral Mass was held the next day, and the church was filled.

The information regarding the last six months of David's ordeal may not be 100% accurate in specific terms. There was so much going on. If I had taken notes, documenting exactly what happened would have been helpful. But the specifics are not important; it was the process of something happening that was so heartfelt and traumatic that words can't describe it. The details I have written about are probably beyond the scope of "Memoirs." This collection of occurrences in my life has expanded from just about me to Verna and me to Verna's family to David and his family, including Donna.

Finally, I used the words "Life-Changing Event" in this story but did not number it five in keeping with the previous four titles using the term. This story has so much different content and is so opposite to the other events. However, the story is **LIFE-CHANGING** in that Verna's and my lives have changed, and we will never be completely happy again. Hence, the adjective—**ULTIMATE!**

87. GRIEVING - COPING - WRAPUP

This last collection of stories has brought my story up to date. What is our "New Normal"? We received around fifty sympathy cards from friends in various places and three Mass cards. We are easing into our abandoned social dinner routine with Verna "Working the Room." We feel sad and happy pangs of pain when a photo of David appears on our Alexa digital photo album. Recently, as I was driving alone doing some errands, I glanced at a beautiful blue sky with gorgeous puffy white clouds and felt the urge to wave my hand and say, "Hi, David," and shed a few tears. That has become a recurring thing since then. I have a moment with David as I look at a recent photo of him and wish him "Goodnight" just before I get into bed.

A big chunk of our lives is gone. We will never be genuinely and completely happy again. David had a saying, "A parent is only as happy as their least happy child." A parent losing a child takes that saying to an indescribable new level.

David and Donna had so much to look forward to, for example, the Boston scene, Martha's Vineyard again, other trips, walks by the Charles River, home-cooked dinners, and sharing a glass of wine. David retired in June and only enjoyed a few months of retirement after working all of those years. He will miss so much, to name a few: not experiencing the joys of grandchildren; sharing retirement years with us; continuing with helping the Syrian refugees (which is one of his many legacies); consulting which he savored and WOW those big bucks; being the keynote speaker at a professional conference in Vienna; reading all of those books I left to him; organizing his collection of photos and videos; enjoying his second cup of coffee in the morning as he read his *New York Times;* writing his memoirs. I was counting on him and Kevin to continue the tradition I hope I started with this epic. I allude to this in an epilogue entitled "FINAL WORDS - A TIME CAPSULE." Now it depends on

Kevin to pick up the ball, and I don't think he will let me down. But who will tell David's story? Perhaps his children Thomas and/or Ellen can include David in their stories. But that will only cover the last half of David's great years. That leaves the task to me. So, when I finally put the pen down after this five-year project, I will catch my breath and put pen to paper again.

On more than one occasion, Verna and I have said it should be us, not David, to be gone. I try to cope by not asking why or being angry. There is no answer, and anger is too negative. We will take one day at a time. David would not like what happened to him to be the cause of our perpetual sadness. I am relying on Faith that David is happy in some other place, no matter what form that may be; that he sees us, may communicate to us in some fashion, and that we will be reunited one day. Hopefully, that will get Verna, me, and his remaining loved ones through the rest of our lives.

FINAL WORDS - I am putting my pen down; no more stories. I was beginning to get the feeling that these "Memoirs" were evolving into a journal with perhaps too much detail, and I better stop. However, if something significant should occur before it goes to press, I will squeeze it into this already "bulging at the seams" chronicle. I will now concentrate on the mechanics of converting this collection of digitized bytes into a handsome bound volume of warm words to be savored by future readers as they flow from the pages through their fingers into the minds and hearts of those who happen to take it off the bookshelf in coming years.

THE END

FINAL WORDS - A TIME CAPSULE

As I mentioned in the Preface of this book, I started writing these stories for our sons, and I have envisioned giving them each a copy, which would be the end of this project. Now that the project is over, my audience has increased, including more family members. Also, they have already received a copy of each story. In a sense, there is no need to do any more than I have already done. The project could be considered finished with these "Final Words." The book you are holding has been created for personal use only. It was not intended for formal or commercial publication, which would require more professional channels and legal consultation. Will that happen? That remains to be seen.

As I alluded to earlier, my mission has been accomplished. As I was writing about my early childhood experiences, I could not help but feel a void because I knew relatively nothing about my parents. Verna knew a little more about her parents' stories. It would have been quite a treasure for each of us if we had a book about our parents like this one.

My final words in this project are to strongly encourage our son, Kevin, to follow in my footsteps and continue the historical saga I have begun. As my imagination runs away with me, I visualize a collection of volumes sitting on a bookshelf about two hundred-plus years from now. Someone from a future generation picks up Volume I of *Made Not Born* and says, "Thank you, Great, Great, Great . . . Grandma and Grandpa, for telling me all about the both of you and starting this tradition."

P.S. Yes, I mean "Volumes." Who knows what future media will look like? Look at how many years "Books" have survived. I love books. Be sure you have a paper copy of your stories alongside ours.